THE GRECO-ROMAN EAST

This collection of papers illustrates how our picture of the Greco-Roman East has changed over the last two decades as a result of new finds, new methods and new interests on the part of classical scholars. The chapters, by a distinguished international cast of contributors, present a view of life in the Eastern empire from the bottom up, and show how a thoughtful use of both new and existing material evidence can shed light on aspects of social and political life that could barely be guessed at from the literary record alone. The evidence of coins, inscriptions and archaeological data is used in the investigation of a wide range of socio-historical issues, including processes of Hellenization and acculturation, the permeability and flexibility of political boundaries at all levels, the interaction of civil and religious authority, and the operation of networks of patronage and power from the highest to the lowest social level.

STEPHEN COLVIN is Associate Professor of Greek Literature and Linguistics at Yale University. He is the author of *Dialect in Aristophanes* (Oxford, 1999).

YALE CLASSICAL STUDIES

VOLUME XXXI

THE GRECO-ROMAN EAST

Politics, Culture, Society

Edited for the Department of Classics by

STEPHEN COLVIN

Associate Professor of Greek Literature and Linguistics, Yale University

PUBLISHED BY THE PRESS SYNDICATE OF THE UNIVERSITY OF CAMBRIDGE
The Pitt Building, Trumpington Street, Cambridge, United Kingdom

CAMBRIDGE UNIVERSITY PRESS
The Edinburgh Building, Cambridge, CB2 2RU, UK
40 West 20th Street, New York, NY 10011–4211, USA
477 Williamstown Road, Port Melbourne, VIC 3207, Australia
Ruiz de Alarcón 13, 28014 Madrid, Spain
Dock House, The Waterfront, Cape Town 8001, South Africa

http://www.cambridge.org

© Cambridge University Press 2004

This book is in copyright. Subject to statutory exception
and to the provisions of relevant collective licensing agreements,
no reproduction of any part may take place without
the written permission of Cambridge University Press.

First published 2004

Printed in the United Kingdom at the University Press, Cambridge

Typeface Adobe Garamond 11/12.5 pt.   *System* LATEX 2$_\varepsilon$ [TB]

A catalogue record for this book is available from the British Library

Library of Congress Cataloguing in Publication data
The Greco-Roman East: politics, culture, society / edited for the Department of Classics
by Stephen Colvin.
p.   cm. – (Yale classical studies; v. 31)
Includes bibliographical references and index.
ISBN 0 521 82875 9 (hardback)
1. Middle East – History – To 622.   I. Colvin, Stephen.   II. Series.
PA25.Y3 vol. 31
[DS62.2]
939′.4 – dc21   2003051486

ISBN 0 521 82875 9 hardback

ΦΙΛΕΛΛΗΝ

Τὴν χάραξι φρόντισε τεχνικὰ νὰ γίνει.
Ἔκφρασις σοβαρὴ καὶ μεγαλοπρεπής.
Τὸ διάδημα καλλίτερα μᾶλλον στενό·
ἐκεῖνα τὰ φαρδιὰ τῶν Πάρθων δὲν μὲ ἀρέσουν.
Ἡ ἐπιγραφή, ὡς σύνηθες, ἑλληνικά·
ὄχ' ὑπερβολική, ὄχι πομπώδης –
μὴν τὰ παρεξηγήσει ὁ ἀνθύπατος
ποὺ ὅλο σκαλίζει καὶ μηνᾶ στὴν Ρώμη –
ἀλλ' ὅμως βέβαια τιμητική.
Κάτι πολὺ ἐκλεκτὸ ἀπ' τὸ ἄλλο μέρος·
κανένας δισκοβόλος ἔφηβος ὡραῖος.
Πρὸ πάντων σὲ συστείνω νὰ κυττάξεις
(Σιθάσπη, πρὸς θεοῦ, νὰ μὴ λησμονηθεῖ)
μετὰ τὸ Βασιλεὺς καὶ τὸ Σωτήρ,
νὰ χαραχθεῖ μὲ γράμματα κομψά, Φιλέλλην.
Καὶ τώρα μὴ μὲ ἀρχίζεις εὐφυολογίες,
τὰ "Ποῦ οἱ Ἕλληνες"; καὶ "Ποῦ τὰ Ἑλληνικὰ
πίσω ἀπ' τὸν Ζάγρο ἐδῶ, ἀπὸ τὰ Φράατα πέρα."
Τόσοι καὶ τόσοι βαρβαρότεροί μας ἄλλοι
ἀφοῦ τὸ γράφουν, θὰ τὸ γράψουμε κ'ἐμεῖς.
Καὶ τέλος μὴ ξεχνᾶς ποὺ ἐνίοτε
μᾶς ἔρχοντ' ἀπὸ τὴν Συρία σοφισταί,
καὶ στιχοπλόκοι, κι ἄλλοι ματαιόσπουδοι.
Ὥστε ἀνελλήνιστοι δὲν εἴμεθα, θαρρῶ.

C.P. Cavafy, 1912

Make sure the engraving is done skilfully.
The expression serious, majestic.
The diadem preferably somewhat narrow:
I don't like that broad kind the Parthians wear. The inscription,
  as usual, in Greek:
nothing excessive or pompous –
we don't want the proconsul to take it the wrong way;
he's always smelling things out and reporting back to Rome –

but of course giving me due honour.
Something very special on the other side:
perhaps a discus-thrower, young, good-looking.
Above all I urge you to see to it
(Sithaspis, for God's sake don't let them forget)
that after 'King' and 'Saviour',
they add 'Philhellene' in elegant characters.
Now don't try to be clever
with your 'where are the Greeks?' and 'what Hellenism
here behind Zagros, out beyond Phraata?'
Since so many others more barbarian than ourselves
choose to inscribe it, we'll inscribe it too.
And besides, don't forget that sometimes
sophists do come to us from Syria,
and versifiers, and other triflers of that kind.
So we're not, I think, un-Hellenized.

trans. Edmund Keeley and Philip Sherrard

Contents

List of illustrations	*page* viii
Preface	ix
List of abbreviations	xi

1   Under the watchful eyes of the gods: divine justice in
    Hellenistic and Roman Asia Minor   1
    ANGELOS CHANIOTIS   (*Ruprecht-Karls-Universität Heidelberg*)

2   Names in Hellenistic and Roman Lycia   44
    STEPHEN COLVIN   (*Yale University*)

3   Caracalla et son médecin L. Gellius Maximus à Antioche de
    Pisidie   85
    MICHEL CHRISTOL ET THOMAS DREW-BEAR   (*CNRS, Paris*)

4   Roman material culture across imperial frontiers? Three case
    studies from Parthian Dura-Europos   119
    NIGEL POLLARD   (*University of Wales Swansea*)

5   *Sympoliteiai* in Hellenistic Asia Minor   145
    GARY L. REGER   (*Trinity College Hartford*)

6   Hellenism on the periphery: the case of Cilicia and an
    etymology of *soloikismos*   181
    GIOVANNI SALMERI   (*Università di Pisa*)

7   Leon son of Chrysaor and the religious identity of
    Stratonikeia in Caria   207
    RIET VAN BREMEN   (*University College London*)

Bibliography	245
Index	271

Illustrations

PLATES

1. Inscription pour Caracalla (partie supérieure) *page* 87
2. Inscription pour Caracalla (partie inférieure) 88
3. Inscription latine pour L. Gellius Maximus 93
4. Inscription grecque pour L. Gellius Maximus 98
5. Un prêtre d'Aesculapius 108
6. Excavation photograph of south apse of Room 4 (caldarium) in F3 bath, showing tubuli 134
7. Excavation photograph of east side of Room 4 (caldarium) of F3 bath, showing rectangular niche 135
8. Excavation photograph showing collapsed fragment of concrete arch with vaulting tubes in F3 bath frigidarium 136
9. Excavation photograph showing primitive pendentive in north-west corner of Room 3, F3 baths 138

FIGURES

1. Inscription grecque pour L. Gellius Maximus 96
2. L. Gellius Maximus prêtre d'Aesculapius 104
3. Plan of the F3 block at Dura-Europos, showing F3 bath and amphitheatre 133
4. Reconstructed elevation of the F3 baths at Dura-Europos 137
5. Schematic depiction of the relationship between the house in F4 and the F3 baths 140

MAPS

1. Caria and environs xv
2. The Roman Near East, showing location of Dura-Europos 120

TABLE

1. Roman and Parthian coins found at Dura-Europos, numbers by reign 129

Preface

The present volume owes its conception to the shared interests in the languages and material culture of Greco-Roman Asia Minor of the original editor of the volume, Andrew Gregory, and his then colleague in the Yale Department of Classics, Stephen Colvin. It follows the established pattern of Yale Classical Studies in bringing substantial contributions by a number of scholars to bear from different points of view on a theme of general interest.

The contributors were invited to explore some of the ways in which our picture of the Greco-Roman East has been changing over the last two decades as a result of new finds, the development of new methods and the emergence of new interests on the part of classical scholars. With its emphasis on the material culture of the Greco-Roman East, the volume complements the extensive, vigorous and innovative work done in recent years on the literature and 'high culture' of the period, notably in the literary movement known, after the phrase of one of its later participants, as the Second Sophistic. The result is a distinct change of perspective. If the literary evidence, rich and varied as it is, offers a 'top down' view of the period, the papers included in this volume show how a thoughtful use of new and existing material evidence can shed light on aspects of social and political life that could barely have been guessed at from the literary record alone. They use the evidence of coins, inscriptions and archaeological discoveries and deploy these in conjunction with the transmitted literary texts, in the investigation of a wide range of socio-political issues. These include the processes (and limits) of Hellenization and acculturation, the permeability and flexibility of political boundaries at all levels of society, the interaction of civil and religious authority, and the operation of networks of patronage and power from the highest to the lowest levels. If the effect is to emphasize the complexity and diversity of the social experience of those who lived even in this one part of the ancient world, then this reflects the situation as it actually existed. Historical writing must be as willing to acknowledge complexity as it is eager to simplify, and not all research leads to a single conclusion.

With its emphasis on political culture and society rather than on literature, the collection begins and ends with papers, by Angelos Chaniotis and Riet van Bremen, on religion and the gods. Its second and penultimate chapters, by Stephen Colvin and Giovanni Salmeri respectively, are on local proper names and the (mis-)use of language, and in the heart of the collection is Gary Reger's study of city formation in the Hellenistic period. The dominant geographical focus is on Asia Minor, but as we write these words in the University department of Michael Rostovtzeff, we feel that Nigel Pollard's paper, which focusses attention on the shifting boundaries of Greco-Roman influence at Dura-Europos, is a particularly appropriate inclusion. The editor is grateful to Cambridge University Press for its agreement to vary its normal practice and allow the fascinating chapter by Michel Christol and Thomas Drew-Bear on Caracalla's doctor and his commemoration in his city of origin to be printed in the language in which it was written.

The editor wishes also to express his gratitude to his colleagues, the contributors to this volume, for their patience on its long road to publication, to the Yale Department of Classics for its support, and to Michael Sharp and Cambridge University Press for undertaking the publication of this volume, as the first instalment in the planned revival of Yale Classical Studies.

Department of Classics John Matthews
Yale University Stephen Colvin

Abbreviations

Abbreviations of journal titles not listed here follow the conventions of *L'Année philologique*

AE	*L'Année épigraphique*
BE	*Bulletin épigraphique* in *Revue des études grecques*
BGU	*Aegyptische Urkunden aus den Königlichen* [later Staatlichen] *Museen zu Berlin, Griechische Urkunden* (Berlin 1895–)
BIWK	*Die Beichtinschriften Westkleinasiens*, ed. G. Petzl (*EA* 22, Bonn 1994)
CEG	*Carmina Epigraphica Graeca*, ed. P.A. Hansen, 2 vols (Berlin 1983–9)
CID	*Corpus des inscriptions de Delphes* (Paris and Athens 1977–)
CIL	*Corpus Inscriptionum Latinarum* (Berlin 1853–)
C.Iust.	*Codex Iustinianus* (*Corpus Iuris Civilis* II: *Codex Iustinianus*, Berlin 1906)
Dura	*The Excavations at Dura-Europos, Preliminary Reports* I–IX, ed. P.V.C. Baur, M.I. Rostovtzeff et al. (New Haven 1929–52)
EA	*Epigraphica Anatolica. Zeitschrift für Epigraphik und historische Geographie Anatoliens* (Bonn 1983–)
EBGR	*Epigraphic Bulletin for Greek Religion*, ed. A. Chaniotis et al. (in *Kernos* 4, 1991–)
HTC	*Les hautes terres de Carie*, ed. P. Debord and E. Varinlioğlu (Bordeaux 2001)
I. Alex. Troas	*Die Inscriften von Alexandreia Troas* (*IGSK* 53), ed. M. Ricl (1997)

IAM	*Inscriptions antiques du Maroc* II: *Inscriptions latines* (Paris 1982)
I. Aryk.	*Die Inschriften von Arykanda* (*IGSK* 48), ed. Sencer Şahin (1994)
IC	*Inscriptiones Creticae*, ed. F. Halbherr and M. Guarducci (Rome 1935–50)
I. Eph.	*Die Inschriften von Ephesos* (*IGSK* XI–XVII), ed. H. Wankel *et al.* (1979–81)
IGR	*Inscriptiones Graecae ad res Romanas pertinentes*, ed. R. Cagnat *et al.* (Paris 1911–27)
IGrSic. et inf. It.	*Inscriptiones Graecae Siciliae et infimae Italiae ad ius pertinentes*, ed. V. Arangio-Ruiz and A. Olivieri (Milan 1925)
IGSK	*Inschriften griechischer Städte aus Kleinasien* (Bonn)
IGUR	*Inscriptiones Graecae urbis Romae*, ed. L. Moretti (Rome 1968–90)
I. Iasos	*Die Inschriften von Iasos* (*IGSK* XXVIII. 1–2), ed. W. Blümel (1985)
I. Keramos	*Die Inschriften von Keramos* (*IGSK* XXX), ed. E. Varinlioğlu (1986)
I. Laodikeia/Lykos	*Die Inschriften von Laodikeia am Lykos* (*IGSK* XLIX), ed. T. Corsten (1997)
ILS	*Inscriptiones Latinae Selectae*, ed. H. Dessau (Berlin 1892)
I. Magn. M.	*Die Inschriften von Magnesia am Maeander*, ed. O. Kern (Berlin 1910)
I. Magn. Sip.	*Die Inschriften von Magnesia am Sipylos* (*IGSK* VIII), ed. Th. Ihnken (1978)
I. Mylasa	*Die Inschriften von Mylasa* (*IGSK* XXXIV–XXXV), ed. W. Blümel (1987–8)
I. Priene	*Inschriften von Priene*, ed. F. Hiller von Gaertringen (Berlin 1906)
I.Rh.Per.	*Die Inschriften der rhodischen Peraia* (*IGSK* XXXVIII), ed. W. Blümel (1991)
IS	*Die Inschriften von Stratonikeia* (*IGSK* XXI, XXII.1–2), ed. M.Ç. Şahin (1981–90)
ISE	*Iscrizioni storiche ellenistiche*, ed. L. Moretti (2 vols, Florence 1967–76)
ISE III	*Iscrizioni storiche ellenistiche* III. *Supplemento e indici*, ed. F. Canali de Rossi (Rome 2001)

I. Smyrna	*Die Inschriften von Smyrna* (*IGSK* XXIII–XXIV), ed. G. Petzl (1982–90)
I. Tralleis	*Die Inschriften von Tralleis und Nysa* (*IGSK* XXXVI), ed. Fj. B. Poljakov (1989)
Labraunda	*Labraunda. Swedish Excavations and Researches* (Stockholm 1955–)
LGPN	*A Lexicon of Greek Personal Names*, ed. P.M. Fraser and E. Matthews (Oxford 1987–)
Lindos	*Lindos. Fouilles de l'acropole 1902–1914* II: *Inscriptions*, ed. C. Blinkenberg (Copenhagen and Berlin 1941)
LSAM	*Lois sacrées de l'Asie Mineure*, ed. F. Sokolowski (Paris 1955)
LSCG	*Lois sacrées des cités grecques*, ed. F. Sokolowski (Paris 1969)
MAMA	*Monumenta Asiae Minoris Antiqua* (Manchester 1928–)
Milet	*Milet. Ergebnisse der Ausgrabungen und Untersuchungen seit dem Jahre 1899* I.3: *Das Delphinion im Milet*, ed. G. Kawerau and A. Rehm (Berlin 1914)
OGIS	*Orientis Graeci Inscriptiones Selectae*, ed. W. Dittenberger (Leipzig 1903–5)
PIR²	*Prosopographia Imperii Romani saec. I. II. III* (2nd edn, Berlin and Leipzig 1933–99)
PSI	*Papyri greci e latini* (Pubblicazioni della Società Italiana per la ricerca dei papiri greci e latini in Egitto, Florence 1912–)
P.Tebt.	*The Tebtunis Papyri* (London 1902–)
RGE	*Roman Documents from the Greek East. Senatus Consulta and epistulae of the age of Augustus*, ed. R.K. Sherk (Baltimore 1969)
RIT	*Die römischen Inschriften von Tarraco*, ed. G. Alföldy (2 vols, Berlin 1975)
RMD	*Roman Military Diplomas* I–IV (Institute of Archaeology, London 1978–)
SEG	*Supplementum Epigraphicum Graecum* (Leiden)
SIG³	*Sylloge Inscriptionum Graecarum*, ed. W. Dittenberger (4 vols, Leipzig 1915–24)

Staatsvertr.	*Die Staatsverträge des Altertums.* II, ed. H. Bengtson; III, ed. H. H. Schmitt (Munich 1962–9).
TAM II	*Tituli Asiae Minoris* II: *Tituli Lyciae linguis graeca et latina conscripti*, ed. E. Kalinka (Vienna 1920–44)
TAM V	*Tituli Asiae Minoris* V: *Tituli Lydiae linguis graeca et latina conscripti*, ed. P. Herrmann (Vienna 1981–9).
Tit. Cal.	*Tituli Calymnii*, ed. M. Segre (*Annuario* 22–3 (1944–5) [1952], whole volume)
Tit. Cam.	*Tituli Camirenses*, ed. M. Segre and G. Pugliese-Carratelli (*Annuario* 27–9 (1949–51), pp. 141–318)
TL	*Tituli Asiae Minoris: Tituli Lyciae lingua Lycia conscripti*, ed. E. Kalinka (Vienna 1901)

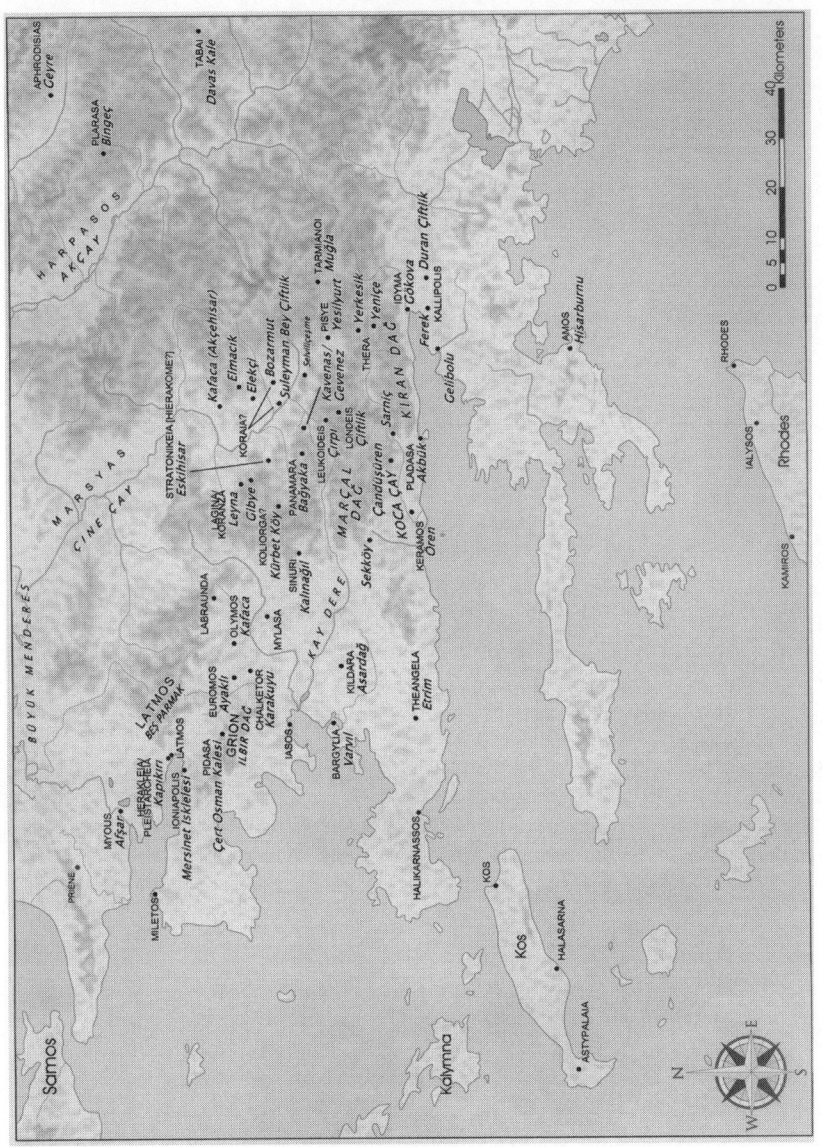

Map 1. Caria and environs

CHAPTER I

*Under the watchful eyes of the gods: divine justice in Hellenistic and Roman Asia Minor**

Angelos Chaniotis

I. INTRODUCTION

In late fifth-century Athens, the sophist Kritias, Plato's uncle and leader of the Thirty, presented in his satyr play *Sisyphus* the following scenario of how belief in gods came about: in the earliest times mortals used to live like animals, subject to the power of the mightiest among them. They knew neither the punishment of the wrongdoer nor the rewarding of the virtuous. It was only at a later stage that they developed laws; but again, only open deeds of violence could be punished. In order to deter the secret offenders as well, a clever-dick invented the gods. He introduced divine powers which could see, hear and know everything – including those crimes which remained unnoticed by mortals. Having observed how frightened men were by celestial phenomena, like thunder and lightning, and how gratefully they received the gifts of the sun and the rain, he thought that heaven was the appropriate dwelling-place of these gods.[1]

Not many Greek thinkers were as bold as Kritias to instrumentalize religion directly and openly by associating the creation of faith in gods with the hope of a more effective implementation of justice (cf. Polyb. 6.56.9–12). More numerous were those who – like Diagoras of Melos[2] – lost their belief in divine powers, observing how many wrongdoers remained unpunished; Babrius narrates the witty fable of a peasant who came to despair when he realized that the gods failed to punish even those who had stolen sacred property (*Fab.* 2):

---

* I am very much indebted to Hank Versnel (Leiden) for many fruitful and entertaining discussions on some of the subjects discussed in this paper. I would also like to thank Hasan Malay (Izmir) for generously providing information on unpublished texts.
[1] Apud Sextus, *Math.* 9.54 (*TGF*, pp. 771–3, ed. Nauck). Translation and discussion: Guthrie (1971: 243–4).
[2] On Diagoras see *Suda*, s.v.; cf. Jacoby (1959: 5) and Guthrie (1971: 236). Compare the views of Diogenes of Oinoanda (fr. 20 col. III = Smith 1998: 132): 'A clear indication of the complete inability of the gods to prevent wrong-doings is provided by the nations of the Jews and Egyptians, who, while being the most superstitious of all peoples, are the vilest of all peoples' (trans. M.F. Smith).

A farmer while digging trenches in his vineyard lost his mattock and thereafter began a search to find out whether some one of the rustics present with him had stolen it. Each one denied having taken it. Not knowing what to do next, he brought all his servants into the city for the purpose of putting them under oath before the gods . . . When they had entered the gates of the city . . . a public crier began to call out that a thousand drachmas would be paid for information revealing the whereabouts of property that had been stolen from the god's temple. When the farmer heard this, he said: 'How useless for me to have come! How could this god know about other thieves, when he doesn't know who those were who stole his own property? Instead, he is offering money in the hope of finding some man who knows about them.' (trans. B.E. Perry)[3]

There were other critical voices as well. And yet, neither the disbelief nor the resignation of alert observers of human society uprooted the idea that the gods – as superior powers, and not as human constructs – did not neglect crime and wrongdoing. That an evildoer can get away with his crimes during his lifetime was, of course, (and still is) a universal experience; but then the faith that divine punishment awaits him in a life after death reduced the frustration of the just – even if it usually failed to discourage the unjust. Already the earliest testimonia of eschatological beliefs colonize the underworld with sinners whose punishment 'furnished a paradigm on which was modeled the punishment in the afterlife of ordinary impious and unjust people'.[4] Furthermore, a sense of justice could be satisfied with the idea that, if a wrongdoer did escape punishment, then at least his relatives or persons associated with him would pay for his deeds (e.g. Solon 13.25–32, ed. West; Plato, *Resp.* 364 b–c). The collective liability of a *genos* is not restricted to the practice of vengeance in Archaic Greece, to the notion of an inherited guilt in Attic tragedy, or to the avenging spirits in popular religion; it can still be found in public documents of the Classical period, i.e. in the Athenian law against tyranny and in a fifth-century verdict against murderers in the sanctuary of Athena Alea.[5] The belief in a collective suffering of divine vengeance for the wrongdoing of an individual had deep roots in Greek religion: the impurity (*miasma*) resulting from the neglect of a religious duty was often regarded as transmissible[6] and was, therefore, potentially

---

[3] Babrius, *Fab.* 2; for this story cf. Versnel (1991: 78).
[4] Sourvinou-Inwood (1995: 70); cf. Mikalson (1991: 120–1). For Egypt cf. Assmann (1997).
[5] Collective and inherited guilt in popular religion: Lloyd-Jones (1983: 35, 90–1), Parker (1983: 198–205), Mikalson (1983: 51), Burkert (1996: 108–13); Athenian law against tyranny: Arist. *Ath. Pol.* 16.10, Demosth. 23.62; inscription of Alea: Thür and Taeuber (1994: 85, 98). Cf. the idea of a collective guilt of mankind for the crime committed by the Titans against Dionysos in the 'Orphic-Dionysiac' tradition; see recently Graf (1993) and my bibliographical reviews in *EBGR* 1996–2000.
[6] Parker (1983: 218–19); Johnston (1999: 54) on inherited guilt and punishment after death in the late Archaic and early Classical period.

collective. As late as the early third century BC the *polis* of Dodona asked the local oracle, 'if the god had sent the bad weather because of the impurity (*akathartia*) of some man' (*SEG* XIX 427).

That ancient notions of retribution have a religious background is well known. It is particularly clear in the belief that disease represents punishment by the gods.[7] However, there is an aspect of this interdependence of religion and law which has received relatively little attention: the question whether and in which way(s) sacred authorities intervened in judicial matters and legal disputes. It is this specific question that I will discuss in this paper, and not divine justice in general. I have chosen Asia Minor as the geographical region for the following survey, though not because evidence for interventions of sacred authorities in judicial matters is lacking from other regions. This is not the case: the relevant evidence ranges from the participation of sacred officials in the cursing of convicts and potential offenders and the verdicts of priests in cases of persons seeking sanctuary (prosecuted persons, convicts, runaway slaves) in Greece to the role of Egyptian priests in legal conflicts among the native population in Ptolemaic Egypt.[8] Two other reasons make Asia Minor a suitable area for such a study: first, the abundance of documentary sources, among which the 'confession inscriptions' of Lydia and Phrygia, the curse tablets of Knidos, dedications with 'prayers for justice', and funerary imprecations occupy the most prominent position; and second, the existence of traditional sanctuaries, some of which had considerable property and most of which exercised significant social and moral influence on the population of small towns and villages.[9]

2. THE EPIGRAPHIC SOURCES: CONFESSION INSCRIPTIONS, PRAYERS FOR JUSTICE AND IMPRECATIONS FOR REVENGE

This paper exploits primarily the evidence provided by the 'confession' or 'propitiatory inscriptions'. These terms designate a group of inscriptions known from parts of Lydia and Phrygia and dating to the first three centuries of our era. So far 142 texts have been published, but many more have been found and await publication. Most texts have been found in the

---

[7] See, e.g., Frisch (1983: 42–3), Varinlioğlu (1989: 39 with n. 11), Versnel (1991: 77), Chaniotis (1995, with further bibliography), Burkert (1996: 102–8), Petzl (1998b: 23–6). For divine retribution see now Harrison (2000: 202–21).

[8] Cursing of convicts: Gschnitzer (1989); *asylia*: Chaniotis (1996a: 78–83); arbitration of Egyptian priests and participation of Egyptian priests in the administration of justice among the native population: Quaegebeur (1993), Anagnostou-Canas (1998).

[9] See, e.g., Zingerle (1926: 47–8), Zawadzki (1952–3: 86–9), Debord (1982), Mitchell (1993a: 187–95), Petzl (1995), Debord (1997), Schuler (1998: 193–4, 247–55), de Hoz (1999: 103–7).

Katakekaumene (north-east Lydia) – mainly in Maionia and in the territories of Saittai and Philadelpheia; other important find spots in Lydia are Sardis and the region between Apollonos Hieron and Tripolis; in Phrygia, confession inscriptions have been found in Akmonia and in the sanctuary of Apollo Lairbenos; a few texts are known from Tiberiopolis in Mysia.[10] The publication of Georg Petzl's valuable corpus (1994, henceforth: *BIWK*), with reliable texts, accurate translations and commentaries, has made a large number of texts widely accessible and permitted a better and more differentiated picture. These texts, written on stone stelae and set up in sanctuaries, contain the confessions of religious offences, crimes and misdemeanours. As far as we can see, the confessions were not made voluntarily, but were forced by divine intervention, i.e. by the prosecution of the guilty person by a divinity through illness, accident, death or destruction of the property.[11] The offences recorded are primarily of a religious nature: disregard of purity regulations (e.g. consumption of forbidden food, entering the sanctuary with unclean clothes or unwashed, sexual intercourse), insult of the gods by ignoring their commands, offences against sacred property and perjury. However, numerous texts mention offences commonly prosecuted by property and criminal law, such as theft, the neglect to repay a debt, cheating, insult, slander, injury, adultery and sorcery.[12]

As we can infer from the longer texts, when a person committed, intentionally or not, a crime or violated a rule and thought that the god was inflicting punishment, he went to a local sanctuary and asked for help. By means of oracles, divine messengers (*angeloi*) or dreams, the god revealed the cause of his anger and the way in which atonement could be

---

[10] The bibliography is vast; I list here some more general studies (not editions of individual texts): Steinleitner (1913), Zingerle (1926), Pettazzoni (1936: 54–115) and (1954: 7–59), Varinlioğlu (1983), Frisch (1983), Petzl (1988), (1991), (1994), (1995: 41–8) and (1997), Versnel (1991: 75–81), (1994), (1999) and (2002), Mitchell (1993a: 191–4), Chaniotis (1995) and (1997a), Ricl (1995) and (1997), Klauck (1996), Schuler (1998: 253–5), Sima (1999), Rostad (2002). M. Ricl's dissertation *La conscience du péché dans les cultes anatoliens à l'époque romaine. La confession des fautes rituelles et éthiques dans les cultes méoniens et phrygiens* (Belgrade 1995; in Serbian, with French summary) was unfortunately not accessible to me; it contains 135 texts: see Ricl (1997) and Petzl (1997: 78–9). For the areas where confession inscriptions have been found see Petzl (1994: vii) (with a map) and Ricl (1997: 36). For the chronological distribution of the material see Petzl (1994: vii and 145) (AD 57–264). A precise date is known for fifty-six texts; most of them (thirty-seven texts) are dated to the period of the Antonines; only three texts can be safely dated to the first century. For texts not included in Petzl's corpus (*BIWK*) see Ricl (1997) and Petzl (1997) and (1998a).

[11] Varinlioğlu (1989: 39), Ricl (1995: 71).

[12] Surveys of the offences attested in the confession inscriptions: Mitchell (1993a: 192–4), Petzl (1994: xii–xiii), Chaniotis (1997a: 354–5), Klauck (1996: 72–5). I regard perjury as a religious offence, since it was not prosecuted by secular law: see Hirzel (1902: 37–41), Plescia (1970: 88–91). The texts not included in Petzl's corpus concern misdemeanours with regard to sacred property (Petzl 1997) and the refusal of a woman to follow a god's request and serve as a priestess (Ricl 1997).

achieved.¹³ However, only a few texts present the facts in their actual chronological sequence; shortening and (much worse) unclear language usually obscure the events. The following text is a good example of the usual course of events (*BIWK* 57):

> Because Trophime, daughter of Artemidoros, also known as Kikinnas, had been asked by the god to fulfil a service and refused to come quickly, the god punished her and made her insane. Now, she asked Meter Tarsene and Apollo Tarsios and Mes Artemidorou Axiottenos, who rules over Koresa. And the god ordered me to register myself for sacred service.

At first sight the procedure seems to concern only the sinner and the divinity, without the interference of any authority, whether secular or sacred. Things are not, however, as simple as that. To begin with, an interference of priests can be recognized in the recording of the confession: in many texts (including the one just quoted) we notice a change of the subject of the verb – from the third to the first person; this may be due to the fact that a priest recorded the confession, possibly made by an illiterate person. In addition to this, it was the priests who transmitted and explained the commands of the gods, usually given in the form of oracles.

The scholars who have studied the confession inscriptions agree that the part played by the priests went beyond these services, although there is some disagreement both in the interpretation of individual texts and in the nature of the activities of the sacred authorities. In the light of the references to offences commonly prosecuted by criminal law as well as in the light of the use of a legal vocabulary in many confession inscriptions, Joseph Zingerle was the first to suggest in 1926, when the known material was rather limited, that trials concerning secular offences took place in the sanctuaries of Phrygia and Lydia; he went so far as to suspect that the priests did not hesitate to assist the gods in carrying out capital punishment.¹⁴ Zingerle's views could not be confirmed by the material available at that time and did not find many followers.¹⁵ O. Eger (1939) rightly pointed out that there is no evidence for trials; he admitted, on the other hand, that accusations must have been submitted to the priests by the wronged party, and that subsequently the priests cursed the guilty party, interpreted the

---

¹³ For the means of communication between man and god see van Straten (1976: 9–12), Varinlioğlu (1989: 39) and (1991: 93), Versnel (1991: 75), Petzl (1994: xv–xvi, 5, 79, 106), Chaniotis (1997a: 354 n. 5), Klauck (1996: 71), de Hoz (1999: 114–24). The importance of reconciliation is stressed by Rostad (2002).
¹⁴ Zingerle (1926: esp. 45–6).
¹⁵ See, e.g., the criticism of Debord (1982: 166), Versnel (1991: 80–1), Petzl (1994: 65, 77, 87–8 and 1995: 43), Ricl (1995: 69–73), Chaniotis (1997a).

signs of the divine will and consulted those who wished to atone for their misdemeanours. Ender Varinlioğlu (1989), the editor of several of the new texts, suggested that the legal vocabulary attested in these inscriptions is occasionally used metaphorically. Marijane Ricl (1995), who has compiled a corpus of these texts (n. 10), came to a similar conclusion: the temples did not act on their own account, she argued, but only when they were asked to intervene by the victims of an offence. The procedure consisted in swearing in the parties and cursing the offenders in order to attract the interest of the gods in the offence. Trials, in the more narrow sense (with judges and verdicts), did not take place.[16] That the priests occasionally served as judges and inflicted penalties has been, nonetheless, maintained by Georg Petzl (1988 and 1994) in the light of a lengthier text: the confession of a certain Theodoros. Indeed, this text (*BIWK* 5, see below, pp. 27–8) resembles the minutes of a trial presided by a priestly council. But in addition to the problems of its interpretation, this text concerns a sacred slave, i.e. a person under the authority of the priests, and thus it is not suitable for general conclusions. My own study of the legal terms and the judiciary elements contained in the confession inscriptions (1997*a*) was conducted after the publication of Petzl's valuable corpus and was based on a larger source material than that available to some of the earlier scholars. Differences in the interpretation of individual texts and in several details notwithstanding, my study confirmed the conclusions of Varinlioğlu and Ricl that trials did not take place in the sanctuaries of Lydia and Phrygia. But I could also find some evidence for negotiations between the priests and the delinquents which allow us to determine the part played by the priests more accurately. This evidence is one of the subjects of the present study; but in order to place the confession inscriptions in a broader religious and social context, I also consider here the evidence provided by further groups of inscriptions.

A group of texts very closely related to the confession inscriptions was found in the sanctuary of Demeter at Knidos; they date to the late second or early first centuries BC.[17] The fact that these texts were written on lead tablets, and that their authors address their curses against persons who had wronged them, brings these inscriptions very close to the ordinary curse

---

[16] Ricl (1995: 69, 'the village temple assumed some of the characteristics of a law-court, but without earthly judges and lawyers', and 71). Ricl also points out that the 'punishment' is often out of all proportion to the crime or the sin.

[17] The most recent publication (with earlier bibliography) is the one by Blümel (1992) = *I.Knidos* nos. 147–59; the most comprehensive recent studies are those presented by Versnel (1994), (1999: 152–3) and (2002: 50–4).

tablets (*defixiones*) of the ancient world. There are, however, significant differences: the culprits are dedicated to the goddess and conditionally cursed; they are to suffer for as long as it takes to make them come to the sanctuary and confess their crime.[18] In the Knidian texts the standard term for the divine pressure exercised on a culprit is πεπρημένος, 'burnt' (only in one case κολαζόμενος, 'punished'). I give a few lines of one of these texts in translation (*I.Knidos* 150 A 1–4): 'I dedicate to Demeter and Kore the man who has made imputations against me, (claiming) that I make a poison (or a potion) against my own man; may he come up to (the sanctuary of) Demeter, with his entire family, burning (or burnt) and confessing . . .' The term *pepremenos* was interpreted by C.T. Newton as 'sold', but it is more probable (also in view of the role of fire as punishment in ancient magic) that it means 'burning with fever' or 'burning in shame'; but the term may also allude to ordeal by fire or hot water, known to have been performed to prove purity or legitimate possession, and to analogous types of oaths of innocence.[19] The interpretation of the term is not without importance, because if an ordeal by fire took place, then the active part played by the sanctuary would be much more significant than just serving as the place where the tablets were deposited. Unfortunately, the material known so far does not allow a decision. Still, the Knidian texts are in many ways very helpful for a better understanding of the involvement of sanctuaries in judicial matters and of the religious mentality which made this involvement possible. The expectation of a confession brings them very close to the confession inscriptions; more similarities can be seen in the nature of the crimes expected to be pursued by the goddesses (theft, slander, embezzlement, bodily injury) and in the expectation of a punishment. As H. Versnel (1994) has pointed out, the main difference is that the Knidian texts ask the gods to do what the confession inscriptions report as already done. The same scholar has also drawn attention to the publicity of these texts and their preoccupation with shame and honour (Versnel 1999 and 2002).

The Knidian texts, with their explicit reference to wrongdoings and their appeal to the intervention of the deities for the satisfaction of the

---

[18] The same idea is expressed in a Christian curse from Alexandria Troas; *I. Alexandreia Troas* 188. 7–8: ποίησον αὐτοὺς πρὸ σοῦ βήματος μολῖν, ἑαυτοὺς ἐσθίοντας καὶ τέκνα καὶ γυναῖκας; M. Ricl, *ad loc.*, has pointed to the similarity of this text to the confession inscriptions and to the Knidian curses.

[19] Burning with fever: Blümel (1992: 85); a long curse tablet referring to 'burning' and 'burning with fever' to death (ἐνπυροῦσθαι, καίεσθαι, φλογίζεσθαι, φλογίζεσθαι πυρετοῖς ἀγρίοις) has been published recently: Kantzia (1997) = *SEG* XLVII 1291. Burning in shame: Versnel (1999: 154). Ordeal by fire: Versnel (1994: 150–4).

wronged party, belong to a distinct group of curses; H. Versnel, who has dedicated a series of penetrating studies to them (1991, 1999 and 2002), has very aptly used the designation 'prayers for justice'.[20] Similar texts, in Greek and Latin, calling the attention of a divinity to an act of injustice, are known from many parts of the Roman empire. Although some of these texts at first sight are very similar to *defixiones*, they share one common feature: they do not force a divinity to harm another person by simply applying magical formulas (like the *defixiones*), but they present arguments to motivate a divinity to act.[21] They inform about the act of injustice (theft, slander, etc.) and they request satisfaction, revenge or both. The use of argumentation is particularly clear in a recently published curse tablet from Oropos (third/second century), whose nature was not recognized by its editor.[22] Someone cursed a series of persons, willing them to be delivered to Plouton and Mounogenes (Persephone), and wishing them death and misery. Unlike ordinary *defixiones*, the curser justified himself: 'I demand that my request be heard, because I have been wronged' (ll. 15–16: [ἀδικο]ύμενος ἀξ[ιῶ πάντα] ἐπήκοα γενέσ[θαι]); 'having been wronged, and not having wronged first, I demand that what I have written down and deposited with you be accomplished' (ll. 25–9: ἀξιῶι οὖν ἀδικούμενος καὶ οὐκ ἀδικῶν πρότερος ἐπιτελ[ῆ] γενέσθα<ι> ἃ καταγράφω καὶ ἃ παρατίθεμαι ὑμῖν; cf. l. 10: ἀξιῶ; l. 45: ἀδικούμενος ὑπ' αὐτῶν). The curser obviously believed that the more or less mechanical application of a curse formulary against the person who had wronged him would not suffice; his appeal to the gods of the Netherworld would be more effective if he presented legal ('I have been wronged') and moral justifications ('not having wronged first').[23] In the cases which concern lost or stolen objects, the victim sometimes asks only for vengeance, as, e.g., in the following *defixio* written on a lead sheet (Hamble estuary, Hampshire, fourth century AD):

Lord Neptune, I give you the man who has stolen the solidus and six argentioli of Muconius. So I give the names of those who took them away, whether male or female, whether boy or girl. So I give you, Niskus [a hitherto unknown deity], and to Neptune the life, health, blood of him who has been privy to that taking-away.

---

[20] Versnel (1991: 68–75, 81–93), (1999: 127) and (2002: 48–50). More material has become known in the last years: Corell (1994), Hassall and Tomlin (1994), (1995) and (1996), Tomlin (1997), *EBGR* (1997) no. 296.

[21] Versnel (1991: 68–9) and (2002: 48–56).

[22] Petrakos (1997: 477–9, no. 746); cf. my commentary in *EBGR* (1997) no. 296.

[23] It should be mentioned in passing that a similar development can be observed in the same period with regard to the notion of pollution, as the purification often requires more than the mechanical performance of a ritual: it presupposes an internalized process of atonement. See Chaniotis (1997*b*).

Divine justice 9

The mind which stole this and which has been privy to it, may you take it away. The thief who stole this, may you consume his blood and take it away, Lord Neptune. (trans. R.S.O. Tomlin)[24]

If I have referred here to texts from Oropos and Britain, it is because of their similarity in content, mentality and (to some extent) vocabulary with analogous texts from Asia Minor.[25] Studies dedicated to a phenomenon in a particular region sometimes tend to overestimate its singularity; these texts remind us that, despite some particular features of the inscriptions of Asia Minor, the ideas concerning divine justice circulated widely in the ancient Mediterranean (and beyond).

A third group of texts, very closely associated with the previous categories in terms of legal, sociological and religious background, but yet very distinct in terms of motivation, are vows addressed to the gods requesting support in various affairs of everyday life, including financial and legal matters. A dedication to Mes Axiottenos at Axiotta, for example, reports the concerns of a woman about whether she would receive some property from her mother; she did get what she wanted and then made the promised dedication.[26] Similarly, Fl. Attalos at Telmessos made a vow to Zeus Olympios, requesting his support in order to obtain the ownership of some pieces of land.[27] Such vows do not allude to disputes and consequently they do not request punishment. Naturally, an unfulfilled vow could easily create the feeling of injustice and dishonour and turn a frustrated person to more drastic means of winning the favour of a god: to curses and prayers for revenge (cf. §3 below).

The belief that crimes did not remain unnoticed and unpunished by the gods is also attested in inscriptions, usually epitaphs, which either mention a crime that had been committed and ask the gods to avenge it or request the punishment of anyone who may have wronged the deceased person.[28] I present only one example of such a prayer for revenge, published recently. In the area of Dorylaion, Helios and Tateis erected a stele, decorated with a representation of hands raised in prayer, on the grave of their slave; an imprecation is addressed to Helios, asking him to avenge the death of their

---

[24] Tomlin (1997: 455–7).
[25] For the wide diffusion of these ideas and similarities in the vocabulary see Versnel (1991), (1999: 155).
[26] *SEG* XLI 1012.4–10: εὐξαμένη | Μηνὶ Ἀξιοττηνῷ, | ἐὰν παρὰ τῆς μητρὸς | λήψομαι τὰ μέρη· λα|βοῦσα ἀνέθηκα τὴν | στήλλην περὶ ὧν εὐ|ξάμην. The word μέρος probably means a share in an inheritance; cf. *BGU* III 895, 35; *BIWK* 18, 28, 71.
[27] *SEG* VI 748: Διὶ Ὀλυμπίῳ Φλάβ[ι]ος Ἄτταλος ὑπὲρ τῆς ἐνκτή[σ]εος τῶν [χ]ωρίων.
[28] For such 'funerary pleas for justice' in Asia Minor see Versnel (1999: 131–2); for examples outside Asia Minor see Björck (1938), Versnel (1991: 70–1) and (1999: 129–31). For the attribution of unexpected death to magic or poisoning see also Graf (1996: 47).

slave (early third century AD): 'they have dedicated this stele for their slave who died a premature death, imploring the testimony of Helios and all the gods, so that they avenge us'.[29]

The expectation of divine punishment is attested in many more inscriptions of Asia Minor than the groups I have singled out here. I should mention in particular the funerary imprecations which threaten desecrators of graves with divine punishment, and the epigraphic evidence for the cult of deities whose name indicates a particular interest in justice. More than 400 funerary imprecations have been found in epitaphs in Asia Minor and in the adjacent islands of Lesbos, Samos, Kos and Rhodes, as well as in epitaphs of 'Anatolians' in Thrace, Macedonia, Athens and Rome – now assembled in a valuable corpus by J. Strubbe (1997).[30] The particular interest of these texts for our subject lies in the fact that their vocabulary often assimilates the divine punishment with a trial (see below p. 29). In addition to this, these texts provide evidence for a strong continuity in religious beliefs, since the earliest text – a bilingual inscription from Kyaneai in Lykia – can be dated as early as the early fourth century BC (Strubbe 1997: no. 376). In the funerary imprecations, but also in other texts as well, we often encounter divinities whose names or epithets imply a very close association with justice. Besides the goddess of punishment Nemesis, whose cult goes back to the Classical period (in Rhamnous and Smyrna) but becomes very popular in the Imperial period, and Dikaiosyne, the personification of Justice, one should mention the all-seeing Sun (Helios Pantepoptes), the Eye of Justice (Dikes Ophthalmos) and Hosios kai Dikaios (or Hosion kai Dikaion, i.e. the personification of Purity and Justice).[31] The latter divine couple is known from more than a hundred monuments (usually dedications, but also a confession inscription and an imprecation). Its cult is almost exclusively limited to Asia Minor (with only four attestations from places

---

[29] *SEG* XLIV 1050.3–11: δούλῳ | ἀώρῳ τήν|δε ἀνέθηκ|αν, μαρτυ|ρούμενο<ι> τὸ|ν Ἥλιον [κὲ] | πάντας | θεοὺς ἵν' ἐγ[δικῆ]|σουσιν ἡμ[ᾶς]; cf. Ricl (1994: 170–1, no. 26); Strubbe (1997: 16), with further examples of epitaphs with representations of raised hands, which may be epitaphs of persons who had met a violent death. A similar Christian prayer for revenge with representation of raised hands (Bahçekonak, Phazemonitis, AD 237/8) has been published recently by Marek (2000: 137–46): 'Almighty lord, you have made me, but an evil man has killed me; avenge me fast!' For another example of raised hands and the explicit reference that the deceased had met a violent death (ὑπὸ βίας) see *I. Beroia* 388.

[30] Cf. Strubbe (1991). For several texts published after Strubbe's corpus see Brixhe (1997) and Brixhe and Drew-Bear (1997).

[31] Cf. in general Versnel (1991: 70–1 with nn. 44–7), Mitchell (1993a: 191). Nemesis: Hornum (1993); cf. Volkmann (1928) and (1934), Chaniotis (1990: 132 n. 28). Dikaiosyne: *TAM* III 731. Helios Pantepoptes: *SEG* XXXVII 1036; cf. *SEG* XVIII 561. Dikes Ophthalmos: *SEG* XXXVIII 1310; cf. Ricl (1991a: 14 no. 25). Ate: *TAM* III.1 268. Hosios kai Dikaios: Ricl (1991a), (1992a), (1992b), Petzl (1992), (1998b).

outside Asia Minor), with a particular density in the areas that have yielded confession inscriptions, i.e. Lydia and Phrygia; it has been suggested that the cult originated in north-west Phrygia (Ricl 1992*a*), but Petzl (1992) has pointed out that the earliest attestation comes from Mysia (first centuries BC/AD). The iconography, influenced by that of Nemesis and Dikaiosyne, sometimes presents Hosios kai Dikaios as one divinity and sometimes as a couple. Ricl's study has shown that, although the iconography reflects the role of Hosios kai Dikaios as protector(s) of animals, agriculture and especially viticulture, the principal function of this deity (or deities) was to remind humans to respect divine and secular laws. It goes without saying that not only deities with names alluding to a special relationship with justice were regarded as patrons of law and right; the epigraphic material leaves no doubt that people could expect any god they invoked to inflict divine punishment.[32]

Since the following study is limited to the active part played by priests in legal disputes, I will be primarily considering the confession inscriptions. The other epigraphic evidence, which I briefly surveyed in this introduction, will be considered only in as much as it attests priestly interventions or offers insights into the religious mentality that permitted the sanctuaries of Asia Minor to become active in legal conflicts.

3. SAVING FACES: DEFENCE AGAINST IMPUTATION, VOWS FOR JUSTICE AND PRAYERS FOR REVENGE

Information about the role of the sanctuaries in legal disputes can be drawn from a series of confession inscriptions, dedications and prayers for justice which show that occasionally the victims of injustice went to the sanctuary and reported this in writing. Two confession inscriptions, both concerning cases of (false?) accusations, are quite revealing. Tatias had heard rumours that she had been giving a magical potion to her son-in-law Jucundus and was, therefore, responsible for his insanity. In order to free herself from what she regarded as slander, she went to the local sanctuary and 'set up the sceptre and deposited imprecations', i.e. she cursed her accusers.[33] Her curse resembled an exculpatory oath, for if her curse was unjustified – in

---

[32] See, e.g., the index of divinities in Petzl (1994) and Strubbe (1997); cf. Klauck (1996: 70–1). Horsley (1997: 55–6) has suggested that divine justice was the common point shared by the gods (Mes, Zeus, Hera, Hermes and Apollo) to whom the Pisidian poet Troilos dedicated an altar (Makron Pedion, AD 126/7).

[33] Cf. a decree of Pednelissos in Pisidia (first century BC), which attests the cooperation of judges with the priestess of Kybele precisely with regard to imprecations (i.e. to accusations) in a legal context (cf. *LSAM* 30 B). The decree is unfortunately very fragmentary, but it is clear that it refers to witnesses and

other words if she was in fact guilty – the unjustified curse would amount to perjury and the gods were expected to punish her. This is in fact what people believed happened in Tatias' case, when both she and her son Sokrates were met by unexpected death soon thereafter. In order to stop the divine wrath, the surviving members of the family had to annul Tatias' curse.[34]

The sociological context of the text cannot be discussed in great detail here. But the 'publicity' of the case immediately attracts our attention: 'Everybody' was observing Tatias' actions and 'everybody' (ll. 5–6: ὑπὸ πάντων) was discussing the incidents. In two very important studies, H.S. Versnel has demonstrated that the background of many curses

judges. *LSAM* 79.1–6: [–] καὶ παρέχηται μάρτυρα ἕνα, ἀποτεισάτω ὁ καταρασάμε|νος σίγλον· ὧι δ' ἂν μάρτυς μὴ ἦι, τιθέσθω τὴν χεῖρα εἰς κε|φαλήν· ἱερεῖα δὲ φερέτω εἰς τοὺς δημοσίους θεοὺς πα[ρὲ]|κ τὸν Πλοῦτον, καὶ ἐσθιέτωσαν οἱ δικασταὶ καὶ οἱ δημόσιοι, διδότω δὲ καὶ Γαλατῶι τέταρτον μέρος, οἷα δεῖν ἐπ[ιφέρειν] εἰς τὸν θεόν. I attempt a translation: 'When (if?) he presents one witness, then the curser (i.e. the plaintiff) shall pay one siglos. But if he has no witness, let him put his hand on his head. And he shall bring sacrificial animals to the public gods, with the exception of Ploutos; and the judges and the *demosioi* (public slaves?) shall participate in the banquet; and he shall give to Galato (the priestess) the fourth part, as it is proper to make offerings to the god (?).' The rest of the decree concerns the duties and the privileges of the priestess.

[34] *BIWK* 69.3–34 (Kula, AD 156/7):

ἐπὶ | Ἰουκοῦνδος ἐγένετο ἐν | διαθέσι μανικῇ καὶ ὑπὸ πάν|των διεφημίσθη ὡς ὑπὸ | Τατιας τῆς πενθερᾶς αὐ|τοῦ φάρμακον αὐτῷ δεδόσ|θαι, ἡ δὲ Τατιας ἐπέστησεν | σκῆπτρον καὶ ἀρὰς ἔθηκεν | ἐν τῷ ναῷ ὡς ἱκανοποιοῦ|σα περὶ τοῦ πεφημίσθαι αὐ|τὴν ἐν συνειδήσι τοιαύτῃ, | οἱ θεοὶ αὐτὴν ἐποίησαν ἐν | κολάσει, ἣν οὐ διέφυγεν· ὁ|μοίως καὶ Σωκράτης ὁ υἱὸς | αὐτῆς παράγων τὴν ἴσοδον | τὴν ἰς τὸ ἄλσος ἀπάγουσαν | δρέπανον κρατῶν ἀμπελοτό|μον, ἐκ τῆς χειρὸς ἔπεσεν | αὐτῷ ἐπὶ τὸν πόδαν καὶ οὕ|τως μονημέρῳ κολάσει ἀ|πηλλάγη. Μεγάλοι οὖν οἱ θε|οὶ οἱ ἐν Αζιττοις· ἐπεζήτησαν | λυθῆναι τὸ σκῆπτρον καὶ τὰς | ἀρὰς τὰς γενομένας ἐν τῷ | ναῷ· ἃ ἔλυσαν τὰ Ἰοκούνδου | καὶ Μοσχίου, ἔγγονοι δὲ τῆς | Τατιας, Σωκράτεια καὶ Μοσχᾶς | καὶ Ἰουκοῦνδος καὶ Μενεκρά|της κατὰ πάντα ἐξειλασάμενοι | τοὺς θεοὺς, καὶ ἀπὸ νοῖν εὐλογοῦ|μεν στηλλογραφήσαντες τὰς δυ|νάμις τῶν θεῶν.

Translation:

Since Jucundus was struck by insanity and it was rumoured by everybody that he had been given a potion by his mother-in-law Tatias, Tatias set up a sceptre and deposited imprecations in the temple, as defending herself against an imputation, although she was conscious (of her guilt). For this reason the gods exercised a punishment which she did not escape. Similarly, her son Sokrates, when he was passing by the entrance which leads to the grove, having a sickle in his hands with which one cuts down vines, the sickle fell on his foot, and thus he died within a day (or: on the same day) suffering his punishment. The gods at Aziotta are great! They demanded that the sceptre and the imprecations made in the temple be annulled; Sokrateia, Moschas, Jucundus and Menekrates, the children of Jucundus and Moschion and grandchildren of Tatias, annulled this, atoning in every way to the gods. Having reported the power of the gods on a stele, we praise the gods from now on.

Commentaries: Zingerle (1926: 16–23), Robert (1983: 518–19), Strubbe (1991: 44–5), Petzl (1994: 89–90), Versnel (2002: 64–5); for pleas for innocence and defence against imputation (cf. ἱκανοποιέω) see Eger (1939: 288–9), Petzl and Malay (1987: 466), Versnel (1991: 76 with n. 83); for the role of gossip see Versnel (2002). For the awareness of guilt see Björck (1938: 127), Petzl (1994: 90). For curses of women who had been the object of similar accusations in Knidos see *I.Knidos* 147 and 150; cf. Versnel (1999: 134).

was the feeling of a person that his or her actions were being carefully observed (and criticized), and that this resulted in a loss of face and dishonour.³⁵ It was under this public pressure of a face-to-face society – not (necessarily) under the pressure of the priests – that Tatias had to defend herself. Her defence, again, was a public performance. She went to a public space – the temple – and publicly declared her innocence by proceeding to a public cursing ceremony. The presence of an audience was important not only as a form of social control, as, again, Versnel has pointed out (2002); it was also important for the manifestation of divine power. Many narratives of miracles underline the fact that a divinity demonstrated its power (by healing or by punishing sacrilege and disbelief) in front of an audience.³⁶

In this text we encounter the expression 'to set up a sceptre'. This phrase appears in several variants in the inscriptions of Lydia and designates the erection of a symbol of divine power – probably in a sanctuary – during a ceremony of imprecation.³⁷ The erection of the sceptre aimed both at preventing future crimes and at punishing offences already committed. The erection of the sceptre seems to have been directed primarily against unknown culprits. 'By this action the crime was transferred to the juridical authority of the god in order that the offender might be unmasked and punished.'³⁸ We may assume that the ceremony was performed by the priests, who are in fact occasionally depicted on stelae with a sceptre (the god's sceptre?) in their hand.³⁹ It is also certain that the expression 'she deposited curses in the temple' in this text does not refer to the common practice of depositing a curse table *in secret*, but to a public cursing ceremony.⁴⁰ Tatias was interested in demonstrating to 'everybody' that the accusations against her were unjustified. We may assume that, similarly, the annulling of the curses by her relatives was a public action as well (cf. §6 below).

---

³⁵ Cf. Versnel (1991: 74, 80–1), and (1999).
³⁶ E.g. *IGUR* 1 148.5 (δήμου παρεστῶτος), LiDonnici (1995: 121) (ὄχλου πολλοῦ περιστάντος). Ricl (1997: 42–3) assumes that *CIG* 4142 refers to a public confession in front of an audience (κὲ συνερχομένου λαοῦ). I suggest reading the text as follows: ὑπὲρ ἑαυτῆς κὲ τῶν ἰδίων πάντων κὲ συνερχομένου λαοῦ (without a comma after πάντων): 'for herself, for all her family, and for the people who come together (frequent the sanctuary)'.
³⁷ Robert (1983: 518–20), Strubbe (1991: 44–5), Petzl (1994: 4, 89–90), Strubbe (1997: 48).
³⁸ Strubbe (1991: 44–5); cf. Zingerle (1926: 13): 'Einleitung des heiligen Rechtsverfahrens durch Aufstellung des Szepters, als Symboles der göttlichen Gerichtsbarkeit'; Versnel (1991: 76): 'ritual opening of the judicial process'; Ricl (1995: 69): 'this procedure signified opening a "trial"'. Eger (1939: 290) has pointed to the difference between σκῆπτρον ἐπίστημι (against unknown offenders) and ἀρὰς τίθημι, ἐπαράομαι (usually against known persons). But see Versnel (2002: 64–5).
³⁹ E.g. *BIWK* 10–12; cf. Strubbe (1991: 44). For representations of Mes with a sceptre see Petzl (1994: 4–5).
⁴⁰ Cf. Strubbe (1991: 45). For the importance of publicity see Versnel (1991: 80–1) and (2002).

The role of publicity is clear also in the case of Menophila (*BIWK* 47, Nea Kome near Kula, AD 146/7); after a dispute with her son Polychronios she demanded satisfaction (εἰκανοποηθῆναι) from the gods. After her son had been punished by the gods and had propitiated them, they asked her to write this incident on a stele; the fact that the sanctuary knew about it leaves no doubt that Menophila (and/or her son) had informed it about the whole affair.

Another victim of slander, Artemidoros, had more luck than Tatias. Hermogenes and Nitonis had made false accusations against him in a case concerning (the purchase of?) wine; this resulted, again, in a loss of face (cf. the use of the verb λοιδορέω). Artemidoros reacted by submitting a tablet to the sanctuary (πιττάκιον ἔδωκεν); it was only natural that a mischance which befell Hermogenes soon after Artemidoros' action was interpreted as divine punishment. Hermogenes recognized the punishment and made the necessary atonements.[41] This shows that he either knew of Artemidoros' action or was informed about it when he went to the temple to propitiate the god. It is quite certain that Artemidoros had not acted in secret, for example by depositing a curse tablet in an ominous place. He must have either submitted his *pittakion* to the priests or made it known in some other way. We know nothing of the procedure – i.e. if it took place in public or if it was connected with the performance of a ritual – but there is some evidence for the assumption that we are dealing with a public action.

A *pittakion*, like the one mentioned in Artemidoros' text, has been recognized in a bronze tablet found somewhere in Asia Minor (first or second century AD): an anonymous person dedicated (ἀνατίθημι) to the Mother of the Gods some lost property, asking her to find the objects, which had thus become sacred property, and to punish the thieves. The public character of the whole action is revealed both by the form of this object and by the text it bears. Despite the small dimensions of this tablet (8 × 5 cm), the existence of a hole for hanging or attaching it with a nail on a wall or another structure shows that the tablet was exposed publicly and could be read. The public nature of the procedure is evident in the text as well:

---

[41] *BIWK* 60 (Silandos or Saittai): Μηνὶ Ἀξιοττηνῷ. Ἐπὶ | Ἑρμογένης Γλύκωνος | καὶ Νιτωνις Φιλοξένου | ἐλοιδόρησαν Ἀρτεμί|δωρον περὶ οἴνου, Ἀρτεμίδωρος πιττάκιον ἔ|δωκεν. Ὁ θεὸς ἐκολά|σετο τὸν Ἑρμογένην | καὶ εἰλάσετο τὸν θε|ὸν καὶ ἀπὸ νῦν εὐδο|ξεῖ. Commentaries: Petzl (1994: 77–8), Versnel (2002: 64). For analogous cases of slander and wrong accusations see *BIWK* 20, 25, 59, 69. For other cases of λοιδορέω see Versnel (1999: 113).

I dedicate to you, Mother of the Gods, all the golden objects which I have lost; in order that she (the goddess) will investigate (the matter) and reveal everything, and in order that those who possess them will be punished in a manner worthy of her power, so that she (the goddess) will not look ridiculous.

The culprit should become known (cf. ἐς μέσον), and people (i.e. observers of the entire affair) should not laugh at the goddesses' inability to regain *her* property, as in the fable of Babrius cited above (p. 1).[42] As in the case of Tatias and Artemidoros, we find again the fear of becoming the laughing stock of close observers, a phenomenon which can often be observed in curses[43] – although in this case the fear is projected to the divinity. We may conclude that, like the tablet of the anonymous victim of theft, Artemidoros' *pittakion* was not a curse tablet, as earlier scholars thought; it was also not a charge submitted in order to open a judicial procedure, as suggested by Joseph Zingerle.[44] It was a 'prayer for justice'.

What the authors of such prayers for justice expected was not (or not primarily) material gain, but moral satisfaction and revenge. These motives also prevail in another 'prayer for justice' from Asia Minor. A certain Apollonios at Kollyda (AD 155/6) 'assigns (to divine justice) the person who threw down the small tablet [a dedication? a confession inscription? a curse tablet?], the person who has removed it, and the accessory to this loss'.[45] But revenge and hope of compensation are not always discernible, as in the following imprecation in an epitaph at Myrikion (Galatia, second/third century): 'Statilia gave, while alive and sane, to someone as a deposit a green garment (?) and two silver armbands. If he does not return the

---

[42] *SEG* XXVIII 1568 (cf. *SEG* XL 1049), with the correction suggested by Versnel (1991: 74) and Ricl (1991*b*): Ἀνατίθημι Μητρὶ θεῶν | χρυσᾶ ἀπ<ώλεσ<α> πάντα ὥ|στε ἀναζητῆσ<α>ι αὐτ|ὴν καὶ ἐς μέσον ἐνε|κκεῖν πάντα καὶ τοὺς | ἔχοντες κολάσεσθα|ι ἀξίως τῆς αὐτῆς δυνά|με<ω>ς καὶ μήτε αὐτ[ὴν] | καταγέλαστον ἔσεσθ[αι]. Cf. Versnel (1999: 145) and (2002: 55), Ricl (1991*b*), Petzl (1994: 77); Ricl suspects a Maionian provenance. For the expression ἐς μέσον cf. Versnel (1999: 155), who points out that it is used in a Latin prayer for justice at Baelo in Spain: *AE* (1988) no. 727: *ut tu evide<s>? immedi.*

[43] For examples see Versnel (1999). In this important study he draws attention to the preoccupation of shame, honour and ridicule in curse tablets.

[44] Curse tablet: Steinleitner (1913: 100), Eger (1939: 287), Latte (1920: 83) ('anklagende Fluchtafel'). Charge: Zingerle (1905: 144) and (1926: 19) ('förmliche Klageschrift'). For the general meaning of *pittakion* see LSJ, s.v.: 'tablet for writing on, label, ticket, written message', but with an inaccurate translation of the term in this inscription ('votive tablet'); for particular meanings see Rupprecht (1971: 9 n. 38c) (receipt), *SEG* XXVII 290 (manumission record), *SEG* XXXIII 1177. 10 and 41 (petition), Anagnostou-Canas (1998: 5 n. 19) (oracular question).

[45] *TAM* v.1 362.2–7: παραγράφε[ι] | Ἀπολλώνιος τὸ|ν βεβληκότα τὸ π[ι]|νακίδιον κ<α>ὶ ἠρκό|<τ>α καὶ σύστορα τῇ | ἀπωλείᾳ. Cf. Zingerle (1905: 143–4), Versnel (1991: 76), Petzl (1994: ix). For συνίστωρ and συνιστορέω (but without this text) see Casanova (1997).

deposit, Hosios and Dikaios and you, Lord Helios, avenge the dead (Statilia) and her living children.'⁴⁶ One can imagine what may have happened. The anonymity of the person who had received and did not return the deposit was not the result of discretion, but probably of the fact that Statilia's children had no clue (or only suspicions) about his identity. Now that the mother was dead, the only way to regain this property would be to make the case public, by drawing both the attention of the god to this incident and the attention of the culprit to the fact that if he took advantage of Statilia's death and did not return the valuables to her heirs, he should suffer divine punishment.

The tablet dedicated to the Mother of the Gods (n. 42) confronts us with an additional element: the dedication to a divinity of lost, stolen or disputed property. A dedication from Kula (AD 176/7), published recently by Hasan Malay, presents a characteristic example; a certain Tatias reports: 'I have bought [–], but having been treated disdainfully, I have "ceded" them to Mes Axiottenos, so that he can do with them as he pleases.' Apparently, this woman had been cheated during a transaction, and her sense of honour was severely damaged (cf. καταφρονουμέ|νη); thereupon she 'ceded' (ἐξεχώρησα) the disputed objects to Mes Axiottenos.⁴⁷ This inscription represents the formal act of cession, making clear to the offenders that the god was now going to investigate the case and punish them.

Tatias' expectations that this would happen were not unfounded: she must have read or known of the confession inscriptions at Kula and in neighbouring areas, which propagated the divine punishment that followed upon such a procedure. The next (fragmentary) text demonstrates this: a certain Apollonios had made a loan to Skollos, who promised under oath to return the money by a certain deadline; when he broke his oath, Apollonios 'ceded' the money (?) to a goddess (παρεχώρησεν τῇ θεῷ). Skollos' (untimely or unnatural?) death was interpreted as divine punishment inflicted by the gods he had invoked in his oath; in order to escape similar punishment, his daughter had to annul the oath and erect a stele. Unfortunately, the text does not inform us about whether she also had to repay the debt – with the interest incurred by the arrears (cf. l. 6: τὸ συναχθὲν κεφάλαιον) – and if so, if she paid this amount to the sanctuary (as the verb παραχωρέω implies), or to Apollonios.⁴⁸ A payment directly to the sanctuary seems to

---

⁴⁶ Ricl (1991a: 40–1, no. 88): Στατιλία ζῶσα προ|νοῦσα παραθήκην | ἔδωκ[έ] τινι ἐρεᾶν (?) π[ρά]|σινον καὶ ψέλλι[α] δύ|ο ἀργυρᾶ. Κἂ[ν] μὴ ἀπο|διδῇ, Ὅσιον, Δίκεον, | Ἥλιε Κύριε, ὑμεῖς ἐκ[δ]ικήσατε τὴν νεκρὰν | καὶ τὰ τέκνα ζῶντα. Cf. Zingerle (1926: 49–50).
⁴⁷ Malay (1994: 70, no. 171): [Τα]τιας ἀγόρασα | [. . .]α καταφρονουμέ|[νη] ἐξεχώρησα αὐτὰ | [Μ]ηνὶ Ἀξιοττηνῷ, ἅτι|να πράξει ὡς ἂν θέλῃ. Cf. Versnel (2002: 53–4 n. 59).
⁴⁸ BIWK 54 (Ayvatlar, AD 118/19):

Divine justice

me more probable; it is attested for another region (Sicily), in the prayer of Kollyra for justice (third century BC?): she dedicated to a sanctuary and its priests not only stolen objects but also the fine (i.e. the payment of twelve times their value).[49]

A ceding to the temple and, consequently, a handing over of the disputed object to the gods may be the background of several confession inscriptions which report the delivery to sanctuaries of immovables. This cannot be proven because of the syncopated form of the narratives, but nonetheless, I present here one such case (*BIWK* 17). A mother cursed her son Apollonios, obviously after a dispute over some real estate. When Apollonios asked the

[–] Ἀπολλωνί|ῳ [– χαλκ]οῦ * μ'. Εἶτα ἀπα[ι]|τοῦντος τοῦ Ἀπολλωνίου τὸν χαλ|κὸν παρὰ τοῦ Σκόλλου ὤμοσε τοὺς | προγεγραμένους θεοὺς ἰς προ|θεσμίαν ἀποδοῦναι τὸ συναχ-θὲν κεφάλαιον. Μὴ τηρήσαντος αὐτοῦ τὴν πίστιν παρεχώρησεν | τῇ θεῷ ὁ Ἀπολλώνιος· κολασθέν|τος οὖν τοῦ Σκόλλου ὑπὸ τῶν θε|ῶν ἰς θανάτου λόγον μετὰ τὴν τ[ε]|λευτὴν αὐ-τοῦ ἐπεζητήθη ὑπὸ τ[ῶν] | θεῶν. Τατιας οὖν ἡ θυγάτηρ αὐτοῦ | ἔλοισε τοὺς ὅρκους καὶ νῦν εἰλα|σαμένη εὐλογεῖ Μητρὶ Ἀτιμιτι | καὶ Μηνὶ Τιαμου.

Translation:

[–] to Apollonios [–] 40 denarii. Then, when Apollonios reclaimed the money from Skollos, the latter swore an oath by the aforementioned [in the lost heading of the inscription] gods to repay the collected sum within a deadline. When he did not keep the agreement, Apollonios ceded (the money) to the god. When Skollos was punished by the gods with death, after his death his daughter was prosecuted by the gods. She annulled the oath and, having atoned, she now praises Meter Atimiti and Mes Tiamou.

It is not entirely clear what we should understand as the object of παρεχώρησεν. In the light of the two other parallels from Asia Minor discussed here (but with different verbs: ἀνατίθημι and ἐκχωρέω) I am inclined to believe that the object of the verb is the disputed amount of money; *contra* Versnel (1991: 78–9): 'the plaintiff hands over the stolen property, the accused and the entire case to the god(s) for final decision'; Eger (1939: 282): 'überanwortet den Skollos der Göttin'. I agree with Zingerle (1926: 35) that Skollos took a promissory oath; cf. Eger (1939: 283 with n. 10). On the contrary, most scholars follow Buckler (1914–16: 178), in the assumption that Skollos swore that he *had paid* the money before the deadline: P. Herrmann, commentary on *TAM* v.1 440, Versnel (1991: 78–9), Mitchell (1993*a*: 192–3), Petzl (1994: 63); but then the text would have been ὤμοσε ἀποδεδοκέναι (cf. *BIWK* 34: ὁμόσε . . . μὴ προδεδωκένε). For interest on outstanding debts (cf. here τὸ συναχθὲν κεφάλαιον) see Rupprecht (1967: 96–9).

[49] *IGrSic. et inf. It.* 25; cf. Versnel (1991: 73). Things are not clear in the case of a certain Tatias (*BIWK* 79): ἐπὶ Τατια Νεικηφό|ρου Μοκαδδηνὴ ἐδάνεισε Γα|[ΐ]ῳ καὶ Ἀφφια τῇ γυναικὶ αὐτοῦ Μ[ο|κ]αδδηνοῖς χαλκὸν προειποῦσα | "[. .]THEPON δανίζω". Ὁ Γάϊος οὖν ἐχρ[ε|οκ]όπησεν αὐτήν. Ἡ Τατιας οὖ[ν χρε|οκ]οπηθεῖσα ἐπεκαλέσετ[ο κατὰ αὐ|τοῦ τὸ]ν θεόν. Μέγας οὖ[ν – |– τ]ὸν Γάϊον καὶ Ε[–|– χ]αρκόν Ο[–]. Commentaries: Herrmann (1978: 419), Herrmann, *TAM* v.1 525 *ad loc.*, Petzl (1994: 103). Tatias had made a loan to Gaius and his wife Apphia. During the conclusion of an oral agreement Tatias named a deadline for the repayment of the money; for such oral contracts and deadlines for the repayment of loans see Rupprecht (1967: 33–5, 68–70). Petzl (1994: 103) suggested restoring a deadline after προειποῦσα ([ἰς] τήμερον?); a Hellenistic inscription from Sicily, published recently, offers an exact parallel: Manganaro (1997: 307 no. 1, l. 5): προεῖπε αὐταμέρι<ν> (again, in the context of a financial transaction). When Gaius proved unable to repay his debt, Tatias 'invoked the god against him'. The lines in which Gaius' punishment and the atonement are described are unfortunately too fragmentary to make any sense. So we do not know whether the creditor 'ceded' her claim to the god, if she just requested revenge, or if she vowed some other reward.

gods twice (together with his brother Eupelastos) what he should do, the sanctuary demanded an amount of 150 denarii; this amount was explicitly connected with specific pieces of property: 'I have given . . . 100 denarii for the house which was bought from Myrmex and 50 denarii for all the cut (?) vines in Promiasse, near the holm-oak' (ἔδωκα . . . ὑπὲρ τοῦ στεγνοῦ δηνάρια ρ΄ τοῦ ἀγορασθέντος παρὰ Μύρμηκος, ὑπὲρ τῶν λυπῶν πάντων τομαίων ἀνπέλων ἐν Προμιάσσῃ ἐπὶ τῇ πρείνῳ ἀπέδωκα ἄλλα δηνάρια ν΄). However, the story did not end there. Another confession inscription concerning the same family (*BIWK* 18)[50] suggests that Apollonios was punished by the gods with death; the gods demanded from his brother and from his heirs (κληρονόμοι) the entire inheritance (ληγάτους) of the mother (Hygie) at Promiasse. I tentatively suggest that when the mother cursed her son, she ceded the disputed property to the sanctuary; in order to annul the curse, the sons had to pay the value of the property in question (or a fine).[51]

The last three texts use verbs which express the permanent transmission of a property title from a mortal to a divinity: dedicate (ἀνατίθημι), cede (ἐκχωρέω), deliver (παραχωρέω). The procedure is always the same: a person who thinks that he (or she) has been treated unjustly hands his claims over to the god. These texts confront us with questions that cannot be answered with certainty: did the 'consecrated' item (money, disputed or stolen property) remain sacred property, and was the victim satisfied with the feeling that he had taken his revenge? Or did the victim receive amends for handing his legal claims over to the god? The first alternative has been favoured by M. Ricl and (more cautiously) H. Versnel.[52] In addition to the meaning of the verbs there are further indications that support this assumption. In one of the texts (n. 47) Tatias explicitly states that the disputed items should remain at the god's disposal (ἅτινα πράξει ὡς ἂν θέλῃ). In another text (n. 42), the victim of theft uses the verb 'to dedicate' (ἀνατίθημι); she requests the punishment of the thief, not the return of the lost objects. One notices that both texts are preoccupied with issues of honour (cf. the words καταφρονουμένη and καταγέλαστος), rather than with material damage; thus, revenge appears to be a plausible aim. A confession inscription suggests that these curses sometimes were effective and the culprits did come to the sanctuary to bring the stolen property to

---

[50] Cf. Petzl (1994: 28).
[51] Herrmann and Varinlioğlu (1984: 7) suspect that the sanctuary charged fees for transactions (cf. below, n. 123). According to Mitchell (1993*a*: 192): 'three brothers had divided up the family vineyards left to them, disregarding a promise that part was promised to the god'.
[52] Versnel (1991: 60, 73–4, 77) and (1999: 153); Ricl (1995: 69).

the gods: it narrates the story of a thief who had stolen a garment from a public bath, disregarding the fact that all potential thieves had already been cursed.[53] The thief was pursued by the god and was forced to bring the stolen garment to the temple. The priests asked him to sell the garment and make a dedication (from the proceeds?).[54] In the light of the other evidence it is tempting to assume that the thief brought the stolen item to the temple in the belief that it had been 'ceded' to the god.

The specific significance of these texts and their difference from ordinary vows can best be seen when we compare them with other evidence. The feeling of dishonour and the wish for revenge were not always stronger than the hope simply to recover the disputed or lost property. We are not surprised to see that in these latter cases the disputed objects were not ceded to the gods. Although we find a legal background very similar to that of the aforementioned prayers for revenge (slander, theft, loans, inheritance), we are dealing with ordinary vows (εὐχαί), based on the principle of *do ut des*:[55] a person requests divine support in a private matter and promises the offering of a dedication. The vow of a certain Menogenes is laconic, but still very revealing: he had made a vow to Meter Aliane concerning a deposit he had given (δοὺς παραθήκην) and was not getting back; he fulfilled his vow when the money was returned to him.[56] Another of these vows concerns itself with theft and possibly with slander: a substantial amount of money (412 denarii) belonging to a certain Agathon had been stolen from a silo. The money was later found in the possession of Crescens, the alumnus of Alkimos and Ekloge. We know of this incident from a vow made to Meter Aliane by the victim's wife, the slave Rhodia, 'with regard to the stolen money' (εὐχὴν ὑπὲρ τοῦ κλαπέντος ἀργυρίου).[57] Rhodia had

---

[53] For a similar preventive curse against thieves see *SEG* XLIII 905 (Amastris, undated); cf. my comments in *EBGR* (1993–4) no. 153.
[54] *BIWK* 3.2–11: ἐπεὶ ἐπεστάθη σκῆ|πτρον, εἴ τις ἐκ τοῦ βαλανείου τι | κλέψι, κλαπέντος οὖν εἱματίου | ὁ θεὸς ἐνεμέσησε τὸν κλέπτην | καὶ ἐπόησε μετὰ χρόνον τὸ εἱμά|τιον ἐνενκῖν ἐπὶ τὸν θεόν, καὶ ἐ|ξωμολογήσατο. Ὁ θεὸς οὖν ἐκέλευ|σε δι' ἀνγέλου πραθῆναι τὸ εἱμά|τιν καὶ στηλλογραφῆσαι τὰς δυ|νάμεις. Commentary: Herrmann, *TAM* v.1 159 *ad loc.*; Petzl (1994: 3–5). For preventive cursing see Latte (1920: 68–77), Wörrle (1978: 230–6), Robert (1983: 519–20), Strubbe (1991: 44–5), Petzl (1994: 4).
[55] For giving in return in dedicatory and sacrificial practice see Grottanelli (1991).
[56] *TAM* v.1 258 (Kula): Μηνογένης Λακίου | θεᾷ Ἀλιανῇ εὐχὴν | δοὺς παραθήκην | καὶ ἀπολαβών. Cf. Herrmann, *TAM* v.1 258 *ad loc*. For a similar problem (λαβόντας . . . παραθή[καν] καὶ μὴ ἀποδίδοντας) see *I.Knidos* 149 and above, n. 46.
[57] *TAM* v.1 257 (Kula, AD 113/14): Ῥοδία | Φλαουίας Μηνογενίδος | δούλη Μη[τ]ρὶ Αλιανῇ εὐ|χὴν ὑπὲρ τοῦ κλαπέντος | ἀργυρίου (δηναρίων) υιβ Ἀγάθωνος | τοῦ ἀνδρὸς αὐτῆς ἐκ ΛΑ|ΝΑΠΟΣΤΩΝ ἐκ τοῦ σειτοβο|λείου καὶ εὑρεθέντος παρὰ | Κρήσκεντι τῷ Ἀλκίμου καὶ Ἐκ|λογῆς θρεπτῷ. Cf. Petzl (1994: x with n. 11). For examples of dedications after divine support in legal matters see Versnel (1991: 65).

probably requested both the discovery of the money and the punishment of the thief; the text does not say what had happened to the money, but it seems probable that it was returned to the owner. The goddess' reward consisted in the erection of the stele. Unclear also is how the thief was punished – and if he was prosecuted by secular authorities in addition to the punishment by the gods. A very similar story is reported in a confession inscription, again from Kula. Theogenes had found a semi-precious blue stone, which later disappeared from his wife's house. Theogenes obviously suspected that his wife, Syntyche, was responsible for the loss – as Agathon had possibly suspected Rhodia for the loss of his money. Being questioned (rather than tortured: βασανιζομένη), Syntyche made a vow (ἐπεύξατο) to Mes Axiottenos, asking him to give her justice (ἵνα αὐτὴν ἱκανοποήσι), i.e. to defend her against this imputation. The thief was soon revealed – it was the neighbour's daughter. This text would have been a dedicatory inscription (like the one set up by Rhodia) had Syntyche fulfilled her vow. But she failed to do so, because her neighbour begged her not to reveal this incident. She was punished herself by the god, and her vow turned into a confession inscription in which she narrates the story, her punishment and her atonement.[58]

The discussion of these texts permits the identification of some common elements, but also a very large variety of aspects. Their protagonists are persons living in the small rural communities of Lydia and Phrygia; they were (or claimed to have been) the victims of wrongdoing: slander, cheating, theft, fraud by a debtor. In some cases they knew who the wrongdoer was; sometimes (particularly in the cases of theft) they did not. None of these texts refers directly or indirectly to an appeal to secular authorities, although this should not be excluded altogether (cf. §7 below). In many cases it was not so much material damage that moved a person to appeal to a god, but rather loss of face: Tatias was the victim of gossip (διεφημίσθη) that she had poisoned her son-in-law; Artemidoros had been cheated and reviled (ἐλοιδόρησαν); Tatias had been treated disdainfully (καταφρονουμένη); an anonymous victim was afraid that he/she and the goddess whom he/she had invoked would become the laughing-stock of others (καταγέλαστον ἔσεσθαι) should a thief remain unpunished; Syntyche and Rhodia may have been suspected for the loss of their husbands'

[58] *BIWK* 59.2–11. Commentaries on this intriguing (and controversial) text: Petzl and Malay (1987: 465–72), Chaniotis (1990: 128–31), Petzl (1994: 75–6), Chaniotis (1997*a*: 368–9 n. 85). On the meaning of βασανιζομένη cf. Petzl and Malay (1987: 466), Versnel (1991: 73 with n. 65) ('tormented by great agonies'), Ricl (1995: 71) ('feeling agony'); cf. the word βάσανος in another confession inscription: Ricl (1997: 37, ll. 9–11): μετὰ πολ|λῆς ἀνάνκης κὲ βασά|νων. On ἱκανοποιέω cf. *BIWK* 47 and 69 (see n. 34 above).

property. In most cases in which the honour of a person had been damaged, the element of revenge prevailed: Artemidoros, Tatias and the anonymous person willingly ceded to a divinity the valuables which had provoked the dispute, expecting as their only satisfaction the revelation of the crime, the punishment of the culprit and his humiliation in the eyes of the entire community.[59]

The fear (and for some the hope) of humiliation was rooted in the publicity given to all these affairs. The 'prayers for justice' (or just for revenge), the accusations, the invocations of the gods, the vows, were displayed publicly; they were meant to be read – possibly to be read aloud by the priests.[60] Not just individuals but entire communities turned publicly to the sanctuaries requesting the divine prosecution of culprits, exactly as they turned to the gods to ask for the fertility of the fields and the protection of the livestock.[61] The 'accusation' was made in public (cf. above p. 13) and the cult personnel became active thereafter. The priests performed the appropriate curse ceremony against the unknown culprit, usually by setting up the symbol of the god, his sceptre (σκῆπτρον ἐπιστᾶναι, cf. above n. 37). The entire procedure was public in nature; unlike the *defixiones* and some 'judicial prayers' which were secretly deposited in an awesome place,[62] these inscriptions of Asia Minor aimed at informing the anonymous or known culprit that he had been cursed, i.e. that he had become the object of divine prosecution. The solemn, public cursing of a wrongdoer led him (or members of his family) sooner or later to the sanctuary. That this happened is reported, e.g. in the confession inscription of the thief who had stolen a garment from a bath (n. 54); here is another typical example: Demainetos and Papias had lost three of their pigs, which mingled with the sheep flock of Hermogenes and his brother Apollonios. Demainetos and Papias requested the return of their animals, but without any success. Thereupon they went to the sanctuary and had the sceptre of Artemis Anaitis and Apollo, the lord of Tiamon/Tiamos, set up (ἐπεστάθη οὖν τῆς θεοῦ τὸ σκῆπτρον καὶ τοῦ κυρίου τοῦ Τιαμου). Even this solemn imprecation failed to make Hermogenes and Apollonios return the pigs. Only when Hermogenes paid for this refusal with his life, his wife, his son and his brother

---

[59] Cf. Versnel (1999: 153).   [60] Cf. Wachsmuth (1863: 569).
[61] *BIWK* 35: ἡ Ταζηνῶν κατοικία ἀδοξήσασα ἐπέστησε τὸ σκῆπτρον; cf. Zingerle (1926: 44–5); Schuler (1998: 254–5); for similar cases see also *BIWK* 3 and 48. For the religious solidarity of the rural population see Gnoli and Thornton (1997).
[62] For examples of 'judicial prayers' which were not set up publicly see Versnel (1991: 81 with n. 113, 90).

propitiated the god, i.e. apparently confessed the wrongdoing and made amends.⁶³

The belief in the effectiveness of 'divine justice' relied entirely upon narratives of its implementation. The confessions of those who had disregarded divine power and the vows of the pious were the visible proof of the punishment which awaits every wrongdoer, sooner or later. This is why the sanctuaries promoted the publicity of these cases by insisting on the erection of inscriptions.⁶⁴ The case of Syntyche (n. 58) is one of the best examples. Mes Axiottenos had heard her prayer and revealed the person who had stolen a semi-precious stone from her house. Yielding to the pleas of the thief's mother, she decided to conceal the whole story. But to profit from the intervention of the gods and to refuse to tell others about it ultimately subverts divine justice, as the priests of Mes Axiottenos certainly knew. Her thirteen-year-old son became sick (or died), and Syntyche was forced to go to the sanctuary, where she confessed the story and – certainly upon the instructions of the priests – dedicated a stele for others to read and draw conclusions regarding the god's power. Syntyche's inscription is inconceivable without the active participation of the priests, and it is this role that we should study more carefully.

4. MAKING SENSE OF TRAGEDY: PRIESTS AS INTERPRETERS OF DIVINE JUSTICE

The persons who came to the sanctuaries were usually persons in despair: they had lost members of their family or their property, they were suffering from disease, they needed help. And they thought that they could find it there. The countless vows in the inscriptions of Asia Minor show that people turned to the gods to be cured, for the health of their family and their animals, for the prosperity of their fields, for a good marriage, hoping

---

⁶³ *BIWK* 68 (Kula, AD 114/15):

Ἑρμογέ|νης καὶ Ἀπολλώνιος οἱ Ἀπολλω|νίου Μίδου ἀπὸ Σύρου Μανδρῶν | πλαζομένων χοίρων τρειῶν Δη|μαινέτου καὶ Παπίου ἐξ Αζι|των καὶ προσμιγόντων αὐτῶν | προβάτοις τοῦ Ἑρμογένου καὶ Ἀ|πολλωνίου, παιδίου αὐτῶν βόσ|κοντος πενταετοῦς, καὶ ἀπαγαγόντων ἔσω, ζητοῦντος οὖν τοῦ | Δημαινέτου καὶ τοῦ Παπίου οὐ|κ ὡμολόγησαν διά τινα ἀχαριστί|αν. Ἐπεστάθη οὖν τῆς θεοῦ τὸ σκῆ|πτρον καὶ τοῦ κυρίου τοῦ Τιαμου, | καὶ μὴ ὁμολογησάν-των αὐτῶν ἡ | θεὸς οὖν ἔδειξεν τὰς ἰδίας δυ|νάμις, καὶ ἱλάσοντο αὐτὴν τελευ|τήσαντος τοῦ Ἑρμογένου ἡ γυνὴ αὐτοῦ καὶ τὸ τέκνον καὶ Ἀπολλώνι|ος ὁ ἀδελφὸς τοῦ Ἑρμογένου, καὶ | νῦν αὐτῇ μαρτυροῦμεν καὶ εὐλο|γοῦμεν μετὰ τῶν τέκνων.

Zingerle (1926: 31–2) assumes that the two brothers repeatedly refused to return the pigs during a judicial procedure; *contra* Eger (1939: 292), Ricl (1995: 71 n. 10) (exculpatory oath), cf. Versnel (1991: 78); Chaniotis (1997a: 367 n. 81). For a similar case see *BIWK* 103: ἐφιώρκησε περὶ προβάτων.

⁶⁴ Zingerle (1926: 21), Frisch (1983: 45), Versnel (1991: 75), Ricl (1995: 73).

to find a lost object,⁶⁵ or in order to pray for justice. Sometimes the priests were able to cure them or at least to make them believe that they had been cured by the gods.⁶⁶ In many more cases they attempted to present the disaster as the punishment for an offence – no matter how important, no matter whether criminal or sacrilegious, premeditated or accidental.

It was not always easy to determine the offence, but an oracle could give a clue. An anonymous person reports: 'I suffered punishment because I was ready (?) and I received the following oracular response: "because you are impure". I have made this dedication in fulfilment of a vow.'⁶⁷ Another man in Maionia, who believed that his disease was caused by the constellation at the time of his birth (κατὰ γένεσιν), was informed by the oracle he consulted ([ἐμαν]τεύσατο) that his sufferings were the punishment for a sin ([κολ]ασθείς).⁶⁸ Oracular responses are believable because they are vague; they rarely answer a question, but they always make people think. In this case the god just pointed vaguely to a previous religious offence; it was now the sinner's business to identify it and to atone for it. The priests were certainly willing to assist him, by interrogating their client in order to discover what had caused the god's anger. Human nature being as it is, it is very doubtful that they ever failed to find an offence – the more so, since the sanctuaries' clients lived near the temples or on sacred land and could easily violate a sacred regulation and offend the gods. A child or an ox had by accident knocked down a stele in a sanctuary (*BIWK* 78; *TAM* v.1 239); a tree had been cut (*BIWK* 10); a boy had entered the sanctuary with unclean clothes (*BIWK* 55). And if the desperate clients had no idea how they had provoked the gods' wrath – and we know in fact of some stubborn (or just innocent) visitors to the sanctuaries who insisted on their innocence – there was always the possibility that they were paying for the crimes or the offences of their forefathers or other relatives (cf. below n. 134). And if their family had been innocent for generations, there was always the

---

⁶⁵ Petzl (1995: 39), Gnoli and Thornton (1997).
⁶⁶ E.g. Chaniotis (1995), with further bibliography.
⁶⁷ *BIWK* 98 (Buldan, second century AD): ΑΠΟ.[. .]Φ [. . . .]|ηνοῦ κολασθεὶς διὰ τό με ἔτ|οιμον εἶνε κὲ κ̣εκληδονίσθε με "ὅτι μεμολυ|μένος εἶ". Εὐξάμε|νος ἀνέθηκα. I have changed the punctuation marks used by Petzl at some points (erasing a comma after κολασθείς and putting a period before εὐξάμενος). Petzl regards the words "μεμολυ|μένος εἶ" as the oracular response. I think that ὅτι is part of the answer: 'Why am I being punished?' – 'Because you are impure'.
⁶⁸ Petzl (1997: 70–1, no. 1) = Petzl (1998a): [Ἀρτέμιδι] Ἀναείτι ἀνέθη|[κε . .]ᾶς Μητροδώρου | [κολ]ασθεὶς εἰς τὰ γό|[νατα?] καὶ εἰς τὰ ἔντε|[ρα. Δό]ξας ὅτι ταῦτα | πάσχει κατὰ γένεσιν, | [ἐμαν]τεύσατο καὶ [. .|. . . .]ΣΟΥΚΕ.[–]. Because of the previous parallel and the use of the verb μαντεύομαι ('to consult an oracle') I assume that the man turned to a sanctuary and was informed by an oracle about the true cause of his illness; Petzl (1998a: 71–4) assumes that he turned to an astrologer or a prophet.

possibility of a sin committed unintentionally and unknowingly. Indeed, some confession inscriptions attest the possibility of atoning for 'known and *unknown* sins' (see n. 120). Needless to say, life did not continue free of minor and major disasters, even after the confession. So several persons came to a sanctuary again and again, after they had discovered that their first confession was not sufficient;[69] probably some of them stopped confessing their sins only in their graves.

The certainty of divine wrath could be more effective than any psychologically guided interrogation. Consequently, the discussion with the priests brought to light small and big offences. Naturally, when the offence was identified, the accused persons tried to defend themselves or begged for forgiveness. Phrases such as 'it escaped my notice', 'I had forgotten', 'I did not know', or 'I did it unknowingly' in the confession inscriptions point, in my view, to excuses put forward by the accused persons.[70] Sometimes the sinners defended themselves by pointing to the exact circumstances under which they had committed their offence. A woman, accused of letting soldiers into a sanctuary (without the priests' permission), responds: 'I wanted to repulse an enemy.'[71] A man punished because he wanted to have sexual intercourse (ἐπεὶ ἠθέλησα μεῖνε μετὰ γυνεκός) adds in his confession:

---

[69] E.g. *BIWK* 17–18; see above, pp. 17–18.

[70] *BIWK* 6: ἐπί με ἔλαθεν κὲ ὑπερέβην τὸν ὅρον ἄθετος ('because I trespassed beyond the boundary stone, as I should not (?), by mistake'); *BIWK* 78: παιδίον ὢν ἀκουσίως κατεάξας στηλλάριον τῆς θεοῦ ('being a child, he shattered a stele of the goddess'); *BIWK* 112: λημόνησα ('I forgot', i.e. to keep a purity regulation); *BIWK* 115: ἔλαθέ [με] ('I did it unknowingly', in the context of the violation of a purity regulation). The participle λαθαμένη in *BIWK* 95 is probably used in the same sense; cf. Petzl (1994: 113); *BIWK* 10: διὰ τὸ ἀγνοεῖν αὐτὸν Διὸς Διδυμείτου ἔκκοψε δρῦν ('he cut an oak of Zeus Didymeites because of ignorance'); *BIWK* 11: ὑπὲρ ἁμαρτίας κατὰ ἄγνοιαν (punished 'for a sin, he committed because of ignorance'); *BIWK* 76: κατὰ ἄγνοιαν ἐκ τοῦ ἄλσους ἔκοψα δένδρα θεῶν ('because of ignorance, I cut trees belonging to the gods from the grove'). I assume that *BIWK* 34 refers to perjury committed unknowingly: ἀγνοήσας ὤμοσεν τὸν θεόν ('he took an oath to the god, because of ignorance'); cf. Pettazzoni (1936: 72–3), Herrmann (1985: 257), Petzl (1994: 41) ('ohne Einblick in den wahren Sachverhalt'). The *lex sacra* of the Labyadai at Delphi probably concerns unintentional perjury as well: *CID* 9 A 16–17: αἰ δ' ἐφιορκέοιμ[ι, Fε]κών (or [κ]α-κῶν?; 'if I commit perjury intentionally'); cf. G. Rougemont's commentary *ad loc.* (pp. 38 and 46). For culpable negligence in Greek law see Maschke (1926: 77–8, 150–9), Jones (1956: 261, 264–5); for *culpa* in Roman law see the bibliography in Nörr (1986: 125 n. 16); cf. Kaser (1975: 346–51). Ignorance of the law was occasionally used as an excuse. See, e.g., the letter of a governor at Phainai (third century AD, *OGIS* 609.29–41): ταῦτά μου τὰ γράμματα ἐν προδήλῳ τῆς μητροκωμίας ὑμῶν χωρίῳ πρόθετε, μή τις ὡς ἀγνοήσας ἀπολογήσηται ('put this letter in a prominent site of the *metrokomia*, so that nobody will defend himself putting forward a "plea of ignorance"').

[71] *BIWK* 114 (Ortaköy): ἐπεὶ ἀνήγαγα στρατιώτας ἐπὶ τὸ ἱερὸν ἐχθρὸν θέλουσα ἀμύνασθαι. Self-defence was used as an excuse in homicide cases in Greek law: Jones (1956: 260, 267). The woman's offence probably is that she let armed persons into a sanctuary; this is forbidden by several sacred regulations: e.g. *LSAM* 68.2–3 (Stratonikeia, Hellenistic?); *SEG* XXXVI 1221.1–4 (Xanthos, third/second century). In Ptolemaic Egypt, soldiers could enter a sanctuary only with the permission of the priests: von Woeß (1923: 133). Mitchell (1993a: 197) has suggested that the priests in Asia Minor did not view the presence of Roman soldiers in their sanctuaries very favourably. Petzl (1994: 135;

Divine justice

'with my own wife, Basilis' (μετὰ τῆς εἰδ[ίας γ]υνεκὸς Βα[σι]λίδος).⁷² References to the young age, and consequently to the limited liability, of the sinner are found in four confession inscriptions (*BIWK* 55: παιδίον ὢν ἐτῶν ἕξ; *BIWK* 58: μήπω οὖσα ἐνῆλιξ; *BIWK* 68: παιδίου αὐτῶν βόσκοντος πενταετοῦς; *BIWK* 78: παιδίον ὢν ἀκουσίως κατεάξας στηλλάριον τῆς θεοῦ). I suspect that these explanations were given by the delinquents in order to exonerate themselves or soothe the gods' wrath. Conversely, there are also cases of incriminating circumstances, which must have been underlined by the priests for didactic reasons. A text castigates a group of persons who schemed against orphans for their malicious deed;⁷³ several confession inscriptions reprimand persons who disregarded and scoffed at divine power,⁷⁴ usually by insisting on their perjury or on pleas for innocence, even though they were conscious of their guilt.⁷⁵

The pleas for extenuating circumstances sometimes worked. A confession inscription quotes a sacred regulation concerning the fines payable to sanctuaries for the annulling of oaths and imprecations (ἵνα λύονται οἱ ὅρκοι, ὁ λύων ὅρκους, ὁ λύων σκῆπτρον),⁷⁶ which prescribed the payment of 175 denarii for the clearing of perjury; the text reports, however,

---

1995: 45) goes one step further and assumes that this inscription reflects a conflict between sacred and secular authorities; the woman let soldiers into the sanctuary, 'um sich gegen den Gott bzw. seine Stellvertreter durchzusetzen'; but in this case the confession inscription would use the word ἐχθρός (enemy) to designate the god or a priest, and I find this hard to believe. The woman's 'enemy' may have been a delinquent who had sought asylum in the sanctuary, against whom the woman tried to mobilize secular authorities.

⁷² *BIWK* 111. This addition is interpreted in a different way by Ramsay (1895: 151), followed by Petzl (1994: 131): 'the last five words are an addition intended to explain the too brief phrase above'.

⁷³ *BIWK* 35 (Tazenon katoikia, AD 210/11). Zingerle (1926: 42) rightly points to the element of *dolus* (λαθραίως) in this text, which is penalized by Roman law: Kaser (1971: 504–13) and (1975: 346–51), Nörr (1986: 90–2, 194–5), cf. Versnel (1991: 97–8 n. 50) and (1999: 131–2). For the moral condemnation of malice (δόλος, ἐπιβουλή) see Chaniotis (1997a: 361 n. 46). Orphans often appear as victims of violence and deceit: Krause (1995: 194–208). For further evidence see Lewis (1989: 102, no. 23).

⁷⁴ *BIWK* 12: κολασθεῖσα ἔτη δ' καὶ μὴ πιστεύουσα τῷ θεῷ; cf. Petzl (1995: 43–6).

⁷⁵ Cf. Petzl (1995: 43–6). See, e.g., *BIWK* 34: ἀπιθοῦντος, cf. Herrmann (1985: 256); *BIWK* 68: οὐκ ὡμολόγησαν διά τινα ἀχαριστίαν, cf. Zingerle (1926: 8); *BIWK* 69: ἐν συνειδήσι τοιαύτῃ, cf. Zingerle (1926: 20) and Björck (1938: 27). The expression ἀτενῶς ὀμόσας in *BIWK* 15 probably refers to persistent perjury; cf. Petzl (1994: 23). Cf. possibly *BIWK* 107: διὰ . . . συνίδησιν. For συνείδησις ('awareness of guilt') cf. Zingerle (1926: 20) and here nn. 34 and 77.

⁷⁶ *BIWK* 58 (Katakekaumene, AD 166/7): Χάριν [ἔ]|δωκαν οἱ θεοὶ Εὐδόξῳ, ἵνα μὴ λυομ[έ]|νων ὅρκων τῆς Ταρσηνῆς λύει Εὔδο|ξος ὑπὲρ τῆς ἰδίας γυναικός. Ἐπεὶ |ὤμοσεν Σάρδιον καὶ παρώρκησεν, διὰ τοῦ|το – μήπω οὖσα ἐνῆλιξ {ουσα} – δαπανή|σας ὁ Εὔδοξος ἐννέα ὀβολοὺς ἔλυ|σε τοὺς ὅρκους καὶ ἐστηλλογ{γ}ράφησε | καὶ εὐχαριστεῖ. Quotation of the *lex sacra*:

"Ἵνα λύονται οἱ ὅρκοι τῷ | ὀνόματι τοῦ Ἀξιοττηνοῦ, ὥστε ὁ | λύων ὅρκους δαπανήσει δηνάρια ἑ|κατὸν ἑβδομήκοντα πέντε· τειμή|ν δὲ λήμψεται ἀφ' αὐτῶν, ἥν ἂν ἐ|περωτήσι, εἰ ταῦτα δικαίως γ{1}εγρ|αμμένα εἰσί, ἵν' ἀνέσστησεν | στήλλην. Ὁ λύων σκῆπτρον θήσ|ει ἐπὶ τὸ ἱερὸν δηνάρια ἑκατὸν ἑβδο|μήκοντα πέντε{1}, καὶ λέλυται τὸ σκῆπτ(ρον?) δικαίως ΕΙΝΡΟΛΥΣΙΝΑΙ λελυμέν<ο>υσ|ς τοὺς θεοὺς κατὰ ὡς ἐπέκρεινα<ν α>ὐτοί.

that the gods did Eudoxos the favour (χάριν [ἔ]δωκαν) of allowing him to annul an oath taken by his wife, who was a minor (again, a reference to extenuating circumstances), through the payment of a much smaller amount (only 9 obols) and the erection of a stele. A similar text concerns a woman who was not in a position to fulfil her vow (the donation of an ox); the god allowed her (συνεχώρησεν) – obviously by means of an oracle (see nn. 13 and 67) – to erect an inscription instead (*BIWK* 61, Ayazviran, AD 235/6). Georg Petzl has convincingly argued that the last lines of another confession inscription quote an oracle given by Meter Phileis, in which the goddess forgives a female delinquent under consideration of the extenuating conditions: when the woman explained that she had committed an offence unintentionally (λαθαμένη), the goddess responded: 'Now I have shown mercy, since (you committed the sin) unconsciously.'[77]

These texts suggest that the priests were instruments of divine justice in a very specific way: they assisted the people who had come to their sanctuaries in agony and in the conviction that the gods were punishing them to identify the cause of divine anger. By doing so they usually found out about more or less important acts of sacrilege, less often about crimes and misdemeanours prosecuted by secular law: a thief brought a garment he had stolen from a bath; Hermogenes admitted that he had cheated Artemidoros; Apollonios confessed that he and his brother had stolen livestock belonging to two foreigners. In all these cases the culprits came to the sanctuary *after* they had been punished by the gods; there is no reference to any additional punishment inflicted by the priests.[78] In the case of the thief, they merely advised him to sell the stolen garment and make a dedication. In other cases they suggested similar remedies: the erection of an inscription, the performance of a ritual, or the spending of money for the sanctuary (cf. §6 below).[79] As we shall see later, they possibly also served as arbitrators when

---

Commentary: Petzl (1994: 71–2). The annulling of oaths is also attested in *BIWK* 34, 52 and 54; for the annulling of imprecations see *BIWK* 69, cf. *BIWK* 17 and 20; see also Strubbe (1991: 45), Petzl (1994: 4).

[77] Petzl (1994: 113). *BIWK* 95: ἐγὼ οὖν ἤλησα (= ἠλέησα?) ἐπὶ (= ἐπεὶ) μὴ ἰδίᾳ συνει[δήσει–]. For συνείδησις ('conscience of guilt') see above n. 75.

[78] Cf. Varinlioğlu (1989: 39), Ricl (1995: 69).

[79] The expiation is expressed with different words: ἱλάζεσθαι, ἐξιλάζεσθαι, ἐκλυτροῦσθαι, λύτρον, θυμολυτεῖν, θυμολυσία, ἱεροποίημα. For ἐκλυτροῦσθαι and λύτρον see Herrmann (1962: 47–8), Petzl (1994: xi with nn. 15–16, 60); for θυμολυσία, θυμολυτεῖν see Malay (1992), Petzl (1994: 31); for ἱεροποίημα (e.g. *TAM* v.1 320–2) see Versnel (1991: 78), Petzl (1994: 91–2) and (1995: 43); for δαπανεῖν see *BIWK* 33, 58, and Petzl (1997: 70–5, no. 2); cf. Varinlioğlu (1991: 92–3), Petzl (1994: 40, 48). For the payment of money see also *BIWK* 38: ἐθήκομεν δηνάρια ἑκατὸν καθὼς ἐπεζήτησαν οἱ πάτριοι θεοί; cf. Versnel (1991: 77) and (2002). Sometimes money was spent on the setting up of a stele: *BIWK* 46 and 58; cf. Petzl (1994: 72). The verb ἀποδίδωμι is used to express both the repayment of a debt to the sanctuary (*BIWK* 8, 17, 18, 28, 36, 46, 63, 71) and the fulfilment of expiation (cf. the expression ἱεροποίημα ἀποδίδωμι in *BIWK* 73 and 74); when used without an

two conflicting parties came to the sanctuary. But did they ever serve as judges or pass judgements?

This has been tentatively maintained by Georg Petzl (1988 and 1994) in the light of a lengthier text – the extremely interesting confession of a certain Theodoros (Silandos, AD 235/6). Indeed, this text resembles the minutes of a trial presided over by a council and has to be discussed in some detail.[80] In this text the confessions of Theodoros alternate with quotations of oracles given by Zeus, thus creating the impression of a dialogue between the sinner and the god.[81] Theodoros, a sacred slave, had violated repeatedly the obligation of sexual abstinence – committing adultery as well, because one of his partners was a 'married' slave. For this reason he lost his sight and presumably sought advice in the temple. Zeus explained, apparently by means of oracular responses, why he had punished him and how Theodoros should atone for his sins. The confession of each sin is followed by the recommendation of a purificatory ritual, which consisted in the transmission of the sin (rather than the illness) to a triad of animals (*triphonon*).[82] Responding to an enquiry by a council (*synkletos*),[83] Zeus finally forgave Theodoros:

---

object, it expresses the general fulfilment of the god's demand: Robert (1964: 30), Herrmann and Varinlioğlu (1984: 2 with note 2).
[80] *BIWK* 5, ll. 2–26:

Ἀκατὰ τὸ ἐφρενωθεὶς ὑπὸ τῶν | θεῶν, ὑπὸ τοῦ | Διὸς κὲ τοῦ (Μηνὸς) μεγάλου Ἀρτεμι|δώρου.' – 'Ἐκολασόμην τὰ ὄματα τὸν | Θεόδωρον κατὰ τὰς ἁμαρτίας, ἃς | ἐπύησεν.'– 'Συνεγενόμην τῇ πε|δίσχῃ τῷ Ἁπλοκόμα, τῇ Τροφίμῃ, τῇ γυ|ναικὶ τῇ Εὐτύχηδος εἰς τὸ πλετώ|ριν.'– 'Ἀπαίρι τὴν πρώτην ἁμαρτίαν προβά|τῳ {ν}, πέρδεικι, ἀσφάλακι. Δευτέρα | ἁμαρτία. "Ἀλλὰ δοῦλος ὢν τῶν θεῶν τῶν | ἐν Νονου συνεγενόμην τῇ Ἀριάγνῃ τῇ | μοναυλίᾳ.' – 'παίρι χύρῳ, θείννῳ, ἐχθύει. Τῇ | τρίτη ἁμαρτία συνεγενόμην Ἀρεθούσῃ | μοναυλίᾳ'. – 'παίρι ὄρνειθι, στρουθῷ, περισ|τερᾷ, κύ(πρῳ) κρειθοπύρων, πρό(χῳ) οἴνου· κύ(πρῳ?) πυρῶν | καθαρὸς τοῖς ἱεροῖς, πρό(χῳ?) α'.– '"Εσχα παράκλητον | τὸν Δείαν.'– 'Εἴδαι, κατὰ τὰ πυήματα πεπηρώκιν.' | Νῦν δὲ εἱλαζομένο αὐτοῦ τοὺς θεοὺς κὲ στη|λογραφοῦντος ἀνερύσετον τὰς ἁμαρτίας. Ἠρωτημαίνος ὑπὸ τῆς συνκλήτου· 'εἴλεος εἶ|μαι ἀναστανομένης τῆς στήλλην μου, |ᾗ ἡμέρᾳ ὥρισα. Ἀνύξαις τὴν φυλακήν, ἐξαφίω | τὸν κατάδικον διὰ ἐνιαυτοῦ κὲ μηνῶν ι΄ περι|πατούντων.

Commentaries: Malay (1988: 151–2) Petzl (1988), Varinlioğlu (1989: 37–40) (with slightly different readings), Petzl (1994: 8–11) (with German translation), Ricl (1995: 72–3), Chaniotis (1997a: 357–60).
[81] Petzl (1988: 155), Varinlioğlu (1989: 38), Petzl (1994: 8–9), Ricl (1995: 72–3).
[82] For this ritual see Chaniotis (1995: 333–4); cf. Varinlioğlu (1989: 48–9), Petzl (1994: xv, 9, 12–13), Ricl (1995: 68, 72), Klauck (1996: 81). Petzl (1997: 75) has expressed his doubts about my interpretation of the *triphonon* as a reference to a triad of animals; but my interpretation is now confirmed by an inscription which will be published soon by H. Malay and P. Herrmann (I owe this information to H. Malay).
[83] It is generally assumed that the term *synkletos* (actually the senate) designates a council of priests: Petzl (1988: 158, 164), Petzl (1994: 10, xiv), Varinlioğlu (1989: 38), Chaniotis (1997a: 359). However, a new text, which will be published by H. Malay and P. Herrmann, suggests that the term designated a council of gods. Hasan Malay has also informed me of a confession inscription he found recently, in which a man, who had been the victim of theft and had appealed to Mes, describes the god as κριτὴς ἀλάθητος ἐν οὐρανῷ.

THEODOROS Because I have been brought by the gods to my senses, by Zeus and the Great Mes Artemidorou, (I have atoned or I have set up this inscription).
ZEUS I have punished Theodoros on his eyes for his offences.
THEODOROS I had sexual intercourse with Trophime, the slave of Haplokomas, the wife of Eutychis, in the 'praetorium'.
ZEUS He takes the first sin away with a sheep, a partridge, a mole.
Second sin
THEODOROS While I was a slave of the gods of Nonnos, I had sexual intercourse with the flutist Ariagne.[84]
ZEUS He takes away with a 'piglet', a tuna, (another) fish.
THEODOROS For my third sin I had sexual intercourse with the flutist Aretousa.
ZEUS He takes away with a chicken, a sparrow, a pigeon. A kypros of barley and wheat, a prochus of wine, a kypros of clean (?) wheat for the priests, one prochus.
THEODOROS I asked for Zeus's help.[85]
ZEUS Look (or see)! I have blinded him for his sins. But, since he has appeased the gods and has erected the stele, he has taken his sins away. Asked by the council, (I respond that) I am kindly disposed, if (or when) he sets up my stele, on the day I have ordered. You may open the prison. I set the convict free after one year and ten months.[86]

Although all the editors of this inscriptions have pointed out that the text recalls a court protocol, they reach different conclusions. According to Georg Petzl a trial did take place in the sanctuary; Theodoros was convicted and was kept in jail (or 'Gotteshaft'); Zeus was impersonated by a priest.[87] Petzl has suggested that a similar punishment is mentioned in another text (*BIWK* 33), interpreting the expression ἐνποδισθ[ῖ]σα ἐν τῷ ναῷ ('fettered in the temple') as a reference to imprisonment in a temple.[88] On the contrary, Ender Varinlioğlu argued that the word φυλακή (jail, prison) is used metaphorically: Theodoros' blindness was his jail; through this punishment the gods restricted his licentious sexual activities.[89] Petzl's interpretation is very appealing. He is certainly right in pointing to the

---

[84] I agree with R. Merkelbach's translation of μοναυλία ('flutist'), *apud* Petzl (1988: 161 n. 42). Cf. the verb μοναυλέω ('play the monaulos': Plut. *Caes.* 52). *Contra* Petzl (1988: 160–1) and (1994: 8 and 10), who points to the metaphorical use of μόναυλος (sc. βίος, i.e. unmarried life: Pl. *Leg.* 6.721D).

[85] In Greek, ἔσχα παράκλητον | τὸν Δείαν. Cf. *BGU* II 601.12: παράκλητος δέδωκα αὐτῷ; cf. Varinlioğlu (1989: 38 n. 6) (Theodoros has begged Zeus); Ricl (1995: 72 n. 19) ('I had Zeus summoned'); *contra* Malay (1988: 152) ('legal adviser'), Petzl (1988: 163–4) ('Rechtsbeistand'), Klauck (1996: 81, 'Anwalt und Fürsprecher'). Henk Versnel suggests to me that the punisher and forgiver may be Mes, Zeus only a mediator.

[86] Petzl (1994: 8): 'da ein Jahr und zehn Monate herumgehen (?)'; cf. Malay (1988: 152).

[87] Petzl (1988: 163–5) and (1994: 10–11).

[88] Petzl (1994: 39): 'die im Tempel festgehalten (?, gehindert?) worden war'; cf. H.W. Pleket, commentary on *SEG* XLI 1038.

[89] Varinlioğlu (1989: 37–9); cf. Ricl (1995: 72–3); Chaniotis (1997a: 357–60).

possibility that priests impersonated the gods in the temple. Such a 'sacred theatre' is well attested in the Imperial period, as R. Merkelbach has demonstrated.⁹⁰ Furthermore, it is conceivable that, since Theodoros was a sacred slave, the priests had the authority to put him away for a period of time – a procedure recalling the 'house arrest' attested in the Serapeum at Memphis in the Ptolemaic period.⁹¹ Finally, the use of legal vocabulary certainly creates the impression of a law suit. We find the words ἁμαρτία and κολάζω, which are not only used in a religious context, but are also the technical terms for offence and punishment in the documentary papyri from the Hellenistic period onwards; we also find the terms παράκλητος (see n. 85) and κατάδικος ('convict').

However, none of these indications is really conclusive. The verbal assimilation of divine justice to secular jurisdiction, which we observe in this text, is very common in texts from Asia Minor which have nothing to do with law suits. In the funerary imprecations divine vengeance is very often assimilated with a trial, with such expressions as ἔνοχος ἔστω θεοῖς ('*he should be liable* to the punishment of the gods'), δίκας τίνειν καταχθονίοις θεοῖς ('*he should be judged* by the gods of the underworld'), λόγον διδόναι τῷ θεῷ ('*he shall account* to the god'), or πρὸς τὸν θεὸν κρίσιν ἔχειν ('*he shall be judged* by the god').⁹² Similarly, the use of legal terms in Theodoros' confession is no proof that his trial took place in a temple and not in heaven (cf. n. 83). In fact it is beyond doubt that in this inscription the Roman terms *synkletos* ('senate') and *pletorin* (*praetorium*)⁹³ were not used in their proper meaning, but metaphorically. Therefore, when we find in the confession inscriptions legal terms (e.g. ἐκζητεῖν, ἐπικρίνειν, συγχωρεῖν, etc.), these do not support the assumption that the temples functioned as courts of justice. In addition to this, the text which Petzl regarded as a possible parallel (*BIWK* 33: ἐνποδισθ[ῖ]σα ἐν τῷ ναῷ ἐκολάσθη ὑπὸ τῶν θεῶν ἵνα ἀναδίξει τὰς δυνάμις αὐτῶν) does not refer to an imprisonment. In all confession inscriptions known to me the verb κολάζειν is preceded by an explanation of why the sinner was punished and followed by the form of the punishment.⁹⁴ It follows that the expression ἐνποδισθ[ῖ]σα ἐν τῷ ναῷ

---

⁹⁰ Merkelbach (1995: 172–3, 178–81).
⁹¹ Von Woeß (1923: 134–5). Of course, in this case one should not attempt to draw more general conclusions based on the particular case of a *hierodoulos*.
⁹² For these expressions see, e.g., *SEG* VI 301, *SEG* XXVII 931, *TAM* II 1028, *TAM* IV 375, Strubbe (1997 nos. 338, 397). Cf. Zingerle (1926: 49–72), Versnel (1991: 68–9, 71, 73, 90).
⁹³ For *synkletos* see above n. 83. For *pletorin* see Petzl (1988: 158, 164).
⁹⁴ *BIWK* 6, 7, 9, 22, 23, 34, 35, 43, 47, 49, 50, 54, 57, 60, 62, 63, 64, 65, 71, 76, 96, 99, 101, 106, 114, 117, 120. The form of the punishment is usually given after the verb κολάζειν: *BIWK* 5, 7, 16, 29, 34, 35, 45, 49, 50, 54, 57, 63, 75, 84, 85, 86, 89, 91, 93, 95, 106, 122.

(used here before and not after ἐκολάσθη) gives the reason for and not the form of the punishment: the sinner was punished because 'she had been detained in the temple', possibly while behaving in an improper way.[95] We should, therefore, disregard these texts as evidence for 'trials' in sanctuaries.

Even if in all the cases discussed so far the role of the priests was limited to the performance of curses, the interpretation of divine will and the performance of rituals for the atonement, this does not mean that they never intervened in legal affairs. But if they did, then it was as arbitrators, not as judges.

5. PRIESTS AS ARBITRATORS AND ADMINISTRATORS OF OATHS

An interesting posthumous honorific decree for Aristodemos, priest of Zeus Pigindenos (first century BC), describes his merits as follows:

he has behaved with piety towards the divinity (εὐσεβῶς διακείμενον πρὸς τὸ θεῖον), he has lived a priestly life (καὶ ἐζηκότα ἱεροπρεπῶς), he has conducted himself in a benevolent and well-disposed way towards justice (καὶ πρὸς τὸ δίκαιον φιλαγάθως καὶ εὐνόως), and he has been a benefactor of the demos (καὶ ὄντα εὐεργέτην τοῦ δήμου).[96]

It is anything but surprising to honour a priest for piety, a priestly life or even benefactions towards the people; but a particular connection with justice requires an explanation. It should be mentioned that the phrase used in this text is not a stereotypical, formulaic expression; therefore, it alludes to specific services of the priest. Two honorary decrees of Laodikeia and Kallipolis for Leon of Stratonikeia, priest of Zeus at Panamara (late third or more probably second century BC), may give us an impression of the ways in which Aristodemos may have contributed to the implementation of law.[97] The decree of the Laodikeis[98] is better preserved; it describes some of Leon's activities in this sanctuary very clearly (*SEG* XLV 1557.4–8): 'Leon, . . . who served as a priest at Panamara in a pious and benevolent way, behaved towards all our citizens who came to the sanctuary in a way which demonstrated his concern with honour (φιλοδόξως), and continually reconciled those who had disputes with regard to oaths (τοὺς διαφερο[μ]ένους ὑπὲρ τῶν ὅρκων συλλύων διετέλει).' The latter expression recurs, but in a fragmentary form, in the honorary decree of Kallipolis (*SEG* XLV 1556.12–13),

---

[95] An alternative is suggested by Petzl (1994: 39): she had been detained to do something the god had ordered her to do.
[96] *SEG* XLV 1515 (Hisartepe in Caria).
[97] *SEG* XLV 1556 and 1557. For the date see P. Gauthier, *BE* (1997) no. 2.
[98] Probably a Seleucid foundation in Caria (and not Laodikeia on the Lykos): see Ma (1997).

Divine justice

which also adds that he took care of the suppliants and other visitors to the sanctuary (ll. 10–11: [–] τῶν ἱκετευόντων [καὶ –] πρόνοιαν ἐποιεῖτο). The sanctuary of Zeus at Panamara, one of the most important religious centres in Caria, attracted visitors from many Carian cities;[99] some of them seem to have been victims of injustice who sought refuge or just support; others came because of disputes over 'oaths' (contracts, exculpatory oaths?). The fact that we have two decrees from the same period (probably the same year) suggests an extraordinary situation, possibly conflicts with regard to debts; but it is also possible that this increased activity in the sanctuary is simply due to the fact that under the priesthood and at the initiative of Leon the asylia of the sanctuary was re-established and many Carian communities were invited to participate in the cult.[100] In any event, it is certain that people came to a widely respected sanctuary in order to solve legal problems.

The expression 'he reconciled those who had disputes with regard to oaths' is rather vague, but it shows that Leon took an active part in the solution of conflicts. The verb συλλύω is adopted from the vocabulary of arbitration (also of international arbitration)[101] and implies a far more energetic intervention than, e.g., the administration of exculpatory oaths. Unfortunately, we lack other evidence for such activities of priests, other than references to their intervention in cases of conflicts between suppliants and their prosecutors.[102]

Studies based on more abundant material suggest that in many cases the adversaries preferred a solution of the conflict outside the court, through arbitration, rather than a trial.[103] This tendency is even stronger in rural communities, and this is where most of the confession inscriptions have been found, in villages and small settlements (κῶμαι, κατοικίαι),[104] in the vicinity of sanctuaries, the gods of which were designated as 'kings' and rulers.[105] Even though some of the sanctuaries were relatively small, their priests were often the next representatives of what we may call an

---

[99] See esp. Oppermann (1924) and Laumonier (1958: 234–9).
[100] *I. Stratonikeia* 7 informs us about Leon's initiative; for the *asylia* of the sanctuary see Rigsby (1996: 425–6).
[101] For συλλύω and σύλλυσις see, e.g., Ager (1996) nos. 63, 64, 74, 83, 90, 109, 114, 137, 146, 158, 161, 171.
[102] Chaniotis (1996*a*).
[103] Scafuro (1997: 68–192, 383–99) (Athens and Rome); Chaniotis (1996*b*: 139–40, 145) (Crete).
[104] E.g. *BIWK* 3: Tarsi; 6: Perkos (or Perkon); 17: Pereudos (or Pereudon); 35: Tazenon katoikia; 68: Azita, Syrou Mandrai.
[105] For examples see Petzl (1994: xiv, 64); Horsley (1997: 55), Schuler (1998: 250). Cf. Zingerle (1926: 9–10); Herrmann (1978: 422–3), Debord (1982: 166), Mitchell (1993*a*: 191).

'authority' – especially in remote villages.¹⁰⁶ The rural population, which sometimes depended on the sanctuaries in one way or another (as sacred slaves, slaves of freedmen of the priests, leasers of the sacred land, leasers of buildings belonging to the sanctuary, or as debtors),¹⁰⁷ naturally turned to the gods and their representatives in order to request a good harvest, healthy offspring, a good marriage, a long-awaited inheritance. The sanctuaries could be for them banks, employers, hospitals and, of course, advisers in simple legal questions,¹⁰⁸ although they did not substitute for the secular authorities in the administration of justice (see §7 below). A similar role was played in Ptolemaic Egypt by the local priests, with the important difference that in Egypt this role was institutionalized.¹⁰⁹ The use of legal terms in the confession inscriptions, vows and dedications not only reflects the legal background of the respective cases, but it also shows that the authors of the texts (often the priests) were familiar with the contemporary legal practices and institutions of Greek – and in part of Roman – law.¹¹⁰

Babrius' fable cited at the beginning of this chapter may provide a slightly different context for some of the legal conflicts with which sanctuaries were confronted: persons could bring their opponents to a sanctuary asking them to take an oath of innocence, and then leave the matter to the god to decide whether this was perjury or not. I suspect that a sacred regulation from Laodikeia on the Lykos (*ca* second century AD) reflects this practice. It stipulates that a person who wanted to make another person take an oath (ὁ θέλων ὀρκ[ίζειν]) had to remain pure and offer a sacrifice.¹¹¹ If this text refers to the practice of bringing an accused person to a sanctuary and

---

¹⁰⁶ We should count on substantial differences among the sanctuaries in terms of property, authority and power. See, e.g., Zingerle (1926: 47–8), Zawadzki (1952–3: 86–9), Debord (1982: 165–8) (for Lydia). On the large number of small rural sanctuaries see also Petzl (1995: 39).

¹⁰⁷ I restrict myself to examples in the confession inscriptions. Sacred slaves: *BIWK* 5, 49, 77, 106; for *hierodouloi* in sanctuaries of Asia Minor in general see Debord (1982: 83–7, cf. 117–24, 165 with n. 29), Mitchell (1993a: 193). Leasers of land or buildings: Petzl (1997); possibly *BIWK* 37; cf. Herrmann (1985: 255), Petzl (1994: 46–7). Debtors: *BIWK* 63; cf. Varinlioğlu (1989: 44 and 49).

¹⁰⁸ Cf. Varinlioğlu (1989: 49), Mitchell (1993a: 193).

¹⁰⁹ Quaegebeur (1993) and Anagnostou-Canas (1998).

¹¹⁰ See the list of more than fifty terms in Chaniotis (1997a: 382–4) with the testimonia, a commentary on the meaning of these terms, and parallels in other documentary sources (esp. in documentary papyri). Numerous terms derive directly or indirectly from the vocabulary of judicial procedures, e.g. ἀναδέχομαι (accept the responsibility for a deed or stand surety for someone) and παράκλητος (called to one's aid in a court). Most of the legal terms are related to the law of property and to inheritance law: e.g. ἀποδίδωμι συναχθὲν κεφάλαιον (repay the collected capital), ἀπόμοιρα (share), ἐκχωρέω and παραχωρέω (cede), ἱκανοδότης (guarantor), κεφάλαιον (capital), ληγᾶτον (*legatum*), μέρος (share in an inheritance), πεκούλιον (*peculium*), πίστις (security), πίστιν τηρέω (keep an agreement), προγραφή (auction) and προλέγω (proclaim in an oral contract). Admittedly some of these words are rather trivial and may be used even outside a legal context, but we also find specialized terms (e.g. ἀναδέχομαι, ἀντίδικος, ἀπελέγχω, κατάδικος, etc.).

¹¹¹ *I.Laodikeia/Lykos* 64 = *MAMA* VI 1 = *LSAM* 88.

making him take an exculpatory oath, it makes sense that it was the duty of the 'plaintiff' to offer the required sacrifice. A confession inscription offers corroborative evidence. An unclear dispute had arisen from the fact that a certain Hermogenes had given security on behalf of Kaikos and Tryphon regarding some sheep (γενόμενος εἰκανοδότης Καΐκου καὶ Τρ<ύ>φωνος περὶ προβάτων). The opponents were given the judgement that Hermogenes should support his claims by taking an oath (ἐκρίθη ὀμόσε τὸν Ἑρμογένην μὴ προδεδωκένε τὰ πρόβατα τὰ Καείκου, 'the judgement was given that he should swear that he had not abandoned?/delivered? Kaikos' sheep'). Hermogenes committed perjury, and although he may have done this unknowingly (ἀγνοήσας, cf. n. 70), he had to pay a high price. His ox and his donkey died, but he insisted on his claims (ἀπιθοῦντος), until the death of his daughter forced him to annul his oath.[112] There is a controversy about whether this exculpatory oath was stipulated by a secular court or by the priests;[113] a third plausible possibility is that an oracle requested Hermogenes to take an oath.[114] But no matter how we answer this question (and I see no compelling reason to prefer one of the three alternatives over another), this text does not provide evidence for trials in the temples of Asia Minor, but it does provide evidence for the importance of exculpatory oaths as a means of resolving a dispute, especially when witnesses or other evidence were lacking.[115] Perjury was then expected to provoke divine wrath. This, again, is probably the context of another fragmentary

[112] *BIWK* 34 (Ayazviran, third century AD?):

[–]ω Ἑρμογένης Ἀπολωνί|ου Βαλέρισς γενόμενος εἰκανοδ|ότης Καΐκου καὶ Τρ<ύ>φωνος περὶ προ|βάτων, ὦν ἐκρίθη ὀμόσε τὸν Ἑρ|μογένην μὴ προδεδωκένε τὰ | πρόβατα τὰ Καείκου· ἀγνοήσας οὖ|ν ὁ Ἑρμογένης ὤμοσεν τὸν θεό|ν. Ὁ θεὸς ἀνέδειξεν τὰς εἰδίας δυν|άμις καὶ ἐκόλασεν τὸν Ἑρμογένην | καὶ ζημίας αὐτῷ ἐπόησεν ἀποκτί|νας αὐτῷ τὰ κτήνη, βοῦν κὲ ὄνον. Ἀπιθοῦντος δὲ τοῦ θεοῦ ἐπέκτινεν α|ὐτοῦ τὶν θυγατέραν. Τότε ἔλυσεν τὸ|ν ὅρκον. Ἀφιὰς καὶ τὰ τέκνα αὐτῆς Ἀλέ|ξανδρος, Ἄτταλος, Ἀπολ<ώ>νιος, Ἀμιο|ν ἐστήσομεν τὴν στήλην καὶ ἐνεγράψομ|εν τὰς δυνάμις τοῦ θεοῦ καὶ ἀπὸ νῦν εὐλ|ογοῦμεν.

Commentaries: Zingerle (1926: 33–5), Eger (1939: 284–6), Petzl (1994: 41–2). Zingerle (1926: 7) identified Hermogenes with the protagonist of *BIWK* 68 (see above n. 63). The cause of this conflict is not clear, because we cannot determine with certainty the meaning of προδίδωμι in this context ('give beforehand, deliver up, give up or abandon').

[113] The assumption that the oath was stipulated by a secular court is held by Latte (1920: 17–18 with n. 33), Buckler (1914–16: 179) and Eger (1939: 285); *contra* Zingerle (1926: 33): 'ein von der Gottheit als richterlicher Instanz einer Prozeßpartei auferlegter Beweiseid'; Petzl (1994: 41) leaves the question open.

[114] Cf. the use of ἐπικρίνω in the meaning 'to answer an oracular request' in *P.Tebt.* II 284.2–3. The same verb is used in *BIWK* 58.20 in connection with the atonement demanded by the gods – again, probably by means of an oracle.

[115] Gagarin (1997), who modifies the traditional view that exculpatory oaths and oaths of purification played a major role in the settlement of disputes in early Greece, does not consider the material from Asia Minor. For exculpatory oaths in Egypt see, e.g., *PSI* 1128 (third century AD). The hopeless situation which leads to an exculpatory oath is described by Babrius, *Fab.* 2: οὐκ ἔχων δ' ὁ ποιήσει, | εἰς τὴν πόλιν κατῆγε πάντας ὀρκώσων.

confession inscription: an anonymous person reports that his legal opponents (ἀντίδικοι) revealed the untruth of his statement (ἀπελεγχθ[εὶς ὑπὸ τῶν ἀν]τιδίκων). The vocabulary suggests the ordinary context of a trial. The fact that this person (and his son) had to propitiate a series of gods for this reason (νῦ[ν ἱλασάμενος] μετὰ υἱοῦ) leaves no doubt that his untrue statement had provoked the gods' anger, i.e. that he had committed perjury.[116] That perjury is the sin most commonly mentioned in the confession inscriptions[117] can best be explained in the light of the exculpatory oaths taken in sanctuaries. One of the moral lessons given in one of these texts is directly connected with this practice: 'he commands not to take an oath or make others take an oath or administer an oath in an unjust way (or for an unjust cause)'.[118]

This evidence leads to the conclusion that the priests of the rural and extra-urban sanctuaries of Asia Minor occasionally arbitrated in legal disputes of the rural population based not only on the power of their gods, but also on their personal experience and authority. A very important service that they could offer – so to say *ex officio* – was the administration of oaths (usually exculpatory oaths), which were often the only means of settling a dispute.

6. 'FEES' FOR THE PROPITIATION OF THE GOD

The confession inscription of Tatias, the 'vicious mother-in-law', confronted us with the phenomenon of the deposition of curses in a temple (§3 above) as a means of refuting unjust accusations. Tatias' claims of innocence were proven false – or at least this is what people believed when Tatias and her family met with accidents and death. To stop further punishment by the gods, it was necessary to annul the curses (*BIWK* 69, ll. 25–7: λυθῆναι τὸ σκῆπτρον καὶ τὰς ἀρὰς τὰς γενομένας ἐν τῷ ναῷ). The text gives us no further details about the procedure, but fortunately we find more information in another confession inscription (*BIWK* 58, see n. 76), which quotes a sacred regulation concerning fines payable to sanctuaries for the annulment of oaths and imprecations: 'In order that the oaths be annulled by the name of Mes Axiottenos (or: the oaths taken through invocation of the name of Mes Axiottenos), the person who annuls oaths shall spend (δαπανήσει) the amount of 175 denarii . . . The person who annuls a sceptre

---

[116] *BIWK* 39. Commentaries: Petzl (1994: 49–50); cf. Ricl (1995: 71 n. 10).
[117] For ἐπιορκέω, ἐπιορκία, ἐπιορκοσύνη and ἐφιορκία see *BIWK* 52, 102, 103, 106, 120. Cf. Chaniotis (1997a: 355 n. 16).
[118] *BIWK* 27: [παραγγέλλων ἀ]δίκως μὴ ὀμνεῖν τινα μήτε ὀρκίζ[ειν] μήτε ὀρκωμότην γίνεσθαι.

(i.e. a curse) shall pay to the sanctuary (θήσει ἐπὶ τὸ ἱερόν) 175 denarii and then the sceptre is annulled justly.' That false oaths were annulled (λύω ὅρκον) is reported in several confession inscriptions (*BIWK* 34 and 54). The following text is certainly related to this procedure: 'I, Diogas Kondon, son of Diogenes, have propitiated Mes of Diodotos (?) for perjury.' Mes is represented on the stele with a sceptre in his right hand. Diogas had probably invoked this god in his oath and then had to propitiate the god by annulling (ἔλοισα = ἔλυσα) the false oath.[119] The aforementioned sacred regulation shows that for the annulment of oaths the gods (i.e. the sanctuaries) charged a fee. Such a fee is mentioned in a confession inscription in a different context: when Chryseros and Stratonikos asked the gods how they could atone for the sins they had committed both knowingly and unknowingly (ἐξ εἰδότων καὶ μὴ εἰδότων), they were asked to pay the sum of 100 denarii.[120] The vocabulary used in these texts (δαπανάω, λύω) provides the context for understanding a series of dedications and confession inscriptions from Lydia and Pisidia which use these or related words (λύτρον, λυτρόω, ἐκλυτρόω) without further explanation of the background.[121]

It was not at all unusual for sanctuaries to receive either money or perquisites for the performance of rituals.[122] The existence of annulment fees suggests that similar charges were paid to the priests for the deposition of curses and for other services, such as the formulation, certification and storage of legal documents (e.g. testaments, contracts, transactions),[123] and the performance of imprecations. A decree of Pednelissos in Pisidia (see above n. 33), which regulates the cooperation of judges with the priestess of Kybele in judiciary matters, attests the payment of a fee by persons who made imprecations in the context of legal disputes (ἀποτεισάτω ὁ

---

[119] *BIWK* 52: Μῆνα ἐξ Διοδότου Διογᾶς Διογένου Κόνδων ἔλοισα ἐξ ἐπιορκοσύνης. Commentary: Petzl (1994) 61, but with a slightly different translation: 'Bei Men ἐξ Διοδότου habe ich, Diogas Kondon, Sohn des Diogenes (mich) vom Meineid losgekauft.' I understand the accusative Μῆνα to be the object of ἔλοισα (= ἔλυσα). Mes must have been the divinity invoked by Diogas in his false oath. Cf. Herrmann (1962: 48), for a similar construction in *BIWK* 51: Μῆνα ἐγ Διοδότου Ἀλέξανδρος Θαλούσης μετὰ Ἰουλίου καὶ τῆς ἀδελφῆς ἐλυτρώσαντο τὸν θεόν.

[120] *BIWK* 38; cf. Petzl (1994: 48). For the expression ἐξ εἰδότων καὶ μὴ εἰδότων (also attested in *BIWK* 51 and 53) see Herrmann (1962: 47–8), Petzl (1994: 60–1), Ricl (1995: 68), Klauck (1996: 74).

[121] For a collection of testimonia see Petzl (1994: xi with nn. 14–16, with further bibliography); cf. Klauck (1996: 79–80). For a new attestation of δαπανάω see Petzl (1997: 70, no. 2). For new attestations of λύτρα see Malay (1999: nos. 111–12).

[122] This is attested in several *leges sacrae*: e.g. *LSAM* 11, 13, 23, 45, 46, 59, 73.

[123] For the possibility that the priests demanded fees or tolls for financial transactions see Herrmann and Varinlioğlu (1984: 5, 7) (cf. *BIWK* 17 and *SEG* XXXIV 1211), Malay and Petzl (1985: 62) (cf. *BIWK* 71), Chaniotis (1997a: 375–6). See, e.g., *SEG* XXXIV 1219: the gods demanded the payment of 72 denarii 'for the house which he has bought' (ὑπὲρ τῆς οἰκίας τῆς ἀγόρασεν).

καταρασάμενος σίγλον). Although there is no explicit reference to this, the payment of fines for the violation of graves to a sanctuary (and not to the city, the *fiscus* or the *aerarium populi Romani*) may be due to the fact that the protection of the grave had been entrusted to the respective sanctuary.[124] The performance of a funerary imprecation (i.e. the invocation of a god or a series of gods) made the gods witnesses to the victims of the violation, and this would explain why the fine for the desecration had to be paid to the sanctuary. Imprecation formulas are not just texts; they presuppose certain ritual actions which should be performed by persons with the relevant knowledge, power or authority. Although I am not at all convinced that all funerary inscriptions which contain imprecations were the result of a ritual performed by priests, in some cases this is explicitly attested. A funerary imprecation at Saittai reports, for example, that the mother and brother of a deceased person 'made an imprecation in order that no one should harm the grave, because sceptres have been set up'.[125] As J. Strubbe (1997: 50) has pointed out, the sceptre probably was erected by the priests inside the sanctuary area. It is in these cases that we can suspect that the sanctuaries received fees for the performance of the imprecations and possibly the fines when a violator of a grave was caught. Similarly, sanctuaries were potential recipients of fines for the violation of wills,[126] probably because they participated in the formulation of the will, or they were the places where the will was deposited, or had performed curses against potential violators.

Many confession inscriptions attest the delivery to sanctuaries of real estate upon request (ἐπιζητέω) of the gods.[127] We should not try to find

---

[124] For the payment of the fine to sanctuaries see, e.g., Strubbe (1991: 34–5) and (1996: 364–6, index). For Lycia see Frézouls and Morant (1985); for Telmessos (to Zeus Solymeus) see Iplikçioğlu (1991: 20) (more than 250 cases). The recipient of the fine is often the person or institution (council, synagogue, professional association) that had been entrusted with the protection of the grave or was expected to take care of it. I give only a few examples. The local *stationarius*: *I.Prusias* 142. The person who took care of the grave: *I.Alex. Troas* 154. The contractor of the estate: *IGR* III 478. The council: *I.Alex. Troas* 98; *I.Laodikeia/Lykos* 122–3. The synagogue: *SEG* XLIV 556. A professional association: *I.Alex. Troas* 122, 151–3, Reynolds (1998).

[125] *TAM* V.1 160 = Strubbe (1997: no. 62): καὶ ἐπηράσαν|το μή τις αὐτοῦ τῷ μνη|μείῳ προσαμάρ-τῃ διὰ τὸ | ἐπεστᾶσθαι σκῆπτρα. Other examples: *TAM* V.1 168 = Strubbe (1997: no. 53); *TAM* V.1 172 = Strubbe (1997: no. 61); *SEG* XXXIV 1231 = Strubbe (1997: no. 55).

[126] E.g. *SEG* VI 673 (Perge): land was bequeathed to the sanctuary of Apollo Lyrboton; the fine for the violation of the will was to be paid to the sanctuary of Artemis Pergaia.

[127] Versnel (1991: 78–9) has shown that the verb ἐπιζητέω is used in different meanings; cf. Herrmann and Varinlioğlu (1984: 2 with n. 5). When it lacks an object it means 'to investigate'; as a transitive verb it means 'to prosecute, to punish'. But in several cases it is used in the meaning 'to demand'; cf. Zingerle (1926: 37) and *BIWK* 15: ἐπεζήτησαν οἱ θεοὶ ἐκ τῆς γυναικὸς αὐτοῦ Καινίδος καὶ τοῦ πεκουλίου τὴν προγραφήν; *BIWK* 18: ἐπεζήτησαν οἱ θεοὶ τὰς ἀνπέλους ... τὰς ληγά-τους; cf. *SEG* XXXIV 1211: ἐπεζήτησαν τὴν ... κληρονομίαν; *BIWK* 36: ἐπιζητήσαντος τοῦ

Divine justice

one generally applicable explanation for all the claims of the gods on real estate and money. Sometimes the gods demanded what was *theirs*, i.e. immovable property bequeathed to the sanctuary and not delivered by the heirs,[128] the repayment of debts,[129] or the delivery of disputed objects which had been ceded to them by victims of injustice (cf. above pp. 16–19). But it is possible that in some cases the delivery of property to a sanctuary was – not unlike the payment of money – part of the process of propitiation, for instance, after a sacrilege.

The payment of a fee and the erection of a stele should not be understood as a *fine*, i.e. as part of the punishment, but as the necessary condition for a reconciliation with the god. The confession inscriptions make a sharp distinction between the punishment (κόλασις, κολάζειν) through disease and other mischances and the atonement (δαπανάω, ἱλάσκομαι, λύω, λυτρόω, ἐκλυτρόω). The latter consisted in the payment of money, the handing over of real estates, the erection of a stele, the performance of rituals and the praising of the gods.[130] This is not without importance for a better understanding of the priests' activities. When the priests demanded the payment of money or the delivery of immovable property, they did not punish the sinners; they simply informed them – as mediators of the divine will – how the wrath of the gods could be appeased. This is particularly clear in the following fragmentary confession inscription. '[–], daughter

---

θεοῦ οἱ κληρονόμοι . . . ἀπέδωκαν; *BIWK* 38: ἐθήκομεν δηνάρια ἑκατὸν καθὼς ἐπεζήτησαν οἱ πάτριοι θεοί; *BIWK* 46: ἐπ[ιζητησά]ντων τῶν [θ]ε[ῶν] ἀπέδωκαν οἱ υἱοὶ . . . τὰ εἰκοσιπέντε δηνάρια διπλᾶ; *SEG* xxxiv 1219: ὑπὲρ τῆς οἰκίας τῆς ἡγόρασεν παρὰ Ἀμμίας Καλλιμάχου ἔδωκα (δηνάρια) οβ', καθὼς ἐπεζήτησαν οἱ θεοί. Cf. also the delivery of food in the context of atonement: *BIWK* 5, 6, 8; cf. Varinlioğlu (1989: 38 n. 10), Ricl (1995: 73).

[128] E.g. Malay (1994: 51 no. 65) (Küpüler near Demirzi): [Ἀ]σκλᾶς Ζωσίμου κατέλιψε | [Δ]ιὶ Σαβασζίῳ κληρονομίαν | ἥντινα ἀπέδωκαν οἱ Διο|δώρου κληρονόμοι. *SEG* xxxiv 1207 (Maionia): ὡς ἐν τῇ διαθήκῃ ἐκέλευσε: "Δία εὐίλατον τῷ κληρονόμῳ, κὲ δωρηὰν χώραν κ' ἀμπέλους τῷ Διεὶ ἀνάφερε τὰ πρὸς Τιλλω"; for ἀναφέρω ('dedicate') see Versnel (1991: 73 with n. 63). Cf. possibly *SEG* xxxiv 1211: the gods ἐπεζήτησαν τὴν . . . κληρονομίαν of C. Iunites. For the bequest of property to sanctuaries see also Debord (1982: 152–3), Petzl (1997: 75) (*TAM* v.1 242) and above n. 126.

[129] This may be the case in *BIWK* 15. When a man insisted on his perjury, the gods asked his wife to put up for auction her property as well (ἐπεζήτησαν . . . καὶ τοῦ πεκουλίου τὴν προγραφήν). The context may be an unpaid debt owed to the sanctuary for sacrilege (perjury); cf. Malay and Petzl (1985: 64). Another equivocal case is *BIWK* 71: Apollonios insulted the god (μεγαλορρημονήσας), possibly by refusing to deliver to the sanctuary some vineyards. The verbs ἀποδιδόναι and παρελκύειν which are used in this text indicate a delay in the repayment of a debt; cf. *BIWK* 63: δανισαμένη . . . καὶ παρελκύσασα; for ἀποδιδόναι, *PSI* v 484.3: παρέλκων οὖν καὶ μὴ ἀποδιδοὺς τὴν γῆν. However, Malay and Petzl (1985: 62) suggest other possibilities (propitiation of a sin or charges for a transaction). One text attests the payment of the *duplum*, but the reason is not stated: *BIWK* 46; Versnel (2002: 67 n. 106) suspects that the perpetrators refused to return an amount of money to the rightful owner. For the payment of *duplum* see Chaniotis (1997*a*: 374 n. 115).

[130] E.g. *BIWK* 5: ἐκολασόμην (l. 5; the punishment is blindness) . . . εἰλαζομένου (l. 20); *BIWK* 6: ἐκολάσαντο (ll. 8–9) . . . ἱλασάμην (ll. 19–20).

of Apollonios, had been detained in the temple and was punished by the gods, in order that she demonstrate their power. By paying monies (δαπανήσασα) she has propitiated the gods and has erected an inscribed stele, and has shown their great power and she praises (them) from now on. During the priesthood of Metras.'[131] The naming of a priest at the end of the text is an unusual feature, attested in only very few confession inscriptions and dedications. I am not convinced that we are dealing here with a local eponymous priest;[132] it seems more probable that we are dealing with a 'false' eponymous, i.e. a sacred official whose name is given in a dating formula not because he was the eponymous official of his community, but because of his participation in the action with which the document is concerned.[133] In the cases of the confession inscriptions in which a priest is named, it is reasonable to assume that he had consulted the sinner, determined the amount of money and the other actions necessary for the atonement, and received the fee (*BIWK* 33) and the real estate demanded by the god (*BIWK* 71) on behalf of the sanctuary.

7. DIVINE JUSTICE AND SECULAR AUTHORITY

This survey of the epigraphic material from Hellenistic and Roman Asia Minor has shown that judicial matters were one of the many issues that the priests of some urban, but primarily of extra-urban and rural sanctuaries, had to deal with. There is no evidence that trials took place in the sanctuaries, that the priests substituted for the secular authorities in the implementation of justice, that they raised charges against delinquents or that they imposed penalties. But they were constantly confronted with acts of injustice: because the gods had been wronged through sacrilege, because the sanctuaries had been wronged by untrustworthy debtors, because the victims of injustice reported this to the local sanctuary and prayed for justice or for revenge, or because the delinquents themselves sought forgiveness in the sanctuary believing that the gods punished them through disease and accidents. Sometimes the priests had to consult persons who could

---

[131] *BIWK* 33 (Uşak): [–]ς Ἀπελλ[ω|νί]ου ἐνποδισθ[ῖ]|σα ἐν τῷ ναῷ ἐκο|λάσθη ὑπὸ τῶν θε|ῶν, ἵνα ἀναδίει | τὰς δυνάμις αὐ|τῶν. Δαπανήσασα [ἱ]|λάσετο τοὺς θεοὺ[ς] | καὶ ἐστηλλογράφη|σεν καὶ ἀνέδειξε | μεγάλας δυνάμις | αὐτῶν, καὶ ἀπὸ νῦν | εὐλογεῖ. Ἐπὶ Μητρᾶ | [ἱ]ερέως. Commentary: Petzl (1994: 39–40); cf. Chaniotis (1997a: 359). For the nature of this woman's offence see above p. 27.

[132] Petzl (1994) 94, with examples of eponymous priests in north-east Lydia. All inscriptions dated by priests (ἐπὶ ἱερέως) are also dated according to the Sullan era; in one case we also find a reference to the local *stephanephoros*, i.e. the actual eponymous official: *BIWK* 71, *TAM* v.1 193 and 241.

[133] For the 'false' eponymous officials see Robert (1989: 606 with n. 8), Dmitriev (1997: 534).

not explain why they were being 'punished' by the gods. The priests could not and did not remain indifferent. Their first task was to determine the cause of the divine anger, sometimes through oracles, more often through discussions. These discussions brought to light the many misdemeanours of everyday life and more or less serious religious offences; but sometimes what their 'clients' confessed was more serious: unpaid debts, theft, perjury.

Often the victims of injustice did more than just present accusations against known and unknown wrongdoers; they cursed them, they asked the gods to reveal the truth, they ceded to the sanctuary stolen or disputed property in the expectation of divine intervention, or they invited their opponents to take exculpatory oaths. Thus they drew the attention of the gods to the legal issue. As many confession inscriptions report, even the most intransigent persons were forced to confess; if they failed to do so, it was the duty of members of their family, their descendants or their heirs to do so.[134] The priests did not give verdicts or impose penalties; they simply informed the delinquents about the ways in which they could expiate the gods and annul false oaths and unjust curses; this could be done through the performance of rituals, the payment of money, and above all the setting up of a stele (στηλογραφεῖν) narrating the incident (see above p. 26), praising the gods and warning others. Of course, during this interaction with delinquents and victims charges were raised and excuses were put forward, aimed at determining the form of the atonement and not the punishment.

Active intervention by the priests is attested primarily in the confession inscriptions of Phrygia and Lydia, but the religious mentality that made their interventions possible was certainly not limited to these regions, as dedications and prayers for justice from other areas of Asia Minor make clear. The appeal to the gods for help in legal disputes, the belief in divine punishment – even after the death of the culprit, the belief in the effectiveness of imprecations, the ceding of disputed property to the gods in expectation of revenge, the importance of honour in such affairs, are phenomena characteristic of the ancient world in general, as Versnel's studies of the prayers for justice have demonstrated.[135] But we should not overlook the importance of local Anatolian traditions as well, some of which

---

[134] E.g. *BIWK* 4, 24, 36, 44, 46, 54, 69, 74. Cf. Zingerle (1926: 37); Eger (1939: 284). Chaniotis (1997a: 373).
[135] Versnel (1991) (1994) (1999) and (2002); cf. Ricl (1995: 70).

certainly antedate Achaemenid rule of Asia Minor.[136] One of these traditions must have been the economic, social and to some extent even administrative importance of some sanctuaries (cf. n. 9). Although recent scholarship does not overestimate the authority of the sanctuaries in Roman Asia Minor, as J. Zingerle once did,[137] there is a tendency to explain the appeals to divine justice as a reflection either of administrative deficiencies or of mistrust towards the civil jurisdiction. M. Ricl (1995: 69–70) observed 'a great tendency among these simple people to settle their conflicts without interference by the state authorities and in a manner inherited from their forefathers, which was probably considered more effective than secular justice'; similarly, S. Mitchell (1993a: 197) argued that 'disputes, even violent ones, were handled by traditional means. It was as dangerous for a villager to turn to outside authorities as it was later for Christians to be forced into using civil courts.'[138]

It is not surprising that these views are better supported with parallels from traditional societies than with the source material from Asia Minor. The gaps in our sources should warn us against generalizations. It would be wrong to jump to the conclusion that the positive evidence we have for an appeal to sanctuaries (see p. 30) demonstrates the replacement of secular authority by the sanctuaries. We simply do not know if the victims of injustice went *only* to the sanctuaries to find justice. The relationship between secular and divine justice resembles the relationship between divine healing and secular medicine. That many sick persons made vows in the sanctuaries begging for a divine cure does not mean that they did not visit medical doctors; in many cases we know for sure that they did both.[139] Similarly, an appeal to divine justice may well have been complementary to a report to the local civil authorities. Wills and funerary inscriptions show that one expected both the gods *and* the secular authorities to pursue violations. One of the funerary imprecations from Termessos is very eloquent: the desecrator of the grave should pay to the fiscus 1500 denarii; 'but if he

---

[136] This has been shown by Varinlioğlu (1989: 48–9) with regard to the ritual of the *triphonon*; cf. Ricl (1997: 36).
[137] Zingerle (1926: 9–10); but see Debord (1982: 165–8).
[138] Cf. Versnel (1991: 68): 'The person in antiquity who had suffered an injustice and had gone to the authorities in vain – if indeed he had bothered to go at all'; Versnel (2002) rightly points out that an appeal to divine justice does not exclude an appeal to courts. Strubbe (1991: 40–1 and 1997: xiv–xv, xvii–xix) suggested that the funerary imprecations may be connected with a decreasing belief in the operation of civil justice, but at the same time pointed out that there is no overall explanation of this phenomenon. I have strong doubts about whether three fragmentary or unclear confession inscriptions can be used as evidence for conflicts between sanctuaries and secular authorities (*BIWK* 13, 49 and 114): see Chaniotis (1997a: 370 n. 94). A new reading of *BIWK* 13 by Hasan Malay, whom I thank for this information, clearly shows that this text at least has nothing to do with a conflict between secular and divine authorities.
[139] Chaniotis (1995: 331 with n. 43).

disregards even this (the fine), he shall be cursed with childlessness'.[140] We should, therefore, avoid generalizations and assume that at least in some cases the appeal to divine justice does not reflect distrust towards secular authorities or a preference for particular traditions, but was simply the result of a hopeless situation (cf. above n. 115).

An interesting (but possibly not very common) case of interaction between religious and secular authorities is narrated by Lucian in his *Alexander* (44). An Epicurean attacked Alexander, the prophet at Abonou Teichos, accusing him of being responsible for the execution of the slaves of a Paphlagonian. His son, who had gone to Alexandria to study, was missing, and the man suspected that the slaves who had accompanied him to Egypt had murdered him. Following Alexander's advice, he brought them to the governor of Galatia, who condemned them to death. However, after their execution, the missing son returned (he had travelled to India), too late for the poor slaves. This story makes sense if we assume that the Paphlagonian consulted Alexander's oracle (either asking about his son's fate or his slaves' guilt) and received a response which confirmed his suspicions. This assumption is strengthened by the fact that Lucian narrates this story in the context of false oracles given by Alexander. It seems that at least in some cases the clients of oracles brought charges to the secular authorities based on the responses they had received.

We happen to know the victims of injustice who appealed to the gods and the priests had no clue about the identity of the wrongdoer (like the farmer in Babrius' fable) because they reported this in their vows and confession inscriptions. We will never know how many others turned to the *kômarchos*, the *eirênarchês*, the magistrates of the nearest urban centre, the governor or the Roman army because no papyri have been preserved from Asia Minor. Gaps in our sources should not be misinterpreted as administrative gaps or as evidence for a mistrust towards the civil administration. Even in the most remote areas there is evidence for some policing of one kind or another (ὀροφύλακες, παραφύλακες, εἰρηνάρχαι, *saltuarii*, etc.),[141] and even the Roman emperor could be confronted with conflicts such as the ones we have encountered here, e.g. the disputes among shepherds or a conflict between mother and son.[142] One notices that serious crimes, such as murder and

---

[140] *TAM* III 742 = Strubbe (1997: 220, no. 331): ὁ πειράσας ἐκτείσει τῷ ἱερωτάτῳ ταμείῳ (δηνάρια) αφ'· εἰ δέ τις κὲ τούτου καταφρονήσει σχήσει ἀτεκνία.

[141] Robert and Robert (1983: 101–9), Mitchell (1993a: 194–7), Petzl (1995: 39–40), Schuler (1998: 112 n. 55, 115, 234–5).

[142] Severus Alexander had to deal with the dispute between the shepherd Mucatraulis and his *dominus* Apollonaris (*C.Iust.* 2.3.9) on 28 September 222; for similar conflicts in confession inscriptions see *BIWK* 34, 68 and 103; Valerianus and Gallienus were confronted with the conflict between a mother and her sons (*C.Iust.* 8.46.4) on 17 May 259; cf. *BIWK* 17, 47.

brigandage, are never mentioned in the texts that concern divine justice,[143] not because people were not murdered or attacked by robbers, but because the civil authorities prosecuted them far more energetically than petty theft and trivial disputes. An epitaph for a young man who was murdered by his wife's secret lover at Alexandria Troas does not contradict this assumption, despite the appeal to Zeus to punish the adulteress: 'I have died a most miserable death because of my wife, the abominable adulteress – may Zeus destroy her. For her secret lover, my own relative, has slaughtered me and thrown me down from a height, like a discus.'[144] The murderer was obviously known; if he is not cursed in the epigram, it is probably because the civil authorities had already dealt with him, whereas the adulteress, who probably had escaped conviction as an accessory to this murder, was left to Zeus's punishment. Again, the appeal to divine justice was not motivated by mistrust of the local or the Roman administration, but by the wish to overcome its limits. We have also noticed that the most common offence mentioned in the relevant texts is one that was not prosecuted by secular law, i.e. perjury. Roman law left its punishment to the gods: *ius iurandi contempta religio satis deum ultorem habet* (*C. Iust.* 412). The sanctuaries of Asia Minor intervened in legal matters not in opposition to the official administration, but compensating for its unavoidable human defects.

The priests possessed only one means of implementing order: the solemn, public imprecations. They informed the culprits that they would be prosecuted by the gods and thus forced them to come to the sanctuaries, confess their offences and make amends (or protest their innocence). This instrument was effective, because the ordinary, small or serious misfortunes of everyday life were understood as divine punishment. It was only a matter of time until the sinner (or one of his relatives) met with an accident. When a sickle fell on his foot, a donkey or a member of his family died, the harvest was bad, he became sick, or his unmarried daughter lost her virginity, he knew that there was a sin which had to be expiated. Sometimes it required some pains until he found his way to the temple to confess his sin.[145] But then, when the repeated calamities of life did break his resistance, the belief of the other villagers in the power of divine punishment became even deeper. This explains why the priests urged the sinners to set up the

---

[143] With the exception of imprecations in epitaphs of persons whose death was attributed to 'foul play' (poisoning or magic); see above n. 28.
[144] *I.Alex. Troas* 90 = Merkelbach and Stauber (1998) no. 07/05/04, ll. 3–6 (second/third century, AD): [θν]ήσκω δ' οἰκτροτάτῳ θα|νάτῳ διὰ τὴν ἄλοχόν μου, | [κ]λεψίγαμον μιεράν, | ἣν περὶ Ζεὺς ὀλέσει | ταύτην γὰρ λάθριος γαμέτης | κἀμὸν γένος ΛΥΧΩΝ | σφάξ[ε] με κάφ' ὕψους δισκοβόλησε.
[145] For examples see Petzl (1995: 43–6).

propitiatory inscriptions: they were the proof (μαρτύριον, ἐξεμπλάριον) of the effectiveness of this divine justice.[146] A funerary inscription from Iulia Gordos expresses this belief very eloquently: 'There exists a goddess of retribution; respect justice!'[147] The certainty of divine punishment could temper the painful consciousness that human beings are often powerless against injustice.

One might be inclined to regard the confession inscriptions as part of a continuous effort on the part of the temples to intimidate the villagers, who would see in every calamity of life the punishment of a known or an unknown sin. But this conclusion is wrong. There is also evidence that these sanctuaries were the keepers of a strict moral order, mediators of legal thought in these areas.[148] The confession inscriptions not only include hard, sometimes meaningless punishments, but also moral instructions, the commands of god (παραγγέλλω): 'I command that nobody should commit perjury', 'I command all men not to disregard the power of god', 'he commands that no one take an oath nor make others take an oath nor administer an oath in an unjust way (or for an unjust cause)', etc.[149]

In one of the *Stories of Mr Keuner* by Bertolt Brecht, someone asks Mr K. if there is a god. Instead of a response, Mr K. asks a question: Would his behaviour change depending on the answer to this question? If yes, then he needed a god. The rural population of Asia Minor certainly did.

---

[146] Ἐξεμπλάριον: *BIWK* 106, 111, 112, 120, 121. Cf. Versnel (1991: 92 with n. 147) and (1999: 153) (for an attestation in Spain). Μαρτύριον: *BIWK* 9; cf. the verb μαρτυρεῖν: *BIWK* 8, 17, 68; cf. Petzl (1991: 132–3), (1994: 17); ὑπόδειγμα τῶν ἄλλων: Ricl (1997: 37, ll. 11–13). See also n. 64.

[147] *SEG* xxx 1480: [ἔστι θε]ὸς Νέμεσις [πρὸς τὰ δίκ]αια βλέπε.

[148] Cf. Zingerle (1926: 47–8), Klauck (1996: 83–5), Petzl (1998*b*: 23).

[149] *BIWK* 27: [παραγγέλλων ἀ]δίκως μὴ ὀμνεῖν τινα μήτε ὀρκίζ[ειν] μήτε ὀρκωμότην γίνεσθαι; *BIWK* 9: παραγγέλλει πᾶσιν ἀνθρώποις ὅτι οὐ δεῖ καταφρονεῖν το[ῦ θε]οῦ; *BIWK* 10: παραγγέλλω δέ αὐτοῦ (sc. τοῦ θεοῦ) τὰς δυνάμις μή τίς ποτε κατευτελήσι καὶ κόψει δρῦν; *BIWK* 110: παραγγέλων πᾶσι μηδὲ ἄναγον ἀναβῆτ' ἐπὶ τὸ χωρίον, ἐπροκήσι ἤ κήσετε (?) τὸν ὄρχις; *BIWK* 123: παραγγέλλω μηθένα ἱερὸν ἄθυτον αἰγοτόμιον ἔσθειν; see also *BIWK* 106, 109, 111, 112, 117, 120, 121 and 124. For these moral instructions see also Pettazzoni (1936: 64), Versnel (1991: 75, 92 with n. 147), Petzl (1991: 143 n. 43) and (1994: 17, 124). Cf. also expressions in the confession inscriptions which indicate the improvement of the delinquent after his punishment, e.g. καὶ ἀπὸ νῦν εὐδοξεῖ (*BIWK* 60); cf. Herrmann and Varinlioğlu (1984: 14 with n. 54), Versnel (1991: 75). For analogous παραγγέλματα see also the *lex sacra* of a cult association at Philadelpheia (*LSAM* 20); cf. Chaniotis (1997*b*: 159–62).

CHAPTER 2

Names in Hellenistic and Roman Lycia*
Stephen Colvin

1. INTRODUCTION

In 70 BC Cicero referred to the people of Lycian Phaselis as Greeks, a useful reminder of the special status that the Lycians had in the perception of the classical world (the approving classical gaze being first Greek, then Macedonian and Roman). It is especially striking if one considers that other areas of south-west Anatolia, at all times the nearest point of contact between the classical world and the East, were more or less bywords for barbarism in Greek and Roman writers as they struggled to define the commonalities of classical culture from which Asia was excluded.[1]

To be accepted as a part of this world the Lycians had been able to fulfil certain criteria. Firstly, they had a respectable mythological pedigree which connected their national ancestors with the peoples, gods and heroes of Greece proper. This was not in itself sufficient, of course, to put one on the right side of the Greek/barbarian divide: even the Persians had been given an ancestry linking them to the Greek hero Perseus, son of Zeus and grandson of the king of Argos. The Lycians, however, had firmer literary-historical ties with the Greek world as a result of their appearance in the *Iliad*, where the Lycian chiefs Sarpedon and Glaukos are important allies of the Trojans, and Glaukos is given a specifically Greek heritage through his grandfather Bellerophon.[2] Secondly, they had played a part in the heroic and historic struggles of the Greeks against the barbarians, starting with the *Iliad* and continuing to the Persian Wars, where the Lycians, like the Greek cities of coastal Asia Minor, strenuously resisted the campaign of the Persian general

---

* I am grateful to Professors Anna Morpurgo Davies and Craig Melchert for corrections and many helpful suggestions.
[1] Cic. *Verr.* 4. 10. 21: 'Phaselis illa, quam cepit P. Servilius, non fuerat urbs antea Cilicum atque praedonum; Lycii illam, Graeci homines, incolebant.'
[2] *Iliad* 6.144–211. An inscription from Xanthos (205 BC) records an alternative, Dorian connection for the Lycians, cooked up by ambassadors from Kytinion in eastern Aetolia who were collecting money to repair their walls (ed. Bousquet 1988).

Harpagos. In the fifth century Lycian cities appear sporadically in the tribute lists of the Athenian League. Finally, a constellation of geographical and political factors led to the absorption of Greek influence considerably earlier than the Macedonian take-over of Asia Minor at the end of the fourth century. Lycian culture seems to have been relatively urbanized from an early date, with civic institutions which were amenable to Greek interpretation; their geographical position was important strategically;[3] and their inclusion in the Persian satrapy of the philhellene Hekatomnids exposed them to Greek as a language of administration and cultural prestige in the early fourth century. Contact with Rhodes from an early date, though not always good-tempered, must have been productive: the Rhodians planted colonists in eastern Lycia, and the Lycian alphabet was taken over from the Greek alphabet of Rhodes. The Lycians, whose experience in the Persian invasions taught them that a wise foreign policy involved prudent recognition of the Power of the day, made full diplomatic use of their special status, and managed to fend off direct outside control of their country till the time of Claudius.

Whatever the Lycians finally developed into, their language shows that their origins lay with other peoples of south-western Anatolia (Carians, Cilicians, etc.), who spoke what may be roughly designated 'late Luwian' languages, descended by various routes from the Hittite-Luwian language family which is attested in cuneiform and hieroglyphic inscriptions in the second millennium BC (approximately seventeenth–thirteenth centuries).[4] Not only are the first-millennium languages clearly related to their Bronze Age predecessors, but similarities in onomastics (both human and divine) also indicate a certain cultural continuity. For example, the personal name Τροκονδας (varieties of which are extremely common in south-western Asia Minor) is a Hellenized form of a name seen in the Hittite-Luwian storm god *Tarḫunta-* (written *Trqqñt-* in the epichoric Lycian alphabet).[5]

Such a demonstrable continuity from the Bronze Age to the Roman period makes Lycia a particularly useful area in which to study the evolving onomastic habits of the locals. The Lycians were writing their own language by 500 BC: we possess around 170 inscriptions in the Lycian language, of which the vast majority (around 150) are funerary. While the repetitive nature of the material means that there is still much in the Lycian language that remains obscure, the presence of a reasonably large corpus, including

---

[3] See Keen (1993) for the shipping routes from the Aegean to the eastern Mediterranean.
[4] The only languages of western Anatolia which seem not to be related to this group are Galatian (Celtic) and Phrygian (Indo-European, but its precise affinities are uncertain).
[5] See Goetze (1954); Houwink ten Cate (1965: 125–31).

bilingual inscriptions, has enabled us to establish the broad outlines of the phonology and the grammar, and to make some headway with the onomastics. The Lycian language finally disappears from inscriptions in the Hellenistic period, but presumably continued to be spoken among certain sections of society and in non-coastal regions for some time. The Greek of the inscriptions is high-quality *koine* from the earliest period: it is only in the later Roman period that lapses in orthography and syntax become pronounced.[6] The orthographic and other variations that are to be found in the Classical and Hellenistic inscriptions show, unsurprisingly, the normal features of south Anatolian *koine*: that is to say, certain traits (mainly phonological, a very few morpho-syntactic) which are found elsewhere in Hellenistic Greek, but may in this case represent a faint influence of the Anatolian substrate language(s). There are, however, no parallels to the extraordinary Greek that has been documented for Phrygia.[7]

Names are an obvious and flexible means of self-definition. Analysis of the changing onomastic habits in Lycia in this period casts some light on how the inhabitants of a community on the fringes of the Hellenic world projected particular social identities onto themselves and their children. Adoption of the Greek language was a necessary part of economic and political survival in the eastern Mediterranean world, but it does not necessarily tell us everything about Hellenization or attitudes to Hellenization. One can adopt foreign names for a variety of reasons before one has embraced the language they are associated with; and conversely, if a particular community is obliged to adopt a foreign language for all or part of the time, there is no guarantee of positive social attitudes towards the new idiom. One way that the community can make a positive statement of its separate identity is by retaining names redolent of its own national history or culture. In the Hellenistic world this was not necessarily the same as retaining an indigenous name in Hellenized form: since the tentacles of Greek mythology spread well beyond the Greek homeland, an onomastic step ideologically intermediate between an indigenous and a Greek

---

[6] By 'lapses' I mean non-standard forms (spellings, constructions) which reveal that there was a gap between the written and the spoken language, and which generally give a useful indication of what developments had taken place in the spoken language. These are 'mistakes' in the sense that the sociolinguistic culture of this period did not allow for variations in the written language to reflect regional or temporal developments (unlike, for example, classical Boeotian inscriptions). See now Brixhe (1999) on 'substrate' influence on Lycian Greek.

[7] Traits of south Anatolian Greek: unusual syllabification (19 per cent of cases in private inscriptions break Threatte's (1980: 64) first 'rule': only 1 per cent in public inscriptions); nasalization (e.g. παραληνψεως: *SEG* XVIII 570.44, 2nd c. AD, Araxa), etc. Phrygian Greek: see Brixhe (1987, esp. 110–16).

name was a name from the corpus of Greek mythology that had local associations.[8]

The rate of utilization of Greek names is not, then, the only relevant factor: the type of name that is chosen can also tell us a number of things about the process of Hellenization. For example, Hellenization that is the result of a bottom-up change in the ethnic make-up of the population (perhaps as a result of artisanal immigration) might reveal itself in the use of popular, humble names, including nicknames, shortened forms and the like. A top-down cultural shift, however, driven by a native elite, would be likely to result in a higher proportion of significant literary and historical names (an onomastic pool qualitatively different, therefore, from the native Greek areas). So far as data are available, the factors that need to be taken into account fall into two broad classes: some are internal to the names themselves (such as names which seem designed to work in both languages), while others pertain to the external conditions of use (including naming differences between men and women, or naming patterns within families).

Lycian names (like their Anatolian predecessors) have a comparable structure to Greek names, perhaps the result of a common Indo-European tradition. Unlike the Roman and Etruscan system of nomenclature, there are no family or clan names: each person has a single name, which may be simple or compound, and additional specification is provided, where required, by addition of a parental name (almost always of the father), or that of a distinguished relative. Occasional instances of a person having a double name will be discussed below.

2. SOURCES

2.1. Inscriptions in Greek

The following discussion is based on epigraphic material which was published and available at the time of writing. The database includes the names of all persons not obviously resident outside Lycia, and excludes Hellenistic monarchs, royal priests in dating formulae and foreign honorands. It is occasionally difficult to decide when a name that has a foreign origin has become truly naturalized in a language. In the present case we shall describe as 'Greek' any name which was in widespread use in the Greek world: this will therefore include names such as Sarapion (but not Maussollos or

---

[8] Cf. Jones's (1939: 41) dry remark: '... the later Paphlagonian kings, discovering their Homeric ancestry, called themselves Pylaemenes'.

Pixodaros). Where figures and percentages are given, these refer to name tokens rather than name types (since the aim of quoting such statistics is to identify trends in the onomastic habits of the region): I have tried to reduce the distortion of the data by eliminating multiple occurrences of the same individual, but may not always have succeeded.

Dates are important for our study: it is often difficult, unfortunately, to date inscriptions from Asia Minor with a high degree of precision, and even more difficult to date inscriptions from early corpora (including *TAM*) and publications which were not dated by the original editor. I have excluded from the database epigraphic material which could not be dated securely to a period before the first half of the first century AD. In some cases I have ventured to place an undated inscription within this period on the basis of the script (a notoriously risky exercise), but in most cases I thought it prudent to exclude undated material. Given these constraints I have divided the data into just three periods: IV denotes the fourth century before Alexander (334); H stands for Hellenistic (arbitrarily 334–129 BC); and LH for the late Hellenistic and early Roman periods (roughly 129 BC–43 AD).[9] Fractions in percentages have been rounded to the nearest whole number. It should be emphasized that since the number of names is relatively small (the total figure is slightly over 1,100 individuals), a margin of error will apply to all statistics quoted. Over 96 per cent of the data comes from the Hellenistic and late Hellenistic periods, which will therefore be the focus of our study; material from the fourth century and earlier is scarce and accounts for around 3 per cent of the data. *Unless otherwise specified, figures quoted refer to names from monolingual Greek inscriptions.* Names from the Greek part of bilingual texts, and from Lycian language texts (whether bilingual or monolingual), are clearly identified.

Most of the names found in Greek inscriptions in Lycia can be labelled as Greek or Lycian (obviously there are varying degrees of Hellenization in the Lycian names, which will be discussed). After these the largest group is Persian. There are a few miscellaneous other names: mainly Carian, but an occasional early appearance of a Roman name.

2.2. Inscriptions in Lycian

Most of the same caveats apply to the Lycian as to the Greek inscriptions, except that the figures quoted must be regarded as even more approximate. This is because of the greater difficulty in interpreting the Lycian

---

[9] In 129 BC the Roman province of Asia was formed; but it was not until AD 43 that Lycia (joined with Pamphylia) was made into a province under direct Roman control.

inscriptions. It is sometimes unclear whether a form is a name, a noun or a title; it is difficult to restore fragmentary texts; and in cases where the same name appears more than once in the corpus it is often impossible to decide with any degree of certainty whether this is due to the same person appearing twice (or more). The total number of names is in the region of 350. The inscriptions can more or less all be dated to the fifth and fourth centuries BC, but it is generally difficult to be more specific within this period.

Louis Robert established criteria, since widely accepted, for establishing whether a name which occurs in a Greek inscription in Asia Minor is to be regarded as indigenous or Greek; the net effect was in general to increase the degree of caution exercised in assigning unusual names to the indigenous substrate.[10] It is unfortunately difficult to apply the same rigour to inscriptions written in the Lycian language, due to uncertainties in interpreting personal names in a barely deciphered language. It may well be the case that names which are currently not properly understood, and which are supposed to be Lycian, may in fact turn out to be Greek names in disguise. Greek names which are most liable to be misinterpreted as foreign are unaristocratic simplex (or shortened) forms, derived from common everyday nouns including plants, animals, etc. Thus, for example, Βρύων (Pinara), which Sundwall connected with Carian Βρυαξις, Βρυασσις, is derived by Robert (1963: 164) from βρύω ('blossom, burgeon'). A particularly difficult case to decide is whether the Lycian *Kuprlli* (Greek Κοπρίλις)[11] started out as a Greek name derived from κόπρος ('dung'), or whether the Greek form is a Hellenized version of a Lycian original. Robert, followed by Zgusta, argued for the Greek interpretation: against this, of course, it could be argued that a Lycian dynast who wanted to choose a Greek name would be unlikely to pick on this one if there were no phonetic similarity to his Lycian name.[12] We might instead expect him to take a name (like Perikles of Limyra, for example) with some historical-political clout. Recent work on copronyms points to the conclusion that they were given by parents (especially, perhaps, those who had already lost children) to avert the 'evil eye'.[13] One would have to assume, if Koprilis were such a name, that the

---

[10] Robert (1963: *passim*), directed principally against J. Sundwall, *Die einheimischen Namen der Lykier nebst einem Verzeichnisse kleinasiatischer Namenstämme* (Leipzig 1913).
[11] *TAM* II 922.1 (4th/3rd c. BC). Kuprlli ruled Xanthos for several decades in the mid-fifth century BC. An (attractive) alternative is to assume that the fifth-century Greek equivalent of Kuprlli was Kybernis: reading Hdt. 7.98 Κύβερνις Κοσσίκα (Keen 1998: 87–90) or Κύβερνισ<κος> Κοσσίκα (Eichner 2000). *Koprilis* would then be a 're-Hellenized' version.
[12] Robert (1938: 175); Zgusta (1964: §683). For *kopros*-names see Bechtel (1917: 611).
[13] Alford (1988: 63–5); Masson (1996: xiv).

dynast's parents had made this decision: since they can hardly have been native speakers of Greek, the assumption seems unlikely.

2.3. Geography

Lycia is more or less bounded by the Indos (modern Dalaman) river in the west; in the east the coastal cities east of the Limyros (Alakır) river were at various times placed inside or outside the Lycian cultural zone. The northern boundary does not run in a continuous line across the peninsula, but is determined by the northern reaches of the three principal river systems as they emerge from their mountainous watersheds (the tail end of the Tauros range): at Araxa (on the Xanthos river, modern Eşen), Arneai (on the Myros river, modern Demre), and Arykanda (on the Arykandos river, modern Suluin). The Indos (Dalaman) plain in the west was a zone of interaction with Caria; in the east the coastal strip from the Chelidonian point west to the Alakır river and north to Phaselis was a zone of Greek (Rhodian) influence, merging into Pamphylian territory around the Gulf of Antalya. The Xanthos valley in the west of the country seems always to have been at the heart of Lycian political and cultural life. For the purposes of this study, western Lycia denotes Telmessos and the Xanthos valley, and central Lycia the territory (wild and mountainous) east of the Xanthos valley and west of the mountains (the Bey Dağları) which separate Limyra from the eastern coastal plain. Eastern Lycian (the least 'Lycian' part of the peninsula) includes all territory east of the Alakır Çay.

The location of the cities in west, central or eastern Lycia is a geographical factor that is likely to have been relevant in the spread of cultural and linguistic habits. Distance from the sea (i.e. a rough north/south axis) may also have been relevant, but is harder to quantify since communication up a river valley such as the Xanthos is easier than the hard walk necessary to get to a place like Arykanda.

The northern uplands do not seem to have been regarded as part of Lycia proper in the epichoric period: the modern plain of Elmalı is bounded to the south by the Susuz Dağ, to the west by the Bey Dağ, and to the east by the Ak Dağ, and is referred to as *Milyas* in literary sources.[14] These uplands will have been open to the influence of the interior, particularly Phrygia. To the west, Boubon, Balboura and Oinoanda comprised an area known to ancient writers as *Kabalia*. Boubon and Balboura (and presumably Oinoanda) were included in Lycia by Sulla after 82 BC; Kibyra was attached to the province

---

[14] Strabo 13.4.17, 14.5.7. The dialect of Lycian known as 'Lycian B' is occasionally referred to as 'Milyan': there is, however, no evidence linking the dialect with the region, and the term is best avoided.

of Asia (earlier there had been a short-lived tetrapolis of the four cities). Data from this northern region are not included in this study.

3. CHANGES OVER TIME

3.1. Regional differences

An obvious question to start with is the proportion of Greek to Lycian names in various populations. By the mid-fourth century the Lycians (especially those of the major cities near the coast) had been in contact with Greeks of various types for several centuries: their adoption of the Greek language at this time in private funerary inscriptions is indicative of an influence that was far from superficial. In the fourth century approximately 66 per cent of the recorded names are still Lycian, but the remaining third are Greek (the Greek sections of bilingual inscriptions, which mostly date to the fifth/fourth centuries, give a roughly similar figure). For the later period the figures are as follows:

	Greek %	Lycian %	Other %
H	79	18	3
LH	76	20	4

The impetus to Hellenize personal names was clearly much reduced in Lycian language inscriptions, for when we compare the figures for the Lycian language (fifth/fourth centuries) the contrast between the early and the late period is even greater: 88 per cent of the names are Lycian, and of the remaining 12 per cent only half are Greek (the others being Persian and Carian). The dramatic change in the figures for the Greek inscriptions of the Hellenistic period suggests an influx of Greeks into Lycia, with a concomitant increase in the Greek influence on the native population; however, it would be simplistic to assume that all the new Greek names were borne by immigrants (where would such a large number of people have come from, and why?) – the situation may rather have been a relatively small influx accompanied by a more profoundly Hellenizing cultural shift. In addition, the very fact of writing in the Greek language may have been conducive to the adoption of Greek nomenclature (the shift in the figures need not, therefore, be a precise indicator of shifting patterns in forms of address in the *Umgangssprache*).

If we analyse the above figures by region (west, central and eastern Lycia) there are some minor variations:

(a) In the fifth/fourth centuries monolingual Greek language inscriptions are very rare in western Lycia. The largest number of bilingual inscriptions comes from this region, however, and around half of the Lycian language inscriptions. While the number of Persian and Carian names remains constant (they belong to dynasts and rulers who appeared perforce in inscriptions in both languages and felt no desire to modify their designation), the number of Greek names is much higher in the Greek portions of the inscriptions:

	Greek %	Lycian %	Other %
Greek (bilingual)	33	56	10
Lycian	8	82	10

In central Lycia, conversely, there are monolingual Greek inscriptions but few bilinguals (the Greek data from the bilinguals – there are only seventeen names altogether – are roughly in line with the monolingual Greek inscriptions):

	Greek %	Lycian %	Other %
Greek	20	80	—
Lycian	5	93	2

In eastern Lycia the inscriptions are too few at this period to provide meaningful data. Greek names outnumber Lycian names in this area; the Greek inscriptions that exist come for the most part from the established Greek settlements at Phaselis, Rhodiapolis and Olympos.

The material, though meagre, points to the conclusion that before the Hellenistic period the central region of the peninsula was least open to Greek influence (access to this region was probably easiest by sea). Use of the Greek language in the west was no doubt due to the seat of regional control at Xanthos and the proximity of Caria; and while settlements in the east of the country seem to have been relatively undeveloped in the early period, the presence of Greek communities led to wider epigraphic use of Greek than might have been expected.

(b) In the third century BC the number of Greek inscriptions jumps dramatically, and with it the proportion of Greek names (the total number of names attested in the Hellenistic period is over fifteen times higher than in the preceding period). However, it is striking that the number of names in eastern Lycia remains very small (about the same level as in the fourth century).

	Greek%	Lycian%	Other%	Total number
Hellenistic period				
Western Lycia	84	13	3	457
Central Lycia	51	46	3	74
Late Hellenistic period				
Western Lycia	77	19	4	354
Central Lycia	73	23	3	179

The figures for western Lycia show heavy Greek influence on the nomenclature from the start. This can be connected with the political importance of the region: Greek craftsmen and artisans who were attracted to Lycia in the turmoil of the late fourth century would naturally have gravitated to the centre of dynastic power. In central Lycia, however, Lycian names hold out in the early centuries, and dip to the same level as the west only in the later period. This seems to reflect a slower rate of penetration of Greek people and ideas into the isolated valleys and mountainous divides of this region.

3.2. Family naming patterns

Another way of viewing the decline in the use of Lycian names is to consider changes in naming patterns within families. In many cases the father of a named individual is specified, and occasionally a grandfather also, which makes it possible to see the period and manner in which residents of the peninsula took a name different from that of their parents. The relatively large number of cases in which Lycians specify a (Lycian) parental name in inscriptions in their own language indicates that this practice need not have been solely the result of Greek influence.[15]

In Lycian language inscriptions there is a high degree of continuity. Approximately 30 per cent of names are followed by a parental name, and of these:

80% are Lycian-name offspring from Lycian-name parents
9% are Greek-name offspring from Lycian-name parents
8% are Lycian-name offspring from Greek-name parents
1% are Greek-name offspring from Greek-name parents
(The remaining involve Persian or Carian names.)

It should be remarked that a large proportion (around half) of inscriptions which attest cross-over naming at this period (Lycian > Greek or *vice versa*) are bilingual inscriptions; families that were sufficiently cosmopolitan to erect bilingual texts are in any case likely to have practised inter-marriage, or to have desired a Hellenized designation for some other reason. Almost all the cases in which Lycian-name parents have Greek-name offspring are in western Lycia; curiously, most of the cases in which the reverse is true (Greek > Lycian) are in the central region (but numbers are small). In

---

[15] Most Greek dialects expressed the relation by the genitive of the parental name. Lycian seems to have had both a nominal genitive and an adjectival suffix which declines for number, case and gender (a possessive construction resembling the Greek patronymic adjective).

Greek inscriptions of the fourth century there are almost no examples of cross-over naming.

In the Hellenistic period the data give a very different picture, pointing not only perhaps to a larger number of Greek-speakers in Lycia than had previously been the case, but also to a deepening trend for indigenous Lycians to give Greek names to their children. Over 80 per cent of names are followed by a parental name, and of these:

9% are Lycian-name offspring from Lycian-name parents
12% are Greek-name offspring from Lycian-name parents
5% are Lycian-name offspring from Greek-name parents
74% are Greek-name offspring from Greek-name parents

In the late Hellenistic period the figures are almost identical, except that Lycian-name offspring from Greek-name parents jump to 11 per cent, with a concomitant decline in the figure for Greek-name offspring from Greek-name parents. If there is any significance in this it might be attributable to a decline in the motivation to Hellenize along the lines of the 'old' Greek world in the expanded and self-confident world of the Hellenic East; in the earlier period there may have been a higher degree of cultural and linguistic insecurity, and a desire to conform to perceived standards of Greekness.

A curious difference between the H and LH material is the rise in genealogical information provided in inscriptions. In the early period eighteen individuals are identified with a grandparent in addition to a parent; this rises to fifty-six in LH inscriptions, plus a couple of instances where great-grandparents are furnished. In both periods about half of the cases represent three generations of Greek names, but the rest are a mixture.

4. GENDER DIFFERENCE AND RELATED FACTORS

In the data presented so far we have been taking no account of the distinction between male and female names. This question needs to be considered for two reasons: firstly, the issue of the role of women in Lycia is intrinsically interesting owing to persistent rumours in the Greek world of Lycian matrilineal naming and social structure;[16] and secondly, ignoring the distinction may distort the picture given by other data, including those we have already considered. When we give parental and grandparental names the usual assumption is that the father and paternal grandfather are meant;

---

[16] Hdt. 1.173, Plut. *De mul. vir.* 248D: further sources quoted and discussed by Bryce (1986: 143–58). See Pembroke (1964) for reasoned dismissal of Lycian matriarchy.

Lycian inscriptions, however, attest to a more prominent social role for women as well as a family structure different from mainland Greece, and caution is in order. One finds in general women playing an active role in the erection of monuments and inscriptions (for parents, offspring and husbands): they are identified by patronym, and may act independently of men. A brother and a sister jointly fund a tomb for their father (Straton and Arsinoe, *TAM* II 472, Patara, H); at Xanthos a monument is erected by Lalla, daughter of the deceased Timanthes, and her two sons, one of whom had been adopted by his maternal grandfather and thus bears his name, while his brother Tlepolemos carries the name of his father, paternal grandfather and great-grandfather (*TAM* II 309, LH). There is also evidence in Lycia for marriage between siblings, most likely non-uterine half-siblings: e.g. *TAM* II 593 (Tlos, LH), a public decree honouring Nanna, wife and sister of Agathokles.

In one case, a funerary inscription from Arsada (*SEG* XXVII 906.3, LH) for a woman named Orsonna gives the names of both (Lycian-name) parents plus their fathers: her paternal grandfather has a Greek name, and her maternal grandfather a Lycian one. Focussing on the paternal line in Orsonna's case (Greek > Lycian > Lycian) would divert attention from some interesting issues. The mention of her mother as a joint sponsor of the inscription is unusual from a Greek perspective, especially as she is identified by a patronymic (the father of a Greek woman ceased to be her legal *kyrios* when she got married, since she thereby became part of her husband's *oikos* and was identified by reference to him). Orsonna's maternal grandfather was named Kleon: the fact that her mother has a Lycian name is less significant than it might be as an onomastic choice, since it is noticeable in Lycia that men are more often given Greek names than women, even within a family. There are probably two related explanations for this: parents may have given Greek names to male offspring on the grounds that men had greater need of a Greek name for advancement in the public world of the Hellenistic city; or men may have been given (or may have taken) a Greek name for public business in addition to the Lycian name they were given at birth.[17]

Lycian names are harder to analyse from this perspective than Greek ones, since it is sometimes difficult to determine the gender associated with a particular name. This is true most often of names occurring in Lycian language inscriptions, but also occasionally of Lycian names which have

---

[17] Or in childhood: we lack knowledge of when and in what circumstances names were given to the new-born in Lycia, and practice varies widely across cultures. See Alford (1988: 29–50).

been rendered into Greek.[18] Lycian, like other languages of the Hittite-Luwian family, does not have a regular morphological distinction between masculine and feminine substantives; indeed, the sporadic loss of opposition between masculine and feminine names in the Anatolian *koine* has often been linked with this feature of the substrate.[19] In addition, the normal word for 'son' in Lycian (*tideimi*) in the expression '*x* son of *y*' can also mean 'child' (non gender-specific, as at *TL* 27.6). Since the default assumption is that a name found in an inscription is masculine, the data may be misleading in this respect. In the following section figures from Greek-language inscriptions only will be used.[20]

The number of female names in Greek inscriptions falls markedly with the end of the fourth century, and remains low for the whole of the subsequent period. In the fourth century female names account for 26 per cent of the total: for the Hellenistic and late Hellenistic period the figure is around 5 per cent. The difference may in part be attributable to the sharp increase in epigraphic activity in the Hellenistic world; while inscriptions were put up only by the very wealthy, the names of aristocratic women had a proportionately greater weight. Connected with this is the broadening of the scope of inscriptions: in the epichoric period the overwhelming majority of Lycian inscriptions are funerary (in which female family members play an important role), while the civic lists and decrees of the later period allow little scope for the mention of women.[21] However, it is tempting also to read into the difference the influence of Greek attitudes to women which were transmitted, presumably, along with the larger package of Hellenistic social and cultural behaviour.

In the fourth century all examples of female names are Lycian, with just a couple of exceptions from Phaselis in the eastern part of the country. Female names give way more slowly to Greek than male names: in the Hellenistic period over 85 per cent of female names are Lycian, dropping to 43 per cent in the late Hellenistic period. By contrast, male names in the fourth

---

[18] E.g. Εδα (*SEG* XLV 1791.2, Limyra, 4th c. BC, ed. M. Wörrle), and *TL* 143: Οσαιμιος (the wife or father of Κοδαρας: Limyra, 5th c. BC) with Wörrle (1991: 221) *ad loc*. Neither is it possible to be sure that some names were not usable by both men and women.

[19] See Brixhe (1987: 77) and Dressler (1966) on fem. names in -ας, masc. names in -α.

[20] Secure identification of female names in Lycian texts is generally the result of apposition to the word 'wife' in the formula '*x* built this [tomb] for himself and his wife'. Since there is evidence from Greek texts that women in Lycia erected tombs in their own right (e.g. *TAM* II 475, Patara: read now Εὐτέρπη Ερμ[ακ]αρταδιος, with *SEG* XLIV 1219.a6), it is possible that names found in such texts without the wife formula may belong to women. At *TAM* II 752 the reverse formula is found: 'Lais purchased this tomb for herself and her husband . . .' In one curious inscription a woman puts up a memorial without naming herself (*SEG* XLV 1786, Limyra, 4th c. BC, ed. M. Wörrle).

[21] Women may occasionally be the subject of honorary decrees by the city: *TAM* II 593, 595, Tlos.

century are already 40 per cent Greek, and this rises to around 80 per cent in the subsequent period. The supposition that the higher incidence of Greek names among men is connected with public or civic activity is given some weight by the correlation between civic status and name type. 7 per cent of the names recorded in Greek inscriptions are marked for high status (that is, the bearers are explicitly given public rank or office): of these, 85 per cent are Greek names and 10 per cent are Lycian. We can add to this the comparative figures for private and public inscriptions: in the fourth century almost all inscriptions are private (mostly funerary), and two-thirds of the names attested in them are Lycian. In the Hellenistic period, however, only 21 per cent of inscriptions are private, and the proportions of Lycian and Greek names in these texts are roughly equal; in the late Hellenistic period Lycian names drop to 26 per cent. In public inscriptions Lycian names are less prominent: in the Hellenistic period, for example, they account for 10 per cent of the total (as opposed to 47 per cent in private inscriptions). Persian and Carian names are for the most part (over 80 per cent) found in public texts in western Lycia (there are no female names among these).

5. ONOMASTIC INGREDIENTS

In this section we shall look at the semantic make-up of names in Greek-language inscriptions. Although the data cannot be quantified as schematically as in the preceding sections, it should nevertheless be possible to arrive at an overview of some of the onomastic patterns of the region. As a control, onomastic data from Athens and Rhodes may give some perspective on the relative frequency of particular names (happily the *Lexicon of Greek Personal Names* now covers both these areas).

The purpose of analysing the semantic constituents of the names is to arrive at some understanding of the avenues by which Lycians came to choose names for themselves in the Greek language. We have now seen that in the Lycian-language inscriptions of the fourth century and earlier the overwhelming majority of names are Lycian, and yet within a relatively short space of time the situation had reversed completely. There must have been certain patterns and methods in the adoption of the new names, and a brief survey of the data suggests a number of possibilities for investigation: (1) Greek theophoric names which were adapted to fit pre-existing patterns and traditional deities; (2) names which had mythical-historical resonances for the Lycians, and which were picked from the resources of the Greek literary tradition primarily for their ideological associations with Greek history and culture (a special category being the names of those figures who had a mythological association with Lycia); (3) the names of Macedonians (soldiers, politicians, etc.) who followed Alexander into Asia Minor; (4) Greek names bearing a superficial phonetic similarity to Lycian names.

5.1. Theophoric names

Roughly a quarter of the names contain an element based on a divine name. This is in line with naming patterns elsewhere in the Hellenistic world, where such theophoric names formed the largest sub-class of name types. The Lycian figure is nevertheless higher than the figure for Attica:[22] the Anatolian (and particularly Lycian) penchant for theophoric names has long been remarked on, and may reflect indigenous naming habits.[23] There are three levels at which a name may be theophoric: in descending order, (i) a person may be given the name of a deity; (ii) a recognizable divine name may form an important part of the personal name, either adjectivally (*Apollônios*) or in compound (*Apollodôros*); or (iii) the personal name may be compounded from the stem of 'Zeus' (thus *Diogenês*). Of these, (i) is rare, while (iii) is somewhat colourless. A particular area of interest in considering theophoric names from Lycia is what local influences may have been in operation. Two obvious possibilities present themselves: influence of indigenous deities, and that of Greek traditions (literary and mythological) concerning Lycia.

(a) Apollo, Artemis, Leto

In the Greek tradition, Apollo is the god most associated with Lycia; by extension, one may look for a prominent position for Artemis and Leto also. Although the use of Apollo itself as a personal name is not attested in Lycia, there is widespread use of Apollo derivatives: more than twenty instances are found in the H/LH periods. This in itself cannot be used as evidence of a special Lycian connection, since the name is also one of the most common theophoric names in Athens (in both Athens and Lycia Apollo accounts for slightly over 10 per cent of theophoric names in the fourth to first centuries BC). However, the relative importance of an Apolline deity in Lycian onomastics becomes clear if one considers a further eight names in *Pyth-* (not particularly common in Athens), and two names which may be connected with a local Apollo cult: three instances

---

[22] Calculated at 15.6 per cent in the period 403/2–30/29 BC by Dow (1937: 218). The term 'theophoric' is found only at Athen. 10.69, where it applies to a name containing any divine element.
[23] See Houwink ten Cate (1965: 124), with references.

of Πανακέστωρ (all from Hippoukome), and half a dozen Ἀγρεοφῶν, a designation of a local deity identified with Apollo.[24] Neither name is found in Athens or Rhodes, and both are characteristic of Caria and western Lycia. Compare also *Pajawa* (*TL* 40, Xanthos), a Greek name in Lycian disguise which must be derived from ΠαιάϜων. Anticipating our discussion of names from Greek mythology and literature, it is worth noting here that Jason (Ἰάσων) is the most frequent name in the mythological category. In Athens the name is not uncommon, but hardly one of the most popular (less than a hundred instances). The frequency may be attributed to a popular derivation of the name from ἰάομαι 'heal' if, in view of Πανακέστωρ, we accept the connection with a local cult of a healing god (liable to be seen in Lycia as an avatar of healing Apollo). There may also be contamination with an Anatolian name Ιασσος which is attested in Hippoukome (*TAM* II 168.d15). In this connection *Ijetruxle* (a rendering of Greek Ἰατροκλῆς, Xanthos, *TL* 38.3) can also be compared, since Neumann must be right in seeing names in *iatros* ('doctor') as theophoric in a local context.[25]

The literal translation of names between classical and indigenous languages (a form of calque) was not uncommon in some areas of the Hellenistic and Roman worlds.[26] A theophoric example which has been tentatively identified in Lycia occurs in the Letoon trilingual (Xanthos, 337 BC), where *Natrbbiyēmi* corresponds to Ἀπολλόδοτον (acc.),[27] a relatively uncommon name in Athens. The evidence for a Lycian deity corresponding to the first half of the compound is unfortunately ambiguous: a word *natri* occurs twice on the north side of the Xanthos stele (Lycian B: *TL* 44.c.33, 48), and this may be the name in question.[28] Conversely, in the bilingual funerary inscription *TL* 6 (Karmylessos, late IV) Ἀπολλωνίδης is rendered with a phonetic approximation *Pulenjda*.

No derivatives of Leto are attested in Lycia (they are found elsewhere on the coast of Asia Minor and on Rhodes), although the goddess appears in inscriptions (in warning clauses on tombs), in a role corresponding to

---

[24] Robert (1937: 486, and *BE* 1981: 650); Bechtel (1917*b*, s.v.): "Ἀγρεοφῶν ist der, der die Erscheinung des Apollon Ἀγρεύς hat.' Compare *Agroitas* (three instances from Hippoukome)? See the discussion of the morphology by Bechtel (1917*b*, s.v. Ἀνεμοίτας).
[25] Neumann (1996: 145). The healing god is perhaps to be connected with *Mandros* (see Sittig 1912: 43–7 s.v. Ἀπόλλων for onomastic evidence of this god in south-west Asia Minor).
[26] Especially common with theophoric names in the Levant (see Jones 1939: 36–41).
[27] The second element is a participle from the verb *pije-* ('give'). The Aramaic text omits this clause.
[28] See Schürr (1998: 155–9) for *turaxssali Na{:}tri (TL* 44. c. 47–8) and Apollo Θυρξεύς (Pausanias 7.21.13). He identifies *Natrbbiyēmi* with a Νετερβιμος attested in Kaunos under Maussollos (Blümel 1990: 30). Laroche (1979: 61–2) sees ἀνάκτωρ in *(a)natr(a)*: but cf. Neumann (1979: 263), (1996: 148).

the Lycian *ēni qlahi ebiyehi* ('mother of the sanctuary').[29] It may be that in Lycian culture the mother goddess identified with Leto (the protector of tombs) was too awful to figure in personal names (so, for example, Ploutos and Persephone in Greek onomastics).

The question of Artemis derivatives in this area of Asia Minor is a knotty one. There is an indigenous name found in various Greek transcriptions, the essential elements of which seem to be *Artima-* (where the first syllable contains an open mid vowel, the second a close front vowel). It is not attested in its simple form in Lycian-language inscriptions: the compound form *Erttimeli*, which is found in the Letoon trilingual (*NLI* 320. 5, rendered as Ἀρτεμηλιν in the Greek version) may be influenced by *Ertemi*, the name of the goddess Artemis (*NLI* 312, Letoon, IV).[30] An additional complication is caused by the possibility of a similar-sounding Persian name.[31] The Lycian Ἀρτ(ε)ιμας is a masculine name: given that the simple form Artemis is in Greek a female name (though compounds such as Ἀρτεμίδωρος may apply to men: e.g. *TAM* II 168.b34, Hippoukome, H), there is no possibility that either language borrowed the name from the other (the regular phonological difference between the two forms makes this unlikely anyway). There is no independent evidence for an indigenous deity with a comparable designation.

There are twenty-two (male) bearers of Artemis derivatives in the published inscriptions from Lycia (Ἀρτέμας, Ἀρτέμης, Ἀρτέμων, Ἀρτεμίδωρος) and one instance of Artemis. Scholars have rightly rejected the view that the use of the name Artemis in coastal Asia Minor must always be due to the presence of a similar-sounding indigenous name.[32] There can be no objection, however, to the assumption that the phonetic coincidence encouraged greater use of male names derived from the Greek goddess. It may also have been the case that men bearing the Lycian name *Artimas* translated it into (for example) Greek *Artemas* for the purpose of civic business and epigraphic record. Although *Artemôn* and *Artemidôros* are relatively common in Athens (over 100 instances), *Artemas* is less common (fewer than twenty-five instances, starting in the Roman period) and

---

[29] *NLI* 320. 34 (Letoon trilingual), *TL* 1.56: see Laroche (1979: 75, 114). Leto and Apollo are also the honoured deities of Arbinas (*CEG* II 888 = *NLI* 324). See Laroche (1980) for Leto's connection with the Luwian mother goddess, and Bousquet (1988: 30) for her cult in Lycia.

[30] Craig Melchert (*per litt. electr.*) suggests that the cluster -rtt- in *Erttimeli* points to a native Lycian word.

[31] In a (possibly spurious) passage of Xenophon's *Anabasis* (7.8.25) there is mention of a Lycian archon called Ἀρτίμας who is an agent of Persia and occurs in a list of Persian regents: cf. Zgusta (1964: §108.5), and Sittig (1912: 60).

[32] Zgusta (1964: §108.11 with n. 415) and Robert (1963: 80–2). Zgusta makes an exception of specific cases such as Termessos (where collocations such as Ἄρτεμεις daughter of Ἀρτειμας are found).

Artemês unattested (it is found at Rhodes, no doubt the result of contact with Asia Minor). Unlike Apollo derivatives, which are evenly spaced over the Hellenistic and late Hellenistic periods, the number of Artemis derivatives jumps in the later period (over 80 per cent of occurrences).

(b) Hermes

By far the most common divine stem in Lycian names is *ERM-*. It is of course impossible to tell from the writing whether this is intended to denote [herm-] or [erm-]; and indeed, since it is unclear whether (or for how long) the aspirate was pronounced in the region, the difference between the two stems may have been ideological rather than phonological.[33] As in the case of Artemis discussed above, the popularity of this onomastic component seems to derive from the phonetic similarity of a Greek deity with an indigenous name: in this case, the Lycian name can be securely identified with an Anatolian deity, Luwian *Arma-* (the moon goddess). The Lycian form of the name is found only in the derived anthroponym *Erm̃menēni* (*TL* 121.4, Limyra).[34]

Greek names in *Herm-* are represented by forty-four tokens (thirteen types): roughly two-thirds come from the Hellenistic period, one-third from the later period. The only two names which are at all common in Athens or Rhodes are *Hermias* and *Hermôn*; some of the names are extremely rare (*Hermaphilos, Hermophantês, Hermoleôn*). As for the names which must be classed as Lycian, there are thirty-seven tokens (eighteen or nineteen types), of which 38 per cent come from the earlier period. There is a slight fluctuation in the rendering of the first vowel in Greek: in six instances (five types) a name is found written both *Arm-* and *Erm-*. Although there is evidence for the Greek world that fathers sometimes chose names for their offspring because of a superficial phonetic similarity,[35] the numbers of

---

[33] Eastern Ionic is psilotic (Ionic speakers once stretched as far as Halikarnassos in Caria). The Lycians were perfectly capable of pronouncing an *h* in their own language, but coy about using it to render a Greek aspirate: cf. *Ijeru* < Ἱέρων, *Exeteija* < Ἑκαταῖος. Greek inscriptions give aspirated consonants in the case of elision (ἐφ' ἱερέως, etc.), but these are often in formulae, and almost always in public inscriptions (and appropriate for *koine* anyway).

[34] See Neumann (1979). For Αρμα-/Ερμα- in Anatolian names and the influence of Greek Ἑρμ-, see Laroche (1951: 145, 147). Cf. Robert (1963: 38–9):

> Ἑρμᾶς se trouve en tout pays grec. Que, dans certaines régions, son succès ait été facilité par sa ressemblance avec un nom indigène, c'est probable. Mais cela ne fait absolument pas d'Hermas un nom 'indigène' . . . Ce théophore abrégé témoigne à l'origine d'un culte Hermès; celui-ci peut-être le dieu grec du gymnase, de l'agora politique ou marchande, introduit avec l'hellénisation; il peut recouvrir une divinité indigène, comme, je pense, en certaines régions de la Pisidie.

[35] Sittig (1912: 156) quotes Μηνόδωρος Μενεκλέους from Lycia. See also Fraenkel's article in *RE* (1936) s.v. *Namenwesen*.

ERM- names in Lycia points to the conclusion that the occurrence of both Greek and Lycian types in father–son or grandfather–grandson relations is indicative of a perceived connection between the two: thus *Hermaios* son of *Armedumnos* (*TAM* II 168.a43), *Hermokratês* son of *Ermatoboris* (*TAM* II 550.20), etc.

(c) Other

After the Letoid trinity and Hermes it is Mên and Zeus who make the most frequent appearance in theophoric names. Neither has any particular local significance. Mên is an Anatolian (Phrygian) deity, but not Lycian (he appears only in Greek names): names in Mên are common in Athens and elsewhere from the third century BC.[36]

5.2. Classical and heroic Greek names

For a non-Greek elite under pressure to Hellenize, the resources of Greek culture and history must have constituted a tempting reservoir of names.[37] Even if for most people the Greek or Macedonian artisans and soldiers who settled in south-west Asia Minor in the late Classical and Hellenistic periods were the most obvious source of Greek names, the 'epigraphic class' (those Lycians with the resources to erect funerary monuments and the desire to leave an inscription in Greek on them) are likely to have set their sights rather higher.

Although no two people would agree exactly which names in the corpus were historically or culturally significant, a conservative 10 per cent of names in the corpus (13 per cent of the Greek names) are instantly evocative of a famous figure from classical history or mythology. So from the canon of Athenian literature one has Aeschylus (5), Aristophanes (3), Demosthenes (6), Lysias (2), Menander (4), Plato (2), Sophocles (1); some of these names are reasonably common in Athens also, though from the above list only Menander is found over 100 times. From Homer there is Diomedes (3), Glaukos (2), Menelaos (3), Patroklos (1), Polydoros (1), Priam (2), Sarpedon (3) and Tlepolemos (8);[38] apart from Glaukos, none of these names is at all common in Athens. Lycian names which are particularly rare in Athens (less than ten instances) include Atalanta, Daidalos, Euterpe,

[36] Mên in Athens: Dow (1937: 220); cf. Masson (1980: 1483–6).
[37] See Clogg (1992: 28) for an analogous attempt to 'Hellenize' the onomastic pool by eighteenth- and nineteenth-century Greek nationalists.
[38] Common all across Lycia. Cf. J. and L. Robert (1983: 168): 'Nom hérophore, le nom Tlépolémos ne se rattache pas en Lycie au grand héros fondateur des trois villes de Rhodes. Mais dans l'*Iliade*, XVI, 416, Patrocle tue un grand nombre d'adversaires ... alors Sarpédon, voyant ses compagnons, ἑταίρους, massacrés, exhorte les Lyciens, v. 419–21; ainsi ce Tlépolémos est un Lycien.'

Hippolytos, Kastor, Meleager, Midas, Patroklos, Peisistratos,[39] Polydoros, Priam, Sarpedon and Tithonos.

The criteria governing the use of mythological names in Athens and Lycia seem to be slightly different: in Athens names may be avoided if the mythological name-bearer comes to an unhappy end, while the Lycians chose names from the literary corpus without a similar sensitivity, especially if a mythological connection with the peninsula could be established. Robert used the term 'herophoric' to distinguish the use of certain locally significant names in Lycia: thus Glaukos ('grey') is not uncommon in Athens, but used in Lycia refers to a particular Homeric figure important for Lycian claims to heroic respectability. So also Sarpedon enjoyed a cult at Xanthos and lent his name, along with Iobates, to a civic division in the city:[40] in a patriotic family of Tlos (*TAM* II 551.22) one Sarpedon named his son Hippolochos, identified in the *Iliad* as the son of Bellerophon and the father of Glaukos. Many (though not all) mythological names which are found in Lycia and are relatively uncommon elsewhere turn out to have a Lycian connection: Daidalos, for example, is said to have died in Lycia and given his name to the city of Daidala (four instances of the name attested). It is not always clear how far such connections should be pushed: an Atalanta is found at Telmessos (*TAM* II 50.a6), but it would be ambitious to attribute this to Atalanta's connection with Artemis (there are also four instances of Meleager, more than in Athens).[41] The appearance of the tragic hero Hippolytos at Kadyanda (*TAM* II 650.3b.7) is surprising – it does not occur at Athens, in line with the usual avoidance of such names. Hippolytos, of course, also had a special relation to Artemis, and had a curiously similar experience to the Lycian hero Bellerophon with an amorous and vengeful step-mother.

It is of course entirely likely that some of the names are the result of influence or import from neighbouring regions: we have already seen that Caria and western Lycia share a number of local peculiarities. Midas (seven instances) is a name particularly associated with the interior (Phrygia, Pisidia and the Kibyratis), whether one regards it as a mythological/heroic name taken over as a personal name, or a personal name borrowed directly

---

[39] For obvious political reasons: see Judeich (1927). The name is common, however, on Rhodes.
[40] On herophoric names see Robert (1978*b*: 282). On Sarpedon see also Robert (1978*a*: 34–5); attested in Lycian B as *Zrppedu* (*TL* 44d.6). Neumann (1996: 148) sees in *Iuba* (*TL* 119.2) a shortened form of Ἰοβάτης.
[41] All from *TAM* II 168 (Hippoukome). A spate of enthusiasm for Aetolian names might be connected with *SEG* XXXVIII 1476 (ed. Bousquet 1988) if the chronology could be made to work. On the other hand, both names have a Macedonian pedigree: Atalanta was sister to Perdikkas II (Diod. Sic. 18.37), Meleager a Macedonian soldier and politician (Diod. Sic. 18.2).

from a local language (presumably Phrygian).[42] Marsyas was another name associated with Phrygia, while the cult of the Dioskouroi in Kibyratis may explain the occurrence of Kastor and Polydeukês (both names rare in Athens).[43]

5.3. Macedonian influence

The wave of soldiers, administrators, merchants and carpet-baggers who followed the Macedonian conquest of Asia Minor in the late fourth century must have had an onomastic influence on the local peoples at this critical period of Hellenization. Clearly not all of them were Macedonian in origin, and of those who were, a large number will have borne Greek names which are not localizable in Macedonia. In the Roman period the practice on the part of new citizens of adopting the names of local Roman dignitaries is easier to trace and is well attested:[44] although there is room for dispute over which names may properly be designated Macedonian, it is nevertheless possible to get a sense of the importance of this onomastic source.

By the crude method of marking up the items in the database as Macedonian or not (on the basis of studies such as Hoffman (1906) and Russu (1938)) we arrive at an overall figure of around 17 per cent for 'Greek' names which were particularly characteristic of the Macedonians (15 per cent for the earlier period, 19 per cent for the later period). While Macedonian and theophoric names almost never coincide, there is a high rate of coincidence of Macedonian names and the mythical-historical names considered above (so, for example, Menander, Meleager, Menelaos, Neoptolemos, Patroklos, Silenos). This may indeed say something about the Hellenization (if such a term is appropriate) of the Macedonians, but makes it more difficult to gauge the resonance of such names in Lycia. It must have been the case, however, that while a name like Patroklos would have sounded very strange in Athens (three instances in the Roman period), such onomastic grandeur struck Lycian ears as appropriate and impressive.

Some of the names that the Lycians used are clearly those of leading Macedonian dynasts and statesmen (Alexander, Antigonos, Attalos, Ptolemaios, Seleukos); some belong to figures who were locally active in southern Asia Minor (thus Achaios, Nearchos, Thibrôn). Others are simply

---

[42] Robert (1954: 78). The name is also found in a Lycian-language inscription (*TL* 141, Limyra). See further Zgusta (1964), who refuses to list it as a proper Anatolian personal name.
[43] Marsyas (*TAM* II 168.a45/51, Hippoukome, and cf. Robert (1954: 89–91)); Kastor (*TAM* II 476.2, Patara) and Polydeukês (*SEG* XLIV 1219.a30, Xanthos, with Robert (*BE* (1973) 456)).
[44] See Lassère (1988: 90).

popular Macedonian names (such as Philotas), or names which were generally widespread in the Greek world including Macedonia (Peithôn).

5.4. Phonetic similarity

The issue of phonetic similarity between Greek and Lycian has already been touched on in the discussion of theophoric names derived from Artemis and Hermes. It can hardly have been the case that, for all names where a similarity exists between a Greek and a Lycian name, the coincidence was the motivating factor in the choice of the Greek name; but the similarity must often have played a role in privileging one name over another.

There are names for which it is fairly clear that the form found in a Greek context could have been transposed with little or no change into Lycian: Dryas, for example, looks like a well-formed Greek name derived from δρῦς ('oak, tree'), while in Lycian it works as a theophoric name.[45] In this case, in the absence of any semantic connection between the two, the Hellenized form can be thought of as a phonaesthetic or merely convenient device which allows the bearer to retain a name with local heritage but which does not sound completely barbaric in Greek. Nor indeed should the significance of the phonetic coincidence be underestimated: in a culture where sound patterns could be deeply meaningful, a name that worked in both languages with minimal adjustment may have allowed the bearer to feel psychologically integrated in both the Lycian and the Greek tradition during a period of traumatic cultural change.

If Dryas was so perfectly flexible that even Robert allowed it to count as an indigenous name, there were other names which could not be converted so neatly but, while indisputably Greek, seem to have had a special relationship with local onomastic elements. For example, the name Monimos (*TAM* II 551.15, Tlos) is a common Macedonian name, with no particular local significance: but given the existence of a non-Greek form Μονεμις in Cilicia, and a Lycian name (female) Μονομμα (*TAM* II 531, Pinara), the suspicion arises that the choice of Monimos was assisted by the existence of a local name. If we allow for the possibility of a sliding scale of coincidence, other names for which phonetic parallels with varying degrees of plausibility can be found include Adeimantos (*Adammñna*), Chrysippos (*Krupsse*), Heliodoros (Ηλις),[46] Hypatos (*Upazi*), Hyperênôr (*Upēne*),

---

[45] Robert (1949: 52), with Plut. *De def. or.* 21.
[46] Ηλις is found in Pisidia (Zgusta 1964: no. 399). One inscription from Termessos (*TAM* III 1.514) gives Ηλις ὁ καὶ Σοζόμενος, which raises the possibility of a semantic connection between father and son in Lycia (*TAM* II 650.3b.15), where Heliodoros is son of Sôsibios.

Oreios (*Urebillaha*),⁴⁷ Orthagoras (*Urtaqija*),⁴⁸ Parmeniôn (*Parmnah*),⁴⁹ Purros, Purrias (*Puresi, Puri-*), Thibrôn (*Trm̃peri, Tubere*), Tlepolemos (*Trbbēnimi*). For Οσειου (gen.) it is unclear whether the 'citation form' should be Greek Ὅσιος or an indigenous name (cf. Lycian Οσετης, Οσανοου, etc.).

This may not seem so implausible if we recall (n. 35 above) that there was a weak tradition in the Greek world of fathers giving names to their offspring with some phonetic similarity to their own. We considered a couple of examples in our discussion of theophoric names: other candidates include Ἑρμολυκος < Λύκων (*TAM* II 650.3a.4), Μηνόδωρος < Μηνόδοτος (*TAM* II 62.1), Νίκανδρος < Νικίων (*TAM* II 1184.1), Νικόλαος < Κολιου (*SEG* XXXVI 1218.3) and Τελεσίας < Τιλομα (*TAM* II 520.1).

The converse of phonetic similarity is the semantic calquing noticed briefly above for *Natrbbiyēmi* and Apollodotos. A generally accepted instance is from the bilingual funerary inscription *TL* 1.25.1 (Tlos, IV), where *Kssbezē* in the Lycian text corresponds to Porpax in the Greek section. Since there is a striking lack of phonetic similarity between the two, and since Greek πόρπαξ has such a specific meaning (handle of a shield), it is not unlikely that Lycian *kssbezē* is a compound word with the same meaning. It is difficult to gauge the extent to which this was practised, however, owing to the limited nature of the evidence and the poor state of our knowledge of the Lycian lexicon. Nevertheless, the bilingual inscriptions overwhelmingly give phonetic transliterations of the names, and there is no reason to suppose that the translation method was particularly common: it would in any case be possible only with names that were semantically transparent, which would exclude categories such as shortened forms.

Lycian names, when given in a transliterated version, are nevertheless allotted to a Greek morphological class and inflected in a regular way (in contrast, say, to the practice of the writers of the Christian scriptures with regard to Hebrew names). There is some variation in the degree of morphological assimilation: for example, in a bilingual from Karmylessos (*TAM* I 6, late IV) *Purihimeti* is rendered in Greek Πυριματις (gen. Πυριματιος), while in a bilingual from Tlos the same name is given as *Πυριβατης (gen. Πυριβατους). In this version the second element has been Hellenized (and indeed allotted to a more sophisticated morphological class), which draws

---

⁴⁷ See Neumann (1978: 129); compare also Lycian *Hura* (*TL* 47.1, 119.1), which is rendered Ορας in the Greek alphabet (*TAM* II 550.17).
⁴⁸ *Urtaqija* is rendered Ορτακια in the Greek alphabet (*TL* 1.25.6, Tlos, bilingual). Cf. also Neumann (1996: 149).
⁴⁹ Neumann (1985: 247).

attention to the fact that the first element Πυρι- is also analysable in Greek (cf. Πυριλάμπης in nearby Rhodes).

6. DOUBLE NAMES

We have suggested that some Lycians (men in particular) may have answered to two names, one Lycian (for private or family use) and one Greek (for public business). There is evidence from inscriptions for double names throughout south-west Asia Minor, particularly in Caria, Cilicia, Lycia, Lydia, Pisidia and Phrygia: the standard formula for recording a double name is ὁ/ἡ καί 'also known as'; in a few cases the second name is simply left in apposition to the first, which can create problems of interpretation. It is difficult, however, to prove that any of the inscriptions from Lycia which contains a double name dates from before the Roman period, which compromises the quality of the evidence: the listing in inscriptions of two names may simply have been a late fashion in the peninsula or perhaps a romantic reassertion of native heritage similar to that evidenced in Laconian inscriptions of the same period. Moreover, the epigraphic evidence casts doubt on the notion that the use of double names was the result of bilingual naming patterns: a quick calculation based on Zgusta (1964) indicates that the number of cases in which a person reports a Greek name and an indigenous name is roughly equal to the number in which two indigenous names are reported. In both cases a large majority of the cases concern women, which might point to a slower rate of adoption of Greek names by women (given that most of the data comes from the first two centuries AD), or might be connected with a vogue for female *Lallnamen* since a considerable proportion of alternative names seem to be offered as a firmer identification for women known familiarly by very common diminutives such as Tata, Ammia and Appia. There are cross-cultural parallels for a smaller naming pool for women than for men.

Double names, then, do not provide unambiguous evidence for the process of Hellenization in the onomastic sphere, since there seems not to have been a convention of recording them in inscriptions on a regular basis for men in the Hellenistic period. An interesting case ('Wien inedita', undated) is reported for Istlada by Zgusta, however, who quotes a text in which a man is designated both Ἑρμαγόρας and Ερμαρας (1964: §355.24).

7. UNFLATTERING NAMES

It is well known that many Indo-European names have a meaning that may generally be characterized as propitious: names which imply glory, might, wisdom, divine connections or other desirable qualities in the bearer. This is especially true of 'heroic' compound names. However, a surprisingly large category of simplex names in the Greek world have more mundane meanings: they may be derived from colour terms (describing hair colour or skin complexion), or words pertaining to the stature or other physical characteristics of a human being. Some of them strike us as distinctly unflattering, in that they are reminiscent of modern nick-names or insulting sobriquets. We saw above (§2.2) the possibility of deriving a name from κόπρος ('dung'); there are few body parts which are not amenable to a similar process of derivation (see Bechtel 1917a: 479–84). Names may also come from adjectives meaning 'hairy', 'fat', 'crooked', 'snub-nosed' and even 'ugly'; or from nouns for animals and plants. Whether such names (or some of them) are to be regarded as apotropaic in origin, and hence crypto-propitious, is not a question which need concern us here.[50]

Greek names from Lycia on the whole fit into the category of heroic or propitious.[51] The small number of exceptions to this include the following:
(a) Insulting: names such as Αἰσχύλος (αἶσχος) are clearly taken over from Greek sources without regard to the meaning of their components. Αἰσχρίων may similarly be a Macedonian import.
(b) Plants, animals and the natural world: Βότριχος (cf. Macedonian Βότρης, with Robert (1962: 249)), Βρύων (above, §2.2), Καυλιος (perhaps Greek καυλός, 'stem of plant, shaft', and sens. obsc.), Κολιος (Greek κολιός, 'green woodpecker', or cf. *Kulida*, *TL* 1.137?), Μόσχος, Νόσσις (Greek νοσσός, Robert (1963: 60–1)), Πρασίδης (πράσον, 'leek', and see Bousquet 1988: 25 for the reading). Heroic animals such as lions and leopards need no apology: neither do names derived from λύκος, which may also play on the word Lycia.
(c) Personal characteristics: Πύρρος, Σιμίας (bilingual, Lycian *Eseimija*).
(d) Trade, profession, activity: Σκοπός.
(e) For Πόρπαξ (hardly heroic) see §5.4 above.

Single-stem sobriquets of this type presuppose a long-established Greek-speaking community in which the frequency of use of such names had accustomed speakers to their oddity. This is precisely what is lacking in a region where Greek has only recently been introduced, and the relative scarcity of this type is unsurprising. It also suggests that a very high proportion of the Greeks in Lycia were Greeks by conversion or assimilation rather than immigrants from the old world.

---

[50] See Ghiron-Bistagne (1988); and §2.2 above for copronyms.
[51] Cf. Bousquet and Gauthier (1994: 356–7).

8. CONCLUDING REMARKS

The onomastic picture in Lycia turns out to be rather different from that in Caria, its neighbour and in many respects the closest social and linguistic parallel. By the Roman period in Caria indigenous names had all but disappeared.[52] In Lycia a rapid increase in the use of Greek personal names can be traced in the Hellenistic period, but a stable proportion of indigenous names continued in use. One can see from examining naming patterns within families that there seems to have been no stigma attached to the use of indigenous names, since Lycian names often appear in the generation following the first attested use of a Greek name: thus for example a man from Kadyanda (*TAM* II 650.1b.2, LH) called Ἀρτέμων has a father with the name Ορνεπειμις and a grandfather Μεγιστόδοτος (and an adoptive father with the Carian name Pixodaros). Brothers and spouses may similarly have names from the two different traditions. Differences between male and female naming patterns point to the conclusion that there was a certain 'bilingualism' in the onomastic habits of the Lycians, whereby men were more likely to have a Greek name in a public text, and may indeed have had two names: to what extent this ambidextrous onomastic attitude coincided with a real bilingual situation, in which Greek and Lycian occupied different social spheres (public and private), is hard to tell. If a functional difference in the use of names must occur in a bilingual context, then we would be encouraged to suppose that the Lycian language survived in spoken form until the early Roman period, in spite of the absence of epigraphic material.

In addition to names which are firmly associated with the two languages in question, there is also a substantial number of ambiguous names which seem designed to bridge the gap. Analogously, the choice of Greek names which have an association with Lycia enable the bearer to reconcile two identities: the Hellenistic and the patriotic. If we can draw a general conclusion from Lycian onomastic behaviour, it is that the Lycians believed their own publicity to the extent that, owing to their privileged status, they saw less of a contradiction between being Lycian and being Hellenized than some of their neighbours in Asia Minor.

Absorption of Greek elements into Lycian culture took place by a number of different routes, and these have left traces in the complex onomastic situation of the peninsula. Interaction with Greek communities in Rhodes and in Pamphylia from the earliest period left its mark: in the case of

---

[52] Robert (1963: 82).

Rhodes, some specific shared names, and in general some Doric phonological colouring; Pamphylian influence is less marked, but can be seen in *Pajawa*. Greeks were doubtless familiar visitors to Lycian ports for many centuries owing to the important position of the country on a shipping route to the eastern Mediterranean. There will also have been contact with Greek settlements to the north for the purposes of trade and (particularly in the period leading up to the Persian invasions) strategic or diplomatic purposes. Ionic influence can be seen in typically Ionic names such as Φιλτῆς, and there may also be Doric influence from cities such as Halikarnassos. Lycia contributed on an irregular basis to the Delian League in the fifth century: the first evidence for large-scale Greek interference was the Athenian intervention during the Peloponnesian War to extract contributions, and the Xanthos stele shows that by the end of this period the Lycians were familiar with the political geography of their noisy neighbours to the west. In the late fifth and fourth centuries there was increasing demand in the dynastic courts of the Xanthos valley for Greek technical expertise: this fuelled, and was in turn fuelled by, an increase in the presence of skilled Greek craftsmen. It is clear that Greek *tekhnê* was valued by this time, not merely as a means to an end (for example, a fine building for a local dynast), but as an end in itself: a Greek inscription on a monument can have had no value except to someone who appreciated the *Greekness itself* of the text. In onomastic terms the choice of the name Perikles by a political leader presupposes a domestic constituency who understood the reference and valued the implications. By the Macedonian period it must have been clear that the destiny of the country was as part of the Greek world: there is a rapid increase in the use of Greek and the adoption of Greek names, many of them taken over from the new Macedonian elite who introduced an impressive onomastic heritage redolent of Greek mythology and high literature. This seems to have encouraged the Lycians themselves to delve into their mythological past for onomastic inspiration and ideological comfort.

APPENDIX: INDEX OF NAMES AVAILABLE FOR THE PRESENT STUDY

Abbreviations (epigraphic sources)

(i) Corpora
NLI *Neufunde Lykischer Inschriften seit 1901*, ed. E. Neumann (Vienna 1979).

(ii) Epigraphic publications

Bean (1948)	G. Bean, 'Notes and inscriptions from Lycia', *JHS* 68, 40–58 at p. 42, nos. 1–2.
Bean (1962)	G. Bean, 'Report on a journey in Lycia in 1960', *AAWW* 99, 4–9 at p. 7, no. 6.
BCH 18	A. Diamantaras, '*Epigraphai ek Lykias*', *BCH* 18 (1894), 323–33 at pp. 325, no. 5 and 326, no. 9.
Bousquet (1988)	J. Bousquet, 'La stèle des Kyténiens au Létôon de Xanthos', *REG* 101, 12–53 at p. 24 n. 9.
Gauthier (1996)	P. Gauthier, 'Bienfaiteurs de gymnase au Létôon de Xanthos', *REG* 109, 1–32 at p. 2, no. 1 and p. 27, no. 11.
HK	R. Heberdey and E. Kalinka (1897), *Bericht über zwei Reisen im südwestlichen Kleinasien* (*Denkschr. Wien* 45).
LS IV	'Neue Inschriften aus Kyaneai und Umgebung', in F. Kolb (ed.), *Lykische Studien* IV: *Feldforschungen auf dem Gebiet von Kyaneai (Yavu-Bergland). Ergebnisse der Kampagnen 1993/4* (*Asia Minor Studien* 29, Bonn 1998), 177–205.
Maiuri (1926)	A. Maiuri, 'Novi supplementi al *Corpus* delle iscrizione di Rodi', *ASAA* 8–9, 313–22 at p. 315, no. 1.
Mendel (1912)	G. Mendel, *Catalogue des Sculptures (Musée Impérial Constantinople)* 1, p. 266, no. 106.
PL	E. Petersen and F. von Luschan (1889), *Reisen im südwestlichen Kleinasien* II: *Reisen in Lykien, Milyas und Kibyratis* (Vienna).
Segre (1932)	M. Segre, 'Due nuovi teste storici', *Riv. Phil.* 10, 446–61 at p. 446, no. 1.
Segre (1938)	M. Segre, 'Iscrizioni di Licia', *Clara Rhodos* IX. 179–208 at p. 183, no. 1.
Wilhelm (1931)	A. Wilhelm, 'Epigramma ek Lykias', *PAA* 6, 319–34 at 327.
Wörrle (1998)	M. Wörrle, 'Leben und sterben wie ein Fürst. Überlegungen zu den Inschriften eines neuen Dynastengrabes in Lykien', *Chiron* 28, 77–83 at p. 78.

* Names from bilingual inscriptions are marked with an asterisk. There is only one listing per individual (where identity can be established).

Ἀβερουνδις	*SEG* XLIII 969.19
Ἀγαθημερος	*TAM* II 551.17; *SEG* VI 778.1
Ἀγαθινος	*SEG* XLIV 1219.a21, b26
Ἀγαθοβουλος	*IGSK* XLVIII 81.3
Ἀγαθοκλης	*TAM* II 550.14, 593.2, 3
Ἀγαθοπους	*TAM* II 62.c5
Ἀγνος	Bean (1962) 6.4
Ἀγρεοφων	*TAM* II 168.b12, 13, 34, 39, 49
Ἀγροιτας	*TAM* II 168.a50, b29, c23, d25
Ἀδειμαντος	*TAM* II 550.28 (bis)
Ἀδεμις	*SEG* XLIII 969.26

Αδλασις	*TAM* ιι 50.b1
Αθανιων	*TAM* ιι 1185.2
Αθηναγορας	*SEG* xliii 969.25
Αισχριων	*TAM* ιι 168.a41, c4
Αισχυλινος	*TAM* ιι 168.c5
Αισχυλος	*SEG* xliii 986.10, 11; *LS* iv 10.5, 6, 13.5
Αιχμων	*TAM* ιι 41a.1, 264.1, 498.4; *SEG* xliv 1219.a24 (bis), 25
Αλεξανδρος	*SEG* xliii 969.9 (bis); Bean (1948) 1.4; *LS* iv 12.2
Αλεξιας	*TL* 1.71.3
Αλεξων	*SEG* xliv 1221.1
Αμιαντος	*TAM* ιι 475.3
Αμυντας	*TAM* ιι 30.1, 550.13 (bis); *SEG* xliv 1218.5; HK ii.28.5; PL 87.14
Ανδρεας	*TAM* ιι 168.a41, 44, 46, b8, 13, 15, 550.12, 650.3.a11, 13, b18
Ανδροβιος	*TAM* ιι 550.20; *SEG* xliv 1219.b1
Ανδρομαχος	*SEG* xxviii 1246.2 (bis), 3, xliv 1219.b29 (bis), 32
Ανδρονικος	*TAM* ιι 550.9, 12 (bis); *SEG* xxxviii 1476.4, xliv 1219.a13, b42; PL 88.8
Ανδρονομος	*SEG* xliv 1219.b19 (bis), 20
Ανδρων	*TAM* ιι 168.d12, ιι 550.27
Αννα	*SEG* xlv 1792.1
Ανθις	*IGSK* xlviii 145.1
Αντιχαρις	HK ii.28.5
Αντιφιλος	*TAM* ιι 597.a1
Αντιγενης	*TAM* ιι 550.4, 25, 552.3, 650.1.b10, 3.a2
Αντιγονος	*TAM* ιι 168.a32; *SEG* xliv 1218.3 (bis), 1219.a22
Αντιοχις	*TAM* ιι 595.1
Αντιοχος	*TAM* ιι 551.8; *SEG* xxviii 1246.26, xxxvi 1220.19; *LS* iv 12.1 (bis)
Αντιπατρος	*TAM* ιι 168.a49, 59, b8, 22 (bis), 24, 26 (bis), 29, 48, c20, d27; *SEG* viii 1246.30; Segre (1938) 1.8
Απολλοδοτος	*TAM* ιι 264.1; *SEG* xxvii 942.3*
Απολλοδωρος	*TAM* ιι 168.a44; Segre (1938) 1.6
Απολλωνιδης	*TL* 1.6.1*; *TAM* ιι 162.2, 168.a54; *SEG* xliv 1219.a7, 18, b31
Απολλωνιος	*TL* 1.72.1; *TAM* ιι 551.2, 552.1 (bis), 3, 752.1; *SEG* xix 870.1, xliii 969.17, xliv 1219.a11 (bis), 13; PL 88.13; Wörrle (1998) 2
Απολλωνις	Bean (1962) 6.9
Αππαδις	PL 27.2
Αρβασιος	*SEG* xlv 1798.1
Αρβινας	*SEG* xxviii 1245. a4*
Αργαιος	*SEG* xliv 1218.11
Αρινδαματι	*SEG* xlv 1813.2
Αριννασn	*SEG* xlv 1800.4
Αρισταγορας	*SEG* xliv 1219.b25; Bean (1962) 6.7; PL 87.2, 89.1 (bis)

Αριστειδης	*TAM* II 550.4 (bis)
Αριστευς	PL 88.32 (bis)
Αριστιων	*SEG* XLIII 986.7
Αριστοδαμος	*TAM* II 550.9, 13, 19
Αριστοδημος	PL 87.13, 88.12
Αριστοκρατεια	*TAM* II 1185.1
Αριστομαχος	PL 88.14
Αριστομενης	*TAM* II 472.2
Αριστοφανης	PL 88.24, 25 (bis)
Αριστονικος	*TAM* II 550.30
Αριστων	*TAM* II 168.b43
Αρμ[.5.]οιυ	*SEG* XXVII 907.i.a1
Αρμαδαπιμις	*SEG* XLV 1789.1
Αρμαις	*TAM* II 550.18
Αρμαπιας	*TL* 1.139.1*
Αρματις	*SEG* XIX 870.2
Αρμεδυμνος	*TAM* II 168.a43, 46
Αρμενος	*TAM* II 309.6; *SEG* XLIV 1219.a22
Αρμοας	*TAM* II 540.4
Αρμοδιος	*TAM* II 168.a48, b15, 50, c5, 550.18, 34, 551.15, 19, 625.1 (bis)
Αρμοστης	*TAM* II 168.c21
Αρμοστος	*TAM* II 168.c1
Αρπαλος	*TAM* II 551.21 (bis), 650.1.b12, 3.b19; *LS* IV 10.10
Αρπιγραμος	*SEG* XLV 1785.2
Αρπιδοβας	Bousquet (1988)
Αρσακης	*TAM* II 550.10
Αρσασις	*TAM* II 473.1, 3
Αρσινοη	*TAM* II 472.1
Αρταπατης	*TAM* II 261.3, 550.16; *SEG* XXVIII 1246.14, XXXIII 1184.6, XLIV 1218.2, 1219.b12, XLV 1803.2, 1825.3
Αρτεμας	*TAM* II 550.29 (bis), 31
Αρτεμηλις	*SEG* XXVII 942.5*
Αρτεμης	*TAM* II 550.18 (bis); *SEG* XXVII 907.i.a2 (bis), a3, ii.1, 4; *IGSK* XLVIII 101.5
Αρτεμιδωρος	*TAM* II 168.a34, 38, b34; *SEG* XLV 1800.3
Αρτιμας	*TAM* II 551.6; *SEG* XLIV 1219.b37, XLV 1807
Αρτεμις	Bean (1948) 1.3
Αρτεμων	*TAM* II 650.1.b2, 3.b6 (bis), b10, 674.1 (bis); Bean (1962) 6.11; PL 88.24
Αρχεδημος	*TAM* II 550.32
Αρχελαος	PL 88.18
Αρχεπολις	*TAM* II 923.1
Αρχεστρατος	*TAM* II 533.4, 5, 551.14, 650.3.b22
Αρχινος	*TAM* II 472.2; *LS* 4: 10.13
Αρχιας	PL 108.6

Αρχων	PL 67.2
Ασεδεπλεμις	SEG XLV 1812
Ασκληπιαδης	TAM II 650.3.b16; SEG XLIV 1219.a18, 26, b14
Αταλαντη	TAM II 50.a6
Ατταλος	TAM II 635, 650.1.a4, a5, a6, 3.b18; SEG XLV 1794
Αφροδισιος	TAM II 168.a55, 60
Αφροδιτη	TAM II 476.1
Αχαιος	TAM II 597.a1; SEG XLIV 1219.b22
Βισιναρις	SEG XLV 1798.1
Βοηθος	TAM II 49.1; SEG XLIV 1219.a29 (bis), b45 (ter)
Βοισκος	SEG XLIV 1219.b24
Βοτριχος	TAM II 551.5, 14; SEG XLIII 969.10
Βουτας	TAM II 533.6
Βρυων	TAM II 550.7 (bis), 533.5; SEG XLIV 1219.b23
Γελλεμις	TAM II 650.3.b5
Γεργις	SEG XXVIII 1245.a1
Γλαυκος	SEG XXVIII 1246.14, 32
Γλαυκων	SEG XLIII 969.15
Δαιδαλος	TAM II 550.15; IGSK XLVIII 1.2; SEG XLIV 1218.1, 1219.b10
Δαλλα	SEG XXVII 906.1
Δαμας	TAM II 168.b28
Δαμεας	TAM II 643.1
Δαπαρας	PL 52.1; Segre (1932) 1.5
Δαρηος	TAM II 596.1
Δελεπιας	PL 87.11
Δελεπιμις	BCH 18: 9.3
Δεξιφανης	SEG XLIV 1218.21
Δεξιος	SEG XLIII 969.20
Δερκυλιδης	TAM II 650.1.b6
Δημεας	SEG XLIV 1218.5, 1219.a7, 21, b25
Δημητριος	TAM II 50.a2, b3, 162.4, 168.a37, c14, d24, 550.10, 23, 551.10 (bis), 18, 768.2; PL 14.2, 87.1, 88.34; SEG XVIII 570.4, XLIII 969.12, XLIV 1219.b27; Maiuri (1926) 1.4
Δημοκλειδης	NLI 312 a1*
Δημοκρατης	TAM II 168.b24
Δημοσθενης	SEG XLIV 1219.b7, 12 (bis), 30, 46; Gauthier (1996) 1.6
Δικαιαρχος	TAM II 168.a58
Δικαιος	TAM II 168.a32, 50, 57
Διογενης	TAM II 168.a56, 389.5 (bis); IGSK XLVIII 81.2 (bis)
Διογνητος	TAM II 50.a5
Διοδοτος	TAM II 595.1
Διοδωρος	TAM II 650.3.a10
Διομηδης	SEG XLIII 969.25, XLIV 1219.a5, 14
Διονυσιος	TAM II 50.a3, 6, 168.b14, 18, 550.17
Διοφανης	TAM II 650.3.a18 (bis)

Δομας   TAM II 168.a53
Δουπων   SEG XLIV 1219.a27
Δρυας   TAM II 550.13, 551.9; Maiuri (1926) 1.4
Δωσιθεος   TAM II 650.1.a3; BCH 18: 5
Εδα   SEG XLV 1791.2
Ειδα   TAM II 543.2
Ειρηναιος   TAM II 548.10, 35, 550.12, 551.1, 3, 4, 597.a3; SEG XLIII 969.26
Ελιδενις   SEG XLV 1791.1
Ελλαφιλος   Wörrle (1998) 2
Ελμιδαυα   TL 1.139.2*
Ελποατις   TL 1.23.1*
Εμβρομος   Bean (1948) 2.1
Επενηνις   SEG XLIV 1219.a9 (bis), b37
Επιδαρσασις   SEG XXVII 905.2; Bean (1948) 1.1
Επιγονος   TAM II 473.2
Επικουρος   TAM II 168.b25
Επικτητος   Bean (1962) 6.5
Επιφρων   SEG XLIV 1219.a8
Ερβιγεσις   SEG XIX 870.3
Εργοτελης   SEG XLIV 1219.b34
Ερεπ[τος?   TAM II 161.1
Εριανθος   SEG XLIV 1219.b17
Εριυασας   SEG XLV 1790.1
Ερμαγορας   LS IV 21.4; PL 88.11
Ερμαδαννας   BCH 18: 9.2, 3
Ερμαδαπιμις   SEG XLIV 1219.b34, XLV 1808.2; PL 95.1
Ερμαδεννας   TAM II 712.1, 2
Ερμαδονεμις   LS IV 13.4
Ερμαδορτας   TAM II 650.3.b11
Ερμαιος   TAM II 168.a32, 43, 47, b42, 550.15, 942.1; SEG XXVII
                  907.i.a2; IGSK XLVIII 2.4
Ερμακαρταδις   SEG XLIV 1219.a6; TAM II 475.1
Ερμακοτας   TAM II 550.16, 551.7, 598.1; SEG XLIII 969.27 BCH 18: 9.1
Ερμακτας   SEG XLIII 969.8
Ερμακτιβιλος   Mendel (1912) 106.2
Ερμανδιμασις   PL 88.29
Ερμανδορτας   TAM II 550.24
Ερμαπιας   TAM II 30.2
Ερμ]απιων   PL 87.12
Ερμα[ρα]της   PL 88.26
Ερματοβορις   TAM II 550.21
Ερματοεορις   TAM II 373.2
Ερματουγγας   SEG XLIV 1219.b35
Ερμαφιλος   TAM II 373.3; SEG XLIV 1219.a23
Ερμεδυμνος   TAM II 168.d25

Ερμενδαδις	SEG XLV 1806.2
Ερμενηνις	SEG XLIV 1219.b8
Ερμιας	TAM II 168.a33, c25
Ερμοας	TAM II 526.1
Ερμοκρατης	TAM II 550.20, 650.3.b9; SEG XLIV 1219.a29, b37
Ερμοκριτος	TAM II 168.c4
Ερμολαος	TAM II 526.9
Ερμολεων	TAM II 168.b36, 41
Ερμολυκος	TAM II 650.3.a4; SEG XXXVI 1218.4, XLIV 1219.a19, b8; PL 88.22 (bis)
Ερμοτιμος	TAM II 168.a36, b23, 31, d26, 650.1.a2
Ερμοφαντος	TAM II 168.a39, 40, d22, 550.11; Segre (1932) 1.5
Ερμων	TAM II 168.a32
Ερμωναξ	TAM II 168.a59 (?), b14, 47, c19; LS IV 13.1, 2
Ερπιας	TAM II 540.6, 550.17, 551.8
Ερπιγρης	SEG XLIV 1219.b17
Ερπιδενηνις	TAM II 475.2; SEG XLIV 1219.b13
Ευαγορας	PL 58.2; SEG XXVIII 1246.46
Ευδημος	SEG XVIII 570.37, 41, XLIV 1219.a17, b21
Ευδρομος	PL 95.2
Ευελθων	TAM II 498.4, 650.1.b7, 9; SEG XLIV 1218.4, 1219.b19
Ευελπιστος	Bean (1962) 6.8
Ευημερις	TAM II 162.3
Ευκλης	SEG XLIV 1219.a20
Ευμενισκος	SEG XXXVI 1220.19
Ευμηδης	SEG XXXIX 1414.a18*
Ευνομος	SEG XLIV 1218.5
Ευτερπη	TAM II 475.1
Ευτυχος	Bean (1962) 6.12
Ευφραινετος	TAM II 263.9
Ευφρανωρ	SEG XLIV 1219.a6
Ζερμουνδις	IGSK XLVIII 113.1, 2, 3
Ζηνοδοτος	TAM II 168.a35, 38, 44, b15
Ζηνων	TAM II 168.a6, 35, 36, 40, 43, c22 (bis), d13, 14, 28, 650.3.b24; SEG XLIV 1219.b24
Ζωσιμος	PL 88.10, 29
Ηγελοχος	SEG XL 1270.1 (bis); LS 4: 12.11
Ηγεμων	TAM II 650.3.b16
Ηγησιλαος	Maiuri (1926) 1.4
Ηγιας	PL 108.2
Ηλιοδωρος	TAM II 650.3.b15
Ηρακλειδης	TL 1.71.2; TAM II 551.5, 596.1; SEG XII 502.5
Ηφαιστιων	TAM II 168.8
Θαλιανδρος	TAM II 903.2
Θειβεσις	NLI 312 a1*

Θεμιστοκλης	*SEG* XLIV 1219.a23
Θεογενης	Gauthier (1996) 11.5
Θεοδοτος	*TAM* II 168.a44; *SEG* XII 502.4
Θεοδωρος	*TL* 1.25b*
Θεοκλης	*TAM* II 650.1.b1, 3.a1,3.a14
Θεοξενος	*SEG* XLIV 1219.b29 (bis)
Θεοφανης	*SEG* XLIV 1219.a8, 14, b24
Θεοφιλος	*TAM* II 650.3.a7
Θερσιπολις	*SEG* XLIV 1219.b18
Θεων	*TAM* II 168.a7
Θηρωνιδης	*TAM* II 168.b21, 39, 44, 46, 51, 650.1.a3, 2.a13
Θιβρων	*SEG* XLIII 969.18 (bis), XLIV 1219.b31 (bis), 32
Θρασεας	*TAM* II 551.13; PL 93
Θρασυμαχος	Maiuri (1926) 1.3 (bis); PL 108.6
Θρυψις	*TL* 1.25.1*
Ιασσος	*TAM* II 168.d15
Ιασων	*TAM* II 509.2 (bis), 551.13; *SEG* XLIV 1219.a19, b15; *LS* IV 10.5, 13.1, 2, 3 (quater); PL 87.13 Segre (1938) 1.5
Ιδαγοας	*SEG* XXVIII 1246.30
Ιδαγρης	*LS* IV 22
Ιδαμας	Bean (1948) 2.2
Ιεροκλης	*TAM* II 372.3; *SEG* XLIV 1219.a32, b32, 33
Ιερων	*SEG* XXVII 942.3*
Ικεσιος	*SEG* XXXVI 1220.18
Ικτας	*TL* 1.56.1*
Ιμβραλος	*TAM* II 923.2
Ιμβρασις	*TAM* II 548.7
Ιππολοχος	*TAM* II 168.b52, c3, 550.19, 551.4, 9 (bis), 18, 22, 580.4; PL 94.1
Ιππολυτος	*TAM* II 650.3.b7
Καδοβορις	*TAM* II 540.1 (ter)
Καιδαρμα	*IGSK* XLVIII 101.6
Καλλικλης	*SEG* XLIV 1219.a28
Καλλικρατης	*TAM* II 533.2; *IGSK* XLVIII 1.3; PL 87.14
Καλλινικος	Bean (1962) 6.10
Καλλιππος	*SEG* XL 1270.1 (bis); PL 86, 87.9, 88.18
Καλλισθενης	*TAM* II 168.b23
Καλλιστρατα	*TAM* II 50.a4
Καλλιστρατος	*TAM* II 550.15, 551.17
Καλλιτελης	*TAM* II 50.a1 (bis), 4
Καρταδις	Mendel (1912) 106.2
Κarταλις	PL 88.9 (bis)
K]αστορ	*TAM* II 476.2
Καυλιος	*SEG* XLIV 1219.b26
Κεδδηβης	*TAM* II 168.a42, 47, 53, b52, c14, 16, 19

Κεισος	PL 52.1
Κενδηρας	IGSK xlviii 101.4
Κενδονις	TAM ii 50.b2
Κενθηβης	TAM ii 168.d23
Κεσινδηλις	SEG xxvii 942.13*
Κινδαβυρις	TAM ii 768.2
Κινδανυβας	SEG xlv 1810
Κινδυοπρας	TAM ii 674.3
Κλε[αδ]ρος	TAM ii 62.c3
Κλειτος	TAM ii 533.2
Κλεοβουλος	TAM ii 650.1.b8; BCH 18: 9.10
Κλεων	TAM ii 389.3, 4; SEG xxvii 906.1; PL 87.12, 88.31
Κοατα	TL 1.134*
Κοδαρας	TL 1.143*
Κολιος	SEG xxxvi 1218.3
Κονδορασις	SEG xxvii 942.9*
Κοπριλις	TAM ii 922.1
Κοτανις	SEG xliv 1219.b21, 22
Κοτων	TAM ii 540.8
Κουαυα	IGSK xlviii 2.4
Κουτος	TAM ii 540.4
Κραισιος	Wilhelm (1931)
Κρατερος	TAM ii 550.10, 12, 598.2, 650.3. b10; SEG xliii 969.24; PL 88.12
Κρατης	SEG xxxvi 1220.19
Κρατιδαμος	SEG xvi 770.1 (bis)
Κρατιππος	SEG xliii 969.7; PL 14.2
Κριν?]αγρος	TAM ii 168.b36
Κρινολαος	SEG xlv 1825.3
Κριτων	TAM ii 168.a50
Κροαδις	SEG xliv 1219.b18
Κρολιμος	LS iv 22
Κτιβιλας	SEG xliii 969.23
Λαις	TAM ii 752.1
Λαλλα	TAM ii 309.2, 712.1; SEG xliv 1219.b40, xlv 1802.2
Λαμισκος	TAM ii 650.3.b20
Λαπαρας	TL 1.6.1*
Λας	TL 1.56.1*
Λειμων	Segre (1938) 1.8
Λεοντιδης	TAM ii 168.d28
Λεοντισκος	TAM ii 168.a54, 550.26; SEG xxxvi 1219.4, xliv 1219.a10, b23, 43
Λεων	TAM ii 160.11, 168.b50
Λεωνιδης	TAM ii 372.2, 475.2, 550.8; SEG xliv 1219.b17, 39, 40
Λυκεας	TAM ii 41.a2

Λυκισκος	*TAM* II 551.24, 650.3.b21; *SEG* XLIV 1218.4 (bis), 1219.a26, b36
Λυκος	Maiuri (1926) 1.3
Λυκων	*TAM* II 650.2.a11, 3.a4
Λυσανιας	*SEG* XVIII 570.36
Λυσιμαχος	*TAM* II 551.3, 22, 597.b1
Λυσιας	*SEG* XLIV 1219.a32, b7
Λυσων	*SEG* XXXVI 1218.4, XLIV 1219.b27, 34; Gauthier (1996) 1.6
Μαμμα	Bean (1948) 2.2
Μαναπιμις	*NLI* 302*
Μανδαλασις	*TAM* II 50.b1
Μαρανδις	*IGSK* XLVIII 161.2
Μαρδονιος	*LS* IV 12.4
Μαρσυας	*TAM* II 168.a45, 51
Μασας	*TL* 1.134*; *TAM* II 650.1.b6, b7, 2.a9; *SEG* XXVII 906.1, XLI 1379.2, XLV 1808.3
Μαυσωλος	*TAM* II 550.15, 551.21; *SEG* XIX 870.2, XLIII 969.23, XLIV 1219.b23 (bis), 38 (ter), 40
Μεγακλης	*TAM* II 650.3.b14
Μεγιστοδοτος	*TAM* II 650.1.b3
Μελαισχρος	*TAM* II 551.15
Μελανδιασις	*IGSK* XLVIII 113.3
Μελεαγρος	*TAM* II 168.a41, c24, 26, d29
Μενανδρος	*TAM* II 168.b20, 30, 309.2, 598.2
Μενεκλης	*TAM* II 168.a33, 40, b38, 40; *SEG* XXXVI 1220.18
Μενεκρατης	*TAM* II 158.3, 160.4; *SEG* XL 1271.1; PL 108.7
Μενελαος	*TAM* II 550.7, 8, 551.23
Μενεμαχος	*SEG* XXVIII 1246.32
Μενεστρατος	*SEG* XXVIII 1246.26, XLIV 1219.a12
Μεννεαος	*TAM* II 526.1
Μενων	*SEG* XLV 1798.2
Μεριμυθος	*IGSK* XLVIII 43.2
Μηνοδοτος	*TAM* II 162.1, 168.b33 *BCH* (1894) 325.5; PL 88.17 (bis)
Μηνοδωρος	*TAM* II 162.1, 4, 168.a7, 31, 35, b35, c24; *SEG* XLIII 969.12
Μηνοκριτος	*SEG* XVIII 570.1
Μηνοφανης	*TAM* II 168.b12
Μηνοφιλος	*TAM* II.650.3.a3; *IGSK* XLVIII 145.3
Μητροδωρος	*TAM* II 168.b27
Μιδας	*TAM* II 168.a37, 49 (bis), 52; *SEG* XLIII 969.19, 28; *LS* IV 13.2
Μικκος	*SEG* XLIV 1219.b35 (bis)
Μιμμις	PL 88.33
Μιστριας	*SEG* XLV 1785.1
Μλααυσις	*TL* 1.139.2*

Μολεσις	*TAM* II 168.a55
Μολλισις	*TL* 1.6.1*
Μονε	PL 94.2
Μονιμος	*TAM* II 551.15, 16 (bis)
Μονις	Bousquet (1988)
Μορασακης	*SEG* XLV 1808.1
Μορνα	*TL* 1.139.2*
Μ]ορωζας	*SEG* XLIII 977*
Μοσχιων	*TAM* II 40.1; PL 53.2
Μοσχος	*TAM* II 551.7, 589.1, 590.3; *SEG* XXVIII 1246.46, XLIII 969.5, 32
Μυρεννεις	PL 94.2
Μυριλα	*TAM* II 489.1
Μυωνιδης	*TAM* II 168.a47
Ναννα	*TAM* II 593.2
Νανος	*IGSK* XLVIII 145.1
Ναυκρατης	*SEG* XLIV 1219.b28 (bis)
Νεαρχος	*SEG* XXXVI 1220.14
Νενις	*SEG* XLV 1796
Νεοπτολεμος	*TAM* II 168.b20, 552.1; Wilhelm (1931)
Νεων	*TAM* II 168.a37
Νικανδρος	*TAM* II 1184.1
Νικανωρ	*TAM* II 550.19
Νικαρης	*TAM* II 1185.10
Νικαρχος	*SEG* XLV 1794
Νικη	*LS* IV 12.4
Νικηφορος	*TAM* II 598.1
Νικιων	*TAM* II 1184.1
Νικολαος	*SEG* XXXVI 1218.3
Νικομηδης	*SEG* XLIV 1219.a27
Νικοστρατος	*SEG* VI 778.3, XXXIII 1184.5
Νικοφων	*TAM* II 550.31, 551.23
Νοσσις	PL 108.6
Ξανθιππος	*LS* IV 21.3
Ξενοκριτος	*SEG* XLV 1789.2
Οασυμμος	*SEG* XLV 1813.1
Οβρα[. . .	*IGSK* XLVIII 1.3
Ονασανδρος	*SEG* XIX 869.1 (bis), 2
Οπλων	*TAM* II 589.2; *SEG* XIX 870.1; PL 88.31
Οπραμοας	*TAM* II 900.2 (bis)
Ορα	*TAM* II 550.17, 551.11, 24
Ορειος	*TAM* II 903.1
Ορενοβας	*SEG* XLIV 1219.a1
Ορθαγορας	*TAM* II 550.16; *SEG* XVIII 570.1, 4
Ορνεμις	*SEG* XXVII 906.2

Ορνεπειμις	*TAM* II 650.1.b3, b8, 3.b9, 674.3
Οροντοδατης	Gauthier (1996) II.2
Ορσοννα	*SEG* XXVII 906.3
Ορτακιας	*TL* 1.25.6*
Οσαιμις	*TL* 1.143*
Οσειος	*TAM* II 712.2
Οσετης	*SEG* XLIII 969.27, 30 (bis); *LS* IV 12.4
Οσονοα	*SEG* XXVII 907.i.3, ii.1
Οσσαπιας	*SEG* XLIII 969.14 (bis), 24
Οσσωνας	*SEG* XLIII 969.15
Οσυβας	*TAM* II 550.14
Ουλιαδης	*TAM* II 168.a54; *SEG* XLIII 986.7, XLIV 1219.b28
Παγκαλος	*SEG* XLIV 1219.b45
Παναγαθος	*SEG* XLV 1805
Πανακεστωρ	*TAM* II 168.b19, 28, 37
Παναθιατις	PL 88.33
Πανταλεων	*TAM* II 160.4, 168.a48
Παπος	*TAM* II 372.1
Παρδαλας	Bean (1962) 6.6
Παρδαλεων	*TAM* II 168.a9, 31, 51
Παρμενισκος	*SEG* XLIV 1219.b18, XLV 1805; PL 53.1
Παρμενιων	*TAM* II 650.3.b13
Παρμενων	*TL* 1.117.6*
Παρπενναυος	*SEG* XLIII 969.17; *LS* IV 23.2
Παρτασις	*SEG* XLIII 969.13
Πασιτενενις	*SEG* XLV 1786.2
Πασιφανης	*TAM* II 550.20; *SEG* XXVII 905.2
Πατροκλος	*SEG* XLIV 1219.b22
Παυα	*TAM* II 903.2
Παυαση	*LS* IV 21.5
Πεδατενδας	*TAM* II 551.20 (ter)
Πεδετερις	*TAM* II 40.1
Περικλης	*SEG* XLI 1380.3, 8, 1382.2
Περλαμος	*SEG* XXXVIII 1476.4; Bousquet (1988)
Περπενηνις	PL 27.1
Πια	*IGSK* XLVIII 161.3
Πιγασις	*TAM* II 168.a28, 39, d11
Πιγραμος	*TAM* II 903.1
Πιγρης	*TAM* II 509.3; *SEG* XXVII 942.13*; *IGSK* XLVIII 2.5
Πιδασις	*SEG* VI 778.3
Πιλλακοας	*IGSK* XLVIII 161.3
Πινταυσις	*IGSK* XLVIII 161.2
Πισιστρατος	*SEG* XLIV 1219.b27
Πιξωδαρος	*TAM* II 650.1.b5, 2.a8, 3.a11
Πλαδαρμα	*TAM* II 543.2

Πλατων	*IGSK* xlviii 161.1; PL 88.13
Πλεισταρχος	*SEG* xliv 1218.11 (bis); PL 88.10
Πλειστομαχος	PL 28
Πλουτογενης	*TAM* ii 168.a34, b32
Πολεμαιος	*SEG* xliii 969.23
Πολεμων	*TAM* ii 168.a33, 52, c3, d15; *SEG* xliii 969.11
Πολυαινετος	*TAM* ii 1184.2
Πολυδευκης	*SEG* xliv 1219.a30 (bis)
Πολυδωρος	*SEG* xvi 773.1
Πολυκαρτης	*TAM* ii 1184.3
Πολυκλεια	*TAM* ii 50.a2
Πολυκριτος	*SEG* xxxvi 1220.14, xliv 1219.b16, 42; PL 67.2
Πολυξενος	*SEG* xliv 1219.b37
Πολυπερχων	*SEG* xliv 1219.b30
Πολυτα	*SEG* xxxviii 1476.91
Πομασας	*SEG* xxxvi 1219.4
Ποπλιος	*TAM* ii 551.1 (Roman)
Ποριματις	*SEG* xlv 1789.1
Πορπαξ	*TL* 1.25.1*
Πορφυρα	*TAM* ii 597.a3
Ποσειδωνιος	*TAM* ii 50.a5; PL 88.15
Πρασιδας	*SEG* xxxiii 1184.4
Πριαμος	*IGSK* xlviii 113.2, 5, 34.2
Πριανοβας	*TL* 1.25.6*
Προμαχος	*TAM* ii 550.24
Πτολεμαιος	*TAM* ii 550.33, 34 (bis), 643.3; *SEG* xliv 1218.1, 1219.b34; PL 88.8, 21
Πυβιαλης	*TL* 1.117.6*
Πυθεας	*TAM* ii 168.d22
Πυθειδης	*TAM* ii 942.3
Πυθιων	*SEG* xxviii 1246.10 (bis)
Πυθοχρηστος	PL 28
Πυθων	*TAM* ii 168.a33, 47, c1 (?), 21 (?)
Πυργων	*TAM* ii 168.a42
Πυριβατης	*TL* 1.25.1*
Πυριματις	*TL* 1.6.2*; *SEG* xli 1379.2
Πυρριας	*SEG* xlv 1800.2
Πυρριχος	*SEG* xliv 1218.6
Πυρρος	*SEG* xxviii 1220.1, 3
Ρ.ομοα	*LS* 4: 21.4
Ριμαρας	*SEG* xlv 1813.1
Σαπια	*NLI* 302*
Σαπιο[-	*TAM* ii 650.3.b8
Σαραπιων	*SEG* xliv 1219.a16
Σαρπηδων	*TAM* ii 551.22; *SEG* xliv 1219.b11; *IGSK* xlviii 34.2

Σατυρος	*SEG* XLIV 1218.12
Σεδεπλεμις	*SEG* XLIII 969.11; PL 108.2
Σεδεπλης	*SEG* XLIII 969.16, 28
Σειμα	*TAM* II 372.1
Σελευκος	*LS* IV 13.3
Σεμριδαρμα	*SEG* XLV 1789.1
Σεραπιων	*TAM* II 551.10
Σεριμυας	*SEG* XLIII 969.13
Σεροτιας	*SEG* XLIII 969.29
Σιγαδρας	*TAM* II 50.b2, 3
Σιδαριος	*TL* 1.117.6*
Σιδωνια	*SEG* VI 778.4
Σιληνος	*SEG* XLIV 1219.a5, b9, cf. PL 88.21
Σιμιας	*SEG* XXVII 942.8*
Σκοπος	*SEG* XLIII 969.31, 32
Σονβρας	*TAM* II 543.1
Σοσσιας	*SEG* XLV 1792.1
Σοφοκλης	PL 93
Σπιγασα	*TL* 1.70*
Στασιθεμις	*TAM* II 261.3; *SEG* XXVIII 1220.2, XLIV 1219.b20; PL 87.10, 88.23
Στρατονικος	*LS* IV 12.11
Στρατων	*TAM* II 50.a3, 168.d12, 472.1, 3; *SEG* XLIV 1219.a20, b45
Στρατωνιδης	*SEG* XLIII 969.10, 22
Συμαδιπυλις	*IGSK* XLVIII 107.1
Συμμαχος	*TAM* II 593.4; *SEG* XXXIX 1414 a18*, XLIV 1218.3
Συνετος	PL 87.10
Συριος	*IGSK* XLVIII 107.1
Συρτιων	*IGSK* XLVIII 43.1
Σωπατρος	*TAM* II 168.b38; *SEG* XLV 1800.2
Σωσιβιος	*TAM* II 650.3.b15
Σωσικλης	*TAM* II 389.4; *SEG* XLIV 1219.b20
Σωσιπολις	*TAM* II 168.a6, 53
Σωσος	*TAM* II 168.a57
Σωτιων	*SEG* XLIV 1219.b28
Τανδασις	*SEG* XLIII 969.16, XLIV 1218.12; *BCH* 18: 9.4 (bis); Bousquet (1988)
Τατα	*SEG* XIX 870.3
Τεδενη[νις	*TAM* II 551.2
Τεδιαρσασις	*TAM* II 533.3
Τεδικτας	*SEG* XLV 1806.2
Τεδιμονεις	*IGSK* XLVIII 107.2
Τεισικρατης	*SEG* XLIV 1219.b46
Τελεσιας	*TAM* II 520.1
Τελητος	*TAM* II 50.b3

Τερμακας	*TAM* II 540.6
Τευινασος	*SEG* XLV 1810
Τιθωνος	*SEG* XLIV 1219.a15, b25, 26, 32
Τιλομας	*TAM* II 520.1
Τιμαγενης	PL 88.28
Τιμανθης	*TAM* II 309.1, 3; *IGSK* XLVIII 161.1
Τιμαρχος	*TAM* II 551.12; *SEG* XLIV 1219.b33
Τιμιαδης	*SEG* XLIII 969.22
Τιμοδωρα	*TAM* II 942.5
Τιμοθεος	*TAM* II 551.19; PL 94.1
Τισευσεμβρα	*TL* 1.25.4*
Τιττα	*SEG* XLIV 1219.b14
Τληπολεμος	*TAM* II 309.3, 5 (bis), 6, 704.3; *SEG* XXVIII 1220.1 (bis), 1220.1, XXXIII 1184.6, XLIV 1219.b30
Τοαλλις	*TAM* II 168.a28
Τριενδασις	*TAM* II 373.1
Τροκονδας	*TAM* II 550.9, 551.11 (bis); *IGSK* XLVIII 113.1
Τρουσαδας	*SEG* XLV 1787.1
Τυριω (?)	*TL* 1.115*
Υπατος	*TAM* II 550.14, 650.1.a4, 2.a6
Υπεραινετος	*TAM* II 597.b1
Υπερηνωρ	*TAM* II 650.2.a12, 3.a6, 7, b11
Υρκανος	*SEG* XLIII 969.20, 29
Φαινιππος	*TAM* II 942.5
Φαρνακης	*SEG* XLIV 1219.b35
Φερεκλης	*TAM* II 551.12
Φιλεταιρος	*SEG* XLIV 1221.1
Φιλινος	*TAM* II 590.3
Φιλοκλης	*TAM* II 550.8, 650.3.a14; *SEG* XXVIII 1246.39; PL 87.9
Φιλοπατωρ	*SEG* XLIV 1219.a28
Φιλοπολις	PL 88.11
Φιλτης	*TAM* II 42.2
Φιλωκλης	*TAM* II 168.d21 (bis)
Φιλων	*TAM* II 168.d13, 942.1
Φιλωτας	*TAM* II 650.1.b1, 2.a10, 3.b17
Φοινιξ	*TL* 1.115*
Χαριδημος	*TAM* II 168.c23, 25
Χαρμιδης	*SEG* XLV 1787.1
Χερσαιος	Gauthier (1996) 11.6
Χρυσιον	*TAM* II 489.2
Χρυσιππος	*TAM* II 551.6
Χρυσογονος	*SEG* XLIV 1219.b30

CHAPTER 3

*Caracalla et son médecin L. Gellius Maximus à Antioche de Pisidie**

M. Christol et T. Drew-Bear

A la mémoire de Hans-Georg Pflaum

Assez rares parmi les inscriptions de la cité d'Antioche de Pisidie sont celles qui se rapportent à des empereurs ou à des membres de la famille impériale. Peu de bases honorifiques de cette catégorie subsistent. Pour l'instant, aucune n'appartient au IIe siècle après J.-C.[1] Mais la rareté de ces textes continue au IIIe siècle, où jusqu'à présent une seule inscription était connue, qui se rapporte à l'empereur Aurélien. Ce document, publié par D.M. Robinson (1926: 227, no. 55), fut ignoré une première fois par l'*Année épigraphique*, et échappa également à G. Sotgiu (1961) lorsqu'elle établit l'appendice de son livre sur l'épigraphie d'Aurélien. Il fut plus tard republié comme inédit par H. Waldmann (1981: 95–96, no. 1 avec une photographie), sans pour autant trouver enfin sa place dans l'*Année épigraphique*. A présent, nous pouvons faire connaître un deuxième texte honorifique d'Antioche pour un empereur du IIIe siècle, dont la présence dans cette ville s'explique par une raison précise.

---

* C'est un plaisir de remercier la Direction Générale des Monuments et Musées pour l'autorisation accordée à Drew-Bear de poursuivre ses recherches, et le Dr. M. Taşlıalan, ancien Directeur du Musée de Yalvaç et des fouilles d'Antioche en Pisidie, pour sa permission de publier ce texte comme pour son aide efficace dans son musée et sur le site antique.
[1] Tel est le cas malgré l'avis de S. Mitchell (1993*a*: 107): dans l'"exuberant atmosphere' qui aurait régné à Antioche, selon l'idée que s'en fait cet auteur, à cause de 'the overwhelming manner in which', dans son esprit au moins, 'the emperor dominated the world view of his subjects', Mitchell imagine que 'it is no surprise that the Roman citizens of Antioch should have defied Roman "custom" by establishing cults of the emperors Vespasian and Antoninus Pius there during their lifetimes'. Mais l'inscription qui, selon Mitchell, attesterait le culte voué par la cité d'Antioche à Antonin le Pieux, n'est autre que celle gravée sur la base d'une statue du médecin L. Gellius Maximus (*CIL* III 6820: notre document II ci-dessous), texte qui n'a rien à voir avec un culte impérial quelconque et, qui plus est, concerne l'empereur Caracalla.

1. INSCRIPTION POUR CARACALLA

En effet, parmi les différents documents venus au jour récemment[2] se trouvent deux fragments de marbre blanc qui doivent être rapprochés afin de former une seule inscription. Ils proviennent d'une base, brisée au milieu et quelque peu endommagée à l'endroit de la cassure. Mais hormis aux lignes 8 et 9, qui ont été ainsi mutilées, le texte est d'une lecture aisée. Ces deux pierres jointives ont été découvertes dans les fouilles menées par M. Taşlıalan, gisant côte à côte non loin au Sud de 'l'avenue à colonnades' qui monte vers le temple d'Auguste, à peu de distance de l'intersection de celle-ci avec l'avenue qui la coupe à angle droit, à l'Est de cette dernière.[3] Cette base porte sur sa face supérieure deux cavités rectangulaires et un canal de coulée, et l'anathyrose est visible sur sa face inférieure. H. 0,95 (fragment supérieur), 0,91 (fragment inférieur); l. 0,71; ép. 0,64; h. l. 0,085 (Planches 1 et 2). L'inscription a été gravée avec soin, et le lapicide a évité de couper les mots à la fin des lignes, parfois en y utilisant des caractères plus petits (ll. 3, 4, 5, 6).

> IMPCAESARI
> M·AVRELLIO
> 3 ANTONINOPIo
> AVG·PARTHICo
> MAX·BRETANNIco
> 6 MAX·GERMANICo
> MAX·PONTIFICI
> [- - - - - - - -]
> 9 X'[. .]II[·]I[- - -]
> COS ·IIII· PI
> PROCOS·

On transcrira:

> *Imp(eratori) Caesari*
> *M(arco) Aurellio*
> 3 *Antonino Pio*
> *Aug(usto), Parthico*
> *max(imo), Bretannico*

---

[2] Parmi les inscriptions impériales d'Antioche que nous comptons publier à court terme figure la grande inscription qui prenait place sur le propylon devant le sanctuaire situé au plus haut de la ville antique, texte qui a déjà fait l'objet d'une brève communication de M. Christol au Xe Congrès international d'épigraphie grecque et latine (Nimes, 1992).

[3] Voir le plan chez M. Taşlıalan (1997: 81).

Planche 1. Inscription pour Caracalla (partie supérieure)

6 *max(imo), Germanico*
max(imo), pontifici
[max(imo), trib(unicia) pot(estate)]
9 *XV[II]II, i[mp(eratori) III]*
co(n)s(uli) IIII, P(atri) P̣(atriae),
proco(n)s(uli)

1.1. Les titres de l'empereur

Cette inscription, gravée sur la base d'une statue de Caracalla, se limite à la titulature du prince, au datif. Comme nous le verrons plus loin, la

Planche 2. Inscription pour Caracalla (partie inférieure)

ligne 9 date ce document de l'intervalle entre le 10 décembre 215 et le 9 décembre 216. L'empereur a reçu une titulature bien développée, qu'il faut rapprocher de la composition canonique, fournie par les documents de caractère juridique que sont les actes impériaux, diplômes militaires, lettres ou édits.[4] Mais on peut relever quelques écarts qui ne sont guère significatifs.

Lignes 1–2. Une partie de la titulature canonique a été éliminée, qui comportait la longue généalogie remontant, sans la mention du *Divus Commodus*, jusqu'à Nerva. Celle-ci est présente sur tous les diplômes militaires de la période 212–217: on la trouve en effet sur le diplôme *RMD* (1954–1977) n° 74, de l'année 212; sur le diplôme *RMD* (1978–1984) n° 131, de l'année 214; sur le diplôme *CIL* XVI 137, de l'année 216; sur le diplôme *CIL* XVI 138, de l'intervalle 213–217. Elle apparaît aussi en tête de la copie de la lettre de Caracalla affichée à Banasa (*IAM* II 100).

---

[4] Voir en général, Magioncalda (1991: 27–50).

Ligne 2. Le gentilice impérial est orthographié sous la forme *Aurellius*, qui est la forme canonique,[5] attestée sur les documents officiels mentionnés ci-dessus, à l'exception de la lettre de Banasa. Mais si l'on reste dans le recueil des *Inscriptions Antiques du Maroc*, on peut relever que cette graphie apparaît sur l'arc de Volubilis, non seulement pour le gentilice impérial mais aussi, vraisemblablement par attraction, pour celui du gouverneur, le procurateur M(arcus) Aurellius Sebastenus (*IAM* II 390–391). Les autorités provinciales et leurs graveurs ont respecté plus ou moins fidèlement l'en-tête des actes impériaux lorsqu'ils ont rendu hommage à l'empereur. Les documents d'Asie Mineure, grecs ou latins, en restent généralement au gentilice *Aurelius*[6] à peu d'exceptions.[7] Toutefois, les trois milliaires récemment mis au jour dans le territoire de la cité de Juliopolis aux limites du Pont-Bithynie et de la Galatie, sur la grande route qui prenait en écharpe l'Anatolie, des Détroits aux Portes de Cilicie, offrent la même forme du gentilice qu'à Antioche de Pisidie.[8]

Ligne 3. Le titre de *Pius* était depuis longtemps devenu habituel. Mais celui de *Felix*, introduit en 209 dans la titulature qui ouvrait les actes impériaux, a été omis.[9]

---

[5] On renoncera à se fonder sur l'opposition entre Rome et les provinces comme le suppose A. Degrassi (1921), à compléter par A. Mastino (1981: 33–34).
[6] Par exemple un milliaire près d'Ancyre: *CIL* III 314; French (1981: 74, no. 40), qui est du début du règne, à la différence de ceux dont on va parler (ici n. 8); ou une inscription de Hiérapolis Castabala (*AE* (1990) 999), qui est plus tardive dans le règne.
[7] On citera à Ancyre *CIL* III: 244 Bosch (1967: no. 259), et une inscription de Sidè (*IGR* III 805) qui a été 'normalisée' par son dernier éditeur, J. Nollé (1993: no. 38), d'après lequel il s'agirait de 'Eine Statue Marc Aurels, Elagabals oder Caracallas': mais Mastino (1981: 33 n. 45) a repris à juste titre ce texte qu'il est préférable d'attribuer à Caracalla plutôt qu'à Elagabal, en raison de la seule mention du titre *Pius*. Nollé écrit abusivement Αὐρήλιον, non par lapsus mais en 'corrigeant' le fac-simile de R.C. Cockerell, suivi à tort, estime-t-il, par Franz dans *CIG* 4344 ('*ex schedis Mülleri Beaufortianis, in quibus extat duplex apographum*') comme par Cagnat dans *IGR*: 'Cockerell kopierte ΑΥΡΗΛΛΙΟΝ; ihm folgten Franz und Cagnat, die Αὐρήλλιον schrieben'. Mais l'orthographe Aurellius ne doit pas être corrigée. Quoiqu'attesté rarement sous Marc Aurèle, il est surtout le gentilice officiellement porté par Caracalla, par Elagabal et par Sévère Alexandre, comme le montrent les diplômes militaires, ainsi que les inscriptions de caractère public: cf. la liste chez Mastino (1981). Pour l'Orient on ajoutera Jones (1978: 289, no. 2) à Boubon (*AE* (1981) 789) et surtout la série de milliaires provenant du territoire de Juliopolis (n. 8).
[8] French (1981: 36–37, nos. 1–3). Ces milliaires, datés de l'intervalle 10 décembre 215 – 9 décembre 216, constituent une série différente par rapport aux textes nos. 40, 42b, 49a de French, qui sont du début du règne.
[9] Cf. *RMD* (1954–1977) no. 73 de juillet 209 et *RMD* (1985–1993) no. 191 de janvier 210. Mais cette épithète est absente de *RMD* (1985–1993) no. 189 et de *AE* (1983) 1789, tous deux de l'année 206, ainsi que du *CIL* XVI 135 de l'année 208. On ne peut utiliser le diplôme *AE* (1995) 1337 a–b (date: 207 ap. J.-C.), en raison de ses lacunes. Ce point n'a pas été relevé par D. Kienast (1996: 162), qui place l'entrée de *Pius* dans la titulature à la date du 4 février 211, sans même évoquer celle de *Felix*. Les titres de *Pius* et de *Felix* ont été, par exemple, conservés dans la titulature impériale qui ouvre le texte de la *cognitio de Goharienis* (*AE* (1947) 182; *SEG* XVII 759) de 216.

Lignes 4–7. Caracalla a reçu les titres de victoire qui apparaissent régulièrement dans sa titulature canonique à partir de la fin de l'année 211 (cf. *RMD* (1954–1977) no. 74, du début de l'année 212). Car l'addition à la titulature d'épithètes de victoire, en l'occurrence le titre de *Parthicus maximus*, remonte vraisemblablement à la mort de Septime Sévère, moment où Caracalla partagea le pouvoir avec Géta (Kienast 1996: 163). On notera accessoirement la graphie *Bretannicus* pour *Britannicus*. On l'interprètera par l'influence du grec Βρεταννικός,[10] ce qui montre l'importance acquise par la langue hellénique dans la colonie de vétérans d'Antioche de Pisidie.

Ligne 9. La principale difficulté pour l'établissement du texte se situe ici, où le chiffre des puissances tribuniciennes a souffert de la cassure. Un examen attentif permet de conclure qu'après les lettres X et puis V, dont il ne subsiste que l'extrémité supérieure gauche, puis deux hastes disparues, se trouvaient le bas de deux autres hastes et enfin, après un intervalle plus large, l'extrémité d'une autre haste. Nous en concluons qu'il s'agissait d'abord de la fin du chiffre XV[II]II, puis d'une séparation de mots qui devait être marquée par un point à mi-hauteur de la ligne (comme ailleurs dans ce texte), enfin de la première lettre du mot IMP.

1.2. Antioche et Caracalla

Cette restitution permet donc d'obtenir la date de 216, année au cours de laquelle Caracalla, qui s'était auparavant déplacé vers Alexandrie, séjourna dans cette ville avant de revenir en Syrie et de s'établir à Antioche de Syrie pour quelque temps. C'est de là qu'il partit pour lutter contre les Parthes à la fin du printemps.[11] L'inscription d'Antioche de Pisidie, comme celles du territoire de Juliopolis dans le Pont, se place dans cette période.[12] Ces milliaires correspondent à des réparations routières. D.H. French (1981: 45) a supposé à bon droit que ces travaux visaient à faciliter l'acheminement des troupes et des moyens en prévision de la guerre contre les Parthes: encore fallait-il préciser de façon plus serrée à quel moment de la période 214–217 il convient de les rattacher. French reprenait simplement ce qu'avait écrit avant lui R.H. Harper pour commenter un milliaire provenant de Podandos.[13] Ce dernier, postérieur au 10 décembre 216, indiquait que des travaux avaient

---

[10] Par exemple *IGR* IV 988 (Samos), 1056 (Cos), 1619 (Philadelphia), et plus récemment, des inscriptions pour Caracalla à Éphèse (*SEG* XXXVI 1030), Takina en Pisidie (*SEG* XXXVII 1186), Aigeai (*ibid.* 1248), et Sagalassos (ci-dessous n. 12).

[11] Nous suivons la chronologie adoptée par Kienast (1996: 162–163); voir aussi H. Halfmann (1986: 224–225 et 229–230).

[12] Noter que la ville voisine de Sagalassos avait déjà sa statue de Caracalla depuis 212: *SEG* XLV 1761 (ici l'empereur porte le titre Εὐτυχής).

[13] Harper (1970: 151); *AE* (1969–1970) 607.

été effectués afin d'améliorer la route empruntant les Portes de Cilicie. Il s'agissait vraisemblablement dans ce cas des préparatifs de la campagne de 217, que d'ailleurs Caracalla n'eut pas le temps de véritablement engager, puisqu'il fut assassiné le 8 avril. En revanche, pour ce qui concerne les milliaires de la région de Juliopolis, ne pourrait-on penser plutôt aux préparatifs de la campagne de 216, qui commença à la fin du printemps, après le retour du souverain d'Egypte en Syrie? Ce groupe de bornes routières se placerait alors dans les premiers mois de l'année 216.

Antioche de Pisidie se trouvait pour sa part sur une autre grande route reliant l'Egée aux Portes de Cilicie: ne peut-on penser qu'il y eut aussi utilisation de ce trajet, d'autant que l'on sait que la *via Sebaste* avait fait l'objet de réparations en 198 ap. J.-C., et que très vraisemblablement durant le IIIe siècle, sinon plus tard encore, le trajet passant par Apamée, Antioche et Iconium fut fréquemment emprunté.[14] L'hommage rendu au prince pourrait être liée à ces déplacements, impliquant le passage de troupes et de hauts responsables du gouvernement de l'Empire. Mais il n'est pas impossible non plus que la proximité du prince, établi en Orient, ait stimulé plus que de coutume les marques de loyalisme à son égard,[15] à l'occasion des grandes fêtes impériales ou dynastiques. Les villes où résidait l'empereur étaient de plus siège de l'activité gouvernementale civile, recevant la visite de plaignants ou d'ambassadeurs venus chercher le secours de la justice impériale.

Mais il est vrai aussi que la cité d'Antioche en Pisidie avait ses propres liens avec Caracalla:[16] car son médecin personnel qu'il tenait en grande faveur, Lucius Gellius Maximus, était issu de cette ville. Lucius Gellius Maximus avait obtenu pour son fils l'entrée dans l'ordre sénatorial,[17] et ce dernier était en train d'accomplir une carrière qui devait comporter alors les étapes séparant la préture du consulat: légat de légion en 219, il avait certainement

---

[14] Nous avons abordé cette question en publiant les inscriptions d'une région s'étendant entre Apamée et Apollonia, en particulier celles provenant d'un *castellum* sis à la frontière de l'Asie et de la Galatie: M. Christol et Th. Drew-Bear (1987). D'autres documents et remarques sur ce sujet ont été présentés par Christol et Drew-Bear (1995: 57–92).

[15] La ville d'Antioche a frappé des monnaies sur lesquelles on voit Caracalla à cheval en costume militaire brandissant une lance, et d'autres représentant une Victoire tenant couronne et palme: autant de témoignages de sa guerre d'Orient. Voir A. Krzyzanowska (1970: 167 avec pl. XXV).

[16] On notera l'inscription qui provient du *tholos* dans la 'Tiberia Platea', sur un bandeau circulaire conservé sur 49 cm. (champ épigraphique: 8 cm.; h.l. 5 cm.) lue]ANTONINIAN[par B. Levick (1967: 103, no. 3) ('it refers to Caracalla or even to Elagabalus rather than to Antoninus Pius or Marcus Aurelius, as Robinson suggested'), mieux: –]*i Antonini Aug.* chez S. Mitchell et M. Waelkens (1998: 156), qui ignorent l'édition par Levick et donnent une photographie peu claire pour la fin de l'inscription, pl. 110 (seulement la partie supérieure des trois dernières lettres est conservée). Il n'est sans doute pas le résultat du hasard que ce monument, auquel sa position près du temple principal de la cité confère toute son importance, porte une inscription pour Caracalla.

[17] Dion Cassius 79.7.1; *PIR*² G 130, cf. 123; Halfmann (1982: 646).

franchi la préture quand l'inscription d'Antioche fut élevée, ce qui permet de supposer qu'il avait un peu dépassé la trentaine, et que son père avait alors franchi la cinquantaine. Sans doute les autorités municipales d'Antioche faisaient-elles élever cette statue à Caracalla en remerciement de quelque bienfait que l'empereur avait accordé à la cité suite à l'intervention de son médecin. Ce personnage est connu par une série d'inscriptions provenant d'Antioche, qui peuvent prêter à réexamen.

2. INSCRIPTION LATINE POUR LUCIUS GELLIUS MAXIMUS

Le premier de ces textes, 'Yalowadj in moschea loco alto', fut publié par Mommsen (1884: 579, no. 1346), d'après une copie de W.M. Ramsay 'celerapio[18] usus', puis mieux par Sterrett (1888: 136, no. 109), qui avait pu en faire un estampage, et ensuite dans le *Supplément* du *CIL* III.1 6820, où sont incorporées les améliorations de l'édition de Sterrett. L'inscription était alors encastrée en haut d'un mur de la vieille mosquée au centre de Yalvaç, où elle se trouve encore: h. visible 1,12; l. 0,48; h. l. 0,03 (Planche 3; obtenue grâce à l'obligeance du Maire de Yalvaç M. Tekin Bayram, qui a bien voulu prêter un engin des pompiers municipaux avec une échelle). Le champ inscrit est entouré d'un cadre mouluré sur tous les côtés (recouvert à gauche par un tuyau en cuivre), mais il a été profondément martelé, en haut comme en bas, de façon à ce que seule subsiste la partie médiane du texte:

```
         [- - - - - - -]
         SE[- - - - -]
   3     ARCH[- - -]
         SANCTI[- - -]I
         DOMINI·N·
   6     ANTONINI
         AVG·DVCENa
         RIO ET A MVSIo
   9     SAC·PERPET·
         DEI AESCVLAPI
         PA[- - - - -]
         - - - - - - - - - -
```

Lignes 1–2 omises dans Mommsen (1884).

Ligne 3. Seulement les deux premières lettres dans Mommsen (1884) et dans la transcription de Sterrett (1888).

Ligne 4. Seulement les quatre premières lettres et le bas des deux suivantes dans Mommsen (1884).

---

[18] Remplacé par 'telescopio' dans le *CIL*.

Planche 3. Inscription latine pour L. Gellius Maximus

Ligne 9. PE*r*P dans Mommsen, corrigeant la copie de Ramsay PEPP.
Ligne 10. Les dernières cinq lettres omises dans Mommsen (1884).
On pourra faire progresser quelque peu l'édition du texte.

Notons que le graveur s'est efforcé de consacrer chaque ligne à un seul mot ou à un petit groupe de mots. Rarement il procède à une coupe, mais il préserve alors la structure syllabique, y compris en réduisant la taille de la dernière lettre (ll. 7 et 8). L'usage des points séparatifs à mi-hauteur de la ligne n'est pas conséquent, car leur suppression permet de resserrer les mots (ll. 8 et 10).

Ligne 4. La lacune à l'intérieur de laquelle il convient de restituer les dernières lettres du mot *sanctissimi* est assez réduite: après les lettres conservées il n'y a de la place pour quatre lettres qu'en supposant que celles-ci étaient plus serrées que les lettres dans la première partie de la même ligne, ainsi qu'il arrive aussi plus bas dans cette inscription.

Ligne 10. Seule la partie supérieure des lettres pointées est conservée.

La lecture du texte et son interprétation ne se fixèrent que progressivement. Il en fut de même pour l'identification du personnage honoré, mentionné dans les deux premières lignes de l'inscription, dont il ne subsiste que le début de la seconde.

Le souci des premiers commentateurs était de bien définir la fonction d'*a Musio*. Pour eux, il ne pouvait s'agir du responsable de la confection d'un pavement mosaïqué, mais d'un fonctionnaire de l'état romain. Pourtant la connaissance du système administratif romain n'était pas suffisante pour que l'on pût éclairer immédiatement quelle était la fonction exercée. Toutefois, O. Hirschfeld (cité dans le supplément au *CIL* III) estimait qu'avec un tel salaire, il devait s'agir du directeur[19] responsable du 'Musée' d'Alexandrie, ὁ ἐπιστάτης τοῦ Μουσείου.

De même faisait difficulté l'établissement de la ligne 3 (= ligne 2 de l'édition de l'*Ephemeris epigraphica* et du *CIL*). La dernière lettre (H) est incomplète. Mais les fac-similés de Sterrett (1888) et du *CIL* indiquent qu'elle commence par une haste verticale. Aussi Hirschfeld (cité dans le *CIL*) proposait de retrouver le mot *arch[ierei]*, datif d'*archiereus*.[20] Ce fut W.M. Calder qui leva la difficulté, en publiant deux autres inscriptions d'Antioche relatives au même personnage que nous allons examiner à notre tour (Calder 1912: 95–96). Calder utilisait surtout une inscription (document no. 4 ci-dessous) copiée en 1912 par Ramsay et Anderson, dont il donnait le texte

---

[19] Dans l'*editio princeps*, Mommsen avait écrit que le personnage semblait 'is esse qui item appellatur *a studiis Augusti*, quoniam huic soli salarium sestertiorum ducenorum aptum est'. Hirschfeld (1905: 363 n. 1) maintenait son point de vue, que Gellius etait directeur du Musée d'Alexandrie.
[20] Hirschfeld (1905: 363) conservait cette restitution *arch[ierei]* encore.

dans le commentaire de son inscription n° 25 (notre document no. 3): car ce texte-là (notre document no. 4) mentionne le personnage sous le nom de L(ucius) Gellius Maximus, φίλος καὶ ἀρχιατρός d'un empereur.[21] A. Stein tira profit de ce texte pour identifier Lucius Gellius Maximus comme père du sénateur qui se révolta en Syrie en 219 ap. J.-C. contre le nouveau pouvoir du jeune Elagabal,[22] et pour identifier le prince mentionné par ce texte à Caracalla,[23] ici qualifié de *sanctissimus*, superlatif qui insiste sur l'excellence des vertus impériales plus que sur la nature divine de l'empereur (*numen*).

Un détail qui ne fut pas remarqué par nos prédécesseurs: les deux premières lettres de la ligne 2 doivent correspondre au début du mot *Se[rgia]*, le nom de la tribu d'Antioche de Pisidie. Cette observation permet de restituer la première ligne du texte. Qui plus est, elle confirme l'hypothèse, acceptée depuis Stein,[24] que ce médecin de Caracalla était originaire d'Antioche de Pisidie.

On parvient donc au texte suivant:

[L(ucio)·Gellio· – ·f(ilio)]
Se[r(gia)·Maximo]
3   arch[iatro]
sancti[ssim]i
domini n(ostri)
6   Antonini
Aug(usti), ducena-
rio et a Musio,
9   sac(erdoti)[25] perpet(uo)
dei Aesculapi,
pa[trono - -]
- - - - - - - - -

Il reste à expliquer l'emploi du latin, qui distingue nettement ce texte des autres inscriptions honorifiques pour Lucius Gellius Maximus, toutes rédigées en grec. Ne faut-il pas supposer que l'érection de cette base résultait d'un décret de la colonie, et qu'il s'agissait d'un hommage public de la collectivité – *decreto decurionum* – à un de ses membres les plus en vue? Le nom de la cité, sous la forme la plus complète, pourrait bien remplir les

---

[21] D'après Calder, 'probably Caracalla or Elagabalus is meant'. Hirschfeld (1905: 363) suggérait Antonin le Pieux.
[22] Stein (1918) et (1927: 322); *PIR*² G 131.
[23] Cette identification se trouve déjà chez Stein (1915: 122).
[24] Stein (1927: 402–403) mais il en était moins sûr dans *PIR*²: '*fortasse*'. 'Likely enough' selon Levick (1967*b*: 118).
[25] *Sac(ro)*: Sterrett (1888: no. 109); *sac(erdoti)*: Calder (1912: 96).

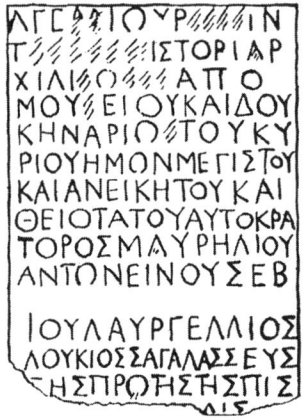

Λ(ουκίῳ) Γ[ελλ]ίῳ . . . . . . υ
Τ Πολυ]ιστορι [ἀ]ρ-
χ[ιάτρ]ῳ [καὶ] ἀπὸ
Μου[σ]είου καὶ δου-
κηναριω[ι] τοῦ κυ-
ρίου ἡμῶν [μ]εγιστου
κα]ὶ [ἀ]νεικήτου κ[α]ὶ
θ[ει]οτ[ά]του Αὐτοκρά-
τορος Μ. Αὐρηλίου
Ἀντωνείνου Σεβ(αστοῦ)
Ἰούλ(ιος) [Α]ὐρ(ήλιος) Γέλλιος
Λούκιος Σαγαλασσεὺς
τῆς πρώτης τῆς Πι[σ-
ιδίας καὶ καλ]λίσ[της

Figure 1. Inscription grecque pour L. Gellius Maximus

quatre ou cinq dernières lignes du texte. En tant qu'*archiater* de l'empereur, Lucius Gellius Maximus était exempté de tout impôt ou liturgie dans sa patrie, dont il était aussi le patron.[26]

3. INSCRIPTION GRECQUE POUR LUCIUS GELLIUS MAXIMUS

Une deuxième inscription honorifique pour Lucius Gellius Maximus fut gravée sur une base de statue, incomplète en bas, pour le compte de Iulius Aurelius Gellius Lucius, citoyen de Sagalassos: celui-ci vint ainsi à Antioche honorer le médecin chez lui. Ce texte fut publié par W.M. Calder (1912: 95–96, no. 25, avec un fac-similé à la p. 96), d'après une copie de M. Hardie, Ramsay et Calder lui-même faite en 1911 et révisée par Ramsay, J.G.C. Anderson et Calder en 1912 (d'où *AE* (1914) 127). Ces quatre savants avaient vu la pierre à 'Yalowadj in the wall of Abudjilar cemetery. The first five lines are faint, and difficult to read'.[27] Pour le fac-similé et la transcription de Calder, voir Fig. 1.

Les premières lignes de ce document avaient résisté à l'interprétation, comme Ramsay le souligna par la suite, ainsi que nous allons le voir. Mais Calder envisageait que L. Gellius Polyhistor, dont il livrait le nom aux

---

[26] Voir Below (1953: 44–48); ce principe était d'ailleurs valable pour tout médecin pratiquant à Rome: voir Nutton (1971*a*).

[27] Calder écrivait (1912: 79): 'I again found several inscriptions, but was harassed in my work and finally ordered to desist by the *Kaimakam*, whose temper had deteriorated in the interval, partly, I think, owing to an outbreak of cholera in his *Kaza*. The result was that my work remained incomplete; some of the more difficult texts, e.g. no. 25, could have been improved by further study.'

lecteurs de son article, puisse être L. Gellius Maximus, duquel l'inscription no. 4 ci-dessous, dont Calder donna une transcription, fournissait d'une façon incontestable la dénomination: Calder supposait que ce personnage pouvait avoir deux surnoms et que les graveurs avaient agi à leur gré avec sa dénomination, explication qui ne résout pas vraiment la difficulté.

Cette inscription est maintenant conservée au Musée de Yalvaç, où nous avons pu l'examiner. Il s'agit d'une base de statue moulurée en haut (h. moulure: 13) et sur les côtés et incomplète en bas: h. 70; l. 60; ép. 50; h. l. 0,02 (Planche 4). Bien qu'elle semble avoir perdu encore plus de sa lisibilité par rapport à son état au début du siècle, même sur estampage, néanmoins on peut encore faire progresser l'édition et donc l'intelligence du texte, au prix d'un minimum de retouches.

On doutera, d'abord et surtout, que le texte soit au datif, comme il a été présenté par Calder: car dans une inscription honorifique en grec on s'attend à trouver l'accusatif.[28] En fait, il s'avère que les savants qui copièrent cette inscription avaient déchiffré quelques *omega* ronds là où manifestement il faut lire, comme nous le verrons, des *omicron*.

Ligne 1. Nous proposons de lire: Λ ΓΕΛΛΙΟΝΜ[ΑΞΙΜΟ]Ν. La correction de la lecture Ω en Ο est logique. Il n'est pas impossible que la barre avant la dernière lettre de la ligne (Ν) soit le reste du Μ, le Ο n'ayant pu être lu.

Ligne 2. Nous proposons de lire: Τ[ΟΝ ΚΡΑΤ]ΙΣΤΟΝ ΑΡ. On peut retrouver Ν derrière la lecture ΡΙ, ce qui fait apparaître le titre de dignité des chevaliers romains, lecture qui s'accorde avec l'essentiel de ce qu'ont lu les premiers éditeurs.

Ligne 3. Nous corrigeons de nouveau la lecture Ω en Ο, soit: ΧΙΑΤ[Ρ]Ο[Ν ΚΑΙ]ΑΠΟ

Ligne 5. Nous proposons cette même correction de nouveau, en changeant aussi la restitution comme il convient: ΚΗΝΑΡΙΟ[Ν] ΤΟΥ ΚΥ.

Le texte donne ensuite la titulature de Caracalla.[29] Ici il est μέγιστος καὶ ἀνείκητος καὶ θειότατος, ce qui est pour les deux premiers éléments un décalque proche de la formule latine *magnus et invictus* qui apparaît en 213 pour ce prince à l'occasion de la guerre germanique.[30] Mais à l'extrême fin du règne (fin 216–début 217), c'est-à-dire à une date voisine de celle du texte d'Antioche, on trouve dans une inscription de Tarragone (*RIT* 83)

---

[28] Sur la différence entre ces deux cas et l'usage en grec voir l'étude de P. Veyne (1962: 68 sqq.).
[29] D'après R. Cagnat et M. Besnier, *AE* (1914) 127: 'l'empereur mentionné est Caracalla ou Elagabal' (cf. ci-dessus n. 21).
[30] Sur cet aspect de la titulature de Caracalla, voir M. Christol (1975: 135 avec n. 26 et 138–139 avec n. 37); Mastino (1981: 60–62).

Planche 4. Inscription grecque pour L. Gellius Maximus

une formulation plus proche de la nôtre, qui peut l'éclairer en relation avec l'activité militaire de Caracalla en Mésopotamie: car on y a inséré dans la titulature du prince la formule élogieuse *invictus et maximus Augustus*. Mais l'inscription latine d'Antioche pour L. Gellius Maximus ne donne à l'empereur que le titre *sanctissimus*, qui ne correspond pas à θειότατος.[31]

[31] Voir sur ce titre J. Rougé (1969: 83–92). Le qualificatif θειότατος doit correspondre plutôt à *sacratissimus*, qui est courant pour les empereurs. *Sanctissimus* est plus rare, il met l'accent sur les qualités exceptionnelles du prince: voir H. Fugier (1963: 278–283), ou du gouverneur irréprochable et vertueux.

La dénomination de l'auteur de l'hommage, *Iulius Aurelius Gellius Lucius* mérite aussi quelque attention. D'abord par sa forme, car elle mentionne à la dernière place le prénom latin. Mais à Antioche même on citera un parallèle avec *Maximus Evius Domitius Valerianus Gaius*.[32] La personne responsable de notre inscription, originaire de Sagalassos, est un nouveau citoyen qui remercie son bienfaiteur: en plus des gentilices impériaux de Caracalla et de sa mère il a pris le prénom et le gentilice du médecin impérial, car c'est à lui qu'il devait vraisemblablement l'intervention décisive.[33] Aussi, même si cette statue fut érigée postérieurement à l'édit de Caracalla, il semble préférable d'admettre que la personne mentionnée entra dans la cité romaine un peu avant, suivant une procédure qui faisait dépendre la faveur impériale de l'intervention d'un personnage bien placé. Sinon il aurait reçu seulement le gentilice Aurelius. Il faut en conclure que les bonnes relations du médecin avec le prince lui donnaient la capacité d'intervenir efficacement comme *suffragator* antérieurement à l'année 212. L. Gellius Maximus aurait pu connaître Caracalla à Rome, mais il aurait pu également entrer dans l'entourage impérial lors du passage de la cour en Asie en 201 ap. J.-C.

Nos dernières observations concerneront la restitution des titres de la cité de Sagalassos, en bas de l'inscription, où la pierre était cassée. Calder écrivait aux ll. 13–14: τῆς πρώτης τῆς Πι[σ/ιδίας[34] καὶ καλ]λίσ[της], sans apporter de vrai parallèle. Il a été suivi par B. Levick (1967*b*: 128), d'après qui le dédicant se décrivait 'as a citizen of Sagalassos, first and fairest city in Pisidia'. Mais nous préférons retrouver un formulaire mieux attesté:[35] τῆς πρώτης τῆς Πισιδίας, φίλης καὶ συμμάχου Ῥωμαίων. On corrigera ainsi à cette ligne la lecture ΛΙΣ en ΑΙΣ.

Nous aboutissons ainsi au texte suivant:

---

[32] Robinson (1926: 221–222, no. 44); *AE* (1927) 170.

[33] Son cas est donc assez proche de celui d'autres notables orientaux qui entrèrent dans la cité romaine au IIe s. ap. J.-C.: T(itus) Pactumeius Aurelius Theon (*BGU* XIII 2244; M. Christol (1993: 405–410)); L(ucius) Aurelius Tarrutienus Demetrius (G. Dagron et D. Feissel 1987: 135, no. 87); Q(uintus) Aelius Egrilius Evaretus, philosophe et ami de Salvius Julianus (*PIR*² A 171, cf. *PIR*² III, p. 76) dont Groag pensait qu'il avait pu recevoir la cité romaine grâce à Q. Egrilius Plarianus (*PIR*² E 49): *CIL* XIII 8159: *ILS* 7776.

[34] Mais son propre fac-similé montre à la fin de la ligne: ΠΙΣ. D'autre part, il convient de restituer *iota* après ces lettres, puisque le lapicide a gardé la coupe syllabique partout ailleurs.

[35] Il suffira de renvoyer à *IGR* III 350–353, p. 148 citée par Calder lui-même, qui n'en a pourtant pas compris la portée. Un autre exemple se trouve dans l'inscription pour Caracalla à Sagalassos, ci-dessus n. 12. Ce titre ne portait pas ombrage à Antioche, parce que cette dernière cité était dans la province de Galatie, tandis que Sagalassos se trouvait dans la province de Lycie-Pamphylie depuis l'époque d'Hadrien, à la suite d'une modification de la frontière détachant la Pisidie de l'autorité du gouverneur de Galatie: voir Christol et Drew-Bear (1991: 397–413).

Λ(ούκιον) Γέλλιον Μ[άξιμο]ν
τ[ὸν κράτ]ιστον ἀρ-
χιατ[ρ]ὸ[ν καὶ] ἀπὸ
Μου[σ]είου καὶ δου-
κηνάριο[ν] τοῦ κυ-
ρίου ἡμῶν μεγίστου
καὶ ἀνεικήτου καὶ
θειοτάτου Αὐτοκρά-
τορος Μ(άρκου) Αὐρηλίου
Ἀντωνείνου Σεβ(αστοῦ)

Ἰούλ(ιος) Αὐρ(ήλιος) Γέλλιος
Λούκιος Σαγαλασεὺς
τῆς πρώτης τῆς Πισ[ι]-
[δίας, φίλης κ]αὶ σ[υμ-
[μάχου Ῥωμαίων]

Ligatures: ligne 13 *tau eta* (deux fois).

Ainsi ce texte qui avait résisté à quelques tentatives de restitution prend un développement plus conforme aux formulaires officiels des membres de l'entourage du prince, et s'insère mieux dans le dossier sur ce médecin de Caracalla originaire d'Antioche. Nous retrouvons plusieurs éléments de la carrière de ce grand personnage, intime du souverain, dont on sait combien l'état de santé était inquiétant à cette époque. Il s'agit de titres ou d'avantages honorifiques et matériels. Surtout, nous pouvons maintenant établir un parallèle étroit avec le texte de l'inscription latine, enchâssée dans le mur de la mosquée qui se trouve à proximité de la grande place centrale. Toutefois, on constatera que le texte latin est plus correct dans sa construction, puisque la qualité de médecin est immédiatement rattachée au nom de l'empereur, alors que le texte grec sépare nettement la mention de la fonction médicale de celle de l'impérial patient.[36]

L'avantage principal de notre restitution du début du texte est de faire disparaître le très rare second surnom, Polyhistor, créé par Calder et ses collègues responsables de la copie qu'il publia, mais qui ne cessait de les intriguer, à l'image de W.M. Ramsay (1916: 133): 'We doubt the restoration of the cognomen of L. Gellius Polyistor. The text is very faint, and these lines at the beginning baffled the united efforts of Anderson, Calder and myself on several occasions.' Mais certains commentateurs ultérieurs se résignaient à le maintenir, à l'image d'Arthur Stein.[37] Désormais toutes

---

[36] Sur le titre de ἀρχιατρός utilisé pour le médecin de l'empereur voir Nutton (1977: 193–198).
[37] Celui-ci le place entre parenthèses et avec un point d'interrogation (Stein 1915: 122); puis il le maintient dans la dénomination du personnage, avec un simple point d'interrogation: 'L. Gellius [Maximus

les hésitations sur la dénomination du personnage peuvent disparaître. De plus, la connaissance d'une nouvelle inscription provenant de Sagalassos (texte VII) permettra de clarifier le contexte de cet hommage.

4. INSCRIPTION D'AELIUS PONTICUS POUR LUCIUS GELLIUS MAXIMUS

Une autre inscription honorifique déjà mentionnée ci-dessus, qui venait d'être copiée dans le quartier de Sofular par Ramsay et Anderson en 1912 lorsque Calder en donna le texte dans son commentaire (1912: 96) sur l'inscription que nous venons d'examiner, ne fut pas reprise dans l'*AE*. Ce n'est qu'à la suite de sa publication par D.M. Robinson (1926: 224, no. 48, avec à la pl. 28 la photographie d'un estampage des lignes 1–5) qu'elle entra dans les recueils épigraphiques.[38]

    Λ(ούκιον) Γέλλιον
    Μάξιμον φίλον
3   καὶ ἀρχιίατρον[39]
    τοῦ Κυρίου

Polyh]istor (?)' (Stein 1918). Mais dans *PIR*² IV G 131, il se résout à appeler le personnage 'L. Gellius Maximus', rejetant le dernier élément supposé en se fondant sur les doutes exprimés par le premier éditeur et par W.M. Ramsay lui-même. L. Robert en revanche (1937: 146) acceptait sans hésiter le nom Λ. Γελλίῳ - - [Πολυ]ίστορι. Des doutes chez Nutton (1971a: 262 n. 7).

[38] *AE* (1927) 171 et *SEG* VI 554, où l'inscription est datée, sans explication, 'a. 200–212 p.'. Mais puisque de toute évidence il s'agit de Caracalla en tant que seul empereur, on ne voit pas l'intérêt de dater ce document du règne de Septime Sévère. D'après Robinson, la pierre était haute de 1,12, large de 0,66, et épaisse de 0,475, avec des lettres hautes de 0,04–0,05.

[39] Dans LSJ s.v. ἀρχιατρός on trouve cet accent, car Hérodien, Περὶ καθολικῆς προσῳδίας θ (1.229, l. 11 Lenz), dans une section où il cite les mots composés (παρασύνθετα) qui peuvent garder l'accent d'origine (φυλάττει) ou le faire remonter (ἀναβιβάζει), le préconise: τὸ δὲ ἰατρός φιλίατρος ἀναβιβάζει καὶ ἐν τῷ ἀρχιατρός καὶ ἱππιατρός φυλάττει. Mais arrivés à l'article ἀρχίατρος les éditeurs de LSJ avaient malheureusement oublié cette doctrine, car dans cette dernière rubrique ils écrivent: ἀρχίατρος (pas de correction dans le plus récent *Supplement*). D'autre part, il existe une attestation du mot bien plus ancien que les deux d'époque romaine qui sont citées par LSJ: *I. Delos* 1573, inscription honorifique pour Παπίαν Μηνοφίλου Ἀμισηνόν, τῶν πρώτων φίλων βασιλέως Μιθραδάτου Εὐπάτορος καὶ ἀρχίατρον.

    De toute façon se pose la question de l'accentuation du mot ἀρχίατρος, accentué ainsi dans ce dictionnaire: puisqu'Hérodien prescrit d'accentuer ἀρχιατρός, pourquoi ne faudrait-il pas écrire également ἀρχιιατρός (comme le font, p. ex., G.W.H. Lampe, *Patristic Greek Lexicon* s.v., ou les éditeurs d'*I. Eph.* IV 1161–1165, 1167, 1677, etc.)? Cf. ὑγίεια, orthographe qui a été réduite plus tard à ὑγεῖα, suite à un changement de prononciation. Sans doute Hérodien codifiait-il l'usage attique, mais il ne cite pas de règle: peut-être n'y en avait-il pas. Cf. H.W. Chandler, *A Practical Introduction to Greek Accentuation*² (Oxford 1881; réimpr. New Rochelle 1983), p. 131 § 423. En fait, le mot ἀρχιιατρος a pu, selon la prononciation employée, porter soit l'un ou l'autre de ces accents, soit, conformément aux règles de l'accentuation grecque, ces deux accents à la fois, rendus nécessaires (souvenons-nous qu'à cette époque le ton était remplacé par le stress) par sa longueur: ἀρχιιατρός comme ἄνθρωπός τις; mais naturellement on l'écrivait avec un seul accent. (L. Threatte, auquel nous devons cette hypothèse, suggère *per litt.* que la forme ἀρχιιατρος 'could also have been encouraged

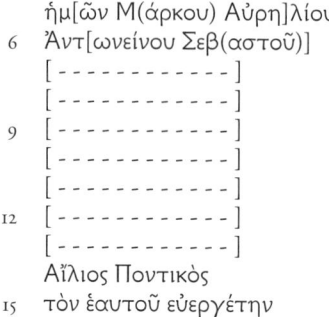

```
         ἡμ[ῶν Μ(άρκου) Αὐρη]λίου
      6  Ἀντ[ωνείνου Σεβ(αστοῦ)]
         [ - - - - - - - - - - - - ]
         [ - - - - - - - - - - - - ]
      9  [ - - - - - - - - - - - - ]
         [ - - - - - - - - - - - - ]
         [ - - - - - - - - - - - - ]
     12  [ - - - - - - - - - - - - ]
         [ - - - - - - - - - - - - ]
         Αἴλιος Ποντικὸς
     15  τὸν ἑαυτοῦ εὐεργέτην
```

Ligne 6. Le début de cette ligne fut copiée uniquement par Robinson.

Lignes 7 sqq. Il manque ici trois lignes d'après Calder, *ca* sept lignes d'après Robinson.

Ce texte aussi comporte une lacune, à partir de la ligne 7, où se trouvait la fin de la titulature de Caracalla, et vraisemblablement la fin des titres de Lucius Gellius Maximus. A première vue nous ne savons pas si le personnage responsable de cette inscription appartenait à la colonie d'Antioche, ou s'il était d'une autre cité d'Asie Mineure. Mais n'aurait-il pas mentionné sa nationalité s'il était venu d'une autre ville? Aussi le considèrerons-nous comme un ressortissant d'Antioche, peut-être descendant des Aelii, affranchis impériaux, connus par une inscription grecque.[40]

Cet hommage apporte sur Lucius Gellius Maximus un autre renseignement: car outre son titre de médecin de l'empereur, il reçoit ici celui de φίλος (*amicus*). C'était lui reconnaître une position privilégiée auprès de Caracalla. Celle-ci ne dérivait pas du rang social, ni de l'importance acquise par une position éminente dans la vie politique, correspondant aux responsabilités institutionelles détenues par le personnage, comme c'était le cas pour les sénateurs et les chevaliers les plus proches de l'empereur qui participaient à ses côtés à l'élaboration des grandes décisions politiques.[41] Elle provenait de sa qualité de médecin, qui lui avait permis d'établir avec

---

by the development of the initial i- of *iatros* to a consonantal glide (as in modern Greek). It is hard to imagine a pronunciation *archyatros* (three syllables).' Cela impliquerait l'accentuation ἀρχίατρος.) Le fait même qu' Hérodien précise l'accentuation pour ce mot, montre qu'il existait des divergences dans la pratique.

Par ailleurs, dans le plus récent *Supplement* à LSJ la forme (reconstituée; non attestée) *ἀρχιατρίνη remplace ἀρχιατρίνη enregistrée dans le *Supplement* précédent. Ceci est une double erreur des plus récents éditeurs; car l'inscription (*MAMA* VII 566, dans un village de la Lycaonie) porte: Αὐρ. Γάϊος ἀρχιειατρὸς ἀνέστησα εἰστήλην θῇ συμβίου μου Αὐγούστης ἀρχιειατρήνᾳ κτλ. Donc les deux *iota* auraient dû être conservés dans LSJ (le deuxième étant noté *epsilon iota*, comme très souvent), et le nominatif devrait être ἀρχιειάτρηνα, sur le modèle: datif ἡμέρᾳ, nominatif ἡμέρα.

[40] Calder (1912: 97, no. 26); H. Waldmann (1981: 96, no. 2 avec pl. X (comme inédit)), d'où *SEG* XXXI 1281.
[41] Crook (1955: 26–28, 123); Millar (1977: 113–116, 119–122).

le souverain une relation de confiance et d'influence, qui le transformaient en confident permanent. Nombreux sont les médecins des membres de la haute société politique ou de la cour dont on évoque la familiarité avec leur patient.[42] A plusieurs reprises, cette proximité et cette intimité valurent aux médecins de cour, dans la littérature qui les fait connaître, qu'ils fussent qualifiés du titre d''ami'.[43]

Cette position s'explique parfaitement par l'état maladif de Caracalla et par sa recherche constante de remèdes. On comprend aisément que Lucius Gellius Maximus, placé comme médecin auprès d'un prince malade, ait acquis par son savoir, sa compétence et, peut-être aussi par son habileté psychologique, un ascendant sur son patient qui lui permettait d'être constamment à ses côtés et de jouer efficacement ce rôle de confident. Aucune autre des inscriptions ne mentionne cette qualité d'*amicus*. Il est donc possible que l'usage de ce terme soit plus un élément d'hommage, issu de la volonté d'un flatteur, qu'un véritable titre comparable à celui dont se paraient des sénateurs ou des chevaliers à la carrière plus brillante. Si Aelius Ponticus avait reçu un bienfait de l'empereur par l'intermédiaire de Gellius Maximus, il est possible que la correspondance impériale le lui signifiant ait eu recours à ce terme pour mettre en évidence celui qui avait joué le rôle d'intercesseur. Il arrive en effet que le prince, dans sa correspondance, utilise ce terme pour un des personnages qu'elle concerne:[44] cette mention ne signifie pas qu'il fasse partie du conseil impérial ni qu'il participe à la prise des grandes décisions, elle correspond plutôt, dans l'esprit de l'empereur, au souhait de valoriser le personnage. Quoi qu'il en soit, l'utilisation de ce terme révèle l'intimité acquise par Gellius Maximus auprès de son souverain, et surtout, pour ceux qui utilisaient son influence, l'efficacité de ses interventions.

5. LUCIUS GELLIUS MAXIMUS PRÊTRE À VIE D'AESCULAPIUS

Encore une autre inscription se rapportant à ce personnage est connue depuis qu'elle fut publiée par Ramsay (1924: 199, no. 35), d'après sa copie

---

[42] André (1995: 91–93, 105–106). Mais André ne connaît pas Lucius Gellius Maximus, et croit (p. 107) que 'la première mention du terme [ἀρχιατρός] pour désigner un médecin impérial figure dans une information juridique adressée en 286 par Dioclétien et Maximien à l'archiatre Aurélius'.

[43] Liste de références dans G. Marasco (1998a: 279, n. 82). Toutefois cet auteur cite en bloc tous les documents relatifs à Lucius Gellius Maximus, alors que, seule, l'inscription dont nous nous occupons à présent comporte ce mot.

[44] Millar (1977: 115). 'This may often be no more than a courtesy to the person referred to, but may in certain cases be intended precisely to demonstrate the emperor's confidence and lend the man authority in dealing with the matter in hand' (des exemples, p. 115 n. 44). Evoquant un membre de sa suite, Germanicus écrit, par exemple: ὁ ἐμὸς φίλος καὶ γραμματεύς (cité par Pflaum 1950: 70).

```
  ΩΟΝΙΑΤΡΟΝ         ]ῳον ἰατρόν
  ΓΕΛΛΙΟΣΜΑ-        Γέλλιος Μά[ξιμος ?
  ΣΑΣΚΛΗΠΙΟΥΔ       ἱερεὺ ?]ς Ἀσκληπιοῦ Δ[ . . .
```

Figure 2. L. Gellius Maximus prêtre d'Aesculapius

faite en 1914 dans le quartier de Kaş: h. 0,29; l. 0,38; ép. 0,41; h. l. (qui gardaient des traces de peinture rouge) 0,035.[45] D'après la ligne verticale sinueuse insérée par Ramsay à gauche du texte, la pierre semblerait être brisée à gauche mais non à droite. Ramsay donna le texte et la transcription qui se trouvent dans Fig. 2.

Le commentaire de Ramsay consistait, en tout et pour tout, de ceci: 'Probably dates about 300 to 312'.[46] Ce fut Robinson (1926: 224)[47] qui identifia le personnage nommé avec le L. Gellius Maximus qui est honoré par l'inscription que nous venons d'étudier. Robinson suggéra de restituer:

```
        τὸ ἡρ]ῷον ἰατροὶ
        Λ. Γέλλιος Μά-
    3   [ξιμ]ος Ἀσκληπιοῦ δ-
        [οῦλος (?) καὶ . . . ]
        [ἀνέστησαν, etc.]
```

On notera qu'à la fin de la première ligne, où Ramsay avait lu *nu*, Robinson donne *iota*. Par ailleurs, au début de la deuxième ligne Robinson déclare avoir lu *lambda*, et au début de la troisième *omicron*.

---

[45] Ces mesures sont données par Robinson (1925: 262), qui précise que les *alpha* avaient la barre brisée, et qu'au début de la première ligne *omega* était certain, comme l'avait déjà signalé Ramsay dans l'*editio princeps*.

[46] Ramsay renvoyait à 'Anderson's article in *JRS* 1913': il s'agit de son 'Festivals of Mên Askaênos in the Roman colonia at Antioch of Pisidia' dans lequel, sous l'intitulé 'the history and significance of the great festival' (pp. 296–300), Anderson développait sa conclusion que 'the sanctuary of Mên at Karakuyu is thus proved to have been one of the centres of pagan revival during the early decades of the fourth century'. Mais non seulement tout cela n'a rien à voir avec L. Gellius Maximus, le raisonnement d'Anderson (suivi par Levick 1967*b*: 87 et 1968: col. 58) est faux en lui-même: car les autorités impériales n'ont orchestré aucun 'revival' religieux au sanctuaire de Men sous le Bas-Empire. Voir L. Robert (1960: 365 et 366 n. 1): 'Je ne crois pas ce groupe d'inscriptions aussi tardif que ne le pense l'éditeur, qui le place après 305'; passages ignorés de S. Mitchell (1993*b*: 10 n. 70), et de nouveau dans sa longue discussion (1998: 12–13). En effet, il y a dans cette série de textes tout un faisceau d'indices – mention des *Pythia* d'Ancyre, termes comme ἐγκριθείς ('choisi') pour participer à un concours stéphanite (auquel on n'a pas été vainqueur), etc. – qui appartiennent au monde agonistique du Haut Empire.

[47] Dans le commentaire sur le no. 48. Bien qu'enregistré dans *SEG* VI 563, ce texte a échappé à Stein dans *PIR*² IV G 131. Dans *SEG* VI 563 cette inscription aussi est datée, sans explication, 'a. 200–212 *p*.' (cf. ci-dessus n. 38): mais puisque Robinson identifia correctement le Gellius de ce texte avec le personnage honoré par notre document IV, on ne comprend pas comment cette proposition de date a pu être suivie sans hésitation par Levick (1967*b*: 125 n. 9).

Malheureusement il n'a pas donné de photographie de cette inscription. Mais il serait peut-être imprudent de rejeter ses lectures.

Robinson y voyait un monument funéraire qui aurait été érigé, pour une personne dont le nom serait perdu, de la part d'au moins deux médecins, dont l'un n'était autre que Lucius Gellius Maximus. Une telle rédaction serait étrange, car la désignation de la profession des personnages responsables d'une épitaphe devrait normalement venir après leurs noms. Qui plus est, la restitution δ|[οῦλος] étonne, autant pour la forme, avec cette coupe en fin de ligne, que pour le fond: car Robinson ne cite aucun parallèle pour son médecin 'esclave d'Asclépios', et l'on serait bien en peine d'en trouver. W. Crönert proposa (dans *SEG* VI 563) de restituer: 'δ|[ιάδοχος *vel simile quid probabilius*'. Qu'un mortel puisse être considéré comme 'successeur' d'un dieu étonne tout autant; et il reste le problème de la coupe en fin de ligne.[48]

Puisque son *nomen* est au nominatif, Lucius Gellius Maximus était donc responsable de cette inscription, avec d'autres ἰατροί si la lecture de Robinson à la fin de la première ligne est correcte. La restitution suggérée par Ramsay à la ligne 3: ἱερεὺ]ς Ἀσκληπιοῦ semble tentante puisqu'il s'agit d'un médecin, mais la lecture de Robinson]ος la rend impossible. Pourtant, nous pouvons accepter cette lecture, tout en gardant la restitution, si nous écrivons: Λ. Γέλλιος Μά[ξιμος ἱερεὺς τοῦ Σωτῆρ]ος Ἀσκληπιοῦ. Mais il reste la fin de la partie conservée. Après la mention d'une prêtrise, il serait tentant de restituer: δ[ιὰ βίου.[49] Cette restitution – ou n'importe quelle autre – amène à supposer qu'il devait manquer au moins quelques lettres aussi à droite, deux au minimum si notre suggestion est correcte. L'inscription serait alors incomplète des deux côtés. Quelle que soit la distribution exacte du texte de ligne en ligne, il doit s'agir de Λ(ούκιος) Γέλλιος Μάξ[ιμος ἱερεὺς τοῦ Σωτῆρο]ος Ἀσκληπιοῦ δ[ιὰ βίου. C'est une fonction qui conviendrait bien à ce grand médecin – et qu'il détenait réellement, comme nous l'apprend la deuxième inscription éditée ci-dessus, qui lui fut adressée en tant que *sac(erdoti) perpet(uo) dei Aesculapi*.[50]

---

[48] Ces deux suggestions semblaient également intéressantes à Nutton (1971a: 262), qui écrivait: 'L. Gellius Maximus is called a "servant" or "successor" to Asclepius.'
[49] A Ancyre on connaît un chevalier ἱερέα διὰ βίου θεο[ῦ Σωτῆρος Ἀσ]κληπιοῦ: Bosch (1967: 343–344, no. 280). Héracleitos médecin et poète, prêtre d'Asklépios et d'Hygie est honoré dans *TAM* II 910, à Rhodiapolis en Lycie.
[50] Levick (1967b: 125) semble ignorer ce témoignage qui est hors de doute, car elle écrit que Gellius était 'probably' prêtre d'Asklépios. Elle continue: 'If this was indeed his position, it is tempting to suppose that he held it in virtue of a connexion with Pergamum.' Déjà Levick (1958: 74–75) estimait que le seul fait que Lucius Gellius Maximus ait été prêtre d'Asklépios à Antioche constituait en soi un 'link between Pisidian Antioch on the one hand and Pergamum . . . on the other'. Or non seulement il

Quel acte accomplissait-il? On a de la peine à croire qu'il s'agit d'une épitaphe rédigée par un groupe professionnel, et en fait rien n'impose la restitution ἡρ]ῷον adoptée par Robinson. On pensera plutôt à une statue, érigée par ce groupe de médecins, représentant Asclépios leur [θεὸν πατρ]ῷον. En partant des lectures de Robinson, on aboutirait ainsi au texte suivant:

[θεὸν πατρ]ῷον ἰατροὶ
[- - ca 15 - - - - - - - - - -] Λ. Γέλλιος Μά[ξι]-
[μος ἱερεὺς τοῦ Σωτῆρ]ος Ἀσκληπιοῦ δ[ιὰ]
[βίου -]

Il faut conclure qu'il existait pendant des générations à Antioche une guilde de médecins, ce qui ne saurait surprendre:[51] car un médecin comme L. Gellius Maximus, assez qualifié pour soigner l'empereur, devait appartenir depuis le début de ses études à un milieu dans lequel cette profession était pratiquée. Comme l'a signalé L. Robert à maintes reprises,[52] tout au long de l'époque romaine les médecins en Occident étaient en général des Grecs. Or Antioche était colonie latine, mais aussi ville grecque fondée par la dynastie des Séleucides, où la médecine a fort bien pu être à l'honneur, ainsi qu'il convenait à une grande cité à l'époque hellénistique. L'épigraphie d'époque romaine, la seule que nous ait livrée Antioche pour l'instant, nous montre qu'un affranchi a construit un tombeau dans cette ville[53] pour τῷ ἑαυτοῦ πάτρω/νι Διο[γενια]νῷ ἐμπε[ιρι/κ]ῷ[54] ἀρχια[τρῷ] et nous connaissons

n'existe aucune raison particulière de croire que Lucius Gellius Maximus détenait ce poste de prêtre d'Asklépios à Antioche grâce à une sienne connexion quelconque – non autrement attestée – avec Pergame; mais qui plus est, Levick (1967b: 125) échafaude une deuxième hypothèse sur cette première: 'If an Antiochian priest of the early third century is connected with Pergamum, Pergamene influence was profound and long-lasting.' Ceci devient à son tour une 'piece of evidence' (sic) qui 'attests the influence of Pergamum upon Antioch'. On trouve cette idée enseignée de nouveau par Levick dans la RE Suppl. (1968: cols. 57–58) comme s'il s'agissait d'un fait acquis. Or rien ne nous oblige à croire que l'Asklépieion de Pergame 'centralisait' l'ensemble des cultes d'Asklépios qui ont pu exister dans telle ou telle ville de l'Asie Mineure. Pourtant Levick a été suivie par Nutton (1971a: 265): 'Gellius' priesthood of Asclepius may derive from a connection with the celebrated Asclepieion.'

[51] Cela malgré Levick (1968: cols. 53–54), pour qui le culte d'Asklépios, pourtant attesté par nos textes nos. 2 et 5 et maintenant encore par notre texte no. 6, doit être classé parmi les 'cultes étrangers', car (à propos des deux premières inscriptions): 'fraglich ist aber, ob dies ein Kult von Antiocheia war'. Peut-être que notre texte no. 6 persuadera du contraire.
[52] Voir en dernier lieu Drew-Bear apud J. Kolendo et V. Bozilova (1997: 179). Pour un médecin le sommet de la carrière était de réussir dans la haute société de Rome, ἐπὶ τῆς ἡγεμονίδος Ῥώμης (SEG XXXII 1261, à Gangra). Ces médecins grecs qui travaillaient en Occident devaient apprendre le latin, aspect du bilinguisme qui a échappé à B. Rochette (1997).
[53] Robinson (1926: 226, no. 52, avec un fac-simile pl. 31); SEG VI 571.
[54] Ainsi A. Wilhelm dans SEG VI 571: 'ἐμπεί/ρῳ Robinson' (mais son fac-simile porte: ΕΜΠΕ/Ω). 'Wilhelm's admirable restoration . . . may be taken as certain' écrivait Ramsay (1933: 318).

à basse époque un conseiller municipal d'Antioche[55] Γ. Καλπ(ούρνιον) Κολλῆγαν Μακεδόνα, non seulement orateur et philosophe mais aussi ἀρχιατρὸν ἐν λόγοις καὶ ἔργοις τὰ Ἱπποκράτους το[λμήσαντα?],[56] ainsi que son parent [Κ]ολλῆγαν,[57] qui était décédé dans sa jeunesse: [τ]ὸν σοφὸν ἰητρὸν εἰκο[σ]τὸν ἄγοντα ἔτος. Ces personnages aux noms romains vivaient à la grecque,[58] qu'ils aient été ou non descendants de colons italiens. De toute évidence ils étaient bilingues, comme le prouvent les inscriptions de L. Gellius Maximus lui-même; car sous beaucoup de points de vue, à l'époque de Caracalla Antioche était une grande ville grecque de l'Asie parmi d'autres. L'existence même de ces médecins, dont l'un arriva au sommet de son art, indique que l'ambiance culturelle d'Antioche était bien marquée par l'hellénisme.

6. UN PRÊTRE D'AESCULAPIUS

Une inscription récemment venue au jour dans les fouilles menées par M. Taşlıalan sur le site de la ville antique, entre dans ce contexte. Il s'agit d'un bloc préservé en haut (mais presque toute la surface supérieure de la face inscrite a été emportée par une cassure) et en bas, et brisé aux deux côtés: h. 0,125; l. 0,235; ép. 0,065; h. l. 0,025 (Planche 5). Les restes du texte se lisent de la sorte:

[- -]AC·AVG·MATER [- -]
[- -]VLAPII SACRVM [- -]

Les A n'ont pas de barre centrale. Ligne 1: il ne reste que les parties droite et gauche des première et dernière lettres respectivement, et la barre supérieure de T a été emportée par la cassure. Les deux barres préservées de E sont obliques.

---

[55] Ramsay (1919: 1–9); Jones (1982: 264–271): *SEG* XXXII 1302. Jones (p. 266) blâme Levick (1967*b*: 126): 'In Antioch, there is no need to see Collega's culture as a relic of the distant past when the city belonged to the Pergamene kingdom [ainsi Levick, *loc. cit.*]: it has nearer parallels in cities of Phrygia, to which Antioch strictly belonged, of Lycaonia not far to the east . . . ' Mais avant de s'aventurer si loin à la recherche de 'nearer parallels' pour la culture de l' ἀρχιατρός Collega (Jones invoque encore la Cappadoce), n'aurait-il pas fallu rappeler son collègue à Antioche même L. Gellius Maximus, τ[ὸν κράτ]ιστον ἀρχιατ[ρ]ὸ[ν καὶ] ἀπὸ Μου[σ]είου?

[56] Ramsay avait suggéré cette restitution, avec le sens 'venturing to do (or imitate)'. Jones le rejeta, tout en admettant: 'I do not see the answer.' Mais cf. Galien, *In Hippocratis aphorismos commentarii vii* 17b, p. 756: φαινόμενα, περὶ ὧν ἐοίκασιν οὐδὲν γιγνώσκειν οἱ τολμῶντες ἐξηγεῖσθαι τὰ Ἱπποκράτους συγγράμματα, πρὶν ἐκμαθεῖν ἅπασαν αὐτοῦ τὴν τέχνην.

[57] *MAMA* VIII 404. On appelle celui-ci μάκαρός τε Μακηδόνος ἠδ' ἱεροῖο / βλαστὸν Κολλήγου.

[58] Notons qu'on louait le conseiller municipal d'Antioche Gaius Calpurnius Collega Macedo (ci-dessus n. 55) comme ῥήτορα ἐν τοῖς δέκα Ἀθηναίων πρώτοις ΚΛ[- -], et comme φιλόσοφον τὰ Πλάτωνος καὶ Σωκράτους ΕΠΑ[- -].

Planche 5. Un prêtre d'Aesculapius

L'emploi du latin et quelques éléments du formulaire rapprochent ce document de ceux qui concernent les notables de la cité. Ce sont souvent des inscriptions apposées sur des bases de statues suite à des décisions du conseil des décurions. De plus, dans ces textes, souvent assez longs, les rédacteurs se complaisaient à détailler les relations familiales du personnage honoré. Ainsi pour Iulia Paulla, *Iuli Paulli senatoris praetori III viri* [pour *VII viri*] *fil(ia), uxor Servi Corneli Dolabellae Pompei Marcelli patris, consularis, flam(inis) Quir*[*inalis ---*].[59] Ici, la personne la plus importante, dont la dénomination était au nominatif, était mère d'un personnage à l'identité inconnue, mais qui était vraisemblablement prêtre d'Esculape, [*sacerdos (dei) Aesc*]*ulapii*. Il serait tentant de rattacher cette personne à Lucius Gellius Maximus, y compris par le style de l'écriture de l'inscription, qui pourrait convenir au IIIe siècle; mais pour l'instant rien ne vient soutenir de façon décisive cette possibilité, sauf la localisation du texte à Antioche. On peut penser que la dame mentionnée à la première ligne appartenait au milieu le plus relevé de la cité, puisque le texte mentionne qu'elle était *s*]*ac(erdos) Aug(ustae)*, c'est-à-dire desservante du culte impérial.[60] Elle a consacré une offrande.

---

[59] Levick (1958*b*: 219–222): *AE* (1960) 35; voir aussi B. Levick et S. Jameson (1964: 97–106): *AE* (1964) 173.

[60] Sur de tels titres à Antioche on peut voir Levick (1967*b*: 88). On mentionnera plus particulièrement l'épouse du procurateur C(aius) Crepereius Gallus, [*sac(erdoti) Div*]*ae* [*Iu*]*li*[*ae*] *Aug(ustae)*, même si une partie de la restitution reste aléatoire (*AE* (1964) 173), ainsi que Paullina, *sac*[-] (*CIL* III 6842). Cf. *Lutatia C. f. sacerdos Augustae* à Malte (*ILS* 121); *Pompeiae Q. f. Catullae sacerd. August., decr. dec.* à Minturnae (*ILS* 6293); *Cantriae P. fil. Paullae sacerd. Augustae Aeclano* (*ILS* 6487), pour des

7. LA CITÉ DE SAGALASSOS HONORE LUCIUS GELLIUS MAXIMUS

A ces inscriptions provenant d'Antioche il convient d'ajouter un texte de la ville voisine de Sagalassos, dont un citoyen a honoré Lucius Gellius Maximus dans sa patrie comme nous l'avons vu. Ce document fut publié par H. Devijver (1996: 140–143)[61] d'où *SEG* XLVI 1680; *AE* (1996) 1514 ne fait que résumer l'article, car il a échappé à l'équipe de rédaction qu'il s'agissait d'une inscription inédite.

    [ἡ βουλὴ καὶ ὁ δῆμος?]
    [Λ. Γέλλιον Μάξι]-
    μον τὸν κράτιστον
4   ἀρχιίατρον καὶ ἀπὸ
    Μουσείου δουκηνά-
    ριον τοῦ Κυρίου ἡ-
    μῶν μεγίστου καὶ ἀ-
8   νεικήτου καὶ θειοτά-
    του Αὐτοκράτορος
    Μ. Αὐρ. Ἀντονείνου[62] Σε-
    βαστοῦ
12 τὸν εὐεργέτην τῆς
    πατρίδος

Devijver estimait[63] que 'L. Gellius Maximus, who hitherto was thought to be from Pisidian Antioch, can now be definitely regarded as a native of

---

impératrices vivantes. Notons qu'Antonia Tryphaena (*PIR*² A 900), reine dans le Pont, qui d'après les *Actes de Paul et Thècle* 27 sqq. aurait habité Antioche à un certain moment de sa vie, était prêtresse de Livie (*SEG* IV 707).

[61] Devijver annonçait que 'the career of L. Gellius Maximus was discussed in detail in the first edition of inscription no. 1 [ce texte], which was found during the 1996 campaign', renvoyant à '*Sagalassos* v, no. 22'. Mais suite au décès de l'auteur, les volumes *Sagalassos* v.1 et v.2 (Louvain, 2000) ne comprennent pas la publication attendue.

[62] *Sic* Devijver (1996: 14, 150).

[63] Devijver 1996: 141. L'auteur continue, sûrement sous l'influence de Levick (1967*b*: 126), qu'il ne cite pas: '[Antioch] was itself under the influence since Hellenistic times of Pergamon and Ephesus, the two cultural *metropoleis* of Asia Minor [? cf. ci-dessus n. 55]. There were links between Antioch and the famous *Asklepieion* of Pergamon, centre of the successful and widespread cult of Asclepius Soter [rien ne le prouve: cf. ci-dessus n. 50]. As priest and adept of the god Asclepius in Antioch . . . L. Gellius Maximus probably maintained ties with the *Asklepieion* of Pergamon [il n'existe aucun témoignage dans ce sens: cf. ci-dessus n. 51]. It is an acceptable hypothesis that L. Gellius Maximus came into contact with the emperor Caracalla in the Pergamon *Asklepieion*, where the latter followed a cure in the second half of the year 214. The emperor met L. Gellius Maximus there and appointed him his personal physician.' Cette hypothèse est gratuite. Contre elle milite le fait que Iulius Aurelius Gellius Lucius de Sagalassos, responsable de notre texte III, avait obtenu la citoyenneté romaine grâce à L. Gellius Maximus avant la promulgation de la *Constitutio Antoniniana* en 212 (voir notre discussion dans le commentaire sur cette inscription): donc empereur et médecin ont dû faire connaissance avant que Caracalla ne vienne à Pergame.

Sagalassos⁶⁴ (τὸν εὐεργέτην τῆς πατρίδος) ... It was presumably to learn the medical profession that he went to Antioch, the cultural capital of the surrounding territory.' Mais d'après sa propre restitution, cette statue du médecin fut érigée sur ordre du Conseil municipal et du Peuple de Sagalassos. Ces corps constitués parlent donc en leur nom quand ils qualifient Gellius Maximus de 'bienfaiteur de la patrie', c'est-à-dire de leur *propre* patrie.⁶⁵ On ne peut donc accepter sa conclusion: 'The case of L. Gellius Maximus... who was long thought to have come from Pisidian Antioch but is now known for sure as a native of Sagalassos, clearly shows how delicate it is to determine a person's geographical origin under the Principate.'⁶⁶

On remarquera que les noms et titres de Gellius comme de Caracalla sont identiques à ceux qui se lisent sur notre texte no. 3, avec la seule exception que l'inscription de Sagalassos omet par erreur καὶ à la l. 5 entre ἀπὸ Μουσείου et δουκηνάριον; car comme nous le montrons ci-dessous, il convient de distinguer entre l'appartenance de Gellius Maximus au Musée d'une part, et son salaire de 200.000 sesterces d'autre part, qui constituent deux éléments séparés de sa carrière. Cette similitude entre les deux inscriptions, qui permet d'associer dans le temps l'érection des statues qu'elles accompagnaient, a son prix pour en éclairer le témoignage, comme on le verra plus bas.

7.1. La carrière de Lucius Gellius Maximus

Au terme de l'analyse de ces documents épigraphiques on peut revenir sur deux sujets essentiels: la carrière du personnage principal, et l'éclat qui en rejaillit sur sa cité.

Le personnage appartient à une famille d'Antioche de Pisidie, sur laquelle nous ne disposons pas, pour l'instant, d'autres documents. Si celle-ci ne possédait pas la dignité équestre, elle devait sûrement appartenir au monde des notables. Dans ce cas, elle aurait, grâce à L. Gellius Maximus, franchi l'étape de l'ordre équestre et aurait atteint le plus haut niveau de la société impériale en deux générations, puisque son fils entra dans

---

⁶⁴ Pour cette raison 'L. Gellius Maximus probably returned to Sagalassos after Caracalla's murder in 217. He was received as a celebrated knight and honoured as: τὸν εὐεργέτην τῆς πατρίδος, presumably around 218–220' (1996: 143). Au contraire, l'expression δουκηνάριον τοῦ Κυρίου ἡμῶν μεγίστου καὶ ἀνεικήτου καὶ θειοτάτου Αὐτοκράτορος indique que cette inscription fut certainement érigée du vivant de Caracalla.

⁶⁵ Ce fait a échappé aux éditeurs du *SEG* XLVI 1680, qui présentent ce texte ainsi: 'important new evidence for Caracalla's ἀρχίατρος [*sic* pour l'accent, qu'on retrouve dans ce volume du *SEG* au no. 2314, trois fois] Λ. Γέλλιος Μάξιμος, now shown to have been a citizen of Sagalassos, not of Pisidian Antiochia'. Voir maintenant sur cette tournure Erkelenz (2001).

⁶⁶ Devijver (1996: 143–144). De même aux pp. 145, 146 (où Gellius Maximus figure parmi les 'equestrian officers from Sagalassos'), 150.

l'ordre sénatorial, par *adlectio*.⁶⁷ Il importe peu de savoir s'il provenait d'une famille de vétérans établis dans la colonie ou de l'élément grec qui s'y était implanté et avait acquis la cité romaine,⁶⁸ car au début du IIIe siècle l'interpénétration des deux groupes devait être assez profonde. Néanmoins, de la même manière que le grec envahissait l'épigraphie funéraire de la cité, le choix de la pratique médicale révèle, comme nous l'avons vu ci-dessus, que l'ambiance culturelle de cette colonie romaine était bien façonnée par les valeurs de l'hellénisme.

La carrière du personnage revêt incontestablement un caractère singulier. Lucius Gellius Maximus fait partie du groupe des chevaliers romains parvenus à une bonne situation dans la hiérarchie des serviteurs équestres de l'empereur grâce à un talent particulier. Ce sont ses compétences médicales qui lui valurent, sans aucun doute, le salaire annuel de deux cent mille sesterces et le titre d'*a Museo*. Ce salaire le plaçait à un niveau assez élevé au sein de la hiérarchie des procurateurs, mais une telle rémunération n'était pas excessive par rapport aux gratifications d'autres médecins impériaux.⁶⁹ Il est vrai que, d'autre part, Lucius Gellius Maximus avait pu assurer à son fils l'accès à l'ordre sénatorial, ce qui est exceptionnel lorsque l'on envisage les limites de l'influence de ces personnages.⁷⁰ S'il n'avait pas le cens d'un million de sesterces, la bienfaisance impériale lui avait assuré les moyens de le détenir.

7.2. Quel Musée?

Lucius Gellius Maximus était *a Musio*, ἀπὸ Μου[σ]είου. Mais de quel Musée s'agit-il? Hirschfeld croyait que l'institution en question ne pouvait

---

⁶⁷ Voir A. Chastagnol (1992: 97–120): cet auteur le range parmi les *adlecti* de Caracalla (p. 120), en supposant qu'il fut admis parmi les anciens préteurs.

⁶⁸ On ne peut trancher d'après l'onomastique seule: cf. les exemples cités par F. Kudlien (1986: 64).

⁶⁹ Q. Stertinius, frère de C. Stertinius Xenophon, médecin de Claude puis de Néron, reçut des empereurs qu'il soignait cinq cent mille sesterces annuels (Plin. *HN*, 29.4.7). Sur ces deux personnages cf. S. Demougin (1992: 396–397, no. 487). Quant à C. Stertinius Xenophon lui-même, il obtint aussi cinq cent mille sesterces de Claude (Plin., *HN* 29.4.8): sur le personnage voir aussi Pflaum (1960: 41–44, no. 16). On trouvera d'autres témoignages sur les rémunérations chez Marasco (1998a: 268–269).

⁷⁰ Voir Marasco (1998a: 278). Toutefois nous n'écririons pas comme lui: 'L'unico medico noto che indirizzò il figlio verso una carriera nell'esercito . . .', car à cette époque la carrière sénatoriale ne se caractérise pas par l'importance des fonctions militaires: si, en 219, le fils du médecin était légat de légion en Syrie, cette fonction n'en était qu'une d'un *cursus* autrement divers. D'après G. Alföldy (1984: 134 et 1985: 177), Dion Cassius (80.7.1) s'indignait que le fils d'un médecin ait pu devenir légat d'une légion. En réalité, le motif de l'indignation de Dion n'était pas ceci, mais plutôt le fait qu'un tel personnage puisse aspirer à devenir empereur de Rome: οὕτω γάρ που πάντα ἄνω κάτω συνεχύθη ὥστε . . . τὸν δὲ ἰατροῦ υἱὸν ὄντα (τὴν ἔφεσιν τῆς ἀρχῆς) εἰς τὸν νοῦν ἐμβαλέσθαι. La discussion peu précise de J. Korpela (1987: 135–136) n'apporte rien.

être que le fameux Musée d'Alexandrie.[71] Il fut suivi sur ce point par Calder[72] et (avec des doutes) par Stein.[73] Mais d'après L. Robert (1937: 146), ce médecin aurait aussi pu être membre du Musée de Smyrne, qui nous est connu par une inscription de Téménouthyrai[74] et qui abritait les archives de la cité. Levick pour sa part a préféré considérer que Lucius Gellius Maximus appartenait au Musée d'Éphèse,[75] qui est attesté par plusieurs inscriptions de cette ville. Celles-ci rendraient attrayante l'hypothèse d'un lien entre le médecin d'Antioche et Éphèse, dans la mesure où se déroulait dans cette dernière cité un concours annuel de médecins, qui étaient regroupés sous le titre οἱ ἐν Ἐφέσῳ ἀπὸ τοῦ Μουσείου ἰατροί.[76] De toute façon, Lucius Gellius Maximus a dû étudier la médecine aussi ailleurs que dans sa ville natale, avant d'acquérir les compétences nécessaires pour soigner un empereur. Serait-ce ainsi qu'il avait noué des liens avec Éphèse (plutôt qu'avec Smyrne, dont le Musée n'est pas connu pour avoir eu une activité

---

[71] Ci-dessus n. 19: à son époque on ne savait pas qu'il en existaient aussi dans d'autres cités.

[72] Calder (1912: 96). Mais l'existence d'un Musée à Éphèse avait déjà été relevée par J. Keil (1905), article resté inconnu de Calder.

[73] Stein (1915: 122): 'Wir haben es nicht, wie Hirschfeld annimt, mit dem Vorsteher des Museions, sondern mit einem Mitglied oder noch wahrscheinlicher nur mit einem im Museion ausgebildeten Arzt zu tun.' Cette dernière hypothèse est naturellement irrecevable. Elle prenait ses racines dans une vieille théorie de Mommsen, selon laquelle le Musée d'Alexandrie aurait servi à former des médecins: cf. F. Poland (1909: 206, note †). Nutton (1971a: 263), parlant de 'the weighty and confident denial of Stein', présente la position de Stein de façon injuste et erronée: car Nutton prétend que Stein refusait d'admettre l'appartenance de Lucius Gellius Maximus au Musée d'Alexandrie, alors qu'en réalité, comme nous venons de le voir, Stein récusait seulement – avec raison – l'idée que Gellius aurait pu en être le directeur. Mais dans PIR² G 131, Stein hésitait entre les Musées d'Éphèse et de Smyrne.

[74] IGR IV 618; Drew-Bear (1979: 295, no. 6): la ville honore le juriste Marcus Aristoneikos Timocratès ἐπὶ τῆς λαμπροτάτης μητροπόλεως Σμυρναίων πόλεως ἡγησάμενον Μουσείου. Une pierre tombale de Smyrne même précise qu'une copie de l'inscription qu'elle porte a été déposée ἐν τῷ ἐν Ζμύρνῃ ἀρχείῳ τῷ [καλου]μένῳ Μουσείῳ. Ce dernier texte a été republié en dernier lieu par G. Petzl, I. Smyrna I 191, avec un commentaire indigent qui ne mentionne même pas l'inscription de Téménouthyrai attestant l'existence d'un Musée à Smyrne, malgré tout ce qu'elle apporte pour notre connaissance de l'institution smyrniote (voir le commentaire de Robert 1937: 147–148).

[75] Levick (1967b: 127 n. 6): 'In view of these ties between Antioch and Ephesus, it is more attractive to regard Gellius Maximus . . . as belonging to the Museum there rather than to those of Smyrna . . . [Robert], or Alexandria . . . [Stein].' Déjà Levick (1958a: 75 n. 6) écrivait: 'ἀπὸ Μουσείου (sic) probably at Ephesus rather than at Smyrna or Alexandria'.

[76] Les inscriptions faisant connaître ce concours ont été publiées par Keil (1905: 128–138): I. Eph. IV 1161–1169; cf. encore VII.1 3239, où il est question d'un ἰατροῦ μετέχοντος καὶ τοῦ περὶ τὸ Μουσεῖον συνεδρίου. Puisque ces documents (sauf le dernier) provenaient des fouilles de l'Église de Marie, Keil (1912: Beibl., cols. 196–197 n. 9) et d'autres (notamment Knoll 1932: 16–26; Miltner 1958: 91) croyaient que le Mouseion aurait pu se trouver au même endroit. Mais cette théorie a été abandonnée par E. Reisch (1932: 3–4) contre Knoll dans le même volume! Reisch préférait y voir un local de change et de vente de marchandises, et cherchait le Mouseion dans le champ de ruines des thermes du port; dans le même sens W. Alzinger (1970: cols. 1636–1637) et S. Karwiese (1989: 42). La bibliographie est donnée de façon partielle et inexacte par Nutton (1971a: 263 n. 8). Voir en dernier lieu Karwiese (1995: 312) et Knibbe (1998: 49).

médicale quelconque)?⁷⁷ Nutton, qui dans un premier temps acceptait cette hypothèse,⁷⁸ a fini par revenir à la solution des premiers éditeurs en adoptant un argument qui a le mérite de la simplicité:⁷⁹ il doit, selon lui, s'agir du Musée d'Alexandrie, car

there is no doubting that the Museum of Alexandria was *the* Museum *par excellence* ... the mere mention of 'Museum', if it is to be intelligible, should indicate either a local Museum or that of Alexandria. There is no firm evidence that the Museum of Ephesus was called simply 'Museum' outside Ephesus ... A purely local Museum at Antioch would appear too trivial, and the most obvious solution would seem to be the Museum of Alexandria, which is described simply as 'Museum' on several inscriptions from Italy and the East.

7.3. Quelles fonctions?

En fait l'appartenance au Musée était vraisemblablement une gratification de caractère honorifique, car on imagine mal le praticien se retirer de la suite impériale et renoncer à accompagner son illustre patient.⁸⁰ Comme le

---

⁷⁷ Pour J. Scarborough (1969: 112), qui confond le père et le fils, L. Gellius Maximus était un 'physician from Ephesus', qui 'apparently was one of an important group of politicians active in promoting the arts in Ephesus and Antioch, taking a cue from Pergamon and its famous Museum'.

⁷⁸ Nutton (1969: 40): 'he had to be content with a procuratorship, probably honorary [cf. ci-dessous n. 89], and membership of the Museum at Ephesus'.

⁷⁹ Nutton (1971*b*: 264–267). Il est curieux que nulle part dans sa longue discussion Nutton ne révèle à ses lecteurs que peu avant il avait lui-même adopté une hypothèse contraire (voir la note précédente).

⁸⁰ On notera la suggestion de Devijver (1996: 142). 'From December 215 to March/April 216 Caracalla was in Alexandreia ad Aegyptum. L. Gellius Maximus was still in his entourage, which explains his presence in the *Museion* of Alexandria.' Mais même si la présence de Caracalla à Alexandrie a pu fournir l'occasion pour l'entrée de Gellius Maximus au Musée, il n'est pas exact (*loc. cit.*) que 'the term ἀπὸ Μουσείου – *a Museo* indicates an office, not mere membership in the *museum* [voir notre paragraphe suivant] ... the question then arises what an imperial *procurator* would be doing in the *Museum* beyond the management of its finances.' Tout en renvoyant aux bonnes conclusions de Nutton (ci-dessous n. 86), Devijver ne les suit pas. Mais il faut séparer dans la carrière de Gellius Maximus les deux éléments, *ducenarius* d'un côté et *a Museo* de l'autre (voir notre discussion ci-dessous); et qui plus est, rien n'indique que Gellius Maximus ait jamais été procurateur (voir Pflaum 1950: 253). Donc les développements de Devijver (1996: 143) ne sont pas pertinents: 'An important text hitherto never involved in the discussion about the exact function of L. Gellius Maximus can be found in Dio. Caracalla hated the philosophers, the Aristotelians ... he abolished their common messes in Alexandria and the other privileges that they had enjoyed ... In connection with Caracalla's bloodbath at Alexandria Dio also states (LXXVII 23.2) that the foreigners were exiled: did this include the members of the *Museum*?' Mais K. Buraselis (1995: 172), pourtant cité par Devijver, adopte avec raison l'interprétation traditionnelle: 'Es dürfte aber im Kontext ... klar sein, daß. ... mit ξένοι (wenigstens hauptsächlich) die Ägypter gemeint sein müssen.' Pourtant Devijver continue: 'In this context a reformation of the *Museum* with financial implications seems quite possible. The abolishment of the privilege of σίτησις for the Aristotelians [mais cf. Buraselis 1995: 175] obviously had monetary repercussions. Did Caracalla establish this *procuratela* to control the accounts of the *Museum* and did he find L. Gellius Maximus, his trusted *archiater*, the most suitable candidate for the job?' Mais cette procuratèle n'a jamais existé: la base de cette hypothèse de Hirschfeld fut détruite en 1912 (Calder 1912: 95–96). Malheureusement Devijver fut suivi par P. Talloen, *Ancient Society* 31 (2001) 308–309.

médecin impérial Aurelius, auquel s'adressent Dioclétien et Maximien, il était de sa fonction de suivre l'empereur: *ob medendi curam comitatu nostro discedere non posse palam sit* (*C. Iust.* 7.35.2 de 286 ap. J.-C.). Cette responsabilité justifiait un certain nombre d'exemptions: *quando iustae absentiae ratio et necessitatis publicae obsequium ab huiusmodi praeiudicio te defendat*. Ce titre signifie donc que Lucius Gellius Maximus bénéficiait de tous les avantages attribués aux pensionnaires du Musée. Mais il n'en exerçait nullement la présidence ou la direction: Stein l'admit (ci-dessus n. 73), puis Nutton l'établit plus longuement. En effet, les premiers éditeurs de l'inscription latine d'Antioche (ci-dessus texte II) avaient profité, comme on l'a vu, des observations et commentaires de Hirschfeld. Celui-ci était tenté de considérer l'anonyme comme le véritable responsable du Musée d'Alexandrie, ailleurs appelé ὁ ἐπιστάτης τοῦ Μουσείου. Ce savant estimait qu'il convenait d'associer le mot *ducenarius* à l'expression *a Museo* pour faire apparaître une responsabilité procuratorienne et le salaire qui en accompagnait l'exercice. Si l'observation transmise en 1884 était encore floue ('*officialis a musio non tesellariorum opus videtur curasse, sed is esse qui item appelatur a studiis Augusti, quoniam huic soli salarium sestertiorum ducenorum aptum est*'), celle qui suivait l'édition du même texte dans le supplément du *CIL* III, en 1902, était bien plus claire: '*officialis a musio non tessellariorum opus videtur curasse, cui salarium sestertiorum ducenorum parum aptum est, sed, ut monet Hirschfeldius* ὁ ἐπιστάτης τοῦ Μουσείου *Alexandreae*'. Ajoutons que l'opinion de Hirschfeld était confortée par sa restitution du mot *archiereus* au début du texte, qui lui permettait d'établir un fort rapprochement avec l'inscription relative à la carrière de Lucius Iulius Vestinus, véritable directeur du Musée.[81]

Pourtant, en 1915, Stein montrait qu'il fallait distinguer entre la direction du Musée et l'appartenance à cette institution. L. Iulius Vestinus devait être considéré comme responsable du fonctionnement de celle-ci.[82] Ses attributions correspondaient à ce que H.-G. Pflaum[83] appelait le 'ministre des cultes et de l'instruction publique en Egypte'. Ses responsabilités étaient comparables à celles qu'avait exercées un peu plus tôt Ti. Claudius Balbillus.[84] En revanche, on ne pouvait, de l'avis même de Stein (1915: 122), interpréter de la même façon ce que nous apprenons sur Lucius Gellius

[81] Voir ci-dessus, n. 20. Sur L. Iulius Vestinus voir les notes suivantes.
[82] Stein (1915: 120); sur ce personnage, avec le même avis, Pflaum (1960: 245–247, no. 105).
[83] Pflaum 1950: 41; 1960: 37 et 245.
[84] Pflaum (1960: 34–41, no. 15); *AE* (1924) 78 (Ephèse): [*–a*]*edium divi Aug(usti) et* [*– e*]*t lucorum sacro*[*rumque omnium qu*]*ae sunt Alexan*[*dreae et in tota Aegypt*]*o et supra mu*[*s*]*eu*[*m*] *e*[*t ab Alexandri*]*na bybliothece et archi*[*erei et ad Herm*]*en Alexandreon pe*[*r annos –*]. Voir aussi Demougin (1992: 447–449, no. 538).

Maximus par l'inscription latine d'Antioche: 'Wir haben es nicht, wie Hirschfeld annimt, mit dem Vorsteher des Museions, sondern mit einem Mitglied oder noch wahrscheinlicher nur mit einem in Museion ausgebildeten Arzt zu tun . . . .' Stein voyait juste dans sa critique de Hirschfeld, mais dans sa contre-proposition[85] il passait outre à ce qui semble maintenant la meilleure interprétation et parvenait à une solution bien moins satisfaisante, car elle s'accordait mal avec le niveau atteint par le personnage quand l'inscription fut gravée. Encore P. Lemerle (1935: 139–140) suivait Hirschfeld en croyant que Lucius Gellius Maximus exerçait la fonction de procurateur chargé de la direction du Musée, *(procurator) ducenarius a Museo*, tacitement supprimant la conjonction *et* à la ligne 8 de son inscription latine à Antioche de Pisidie (notre texte no. 2 ci-dessus).

Enfin Nutton a apporté à ce problème des solutions heureuses.[86] D'abord en revenant soigneusement sur la distinction entre direction du Musée d'Alexandrie et appartenance à cette institution: c'est ainsi que, pour lui, les deux personnages qualifiés par Pflaum (1950) de *(procurator) a Museo Alexandreae*, deviennent de simples membres du Musée. Ensuite en établissant que Lucius Gellius Maximus entre dans cette catégorie. Enfin, en examinant, avec une conclusion négative, la possibilité d'interpréter l'expression *a Museo* comme l'équivalent de *procurator a Museo*. Il critiquait ainsi un point de vue de Pflaum qui, vraisemblablement influencé par l'œuvre de Hirschfeld, avait enregistré une fonction intitulée *archiereus Alex. et totius Aeg. et a Museo Alexandrino* (Pflaum 1950: 253). Ce faisant, notre maître tentait d'exprimer ce que les inscriptions relatives à Ti. Claudius Balbillus et à L. Iulius Vestinus nous apprenaient. Mais, à la place de l'expression *supra Museum*, qui apparaît dans le *cursus* du premier, et à la place de l'expression ὁ ἐπιστάτης τοῦ Μουσείου, qui apparaît dans le *cursus* du second, il utilisait l'expression *a Museo* que l'on trouve aussi dans d'autres documents.[87] Par la suite, en ayant peut-être mieux approfondi la question, il distinguait entre le *(procurator) supra Museum (CC)* et le *(procurator) a Museo Alexandreae (CC)*, comme si la formulation relative à cette fonction avait évolué dans le temps.[88] Observons toutefois

---

[85] Celle-ci fut peut-être motivée par la réputation excellente qu'avaient partout les medecins formés à Alexandrie (voir p. ex. Ammien Marcellin 22.16).

[86] Nutton (1971*b*: 265–267). Pour l'appartenance du personnage au Musée d'Alexandrie, Nutton a été suivi par N. Lewis (1981: 149–158).

[87] On peut penser que Pflaum, qui faisait grand cas des travaux de Hirschfeld (voir 1950: 1; 1960: 2–3), a été influencé par ce savant qui, à propos du titre du responsable du Musée d'Alexandrie, avait écrit (1905: 363 n.1): 'Sein Titel ist im zweiten Jahrhundert ἐπιστάτης τοῦ Μουσείου . . .; lateinisch *a museo*, vgl. C. III, 6820.'

[88] Pflaum 1960: 1089 (fastes). En revanche, si à plusieurs reprises Stein est revenu sur L(ucius) Gellius Maximus, ses origines et sa carrière (voir ci-dessus n. 22–24), jamais il n'a profité d'une de ces

que, curieusement, il ne faisait pas entrer Lucius Gellius Maximus dans le dernier groupe. On ne peut que se rallier à la démonstration de Nutton (1971: 268–269) quand il reprend les arguments de Stein lesquels, contre Hirschfeld, insistent sur la distinction entre *a Museo* et ὁ ἐπιστάτης τοῦ Μουσείου, puis quand il conclut que le premier de ces titres signifie simplement 'member of the Museum'. Il devient donc évident que dans l'inscription latine d'Antioche, comme dans l'une des inscriptions grecques, l'indication *ducenarius* se réfère explicitement au salaire octroyé par Caracalla à son médecin.[89] Mais il est tout aussi assuré, comme nous l'avons indiqué un peu plus haut, que la qualification d'*a Museo* doit apparaître comme une gratification supplémentaire.

8. CONCLUSION

Par ailleurs, on est en droit d'expliquer par sa position auprès du prince la multiplicité des hommages que ce personnage reçut dans sa cité d'origine. Il était en effet bien placé pour faire progresser les demandes qui se multiplièrent quand l'empereur traversa l'Asie Mineure[90] et séjourna dans les provinces orientales. Pendant un certain temps on pouvait dire que le prince était présent. Et quand Caracalla s'établit en Syrie, il demeurait aisément accessible. Les ambassades ou délégations pouvaient se multiplier ou se répéter. Un notable d'Ancyre ne démarcha-t-il pas trois fois le prince afin d'obtenir un concours pour sa cité?[91] Lucius Gellius Maximus disposait d'une position avantageuse pour jouer le rôle d'intermédiaire ou d'intercesseur. Mais c'était aussi sa cité d'origine qui en profitait, car un de ses enfants se trouvait dans la suite impériale: les hommages qui étaient rendus au médecin venaient rehausser l'éclat de sa patrie.

On peut interpréter l'hommage adressé par Aelius Ponticus comme un témoignage de reconnaissance pour services rendus. C'était apparemment l'hommage d'un particulier. Il en va différemment pour le texte rédigé par Julius Aurelius Gellius Lucius de Sagalassos, maintenant que l'on dispose de l'inscription parallèle provenant de cette ville de Pisidie, qui faisait

---

occasions, en particulier dans *Der römische Ritterstand* (1927), pour traiter du problème institutionnel qu'il avait en parti résolu dans les *Untersuchungen* de 1915 (voir ci-dessus n. 73).

[89] On ne comprend pas pour quelles raisons, au terme de sa démonstration, Nutton (1971*b*: 270–272) considère encore que l'indication *ducenarius* signifierait que Lucius Gellius Maximus aurait pu être procurateur à une étape antérieure de sa carrière, ni pourquoi il éprouve le besoin de relancer les discussions. Marasco (1998*a*: 277; puis 1998*b*: 253) l'appelle aussi invariablement *procurator ducenarius*.

[90] Sur le passage de Caracalla à Ancyre et sa région voir en dernier lieu Christol et Drew-Bear (2000).

[91] Il s'agit précisément des *Megala Asklepieia*: voir Robert (1960: 358–366). Naturellement il devait y avoir un culte d'Asklépios à Ankara avant la création de ce concours.

alors partie de la province de Lycie-Pamphylie. Nous avons noté entre ces deux dernières inscriptions d'étroites ressemblances de formulaire, tant pour définir la position de Lucius Gellius Maximus que pour dénommer l'empereur lui-même. Si à Sagalassos l'hommage est celui de la cité, à Antioche c'est celui d'un particulier. Mais les ressemblances sont telles que ces deux inscriptions s'accordent étroitement. Ne pourrait-on pas envisager qu'à la suite de l'hommage municipal rendu par la cité pisidienne, un de ses notables les plus éminents, qui devait beaucoup à Lucius Gellius Maximus, aurait ajouté son propre hommage dans la cité d'origine du médecin, presque voisine? Julius Aurelius Gellius Lucius prend tellement de soin non seulement à décliner sa qualité de citoyen de Sagalassos, mais à fournir de surcroît la titulature de sa cité, que l'on peut supposer qu'il se sentait investi d'une responsabilité dépassant sa personne. Ainsi l'hommage qu'il rendait à Lucius Gellius Maximus dans la ville d'Antioche prenait sans aucun doute une dimension plus large, et il rejaillissait sur sa propre patrie.

Mais il y avait aussi pour Antioche des profits plus concrets. L'inscription latine en son honneur prend soin de qualifier Lucius Gellius Maximus de *patronus*. Et nous avons vu que l'usage du latin doit répondre à la mise en exécution d'un décret municipal, qui pouvait suivre l'octroi d'un bienfait impérial. L'inscription adressée à Caracalla ne fait certes pas intervenir le médecin de façon explicite. Mais elle s'insère dans ce contexte. A tout le moins on ne peut l'examiner sans se référer à la personnalité et à l'influence de Lucius Gellius Maximus. On comprend aisément ainsi pourquoi en lieu public, à Antioche de Pisidie entre 214 et 217, on honora le prince et son médecin.

Après la rédaction de notre texte est paru: E. Samama, *Les médecins dans le monde grec, sources épigraphiques sur la naissance d'un corps médical* (Genève, 2003). Samama ne reproduit pas dans son recueil de textes l'inscription latine pour L. Gellius Maximus, notre texte no. 2 – bien que celle-ci provienne de la même ville que les inscriptions grecques honorant le même personnage, et bien que ce document constitue un acte official de la Cité d'Antioche, témoignage donc très important pour le sujet du livre.

Aux lignes 1-3 de notre inscription no. 3, Samama écrit (431 no. 332):

Λ(ουκίῳ) Γ[ελλ]ίῳ Ρ[. . . .]
Τ[. . . . . .]ιστορι [ἀ]ρ-
χι[ατρ]ῷ κτλ.

Elle recopie ainsi la désignation entière du personnage au datif, sans reconnaître à la ligne 1 son *cognomen*, donné pourtant par toutes les autres inscriptions dans les deux langues, ni son titre κράτιστον à la ligne 2. Par ailleurs, Samama améliore la fin du texte en y ajoutant *suo Marte*, après le titre *καλ]λίσ[της, une ligne supplémentaire qui comporte la restitution [πόλεως].

Notre inscription no. 4, attribuée à Antioche par la première édition comme dans toutes les éditions et commentaires postérieurs, vient pour Samama (p. 435) de la ville de Timbriada en Pisidie, au Sud-Est du lac Egridir: car elle seule confond Sofular quartier de Yalvaç,[92] le bourg turc au-dessous de l'acropole d'Antioche, avec Sofular, village turc près du site de Timbriada.[93] Samama n'a donc pas regardé l'édition de ce texte par D.M. Robinson qu'elle cite, car la provenance y est indiquée sans ambiguïté.

Pour notre inscription no. 5,[94] où Robinson a proposé Ἀσκληπιοῦ δ/[οῦλος et Crönert a suggéré δ/[ιάδοχος, Samama (431 n. 6) estime que 'on peut aussi penser à δ[μῶοι]', ce qui est un équivalent poétique (homérique) du mot δοῦλοι: mais que viendrait faire la poésie ici?

Samama prétend (p. 436) que notre inscription no. 7 fut publiée par 'M. Waelkens, *Sagalassos* v, no. 22', alors qu'en fait, comme nous l'avons écrit dans notre n. 61, 'suite au décès de l'auteur [H. Devijver], les volumes *Sagalassos* v.1 et v.2 (Louvain, 2000) ne comprennent pas la publication attendue.' Ainsi force est-il de constater que Samama n'a jamais vu cet ouvrage qu'elle prétend citer.[95] Cette constatation seule permet de juger de la qualité de son travail.

---

[92] 'Inscription copied . . . at Yolowadj-Sofular in 1912' écrivait Calder (1912: 96).

[93] Samama (2003: 435 n. 29) l'appelle 'Sofilar', déformation du nom qui serait impossible en turc. Sur Timbriada voir C. Brixhe, T. Drew-Bear et D. Kaya, 'Nouveaux monuments de Pisidie', *Kadmos* 26 (1987) 122–170, avec une photographie du site du village de Sofular à la pl. 1 et une description de ce village, avec explication du sens du toponyme, 126–127.

[94] Apparemment par simple lapsus, dans cette inscription Samama donne une quatrième ligne comme ayant été lue, qu'on trouve dans nulle autre édition. Elle date ce texte (son no. 331) du 'début IIIe s. *p. C.*', alors qu'elle date notre inscription no. 3 (son no. 332, p. 431) de '214–217 *p. C.*', et notre inscription no. 4 (son no. 337, séparée des autres car pour elle ce document viendrait de Timbriada) de '212–217 *p. C.*'. Comprenne qui pourra.

[95] Le lemme de Samama est fictif, car après cette fausse indication du lieu de publication, elle écrit à la ligne suivante: 'Cf. H. Devijver, *Ancient Society* 1996' etc., qui est en vérité la source d'où elle a recopié ce texte (en y introduisant de son cru une erreur d'accentuation à la l. 4: cf. ci-dessus n. 39, et un contre-sens dans la traduction: 'archiatros du Mouseion').

CHAPTER 4

Roman material culture across imperial frontiers? Three case studies from Parthian Dura-Europos

Nigel Pollard

The discovery of characteristically Roman artefacts and technology beyond the political frontiers of the empire has long stimulated interest among archaeologists and historians, one of the older studies being that of Wheeler (1954). The economic permeability of the Roman frontier and the concept of the frontier as a zone rather than a line has been emphasized in more recent studies such as the historical analysis of Whittaker (1994). For two centuries of its history Dura-Europos in Syria lay within about 200 km of the Roman frontier but beyond Roman political control. It also lay on a major land- and sea-route between East and West, and has yielded documentary evidence of long-distance trade passing through the city. Thus it seems logical to look at Dura for evidence of Roman material culture spread beyond the imperial frontier. This was certainly an issue considered by the Franco-American excavators of the site in the 1920s and 1930s, and they drew what were, for their time, sensible conclusions. However, some of these conclusions are due for re-evaluation in the light of more recent studies of Roman architecture, pottery and numismatics.

The following consists of three case studies of aspects of Roman material culture at Dura between the establishment of the Roman province of Syria and of direct Roman political control over that city. The general aims are to establish whether there is archaeological evidence for the involvement of Parthian Dura in the economy of the Roman empire across the imperial frontier; whether there is evidence of technological influence across the border; and whether there is evidence of change in the level of that involvement and influence. The three case studies deal with pottery, an important form of archaeological evidence for trade throughout the Roman empire; with coins, artefacts of obvious relevance to economic questions; and with bathing technology.

Dura-Europos was founded as a Seleucid colony perhaps shortly after 312 BC (Grainger 1990: 46) and came under Parthian control *ca* 113 BC (Bellinger 1949: 201). After Pompey's establishment of the Roman province of Syria,

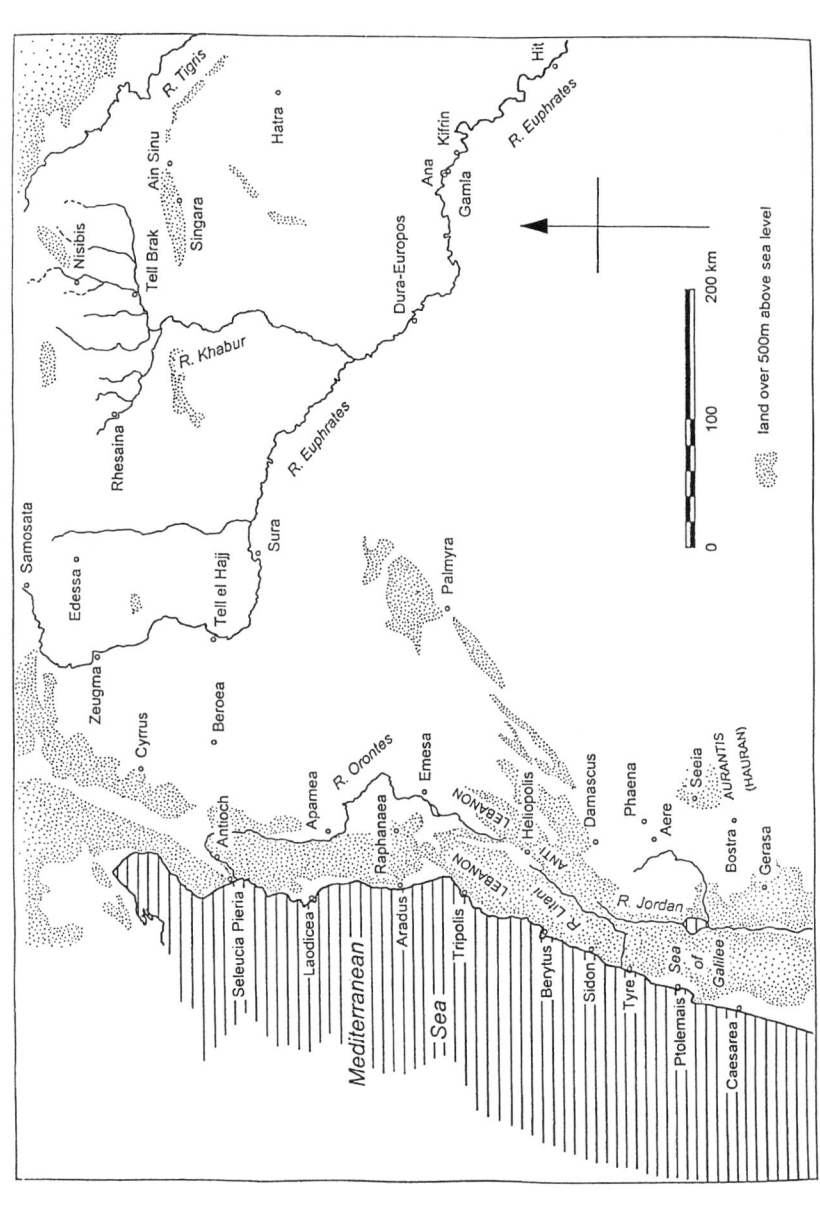

Map 2. The Roman Near East, showing location of Dura-Europos (drawn by David Hopkins)

Dura remained under Parthian control until AD 115, when it briefly came under Roman control (*Dura* IV, 56–65). However, the Romans withdrew from the city by AD 117 (*Dura* VII–VIII, 129–32), and it remained Parthian until AD 165/6, when it was conquered by Lucius Verus' armies. The Roman frontier in this area was not a simple linear feature, and its historical development is often unclear. However, Dura was about 200 km from both Sura on the Euphrates and Palmyra in the steppe (Map 2). Sura seems to have been under Roman control by the Flavian period, and is often regarded as the limit of Roman power before Roman expansion into the middle Euphrates in AD 165–6, as it was after the loss of Roman control of that region.[1] Palmyra may have been under direct Roman control as early as AD 19, but this certainly seems to have been the case by the Flavian period.[2] Thus we can say, broadly, that Dura was within about 200 km of the Roman empire for at least part of the period of Parthian control.

Very broadly speaking, the material influence of the Greco-Macedonian world can be seen in the city's early phases in, for example, the black-slipped fine pottery typical of the Hellenistic world (Cox 1949: 2–6), and in Greek architectural influences on some public buildings (Downey 1988: 76–86). However, through the period of Parthian control (and, indeed, through much of the Roman period), the site was dominated by aspects of material culture common to much of Parthian Mesopotamia, including cities such as Seleucia on the Tigris and Hatra, and, in some respects, eastern Syria, notably Palmyra. The fine table pottery was mostly 'Parthian' green-glazed ware (Toll 1943), most temples were of 'Mesopotamian' courtyard plan (Downey 1988: 89–128) and houses were typically of a distinctive courtyard plan (Perkins 1973: 21–3), constructed in mudbrick with flat roofs. However, some artefacts and technologies found in Parthian Dura had their origins within the Roman empire.

1. 'ROMAN' POTTERY IN PARTHIAN DURA?

The first category of artefacts considered consists of pottery, particularly Eastern Sigillata A (ESA). This is a glossy red-slipped tableware produced from the second century BC to the second century AD, probably at a single

---

[1] The construction of a road between Palmyra and Sura by the *legatus pro praetore* Ulpius Traianus in AD 75 (*AE* 1933: 205) suggests Sura was under Roman control by then.

[2] Conclusions based on apparent Palmyrene acceptance of a pronouncement of Germanicus recorded in the tax law of Palmyra (*OGIS* II 629 = *IGR* III 1056) or, alternatively, the construction of a road between Palmyra and Sura by the *legatus pro praetore* Ulpius Traianus in AD 75 (*AE* 1933: 205). Of course, the well-attested presence of Palmyrenes in pre-Roman Dura-Europos, discussed most recently by Lucinda Dirven (1999), is categorical evidence for human contact across the imperial frontier.

location somewhere to the north of Antioch (Slane 1997: 272). While its earliest production pre-dated the Roman annexation of Syria and ESA was not 'Roman' in the sense of being a Roman introduction, it continued to be produced within the Roman province of Syria, and some later forms show the influence of Italian terra sigillata. The forms and brief descriptions of fabric published by Cox (1949) of a moderate number of red-slipped sherds excavated at Dura (by the Yale University/French Academy of Inscriptions and Letters mission in 1928–37) enable them to be identified as ESA.[3] Cox's account included datings based on early excavations, but ESA has been much studied since then, including a major typological catalogue by Hayes (1985) and, most recently, an important study based on a long stratified sequence at Tel Anafa in Israel (Slane 1997). The dating of some forms has been changed to some degree on the basis of stratified evidence. For example, Cox (1949: 11) considered that numbers 63 and 64 in her catalogue were examples of a first-century BC form, while Hayes (1985: 28) considers the form (his form 30) to date to *ca* AD 10–50. At Tel Anafa (as TA 21, Slane 1997: 304–5) the form appears in Rom 1B and Rom 1C contexts, in the first half of the first century AD.

Cox's synthesis of the import of ESA to Dura suggests that there was a substantial decline after Dura passed into Parthian control, with a very low level of imports thereafter. She states: 'earlier Hellenistic "Pergamene" sherds are almost as numerous as the later Hellenistic and the Roman sigillata, which together cover a period four times as long . . . imports of "Pergamene" continued in Parthian times but they were no longer common . . . the local potters now turned to the production of Parthian pottery' (Cox 1949: 24), and 'for more than three hundred years the infrequent imports were such as might gravitate to any somewhat isolated settlement in Mesopotamia irrespective of its political affiliations' (Cox 1949: 26). If this was the case, one might assume that it was the result of the separation of the production area of ESA from Dura by a political boundary after the earliest imports of ESA – initially the boundary between the Seleucid and Parthian kingdoms, subsequently that between the Roman empire and the Parthian kingdom. The numbers of sherds involved are low (in single figures for any given form) in both the Seleucid and Parthian/Roman periods, and green-glazed pottery in the Parthian tradition is more common (Toll 1943). However, re-evaluation of the chronology of the ESA found at Dura shifts the chronological emphasis somewhat. It suggests that the level of

---

[3] I have not examined this material in person, but have relied entirely on published accounts, especially that of Hayes (1985), who equated the Dura sherds to his own ESA forms.

imports of ESA to Dura perhaps *increased* after the creation of the Roman province of Syria, and their relative levels over time correspond roughly to those found at a site within the Roman empire, Hama/Epiphania, while Dura lay within the Parthian empire.

For the most part the ESA forms represented in substantial numbers at Hama (originally published by Christensen and Johansen (1971), recently re-evaluated by Lund (1995a)), within the Roman empire, are also relatively well represented at Dura, regardless of whether they were produced before or after the establishment of the Roman province of Syria. For example, Hayes's (1985: 14–16) forms 2–4, which begin as early as the second century BC, are represented by remains of 145 examples at Hama (Lund 1995a: 136) and about 25 examples at Dura (Cox 1949: 7–8, group I, cf. Slane 1997: 285–8, TA 13).[4]

Forms produced after the establishment of the Roman province of Syria include the following:

Hayes 12, dated (Hayes 1985: 19–20) to *ca* 40 BC–*ca* AD 10, was represented by thirty-two examples at Hama (Lund 1995a: 136) and six or seven at Dura (Cox 1949: 11, group V, no. 62).

Hayes 28 was dated (Hayes 1985: 27) to *ca* 25 BC–*ca* AD 30. This form equates to TA 22 at Tel Anafa (Slane 1997: 306–7), where it appears first in Rom 1B (early first century AD) excavated contexts. Fragments of about thirty-one examples were excavated at Hama, about twelve at Dura (Cox 1949: 10, group IVb, especially nos. 59 and 60).

Hayes 30, as noted above, was dated by Hayes (1985: 28) to *ca* AD 10–50. At Tel Anafa (Slane 1997: 304–5) the form was classified as TA 21 and appears in Rom 1B and Rom 1C contexts, in the first half of the first century AD. At Hama this form was represented by twenty fragmentary examples (Lund 1995a: 136), at Dura by six or seven (Cox 1949: 11, nos. 63–4).

Hayes's forms 34–7, grouped together, were dated by him (1985: 29–31) generally to the first century AD and at Tel Anafa, as TA 23, they appear to be 'essentially a Claudian-Neronian form' (Slane 1997: 308). Sixty-three sherds apparently relating to this form were excavated at Hama (Lund 1995a: 136) and twenty-six at Dura (Cox 1949: 12, group VIb, nos. 65–8).

---

[4] Since the groups, sub-groups and forms in Cox's publication do not always coincide with those used elsewhere, it is not always easy to be certain of the numbers of a given form in Hayes's typology excavated at Dura merely by adding up Cox's numbers. These numbers are often confusing, since there are many vague references to additional examples belonging to a group, sub-group or form, which were found but not illustrated or numbered individually in Cox's catalogue.

It is quite difficult to see what Cox describes as a decline after the establishment of Parthian control of Dura, or any particular decline after the establishment of the Roman province of Syria. Instead, one gets the impression that ESA imports to Dura were at their peak in the second half of the first century BC and the first half of the first century AD, just as they were at Hama. As at Hama, there was little late first-century AD and second-century material, despite the fact that ESA was still produced at this period and is found on other sites (Lund 1995a: 137).

In fact the relative absence of ESA at Dura from the later first century AD onwards seems to relate to distribution factors applying equally to parts of Syria east and west of the Roman political frontier. Kenrick, for example (1981: 439), has commented on the absence of second-century ESA forms in the Qoueiq valley survey area to the north of Aleppo/Beroea, well within the Roman province of Syria. There is certainly less ESA from Dura than from Hama, but even if this is a real difference (and not one based on the scale of excavation or rate of recovery of pottery) it is probably because the former site was further from the production areas (perhaps as much as four times the distance as the crow flies), not because the frontier of the Roman empire intervened. The direct, overland distance is certainly less important than access to rivers such as the Orontes and the Euphrates, but undoubtedly it was a more complex and expensive process to bring ESA from its production area to Dura than to Hama. In general the evidence of ESA suggests that Dura participated in a modest way in a regional economy which included Roman and Parthian Syria.

However, it is difficult to take this conclusion further and suggest that Parthian Dura participated in a wider Roman/Mediterranean economy. There is no suggestion in Cox's catalogue that non-Syrian red-slipped finewares reached Parthian Dura, while Hama received modest quantities of Italian and Cypriote sigillata (Lund 1995a: 137–8). There is only one published amphora from Dura apparently imported from the Mediterranean which might belong to the period between the establishment of the Roman province of Syria and the extension of direct Roman control over Dura (Dyson 1968: 7–8). An Aegean origin seems likely on the basis of similarities of form to known Aegean amphorae, and Dyson cites a parallel in a post-75 BC deposit in the Athenian Agora (Robinson 1959: 20, F92). Of course, this absence of Mediterranean material is mostly due to the costs and difficulties of importing such pottery from the Mediterranean coast to Dura. This would require some overland transport, even if the river systems of Syria were exploited as much as possible. However, some Mediterranean material such as African Red Slip finewares (Cox 1949: 14–16, as Late Roman A ware) *did* reach Dura after the city came under direct Roman political control, despite the problems of transport. This suggests that the political incorporation of Dura within the empire did have some impact on Dura's involvement in certain forms of long-distance trade with the Roman Mediterranean, perhaps through the extension of army supply networks or of particular forms of civilian trade.

But generally, all this imported material was found in small quantities relative to the Mesopotamian green-glazed ware, and its importance must not be overstated.

2. 'ROMAN' COINAGE IN PARTHIAN DURA?

The next category of artefacts from the Roman empire found at Dura consists of coins. Many of the 'Roman' coins excavated at Dura were produced before the Romans gained political control of Dura in AD 165, and some or all of them (see below) may actually have reached Dura before then.

There are several categories of 'Roman' coins represented in the published material from the excavations of the Yale University/French Academy of Inscriptions and Letters at Dura. First there are denarii (Bellinger 1949: 30–53), almost all of the mint of Rome. These range in date from Republican issues of Marcus Antonius to the reign of Gordian III. About 300 of the 924 denarii published were minted before AD 165, 224 of them from contexts recognized as hoards. The most numerous were from the reigns of Vespasian (39), Domitian (13), Trajan (75), Hadrian (57), Antoninus Pius (36), Faustina Senior (23), M. Aurelius (13 definitely before AD 165) and Faustina Junior (13 definitely before AD 165). Another category is the so-called Roman Imperial bronze of the eastern provinces, with the imperial portrait and Latin legends on the obverse and the letters SC in a laurel wreath on the reverse. Most were minted in Antioch, but some were minted at other Syrian centres, and some, apparently, were even produced at the mint of Rome for circulation in the east (Butcher 1996: 103–4; Carradice and Cowell 1987; Howgego 1985: 21–4). These coins are characterized in the Dura excavation reports as 'senatorial' issues of Antioch (Bellinger 1949: 73–7). Examples from Dura range from the reign of Augustus to that of Marcus Aurelius. A total of 463 were definitely minted before AD 165, only seven came from identified hoards: 163 were dated to the reign of Claudius, with 125 of Domitian, 31 of Nerva, 41 of Trajan. There was also a handful of pre-AD 165 bronze coins of the mint of Rome (Bellinger 1949: 61–2). Very few of the tetradrachms found at Dura, mostly minted at Antioch, with Greek legends and an imperial portrait (obverse) and an eagle (reverse), were produced before AD 165: only thirteen (seven from hoards) from a total of 2,346; the rest were overwhelmingly of third-century AD date (Bellinger 1949: 12–29). A further 32 (sixteen from hoards) were imitations of tetradrachms of the Seleucid king Philip Philadelphos, minted at Antioch after the formation of the Roman province of Syria (Bellinger 1949: 12). The final category consists of civic bronze coinages of cities within the Roman empire. Modest numbers of such coins minted before AD 165 (of cities such as Seleucia Pieria, Beroea, Laodicea, Hierapolis and Aradus) were excavated at Dura (Bellinger 1949: 81–9).

Collectively, all these categories of coins are referred to below as Roman because they were minted within the Roman empire. However, the tetradrachms, SC coinage and civic bronzes fall into the category generally called 'Greek Imperials' or 'Roman provincial' by numismatists, and the use of the term Roman here is not intended to imply any particular relationship with Roman authority.

The crucial question, for current purposes, is when and how these coins reached Dura. Some or all may have reached Dura shortly after their minting. Others may have circulated for much longer periods and reached Dura much later than their dates of minting, perhaps not until Dura came under direct Roman control in AD 115 (Trajan) or subsequently in AD 165–6. For example, denarii minted after Nero's weight reforms of AD 64 might have continued to circulate until after AD 165. Earlier examples were struck to a heavier standard, and so, if they survived, they were probably taken out of circulation and kept, as their bullion value exceeded their face value. In fact all the denarii from Dura post-date the Neronian reform, except for three of M. Antonius, which Bellinger (1949: 126, 203) noted were struck light initially and of reduced weight due to wear, and so may have circulated alongside post-reform issues. Thus, at least in theory, all the denarii found at Dura may have been in circulation as late as AD 115 or even AD 165 and reached the city with the Roman army. Bellinger (1949: 169) suggests that hoards 3 and 4, which together contained 370 denarii, nearly half minted before AD 165, were buried in AD 218, 'showing the varieties of wear that one might expect if they had come in in a single payment in 218 from money in normal circulation'. Otherwise Bellinger's catalogue does not provide much information about wear or weight, which would be helpful to determine how long they had been in circulation.

Another form of evidence for where particular coins may have been at certain dates is provided by countermarks. These are marks applied to coins after they have been minted, for a range of possible reasons (Howgego 1985). They rarely have explicit dates, but sometimes it is possible to suggest a date at which certain countermarks were applied. For example, twenty-four of the SC bronze coins from Dura (Bellinger 1949: 74–6) bear a countermark of a standing Athena. Howgego (1985: 150, no. 245) suggests that this mark was associated with Domitian and was probably applied in Antioch between AD 83 and 96. Two of the coins from Dura thus countermarked were minted in the reign of Claudius (Bellinger 1949: 74, nos. 1604e, 1604f), so it appears that these had remained within the Roman empire for at least thirty years before they were countermarked, and reached Dura only then or perhaps much later. Certainly their appearance at Dura was not contemporary with their minting. Other countermarks relate to legions. For example, LXV on an SC dupondius minted under Claudius (Bellinger 1949: 74, no. 1604c) probably relates to *legio XV Apollinaris*. Howgego (1985: 257, no. 739) suggests that this post-dates that legion's transfer from Pannonia to Cappadocia in the reign of Trajan. The most likely explanation of the coin's appearance at Dura is that it had remained within the Roman empire from the time when it was minted to the reign of Trajan, when it was countermarked by the legion. Subsequently it reached Dura, either with soldiers in AD 115–17, or perhaps after AD 165.[5] Similar arguments might apply to coins countermarked by *legio X Fretensis*, which Howgego suggests were brought north from that legion's base at Jerusalem for Trajan's Parthian war (Bellinger 1949: 74–5, nos. 1604a, 1604b, 1625d; Howgego 1985: 252–3).[6]

Stratigraphic evidence for when particular coins were in use in Dura is less helpful than one might hope, as few definitively datable sealed deposits were published in the excavation reports. However, two Roman coins – an unspecified silver issue of Domitian and a bronze coin of Trajan – were found in tombs sealed under a debris layer dated to ca AD 160 (*Dura* IX.2, 4, 33, 77, 132). This would suggest that these coins probably reached Dura before the definitive establishment of Roman control over the area, although the argument is rather circular, as the presence of these coins and

---

[5] Of course, there is some possibility of more complicated patterns of circulation across the imperial borders in both directions, but these simpler explanations seem more likely.

[6] Bellinger (1949: 203) suggested that many Claudian coins found at Dura, including some with legionary countermarks, reached the city in the immediate aftermath of Corbulo's campaigns in the East in the reign of Nero, and the countermarks might belong to that period. Certainly both legions *X Fretensis* and *XV Apollinaris* participated in those campaigns. However, Howgego's later dates for the countermarks are to be preferred, partly because some Flavian coins (including one at Dura – Bellinger 1949: 75, no. 1625d) bear the same countermarks, and also because the *X Fretensis* countermark is found on many coins from around Jerusalem, suggesting a date after that legion's deployment there in AD 69 (Howgego 1985: 252–3, 257). The only possibility which would confirm Bellinger's dating is that these later countermarks and the identical or similar ones found at Dura were applied at different times.

the absence of later ones is part of the excavators' evidence for dating the deposition of the debris layer.

In his synthesis of coin use at Dura, Bellinger (1949: 195–210) asserts quite strongly that Roman coinage was widely used in Parthian Dura. For example, he states that there were 'times when Dura was certainly a Parthian city but used Roman bronze' (1949: 200); that 'Antiochene tetradrachms [the Roman period imitations of Philip Philadelphos] . . . continued to be used in the actually or potentially hostile territory of the Parthians' (1949: 202); that after Nero's reign 'the supply of denarii is constant, while the Parthian drachms disappear entirely' (1949: 203). Bellinger (1949: 204) also suggests that while Trajan's conquest of Dura meant the arrival of more Roman coinage in the city, the subsequent loss of Roman control had no major impact, with issues of Hadrian circulating there alongside little Parthian coinage. As indicated above, there is relatively little definitive evidence for when the Roman coins came to Dura, so Bellinger bases his argument to a great degree on the absence of Parthian and other Eastern coinages (notably civic issues of Seleucia on the Tigris) at certain periods. He assumes that Dura was a highly monetized community, and if there was little or no Parthian coin there at a given period, then the vacuum must have been filled by Western coins.

Certainly superficially Table 1, showing the numbers of certain categories of Roman and Parthian coins by date of minting, gives the impression of a shortfall of Parthian coins (particularly of silver) being filled by Roman coins, from the Flavian period in particular. But the reality was surely much more complex, and the true picture much more blurred. Probably many Domitianic SC issues came to Dura during the brief period of Roman control under Trajan, for example, while the civic issues of Seleucia on the Tigris continued to circulate. Reckoning in documents from Dura is typically in drachmas until after the Roman occupation (Bellinger 1949: 203 n. 29) and this might refer primarily to Parthian coins. However, it could also refer to the 'Roman' tetradrachms mentioned above (see Bellinger 1949: 204 n. 31, although examples dating to before AD 165 are relatively rare at Dura), or even to drachma equivalents of other coins such as denarii. Otherwise Parthian coins might be underrepresented in the archaeological record for reasons connected with survival and recovery. They may have fallen out of use after the Roman occupation, been melted down, or, because they were deposited earlier, merely failed to survive in numbers equivalent to their Roman counterparts. It is very difficult to form any strong impression of the coinage in circulation at Dura due to the lack of well-dated excavated contexts relating to normal use and loss.

Table 1. *Roman and Parthian coins found at Dura-Europos, numbers by reign*

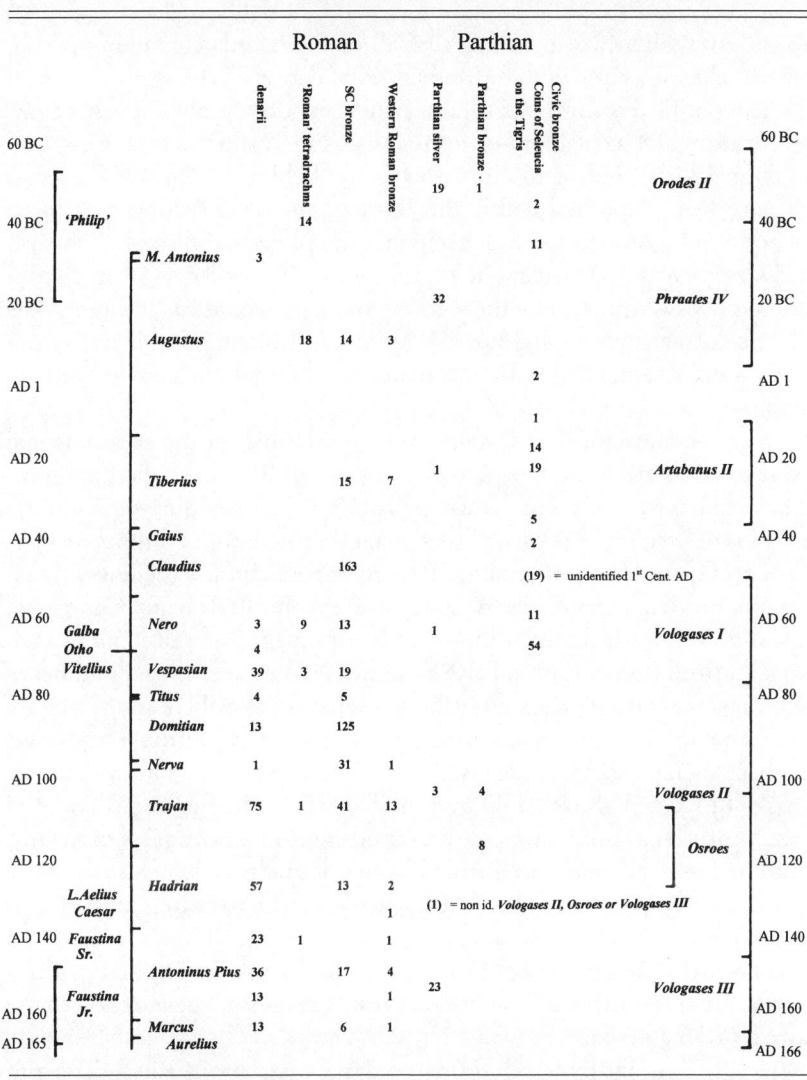

Source: adopted from Bellinger (1949).

The high proportion of coins (especially silver) from hoards also complicates this picture, as these do not represent normal circulation, use and loss – they relate to special circumstances and the deliberate choice of coins to put away. It is worth noting that all of the hoards containing pre-AD 165 Roman coins also contain Roman coins dating to the period of direct Roman political control of the city. Thus these do not provide any definitive evidence of availability of Roman coins in Parthian Dura. Only one excavated hoard out of twenty-two (no. 13, Bellinger 1949: 178–9) seems to have been deposited before the Roman conquest: Bellinger dated its deposition to 150–130 BC. It is likely that the pattern of discovered hoards at Dura relates to particular circumstances in the period of Roman control and perhaps is distorted by the recovery of earlier hoards in antiquity. The absence of Parthian period hoards containing Roman coins is not necessarily a decisive indication that Roman coins did not circulate in Parthian Dura.

What circumstances and agents were responsible for the appearance of Roman coins at Dura? The physical presence of Roman soldiers and officials is one possibility. This would explain, for example, the large numbers of coins minted in the reign of Trajan, including denarii, SC bronzes, a wide variety of coins of civic mints and Western imperial bronze. Bellinger (1949: 204) notes that some of the Western bronze coins of Trajan's reign found at Dura were so little worn that they had probably arrived uncirculated, straight from Rome. It would also account for an indeterminate number of pre-Trajanic coins which were still in circulation elsewhere in the empire and came to Dura during the brief period of Roman control. These coins perhaps include some earlier issues of SC bronze with legionary countermarks (discussed above). Likewise most or all of the numerous issues of Antoninus Pius could have come in after the Roman conquest of AD 165, and the same may have been true of issues of Hadrian, which surely were still in circulation then. There is no particular reason to assume, as Bellinger did (1949: 204), that these were the normal coinage of Dura between AD 115 and 165, although the political vacuum in the middle Euphrates at this period (Potter 1991) may have meant greater than usual penetration of the area by Roman coinage.

A second means by which Roman coinage may have reached Dura also involves the Roman army, but in a less direct way. Payment of large numbers of soldiers and purchase of army supplies for large-scale campaigns may have led to particularly large quantities of coin circulating in frontier areas of the Roman empire. Some of these coins may have crossed the normal frontier and been spent or lost by soldiers on campaign. Some may have been used to purchase supplies by the army or civilian contractors, even across imperial frontiers from nominally hostile territories (Whittaker 1994: 114, 118). Alternatively, such coins may have been spent by the army within the empire and gradually found their way, by civilian means, across the frontier. Some of the types of Roman coin found at Dura may have been used primarily by the army. For example, denarii in general may have found their way into the regional economy initially as payment to soldiers. It has been suggested that the SC bronze issues had a close association with military finance, not least because many of these coins, including examples from Dura, received legionary countermarks (Howgego 1982: 1–20; 1985: 21–3). Carradice (1983: 160) has suggested that the SC issues of the reign of Domitian, numerous at Dura, were specifically issued for soldiers. Bellinger (1949: 203) linked the issues of Claudius and Nero excavated at Dura to Nero's Armenian wars, suggesting that they reached Dura via Edessa (although see the discussion of the dating of the legionary countermarks above, which implies that some of these coins did not reach Dura until much later). It is quite likely that some coins found at Dura (and many Roman coins in general) originally came into the regional economy through some form of military payment or purchase of supplies. However, military needs probably led to the minting of particularly large issues of coin from time to time. These large issues would have remained in circulation for a long time and been well represented in later deposits, so the time and place of their use and deposition at Dura might have had only a very indirect relationship to the specific campaign for which they were originally minted.

Finally, the coins may have reached Dura through civilian means. Long-distance trade passing through Dura may have been subjected to civic customs dues exacted in cash, as was certainly the case at Palmyra (as shown in the inscribed tax law *OGIS* II 629 = *IGR* III 1056). There is evidence of officials who may have collected such dues at Dura (*Dura* II, 115–39 *passim*, 156–8), apparently early in the Roman period, although it is not clear whether they were civic or imperial taxes or both at that time. Additionally or alternatively, it may be that Roman coinage was in normal day-to-day civilian use for basic economic transactions in a network of communities stretching from the Roman frontier to Dura and perhaps beyond. This seems to be the situation envisaged by Bellinger when he refers to Parthian Dura and other western Parthian territories as allowed to be 'economic dependencies of the West whatever the political condition' (1949: 201).

Thus any attempt to consider the degree to which Roman coinage reached Dura before the city came under Roman political control is weakened by the absence of dated archaeological deposits including coins relating to normal circulation and loss. There were no hoards containing Roman coins deposited before the Roman conquest of the city, although the peculiar nature of hoards in general and the lack of excavated pre-Roman hoards from Dura mean that this evidence is far from decisive. Probably some coins found their way across the frontier from the Roman empire to Parthian Dura, but Bellinger's picture of regular day-to-day economic activities being conducted in Roman coin may go too far. It seems more likely that a high proportion of the pre-AD 165 Roman coinage was in normal circulation either in AD 115 and arrived then with the Roman army under Trajan, or was in use in AD 165 and reached Dura at that date.

3. A TECHNOLOGICAL-CULTURAL CASE STUDY? THE F3 BATH BUILDING

A third case study of possible influence across imperial frontiers on the material culture of Dura-Europos is a technological and architectural one with cultural implications. This relates to the small bath building in block F3. In his publication of this building, Frank Brown assigned to it a construction date in the third quarter of the first century AD (*Dura* VI, 5; 77). This dating, to the period of Parthian control of Dura, has been cited by many later scholars, such as Nielsen (1993: 44, no. C360) in her catalogue of Roman-type baths, and Wilson (1992: 112, 127) despite Ann Perkins' (1973: 25) considerable and sensible doubts about this chronology. If Brown's proposed dating is correct, then this bath building is an important and fascinating example of a Roman technological 'package' found outside the empire, with a hypocaust heating system, widespread use of kiln-baked bricks of Roman shapes and sizes, concrete domes and vaults and vaulting tubes. There is nothing like it in Parthian architecture (Colledge 1977: 56–7). The import of the technology has cultural implications too, suggesting the development of a taste for Roman-style bathing on the part of an element of the population of Dura, perhaps through contact with urban communities on the Roman side of the frontier. However, as will be shown, the excavators' date for the building is far from reliable, and it is more likely that these baths were built at a period when Dura lay within the Roman empire.

The core of the building (described in *Dura* VI, 49–72, 76–7) consists of four rooms: a frigidarium (F) with walls of gypsum and sandstone rubble, and three rooms with underfloor heating and walls of regular gypsum blocks laid with mortar (Fig. 3). The heated rooms (H) had tubuli sandwiched between the stone and the plaster. One heated room, presumably the caldarium (C), had apsidal and rectangular niches with remains of bathing pools

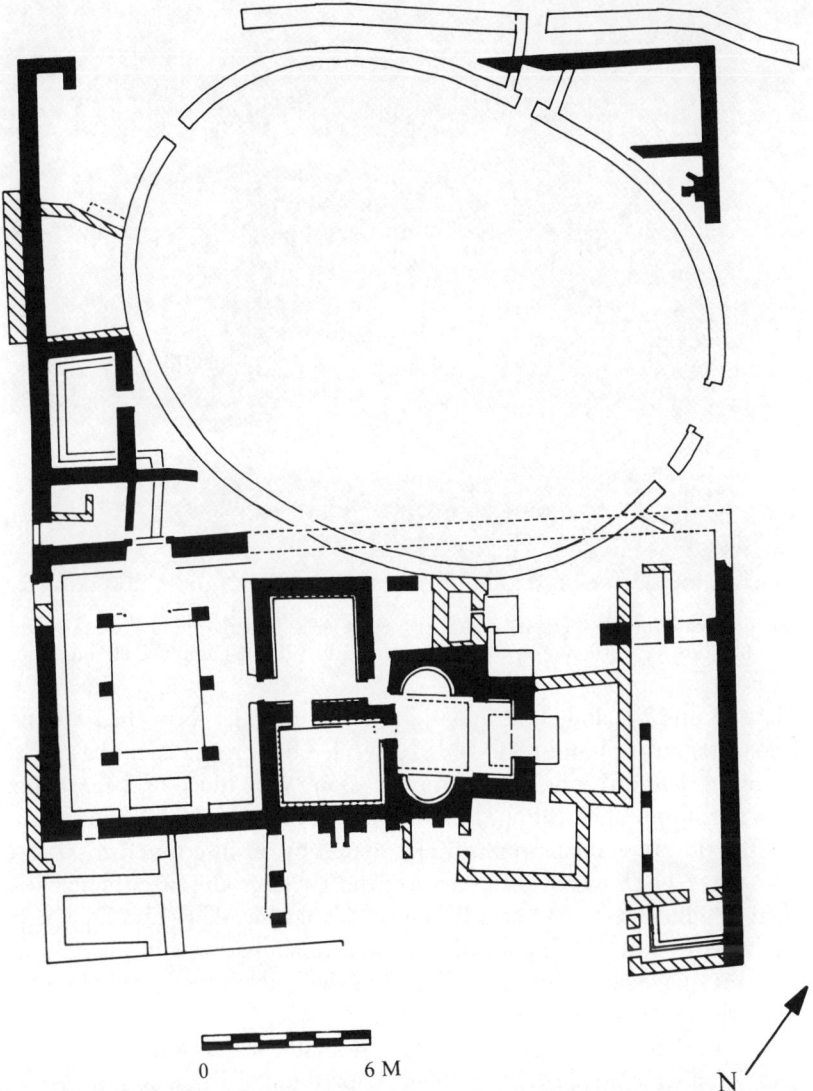

Figure 3. Plan of the F3 block at Dura-Europos, showing F3 bath and amphitheatre (redrawn by David Hopkins from an original by Van Knox, *Dura* VI, pl. 3) (by permission of Yale University Art Gallery)

Plate 6. Excavation photograph of south apse of Room 5 (caldarium) in F3 bath, showing tubuli (by permission of Yale University Art Gallery, Dura-Europos Collection)

(Plates 6 and 7), and the frigidarium, in its original form, had a large, deep rectangular plunge pool, which was filled in during a later phase. The rooms on the north side of the complex, along with much of the evidence for water supply and heating, and for drainage, were badly damaged by the construction of a small amphitheatre, dated by an inscription to AD 216 (*Dura* VI, 76). However, the excavators did locate in this area the remains of seats, which they suggested belonged to a latrine. They also suggested, partly because of the absence of structural remains under the arena, that there may have been a palaestra linked to the bath in that area before the amphitheatre was built (*Dura* VI, 56–7).

Besides the existence of a hypocaust, several features of the baths' construction are intrusive to the Parthian architecture of Dura, and suggest an origin within the Roman empire. One is the extensive use of flat, square, kiln-baked bricks typical of Roman architecture.[7] Some were 26–7 cm square by 4.5–5 cm thick, with bipedalis-type bricks 58–60 cm square by 5–6 cm thick. Apparently less common were bricks 36–8 cm square by 4.5–5 cm thick. Overall they were comparable but not identical in size to

---

[7] That is not to say that baked brick was not used in Parthian architecture – for a summary see Colledge (1977: 56–7).

Plate 7. Excavation photograph of east side of Room 4 (caldarium) of F3 bath, showing rectangular niche (by permission of Yale University Art Gallery, Dura-Europos Collection)

the bricks used in the undoubtedly Roman period baths in blocks M7, C3 and E3 at Dura, and very different from the thick, rectangular mudbricks typical of the site.[8] In the F3 bath, the bricks were mostly used in the hypocaust, where mudbrick would not have been suitable anyway. The only other structures making extensive use of baked bricks at Dura were the M7, C3 and E3 baths, where they were used to build walls as well as the hypocaust (*Dura* VI, 84–105).

Other elements intrusive to Parthian architecture used in the F3 bath building include, apparently, the use of concrete vaulting as a roofing material and the use of vaulting tubes. The pool in the frigidarium was surrounded by piers made of gypsum blocks. Found collapsed in that room was a fragment of concrete vaulting with nine lengths of hollow terracotta tube embedded in it (Plate 8). These tubes were ribbed, 36 cm long, 10.5 cm in diameter, with one end open and a nozzle at the other (*Dura* VI, 49–50).

---

[8] The 26–7 cm size and the bipedales of 58–60 cm work well as modules of a Roman foot. The 36–8 cm size is less usual. The latter were used in the levelling course below the pilae of the hypocaust (*Dura* VI, 52), which initially might lead one to suppose that the Roman bath was built on a pre-Roman structure that used 'non-Roman' bricks. However, the situation is more complicated, as a few of these bricks are used higher up in the hypocaust of the F3 bath and to some degree in the later, undoubtedly Roman period baths. Thus they seem as likely to be Roman as the other bricks.

Plate 8. Excavation photograph showing collapsed fragment of concrete arch with vaulting tubes in F3 bath frigidarium (by permission of Yale University Art Gallery, Dura-Europos Collection)

The curve preserved on the vaulting fragment led Brown to suggest that it was part of a series of arches spanning the piers, supporting the roof of the frigidarium. A fully vaulted roof is one possibility for this, although Brown (*Dura* VI, 50) felt that the piers were too slight to support the roof. It was reconstructed (Fig. 4; by Brown and Knox, *Dura* VI, 50 with pl. 3) in atrium form, although Brown thought that a flat roof (typical of Dura) supported on the arches over the piers was equally likely.

Brown also suggested that the heated rooms of the bath suite had been roofed with concrete domes, perhaps also containing vaulting tubes (*Dura* VI, 54–5). This proposal was based on the survival of flat blocks spanning the corners of the rooms (Plate 9), apparently acting as a basic version

Roman material culture across imperial frontiers? 137

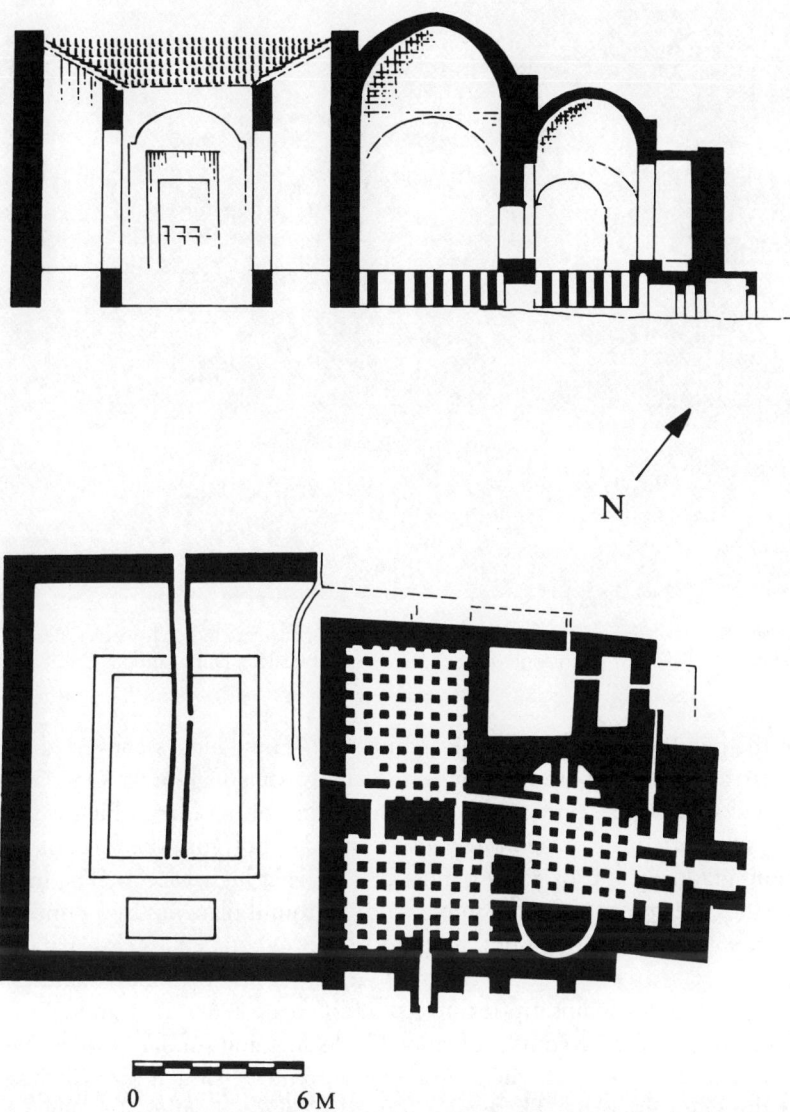

Figure 4. Reconstructed elevation and plan at hypocaust level of the F3 baths at Dura-Europos (redrawn by David Hopkins from an original by Van Knox, *Dura* VI, pl. 3) (by permission of Yale University Art Gallery)

Plate 9. Excavation photograph showing primitive pendentive in north-west corner of Room 3, F3 baths (by permission of Yale University Art Gallery, Dura-Europos Collection)

of the pendentives of Byzantine architecture. These blocks converted the squarish rectangular ground plans into roughly octagonal forms. One room provided surviving evidence of a further course of masonry which would have converted the octagon into a sixteen-sided polygon, the form of the room gradually approximating more to a circle at higher levels. The most obvious means of roofing a room of such a ground plan was by a dome of some sort, possibly of masonry but most likely of concrete. A close parallel can be seen in a sanctuary at Omm-es-Zeitun, in the Hauran of southern Syria, dated by an inscription to AD 282 (Vogüé 1865: 43–5 and pl. 6). This preserved three courses of stone blocks forming similar 'pendentives rudimentaires' in the corners of a square room of similar size to those of the Dura F3 bath.[9] These were topped by the remnants of a concrete dome. Likewise, concrete half-domes would have been the easiest way of roofing the apsidal recesses in the caldarium of the Dura F3 bath. However, no concrete debris was actually found in these rooms in the course of excavation (*Dura* 6, 55).

---

[9] This might imply that the technique was, in some sense, Syrian, but it appears as a product of the *Roman* architecture of Syria, and the use of concrete certainly suggests a Roman origin or adaptation.

Vaulting tubes were not found anywhere else in Dura, and concrete vaults were rare and otherwise confined to the Roman period, notably to the M7, E3 and C3 baths, where the debris from the vaults was found collapsed into the rooms they had roofed (*Dura* VI, 85–6, 91, 96–7). The excavators suggested that some of the distinctive features of the F3 baths, including the vaulting tubes, were not intrusive Roman introductions, but Eastern characteristics which subsequently spread throughout the Roman empire (*Dura* VI, 58–63). Such theories of eastern origins were quite common (and reasonable) in the aftermath of the Dura excavations, when scholars employed evidence from Dura to propose that certain features of later Roman art and architecture derived from Eastern sources, including aspects of late antique painting (for example Breasted (1924)). Confidence in some of these theories has diminished due to the subsequent lack of supporting evidence found elsewhere in Syria. This is certainly true of vaulting tubes, which do not appear to have been found on any other site in Syria, and which are very rare elsewhere in the Roman East, despite decades of excavation of urban sites like Palmyra and Apamea.[10] Their use at Dura seems to have been imported, and to relate to their use in the Roman empire. The next question is when the vaulting tubes, and the other apparently Roman features of this building, actually reached Dura. Were they, as Brown implies, a product of the Parthian period, a technology transmitted by, presumably, civilian means across the imperial frontier? Or do they actually belong to the period of Roman control of Dura, transmitted more directly from the centre of the empire?

Despite the perceptions of the F3 bath as a well-dated structure, the only apparent certainty in its chronology is that it was superseded by the construction of the amphitheatre dated by an inscription to AD 216 (*Dura* VI, 77–80). The bath provides some evidence of remodelling between its construction and abandonment, including three successive paving levels in the frigidarium and the filling in of the frigidarium pool (*Dura* VI, 68–72). Brown suggests that evidence of burning in some rooms meant that the bath was destroyed by fire at some point prior to its abandonment. The evidence for the absolute dating of the phases of remodelling and for the bath's construction is not very precise.

The published date for the construction of the bath, the mid-first century AD, is based on the following observations and assumptions (Fig. 5):

(i) The bath construction pre-dated construction of a house in the adjacent block, E4 (*Dura* VI, 4–5, 77). This assumption regarding their

---

[10] Wilson (1992: 125–9) has published a list of documented vaulting tube use on sites throughout the Roman empire, and the only Eastern contexts he records are Dura and a Byzantine church at Nazareth.

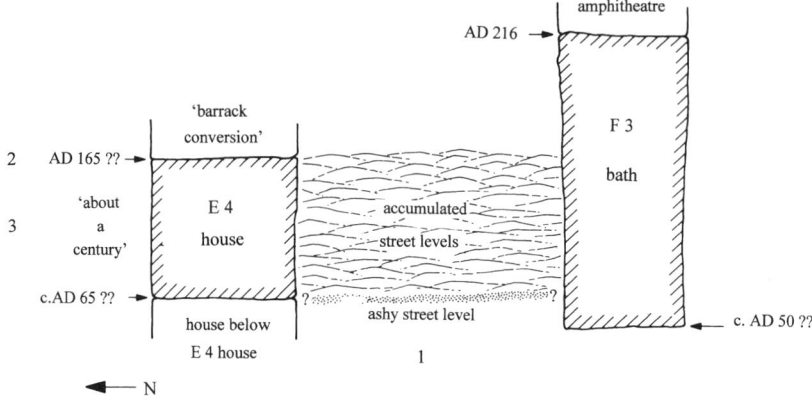

Figure 5. Schematic depiction of the relationship between the house in F4 and the F3 baths (drawn by David Hopkins)

interrelationship was based on observation of successive surfaces in the intervening street and also on the observation that ashy material (which Brown assumed was waste from the bath's furnaces) was common in street levels apparently pre-dating the E4 house.

(ii) The E4 house was converted into smaller units, interpreted as barracks, ca AD 165 (*Dura* VI, 28, 31). The date is very approximate, based solely on the likelihood that the first Roman garrison was installed in Dura at about that time, when the city came under Roman control.

(iii) The E4 house was built in the third quarter of the first century AD (*Dura* VI, 31). Brown derived this date by extrapolating back from the AD 165 date (see (ii) above) supposed for the conversion and assuming it took about a century for the adjacent street levels to rise 0.55 m between the time of the house's construction and its conversion.

Clearly there are a number of problems with all these assumptions.

(i) It is clear that Brown was much less certain about the interrelationships of F3, E4 and the intervening street levels than the published account suggests. Unpublished notes in his hand contain numerous crossings-out, apparently evidence that he was undecided when discussing the issue of whether the bath pre-dated or was contemporary with a street level contemporary with the construction of the E4 house.[11] Also, as Perkins (1973: 25 n. 1) points out, the ashy material in the street level apparently pre-dating

---

[11] Unpublished notes labelled 're. E4 so. st.' in the Dura archive of the Yale University Art Gallery. I am grateful to Dr Susan Matheson, curator of the archive, for allowing me access to this unpublished material. The notes appear to be preparatory material for writing up the published preliminary reports. Unfortunately it has not been possible to locate primary excavation notes regarding this building, or, for example, section drawings relevant to its excavation.

the E4 house might just as easily relate to the destruction of an earlier building whose remains were found under the E4 house (*Dura* VI, 4–5) as to waste from the F3 bath. She mentions that the ashy layer also contained plaster and mudbrick remnants, more appropriate for debris from a mudbrick house than furnace waste (1973: 25 n. 1).

(ii) There is no particular reason to assume that the conversion of the E4 house took place as early as AD 165, even if the conversion is correctly identified as a barracks. The date is a purely notional one, and the change could have taken place as late as AD 216. Brown provides some evidence (*Dura* VI, 30) that the conversion took place before the amphitheatre was built.

(iii) The assumptions about the extrapolated construction date of the E4 house seem quite speculative. The excavators suggested that the accumulation of street fills between the construction of the house and its conversion took about a century and was gradual and regular. Personal experience of excavating fills in mudbrick-built communities suggests that such fills can accumulate very quickly, often as the result of deliberate raising of street or building levels. The excavators also note (*Dura* VI, 32) that there were hardly any recognizable pre-Roman finds from the E4 house. If it was originally constructed as early as AD 165, one might expect them to have found more residual Parthian period material.

Thus the grounds for dating the F3 bath to the mid-first century AD are quite tenuous. The relationship with the E4 house is unclear, and the dating of that house is uncertain. Fundamentally, all we can say with any certainty is that the bath was built before AD 216, and long enough before for some remodelling to have taken place before it was abandoned.

What other evidence might be applied to this dating problem? The well-documented and dated use of vaulting tubes in Roman architecture is mostly a phenomenon of the North African provinces from the later second century onwards.[12] The Dura vaulting tubes look quite similar to the North African examples (apart from being slightly longer), although their

---

[12] Wilson (1992) has attempted to show that their use went back as early as the third century BC, citing examples from datable contexts at Morgantina. However, the Morgantina examples are rather different from the African ones. He (107) states that the former were exceptionally long (*ca* 70 cm) and smooth, while the African examples ranged from 7 to 32 cm long and tended to be ribbed. His attempt to show the continued use of this technology over 400 years, from Morgantina to Roman North Africa, breaks down due to the very few, poorly documented and poorly dated examples he is able to cite, which contrast with the numerous and relatively well-dated examples from the late second century onwards in Africa. He assumes that the Dura vaulting tubes are well-dated early examples, whereas, as we have seen, their date is not at all secure. The Dura examples are more like the African versions than the Morgantina ones, although they are a little longer than the African examples (36 cm). Wilson's alternative suggestion (1992: 121), that the African use of vaulting tubes was a rediscovery or independent invention of a technology which had been used briefly in third-century BC Sicily, seems more plausible.

use seems a little unusual. Instead of being used as a support for concrete poured on top of them, in place of wooden centring (the lower surface being plastered flat), the Dura tubes were actually embedded in the vault, apparently to lighten it, rather like the amphorae used, for example, in the Circus of Maxentius near Rome. However, the similarities are such that, I believe, we can see the Dura tubes as being related to the use of tubes in North Africa.

Certainly hypocausts and some of the other features of the Dura baths (concrete vaults, Roman-style baked bricks) were used in Roman provinces adjacent to the Parthian empire, and the concepts, architects and artisans required could have made their way to Dura. Likewise, the plan of the building has no very specific and obvious geographical origin. The compact rectangular form can be found in many parts of the Roman empire where small bath buildings were fitted into crowded urban contexts. However, vaulting tubes are *not* found at all in adjacent provinces. They seem to have been primarily a central Mediterranean technology, from Africa (or, as Wilson 1992: 112 suggests, Sicily and Italy). The Roman army seems the most likely agency for the transmission of this construction technique from the central Mediterranean to such a distant location. One might compare the use of vaulting tubes in Britain. They appear at York, Carleon and Chester, the sites of legionary fortresses, all apparently in the context of legionary bath buildings (Wilson 1992: 118–19). As at Dura, the construction technique seems to have been directly imported from the centre of the empire, as it is not recorded in Germany or northern Gaul (Wilson 1992: 118). Mason, who published the vaulting tubes from the tepidarium of the baths within the Chester legionary fortress, suggested that their use there related to an early third-century rebuilding, and proposed that an African military architect was responsible (Mason 1990: 222).

The Roman army was present in Dura briefly from AD 115 in the course of Trajan's Eastern conquests. The city came under Roman political control in AD 165–6 and presumably the first garrison was installed then. Certainly there was a Roman garrison by *ca* AD 192.[13] The brief occupation under Trajan may have been too short for the construction of a bath building, and, if the Roman army was responsible, a date after AD 165 (but before the construction of the amphitheatre in AD 216) seems more likely.[14] Perkins

---

[13] There was a detachment of Palmyrene archers at Dura by AD 168, and a regular auxiliary cohort of the Roman army is attested by *ca* AD 192 (Welles, Fink and Gilliam 1959: 24–5). However, it is quite likely that such troops were there at an earlier date.

[14] Although as Potter (1991) has suggested, it is likely that the middle Euphrates was something of a political vacuum between Trajan's campaigns and those of Lucius Verus, and a brief, undocumented Roman military presence there at that time is not impossible.

(1973: 25) suggested that the bath was built for the use of a small late second-century Roman garrison.

Interestingly, there is considerable evidence for the presence of individual members and (probably) a vexillation of the North African *legio III Augusta* in Syria and elsewhere on the eastern frontier throughout the second century AD (references in Ritterling 1924: 1499–1501), so it is quite possible that an African military architect was present in Dura at some time.

Finally, it should be noted that a figure of a Victory on a globe was painted on the first coat of plaster on one of the piers in the frigidarium (*Dura* VI, 51, 63–7, pl. 41.1). Depictions of Victory are certainly found in pre-Roman and non-military contexts at Dura, but the symbolism would be appropriate for a bath used by Roman soldiers shortly after the conquest of the region. Stylistically, the figure contrasts quite strongly with another Victory on a globe (*Dura* II, 181–93), painted on a wooden panel. The latter was characterized by the excavators as 'more oriental', and certainly it has, for example, a distinctive Parthian hairstyle, with a topknot and masses of hair bound over the ears. The contrast with the F3 Victory is quite striking, and emphasizes the latter's intrusive character in Parthian Dura. As Perkins (1973: 125) states, 'her appearance at Dura is probably due to Roman influence'.

Thus it is clear that the F3 bath at Dura is not at all securely dated to the Parthian period, although many scholars continue to accept the published date.[15] The Parthian dating would imply a rare and interesting example of the transfer of a technological package and associated cultural values across an imperial frontier, probably by civilian means. However, it seems more likely that this bath was a construction of the Roman period, probably introduced by Roman soldiers for their own use. Elsewhere (Pollard 2000: 52–3) I have suggested that the later bath buildings at Dura were exclusively for military use and a manifestation of the cultural insularity of the Roman army in the city. I believe this is true of the F3 baths too, and that they do not provide evidence for what Brown called 'the intensive Romanization of municipal life' at Dura in the Parthian period, any more than the later baths do for the Roman period (*Dura* VI, 104).

CONCLUSIONS

These three case studies have shown rather mixed results in the search for evidence of Roman material influence in Dura in the Parthian period.

---

[15] After this paper was essentially complete, I discovered that Mathilde Gélin (2000: 57 n. 22) recently drew similar conclusions about the dating of these baths.

The analysis of ESA pottery suggests that imports from its area of production in Roman Syria were not particularly diminished by the establishment of the Roman province, and that what Cox viewed as a decrease in those imports in the later first and second centuries AD was more likely the result of changes in the production and/or export of the pottery which affected the Roman province as well as Parthian Syria. If this is so, then Parthian Dura participated in a modest level of cross-border, intra-regional trade in pottery. However, the quantity of green-glazed Parthian-type pottery excavated at Dura greatly outweighed the imported 'Roman' pottery. Nor is there evidence of import of fineware from the wider Roman Mediterranean world until after the establishment of Roman political control over the site, when African Red Slip ware reached the site.

Probably some coins produced within the Roman empire reached Dura while it was under Parthian control, but it is difficult to tell what proportion of the 'Roman' coins from the site came in later, with the physical presence of the Roman army in AD 115–17 and after AD 165, and with direct Roman political control. Reconsideration of the evidence tends to emphasize the role of the army in bringing in coinage which had been in circulation for some time and to diminish the participation of Parthian Dura in a regional economy that crossed the imperial frontier.

Finally, the case study of a 'Roman' bath in Parthian Dura suggests that it was actually a Roman bath, probably to be attributed to the early years of Roman military occupation, rather than an exciting example of cross-border transfer of technology and of associated cultural values.

Undoubtedly Dura participated in long-distance trade between empires and, to some degree, in a regional economy that crossed imperial frontiers. However, the impact of this cross-border economic activity on the surviving archaeological evidence from Dura is perhaps less than one might expect. In this case it may be that categories of evidence traditionally used to study trade and 'Romanization' in archaeological terms are of less significance than perishable goods, such as spices and textiles, which are often assumed to have been the subjects of long-distance trade between East and West.[16]

---

[16] At Dura, of course, there is the possibility of studying some of these perishable commodities. For example, Pfister and Bellinger (1945: 53–4) published some fragments of Chinese and Indian silk from the site. However, it is difficult to separate out trade commodities from textiles worn locally, and to date such items.

CHAPTER 5

Sympoliteiai *in Hellenistic Asia Minor**

Gary Reger

Twenty-seven years ago, publishing an inscription that treats the absorption of Kyrbissos by Teos in Ionia, Jeanne and Louis Robert offered some general remarks on the mechanisms by which one town absorbed another in Asia Minor in the Hellenistic period:[1]

With Airai and Kyrbissos absorbed by Teos just as Dios Hieron submitted to Kolophon, we have examples of this phenomenon so characteristic of the Hellenistic period: the documents, and especially the Athenian Tribute Lists, show for the fifth century a pullulation of political entities, tiny independent towns having a small plain as their territory, on the coast or in the interior, a cultivatable valley surrounded by hills furnishing pasturage and wood. . . . Many of these entities – sometimes the majority – disappear later, absorbed by their more powerful neighbours by means of *synoikismoi* or *sympoliteiai*. We will recall below the cases of Miletos and Smyrna. It was the same for the expansion of the territory of Mylasa in Caria, for Erythrai which absorbed five other entities in the peninsula. In this case [that of the texts treated in this article], there was no royal intervention. But the impulse toward concentration came from kings, whether Antigonos the One-Eyed for the ultimately failed *synoikismos* of Teos and Lebedos . . . or Lysimachos for Arsinoe, the New Ephesos, or Antigonos and Lysimachos for Alexandreia in the Troad. In the two latter cases we can also simultaneously follow the movement toward concentration and the resistance to the *synoikismos* which resulted in the reconstitution, in one form or another, of the cities temporarily absorbed.

---

* I cannot adequately express my gratitude to Jeanne Robert for entrusting to me the material she and her late husband Louis Robert collected for their book on Mylasa. I am preparing the inscriptions and other material for publication in an extensive monograph setting Mylasa in its regional context; this paper is part of the *prolegomena* for that large project. Glen Bowersock, Christian Habicht, C.P. Jones and Léopold Migeotte have been instrumental in the realization of this project; Wolfgang Blümel has shared with unstinting generosity the results of his work in Caria. I am also grateful to Alain Bresson for allowing me to see the unpublished texts in *Hautes terres de la Carie* (hereafter *HTC*) with his extensive and deeply learned commentaries, and for providing in advance of publication Gauthier (2001) and Migeotte (2001). Angelos Chaniotis also generously shared unpublished work (Chaniotis [forthcoming]). Riet van Bremen read an early version of this paper and saved me from many errors; Marie-Christine Marcellesi put me onto important bibliography I would otherwise have missed.

[1] Robert and Robert (1976: 174–5).

In a few sentences the Roberts summarized or adumbrated many of the issues that arise in respect to the creation, in Hellenistic Asia Minor, of new political entities by means of absorption of their neighbours, including the problem of terminology (*synoikismos* or *sympoliteia*), the source of the motivation for the absorption (the interests of the Hellenistic monarchs, or local pressures unconnected with the desires of sovereigns), the existence of a predominant partner in these absorptions (Teos here), the resistance to absorption shown in many cases by the smaller entities, and the efforts, sometimes successful, by absorbed entities to reassert their independence in the face of their more powerful predatory neighbours.

The *sympoliteia* as a political phenomenon deserves a comprehensive study.[2] The main focus of much (but not all) scholarship has been either the *sympoliteiai* of the Classical period or the Hellenistic *sympoliteiai* of mainland Greece by which the Achaean and Aetolian Leagues were constituted; there was a few years ago an excellent study of the *sympoliteiai* of some Lycian cities that seem to have begun in the later Hellenistic period and to have continued well into the first three centuries of the Empire.[3] But a great deal of material, offering detailed accounts of particular *sympoliteiai*, has mostly been treated in specialized articles, typically in connection with the publication (or republication) of a particular inscription.[4] The comprehensive treatment that cries out to be done would require far more space than available in the confines of a brief chapter. My more modest aims are threefold: first, to explore some aspects of the phenomenon, starting from the Roberts' observations; second, to emphasize some features of Hellenistic *sympoliteiai* in Caria – the impetus to *sympoliteiai* in Hellenistic Caria, especially in the third and second centuries BC, was markedly strong, and the rich evidence gets richer all the time;[5] finally, to consider the role that the so-called Rhodian *synoikismos* of 408/7 may have played in providing its neighbours with a model of how to bring together formerly independent entities into a larger political whole.

The richness of the data from Caria in particular may be illustrated by a recently published inscription from Bargylia.[6] The text, which is inscribed

---

[2] As called for recently by Schuler (1998: 43 n. 155).
[3] See the works cited in nn. 12 and 90 below. For a recent study of the various Greek leagues in the fourth century see Beck (1997).
[4] A number of examples are cited in what follows; the Roberts' article is itself a classic example.
[5] To attempt a full account of the Carian *sympoliteiai*, bedevilled as they are by problems of chronology and motivation, is a major task to be reserved for another context (see n. 1). Compare Gauthier (2001: 117).
[6] Blümel (2000a); an improved text, based on work by Charles Crowther and Andrew Meadows and incorporating suggestions by Wiemer (2001), appears in the appendix to the paperback edition of Ma (1999), i.e. Ma (2002: 380); but for a critique of some aspects of Wiemer's restorations, see now Dreyer (2002: 123–4).

on a large marble block that may have been part of a building, is only partly preserved. It mentions loans made by decrees (ψαφίσματα, l. 9: the dialect here and elsewhere – e.g. ποτί at l. 10 – is the only evidence for the identification of the decree as Rhodian) and 'war waged by King Antiochos against King Ptolemaios', [σ]υνστάντος δὲ πολέμου βασιλεῖ Ἀντιόχωι ποτὶ βασιλῆ Π[το]λεμ[αῖον] (l. 10).[7] Thanks to Charles Crowther's observation that the *sigma* in l. 12 of Blümel's text is actually a *rho*, we can restore ll. 11–12: κυριεῦσαι τοὺς παρὰ βασιλέως Ἀντι[ό]χο[υ–| Κιλλά]ρων καὶ Θωδασων ('the troops of Antiochos got control of Killara and Thodasa'). Killara is a variant for Kildara, a town located about 11 km south-east of Bargylia (see map, p. xv). *Thodasa is previously unattested[8] but clearly must have been situated close to Kildara since Antiochos' troops took both together (perhaps anticipating the arrival of Ptolemaic forces operating around Theangela; see the incomplete ll. 12–13). Circumstances strongly suggest that we should restore these new Thodaseis at l. 13 as well (they fit the space available well):[9] 'the Killareis and Th[odaseis] entered into a *sympoliteia*', καὶ συμπολιτεύεσθαι Κιλλαρεῖς καὶ Θ[ωδασεῖς] (l. 13). The precise historical circumstances and date of the events described remain under debate. In the current state of the text it is impossible to say for sure to whose impetus was owed, and whose interests were served by, the *sympoliteia*. But it is tempting to speculate that Antiochos was the instigator of this *sympoliteia* between two towns that had just come into his possession from the Ptolemies. Kildara and presumably Thodasa lay close to the border of Ptolemaic-controlled territory; both small places, they might have benefited from increased security if joined (forcibly?) together. We can see Antiochos (or his agents) operating in an analogous manner at Theangela at roughly the same time or in 197, when he repopulated that city after its capture from the Ptolemies: τὸν δῆμον συνοικισθῆ[ναι].[10] If this reconstruction

---

[7] Perhaps a reference to a recently enthroned Ptolemaios V if the beginning of the following line, [τὸν] νῦν βασιλεύοντα, should be read continuously with the end of l. 10.
[8] Blümel (2000*a*: 96).
[9] Θ[εαγγελεῖς] is too long, and the interpretation offered above of ll. 11–12 precludes the possibility that the inscription was continued on another stone. The Θεμισσεῖς, mentioned by Steph. Byz. (s.v. Θεμισσός), incorporated into the territory of Stratonikeia by the *senatus consultum* of 81 BC (*IS* 505; cf. Robert 1937: 561–6), might be another candidate, if their town lay somewhere west of Keramos, incorporated into Stratonikeia at the same time. But its exact location remains unknown, and many toponyms beginning with *theta* are known from Caria but are still unlocated; see the list at Blümel (1998*a*: 167). The debate about the relevance of this text to the historicity of the 'secret treaty' between Philip V and Antiochos III to divide up the possessions of Ptolemaios in Asia Minor need not detain us here; see Wiemer (2001), Ma (2002: 380–1), who suggests that the events it describes could be placed among the operations of 197–196, and Dreyer (2002), who dates the events described in the inscription to 201 BC (at p. 201) and offers a different historical interpretation focussed on the secret treaty. None of these discussions has much to say about the *sympoliteia*.
[10] Robert (1936: 98, l. 3), with Robert's commentary *ad loc.* Generally, see Reger (1999: 87–8) and now Ma (1999: esp. 63–73, 82–94). There is now good evidence that Theangela was placed under

is right, it points toward the role of kings in the creation of *sympoliteiai* in Hellenistic Asia Minor. We shall return to this matter below.

I

The Greeks, as is well known, did not use terms for constitutional structures consistently either in time or space.[11] In the Hellenistic period *sympoliteia* covered two broad types of political organization: the 'federal state' with shared citizenship arrangements and super-*polis* political institutions, like the Achaean or Aetolian Leagues,[12] and the political union of two coterminous *poleis* which could – but did not necessarily – lead ultimately to the disappearance of one of the partners. As Hatto Schmitt has recently stressed, the element that linked these two types of *sympoliteia* conceptually was the creation of a common citizenship.[13] But while the lineaments of the federal type of *sympoliteia* are familiar, the second type, which was especially common in Hellenistic Asia Minor, remains more obscure. In part this is due to the looseness of terminology. Polybius provides a nice instance of imprecision in the use of the term *sympoliteia* in a discussion of Cretan affairs of 170/69 BC. The town of Kydonia committed a shocking offence against Apollonia:

> For, even though they [sc. the Kydoniatai] had not only friendship, but also *sympoliteia* with the Apolloniatai and a general sharing of all the rights thought to belong to men, and even though a sworn treaty (ἐνόρκου συνθήκης) about these matters was deposited with Idaian Zeus, they broke their agreement (παρασπονδήσαντες) with the Apolloniatai, captured their city, killed the men, stole their property, and divided up and kept their women and children and city and territory. (Polyb. 28.14.3)

Despite Polybius' explicit use of the word *sympoliteia* to describe the relationship, scholars are generally agreed that the actual arrangement must have been an *isopoliteia*. The territories of the two towns were not

---

the control of Halikarnassos during the period of Philip V's brief suzerainty over part of Caria; later, recovered by Antiochos, Theangela regained its independence. It is hard to place texts without precise dates in the correct order within a complicated and rapidly changing historical context. On Theangela and Halikarnassos see Descat (1997), with references. On the meaning of συνοικίζομαι see below.

[11] See, for example, the discussion of *synoikismos* and *metoikesis* in Demand (1990: 9–10).

[12] The starting place now for study of the *Bundesstaat*-type of *sympoliteia* is Giovannini (1971). For recent discussion of the Aetolians see Scholten (2000) and Grainger (1999). For a recent general discussion of the phenomenon see now Corsten (1999). On the Achaean League see still Urban (1978). Such a federal-type *sympoliteia* is known also from Crete in the late fourth century, the *koinon* of the Oreioi; see Chaniotis (1996*b*: 421–2).

[13] Schmitt (1994: 35).

coterminous,[14] and Angelos Chaniotis has recently noted that the phrase 'general sharing of all the rights thought to belong to men' (κοινωνία πάντων τῶν ἐν ἀνθρώποις νομιζομένων δικαίων) echoes the expression μετέχειν θίνων καὶ ἀνθρωπίνων πάντων found in Cretan *isopoliteia* agreements.[15] Thus it seems sure that here Polybius has used the word loosely, to describe a shared citizenship, and not in a 'constitutionally' fixed manner.

Synoikismos can range in meaning from the physical union of two or more settlements[16] to simply 'resettle', 'settle', or even just 'occupy', as in Antiochos III's letter of 213 BC to Sardis (in which he orders wood to be supplied 'for the resettlement of the city', εἰς τὸν συνοικισμὸν τῆς πόλεως, which had been devastated in the siege against the rebel Achaios),[17] or in Polybius' reference to Megalopolis as the 'inhabited city of the Megalopolitans', συνοικιζομένη τῇ Μεγαλοπολι<τῶν πόλει> (Polyb. 4.25.4). Despite the etymological emphasis of *synoikismos* on physical living arrangements, the word was in fact always available to cover the amalgamation of political institutions also, without necessarily implying a physical restructuring of settlement patterns.[18] Thus, while *synoikismos* might implicitly emphasize the physical joining of separate settlements and *sympoliteia* political and citizenship arrangements, in fact the overlap between the two terms was considerable, and an action described as a *synoikismos* could be a purely political restructuring.[19]

---

[14] Muttelsee (1925: 37–8); Guarducci, *IC* I, p. 3, II, p. 112; Walbank (1979: 348). See also Diod. 30.13. For coterminousness as a necessary condition see Robert (1962: 54–64, 272), who also gives an outline of the problem and much of the evidence. The book in which Robert promised to treat the phenomenon (272–3 n. 9) never appeared. The example of a supposed Parian–Thasian *sympoliteia* would seem to violate the rule of coterminousness, but this arrangement, inferred from a couple of inscriptions, is now to be rejected: see Ehrhardt (forthcoming) (*non vidi*), Pouilloux (1989), and especially Berranger (1992: 311), and cf. Berranger-Auserve (2000: 108). On the other hand, there are some possible candidates for *sympoliteiai* between non-coterminous towns. For the supposed Keramos–Stratonikeia example, see below.

[15] Chaniotis (1996b: 285–7). See, for example, the *isopoliteia* treaty between Hierapytna and Itanos of the late third century: [κατ]ὰ ταὐτὰ δὲ καὶ τ[ῶι Ἱαραπυτνί]ωι ἐν Ἰτάνωι μετέχοντι θε[ίων τε] καὶ ἀνθρωπίνων (*IC* III iv.6; *Staatsvertr.* III 579; Chaniotis 1996b: 234–5, no. 20).

[16] Cf. Reger (2001: 161–2).

[17] Gauthier (1989: 13, no. 1 l. 3), reprinted with translation at Ma (1999: 284–5, no. 1); cf. Gauthier's commentary at pp. 22–3, with reference to the important discussion at Robert and Robert (1983: 188–91). On Achaios see now Ma (1999: 54–63). One may wonder whether the *synoikismos* of Apollonis in Lydia undertaken by one of the brothers of Eumenes II toward the middle of the second century was not also of this type; *TAM* v. 2 1187. And see the inscription from Theangela cited above.

[18] See already the situation in Archaic and Classical Attica: Luce (1998).

[19] Schmitt (1994: 36) cites Thür and Taueber (1994: 130–52, no. 15) (originally published by Plassart 1915: 105–8; *Staatsvertr.* II 297) of 360–350 (Thür and Taueber 1994: 139–40, refuting Dušanic 1978: 334–5) as an example from the Classical period in which *synoikia* is used apparently only of political union, but Nielsen (1999: 54) treats it as indicating an 'absorption by Orchomenos of Euaimon'; likewise te Riele (1987: 187). Thür and Taueber (1994: 134–5 n. 2) point out, rightly, that the agreement

II

A number of *sympoliteiai* attested in Asia Minor for the Hellenistic period resulted from the decisions of kings or their representatives. Many of these were of course foundations, or more typically refoundations, in which existing cities were combined or moved and graced with a dynastic name. The most famous example is perhaps the *synoikismos* of Teos and Lebedos ordered by Antigonos Monophthalmos but perhaps not carried out. The hand of the king is visible everywhere in the procedures, down to involvement in the minutest details.[20] Antigonos' more successful foundation was of course Alexandreia Troas.[21] This city was founded as Antigoneia, probably between 311 and 306, by the *synoikismos* of seven other cities in the Troad. Several of these towns either maintained a separate identity or managed to extricate themselves from subordination to Alexandreia in the course of the Hellenistic period;[22] on the other hand, Chrysa is attested in an inscription of the early second century BC as a fort, φρούριον, of Alexandreia (*I. Alex. Troas* 4) – a status repeated in other cases of subordinated polities.

Another famous episode of *synoikismos* for which a king was responsible concerns Ephesos. King Lysimachos, recent victor in western Asia Minor, relocated the city of Ephesos to the site on which it remained for the rest of its history, renamed it Arsinoe, and augmented its population with people forcibly transferred from several towns, including Kolophon and Lebedos, which ceased to exist for a time.[23] Phygela (or Pygela) was reduced to a fort, in the charge of an official appointed by the king; the Ephesians were careful to continue to observe the religious festivals that took place there.[24] Local dynasts also indulged in this procedure. In Caria Pleistarchos

---

presupposes the physical transfer of a large part of the population of Euaimon to Orchomenos. See the good general discussion by Hornblower (1982: 79–81, 83–5), who stresses the two aspects of *synoikismoi*: political and physical.

[20] Welles (1934: 3–4). See now Cohen (1995: 188–9). That the *synoikismos* was in fact carried out has been argued recently on the basis of *SEG* 11 579 and xxvIII 697 by Ager (1998: 10–12). As Schmitt (1994: 37–8) has argued, the union of these towns should be regarded as an 'incorporating *sympoliteia*' ('Eingemeindungs- Sympolitie'). See also *Tit. Cal.* 12 (more at n. 35); *Milet* 1.3 149 (see below), *SIG*³ 647 (with n. 58). See also the very useful list of *sympoliteiai* (from which Schmitt borrows) at te Riele (1987: 187–8).

[21] See the discussion of Marijana Ricl, *I. Alex. Troas*, pp. 4–9. Also Cohen (1995: 145–8), Cook (1973: 198–204); on Antigonos' policies, which also embraced Smyrna and Kolophon, see Billows (1990: 294–5).

[22] On this 'force centrifuge des communautés absorbées' for Alexandreia see Robert (1951: 1–12, 35–6).

[23] The best treatment of this episode is now Robert and Robert (1989: 78–84). See also now Étienne and Migeotte (1998: 149–50) and Ager (1998: 6–8). Sources and brief summary of the history at Cohen (1995: 177–80), see also pp. 183–7 (Kolophon) and pp. 188–91 (Lebedos). A general overview of Lysimachos' activities as a founder of cities appears in Lund (1992: 174–7). I have not been able to make use here of Gattoni (1992).

[24] See the discussion in Robert (1967: 36–40) (*OMS* v 376–80); Robert and Robert (1989: 80–1).

renamed Herakleia under Latmos Pleistarcheia. Indeed, he may have been responsible for the original foundation, which involved the movement of the Carian town of Latmos by a few hundred metres; we now know that Latmos still existed, under its old Carian name, into the penultimate decade of the fourth century.[25]

The inscription that provides us with proof of Latmos' continued existence as Latmos at this late date is in fact a text full of interest for our purposes here. Though incomplete at the top and bottom, it preserves in forty-three lines a large part of the terms and conditions of a *sympoliteia* between Latmos and its neighbour Pidasa. The motivating personality behind this action was clearly the Carian satrap Asandros. The text calls for the complete absorption of Pidasa into Latmos, though perhaps not the demolition of the urban centre of Pidasa. A new tribe, the Asandris, was to be created at Latmos and filled by selecting members from all pre-existing tribes (*phylai*) in Latmos and phratries in both Latmos and Pidasa.[26] The remaining Pidaseans were to be distributed equally into the other tribes, and they were to enjoy full participation in the religious celebrations of the tribes and the phratries. The finances of both cities were to be unified, 'and nothing is to belong solely to either of the *poleis*', ἴδιον δὲ μηθὲν εἶναι μηδετέραι τῶν πόλεων (ll. 16–17). The Latmians were to provide the Pidaseans with suitable housing for one year – a clause showing clearly the intention utterly to terminate Pidasa's independent existence as a settlement. For a term of six years, Latmians were to marry only Pidaseans and Pidaseans only Latmians. Offices were to be common. Pidaseans were permitted to construct houses for themselves in the *polis* of Latmos (here *polis* is used clearly in the urban sense) on public land wherever they wished. Various oaths and publication requirements follow – most notably at the sanctuary of Zeus Labraundos, which must be, as Philippe Gauthier and C.P. Jones have argued,[27] the sanctuary north of Mylasa.

These terms make it abundantly clear that the predominant partner in this *sympoliteia* was Latmos. Pidasa as a *polis* would cease to exist by the terms of this agreement: every Pidasean would become a Latmian by tribal and phratral registration and by residence. The drafters of this agreement worked hard to anticipate and prevent possible sources of resistance. It is typical of the language of decrees that bring outsiders into a closed group

---

[25] See the summary at Cohen (1995: 261–3). The inscription is Blümel (1997); text reprinted in *SEG* XLVII 1563. For commentary see Habicht (1998), Blümel (1998*b*), Jones (1999*a*) and P. Gauthier, *BE* (1999) 462. The date is 323–313 BC (close to 313 according to Gauthier).

[26] Jones (1999*a*: 1–2), Pidasa possibly 'to continue as a subordinate *polis* in union with Latmos'. Habicht (1998: 9); for a different interpretation of this passage see Jones (1999*a*: 3–6) (cf. Brixhe, *BE* (2000) 540).

[27] At *BE* (1999) 462; also Jones (1999*a*: 6–7).

(e.g. *proxenoi* awarded citizenship) to make explicit the newcomers' right to participate in the group's religious life. Such participation was a fundamental marker of belonging. The specificity of the language here[28] seems to suggest a desire to cut off any possibility that the newly enfranchised Pidaseans might be treated as second-class citizens within their tribes or phratries. This fear was not theoretical, as we shall see in the case of the *sympoliteia* of Olymos and Mylasa. The Pidaseans were required to move physically to the urban centre of Latmos. It would be very interesting to know the fate of Pidasa: was it to become a fortress, like Kyrbissos after its absorption by Teos, or as indeed Pidasa itself became later? Finally, the requirement for intermarriage between Latmians and former Pidaseans for six years aimed to prevent any lingering sense among either group of continuing self-identity, by creating the complex social, economic and political links that marriage fostered between the people who had previously been citizens of different *poleis*. In the later *sympoliteia* between Miletos and Pidasa, the Milesians granted Milesian citizenship to all women married to Pidaseans, regardless of their *polis* of origin, as long as they were Greek – could this perhaps reflect continued interrelations between the Pidaseans and their Carian neighbours?[29]

The interests of Asandros are not hard to fathom.[30] Pidasa, whose location is now known, overlooks the routes of communication between Miletos[31] and Mylasa. Mylasa was Asandros' headquarters, and he was no doubt anxious to secure access between his capital and the most important port of western Caria; when the Milesians absorbed Pidasa in the 180s, they transformed the *polis* into a fortress for reasons that are plain in the local military and political context of that decade (see below for all this in more detail). In any case, the arrangement promoted by Asandros did not last, for Pidasa was again an independent *polis* in the third century until its absorption by Miletos.

Another example of a *sympoliteia* promoted by royal authority is that between Smyrna and Magnesia by Sipylos.[32] Before the *sympoliteia*, Smyrna had been steadfastly loyal to the Seleucids. It remained faithful during

---

[28] See ll. 10–13: τοὺς δὲ λάχοντας Πιδα[σ]εῖς μετέχειν ἱερῶν πάντων, τοὺς μὲν φράτο[ρ]ας τῶν φρατορικῶν, τὰς δὲ φυλὰς τῶν φυλετ[ικ]ῶν, οὗ ἂν [ἕ]καστοι λάχωσιν.

[29] See the interesting discussion by Vérilhac and Vial (1998: 72–3), citing also an inscription from Amyzon (Robert and Robert 1983: 35–6), but of course without knowledge of this new inscription.

[30] On Asandros see now O'Sullivan (1997) and Descat (1998: 180–4).

[31] The importance of Asandros' role in 314/13 as eponymous *stephanephoros* in Miletos (*Milet* I.3 122.101) is rightly stressed by Habicht (1998: 10).

[32] The text has been published and studied many times, including as *I. Smyrna* 573, *I. Magn. Sip.* 1 (with an extensive commentary by Th. Ihnken), *OGIS* 229, *Staatsvertr.* III 492. The most recent edition and detailed study is that of Rigsby (1996: 95–105), which see for previous bibliography.

the Laodikeian war (the Third Syrian War), and honoured Seleukos II by decreeing divine honours for his father Antiochos II and his mother Stratonike; in return, Seleukos secured for Smyrna 'autonomy and democracy', and wrote to 'kings and dynasts and cities and tribes' asking them to grant *asylia* for the sanctuary of Stratonikis Aphrodite and for the *polis* to be accepted as holy and *asylos*. In the context of the favour shown by Seleukos to Smyrna, the Smyrneans then sent an embassy to the soldiers at Magnesia (who formed two distinct groups) proposing that they keep faithfully in friendship and alliance forever with Seleukos; and that if they should guard the king's interests and have the same friends and enemies as him they would receive appropriate awards from the king and from the *demos* of Smyrna. The soldiers took the hint and sent an embassy to Smyrna proposing 'friendship' (φιλία), which the Smyrneans accepted. The agreement that follows in effect absorbed the soldiers at Magnesia into the body-politic of Smyrna.

Royal interests figure also in the incorporation of Kalymna into Kos by *homopoliteia*. Kos enjoyed excellent relations with the Ptolemies throughout the third century; the kings left the island independent, showered it with benefits, and offered protection in times of crisis.[33] The Kalymnians, too, had benefited from their association with the Ptolemies.[34] The connection between the *homopoliteia* that made Kalymna part of Kos in the later third century and Ptolemaic interests becomes explicit in the oath sworn by the Kalymnians to restore the arrangement, broken off during the first Cretan War: 'I will also abide by the friendship and alliance with King Ptolemy and by the agreements that have been ratified by the *damos* with its allies', ἐμμενῶ δὲ καὶ τᾶι ποτὶ βασιλῆ Πτολεμαῖον φιλίαι καὶ συμμαχίαι καὶ ταῖς συνθήκαις ταῖς ποτὶ τοὺς συμμάχους τῶι δάμωι κεκυρωμέναις.[35]

Finally, we may consider a last example from the third century concerning the Carian town of Chalketor. An inscription found there records the ratification of an order to create a *sympoliteia* between an unknown town and Chalketor; the details are left to the local *strategos*, one Iason, to work out. The king 'has written to the *boule* and the *demos* that he is adding to the boundaries of the *polis* the *demos* of the Chalketoreans so that sharing

---

[33] See the long discussion of evidence then known in Sherwin-White (1978: 90–124). See also now Segre (1993: ED 17 and ED 229) with Habicht (1996: 83–94).
[34] For example, by the receipt of dikasts (*Tit. Cal.* 17; cf. also *I. Iasos* 82, which Bagnall (1976: 91 n. 45) has suggested may be part of this text).
[35] Herzog (1942: 5, no. 2, ll. 18–20) (*Tit. Cal.* 12, *Staatsvertr.* III 545); translation of Sherwin-White (1978: 126), who has illuminated the political situation (pp. 124–9). See Höghammar (1993: 88–93); Krob (1997: 437) (a good summary). Cf. also Thomas Ihnken, *I. Magn. Sip.* p. 46. There is no evidence for the *sympoliteia* between Arykanda and Tragalassa suggested on the basis of *I. Aryk.* 1; see Wörrle (1996: 158).

citizenship equally and similarly (the *demos*) may participate in the same things with you', γέγραφεν τῆι βουλῆι καὶ τῶι δήμωι ὅτι προσ[ο]ρίζει τῆι πόλει τὸν τῶν Χαλκητορέων δῆμον ἵνα συμπολειτευόμενος ἐπ' ἴσηι καὶ ὁμοίαι τ[ῶ]ν αὐτῶν ὑμῖν μετέχηι (*I. Mylasa* 913.2–6). The language is couched in terms of a favour to the unnamed town from the king, who is extending its boundaries to gobble up Chalketor. This is a theme that recurs in other instances of *sympoliteiai* undertaken by royal order or with royal assent. That the *sympoliteia* occurs by expansion of boundaries shows also that the two towns were coterminous and that the arrangement involved an actual absorption of Chalketor by the other *polis*, in the sense that (from an outside perspective) where there had been two *poleis* with their *chorai* there was now but one of each. The king stresses the place of the Chalketoreans within this new entity as fellow-citizens, indeed of the whole *demos* of the Chalketoreans as sharer in citizenship with its new partner. No doubt the actual arrangements necessary to carry out this *sympoliteia*, left in the hands of the *strategos* Iason,[36] must have entailed the elaboration of detailed and difficult specifics such as we see in some other texts. As far as we can tell from the preserved parts of this inscription, the Chalketoreans were not required to abandon their town, as the Pidaseans were twice. In this respect – unless there were other terms – the *sympoliteia* of Chalketor with its unknown neighbour resembled that of Keramos with a likewise unknown neighbour. That arrangement, which came apart after a time of troubles, involved no physical movement of Keramos or its citizens, for the town continued to enjoy a healthy existence from the Classical period well into the Roman Empire.[37] Likewise Euromos was for a time linked by *sympoliteia* to its powerful neighbour Mylasa, but the arrangement collapsed and Euromos continued to exist as an independent entity.[38]

It would be interesting to know the motivation of the king who ordered the incorporation of Chalketor into one of its neighbours. Some time in the last quarter of the third century, perhaps precisely in 201 BC, Euromos – one of Chalketor's neighbours and suggested by L. Robert as its partner in the

---

[36] Cf. Blümel's commentary at *I. Mylasa* 913. Mylasa (Welles) and Euromos (Robert) have been proposed as the second town. See Robert (1934: 525), Welles (1934: 134–5), Marek (1982) with J. and L. Robert, *BE* (1983) 401; Crampa (1968: 176–7), Laumonier (1958: 162–3). L. Robert (1978c: 517); Cohen (1995: 261). Gabrielsen (2000a: 168–9) offers a somewhat speculative reconstruction of the history of Chalketor in the Hellenistic period. I do not know the basis of the claim that 'by the first century B.C., Mylasa had succeeded in snatching Chalketor from Euromos, adding it to its existing dependencies' (169). The entry for Iason in Grainger (1997: 95) is incomplete.
[37] *I. Keramos* 6.4: ἐν τῶι τῆς συμπολιτείας χρόνωι. Further discussion below. See now Spanu (1997), especially on the architectural history of the site.
[38] *I. Mylasa* 102.14–15. See the discussion below.

sympoliteia – was renamed Philippoi after Philip V of Macedon. Blümel has suggested that the expansion of Euromos' territory by the incorporation of Chalketor may have been an element in the reorganization of – and favouritism toward – the newly minted royal foundation. It has also been suggested recently that this reward drew the envy of the neighbouring Mylaseans, whose territory would have abutted on that of Euromos once they had absorbed Olymos.[39]

The interests of the Hellenistic kings (often enforced by their local representatives) in the *poleis* of Asia Minor are well known and need no particular emphasis here. The range of reasons, stated or suspected, which might induce a king to promote a *sympoliteia* runs the gamut. Lysimachos' refoundation of Ephesos has been rightly seen as providing the king with an important base for his operations; the brilliance of its location, which continued to be the city's home well into the Byzantine period, had first and foremost a significance for Lysimachos. Defence certainly was often at the top of their considerations, whether in making the situation of a city more easily defensible – perhaps, in some cases, by agglomerating populations to increase the number of men available for duty or to decrease the number of urban centres that needed to be defended[40] – or in punishing cities that had resisted royal power and might serve as loci of future discontent. No doubt increasing the size of a city's territory by adding another to it was a way to reward past and guarantee (one would hope) future loyalty. Fewer urban centres would also mean fewer garrisons – and so lower expenses and reduced opportunities for ambitious commanders to be tempted to rebellion. Certainly these considerations might be especially compelling in territories bordering on land under the jurisdiction of another king – in Caria alone, one might think of the *sympoliteia* of Kildara and a neighbour, perhaps Thodasa, or the foundation of Stratonikeia in the early third century, both on the marches between the Ptolemaic and Seleucid empires. Kings also had interests in improving the cities under their control, be it by building walls, expanding harbour facilities, or showering other benefits on them;[41] such improvements could serve military ends by (for example) making the

---

[39] The name is attested in an inscription published by Errington (1986): *SEG* XXXVI 973; P. Gauthier, *BE* (1987) 294; Ma (1999): 338, no. 29, text and translation); Cohen (1995: 261). Blümel in *I. Mylasa* II, p. 109. Gabrielsen (2000a: 168–9). See further below.

[40] One might consider the difficulties of defending great runs of fortification walls, like those of Herakleia by Latmos or the greatly expanded walls of Kolophon (which was in *sympoliteia* at the time with its neighbour Notion) of the late fourth century that incorporated the *palaia polis*: see Migeotte (1992: 214–23, no. 69), with full bibliography; Cohen (1995: 183–7). On fortifications see now McNicoll (1997: 75–105, 75–81 on Herakleia).

[41] For harbours see the examples listed at Jones (1992: 97–100); for benefits generally, the catalogue of Bringmann and von Steuben (1995).

supply of a city by sea easier, and fiscal ends by increasing revenue and so taxes. All of these ends might sometimes be most easily achieved through *sympoliteiai*, whether the partners were willing or not. Nor should we too readily dismiss the example of Alexander, whose shoes his successors strove to fill: Alexander's example as a founder of cities, reshuffling populations, recreating, relocating and renaming towns, played a fundamental role in the kings' self-advertisement, their self-presentation.[42]

III

The surviving lines of the inscription recording the absorption of Kyrbissos by Teos illustrate nicely some of the reasons that the predominant partner might have for taking over a smaller neighbour. Kyrbissos lay on the border of Teian territory. It had a fortress and a small population. The Teians' chief interest as revealed by the inscription was to guarantee the security of this fort. Strict regulations were imposed on the choice of a *phrourarchos* – rotated every four months – and his troops; care was taken to ensure that everyone would be properly armed and paid, and even the guard dogs properly fed. Here the overwhelming interest was clearly the security of Teos. Similar considerations operated in the absorption by Smyrna of Magnesia by Sipylos: Magnesia was to be turned over to an official sent by Smyrna, who would keep the keys, guard the city and keep it secure for Seleukos. That is to say, the Smyrneans obtained an expansion of their territory and firm control of a crucial fortress along with the troops occupying it.

Similar interests governed the Milesians in their absorption of neighbouring Pidasa by *sympoliteia* in the 180s, perhaps exactly in 187/6 BC.[43] The Milesians gained in security and expanded their territory. The security arrangements appear in the clauses of the agreement which call for the reconstruction of the walls of the fortress at the settlement of Pidasa and the dispatch by Miletos of a *phrourachos* and *phrouroi* who were to remain in the countryside (χώρα) and guard the region as the Milesians thought best (ll. 15–18). The expansion of Milesian territory occurred by the incorporation of the Pidasean *chora* into Miletos; this was facilitated by the construction of a new road suitable for wagons between Pidasa and Ioniapolis.[44] Broad economic concessions granted to the Pidaseans suggest the agricultural productivity of the new territory.

---

[42] See now the rich collection of evidence in Cohen (1995).
[43] *Milet* 1.3 149. See Wörrle (1988c: 428–48). For a date of exactly 188/7 see Errington (1989: 288), who gives the other suggestions; Peter Herrmann, *Milet* VI.1 (Berlin 1997) p. 184, remains agnostic. Gauthier (2001: 117): 'peut-être déjà 187/186'.
[44] See Peschlow (1977–8) for the location of this site.

The security advantages Miletos derived from this *sympoliteia* were probably connected, at least in part, to relations between Miletos and Herakleia under Latmos. One clause of the agreement, to which Philippe Gauthier has drawn attention, required the Milesians to act as advocates for the Pidaseans about land recently restored to them in case a dispute should arise (ll. 37–8). Taking up a suggestion of Michael Wörrle, Gauthier sees in this disputed land territory granted by Zeuxis, the powerful local agent of Antiochos III, to Herakleia a few years before. The loss of this territory would give the Herakleians reason to be angry at the Pidaseans, and the Pidaseans (as Gauthier has argued) reason to seek protection of a more powerful neighbour.[45] But the *sympoliteia* did not inaugurate tension between Miletos and Herakleia. Miletos had absorbed Myous by *sympoliteia* some time in the third century BC (Strabo 14.1.10 (636)). About 186–185 BC the Milesians fought a war with Herakleia caused in part by dispute over territory that the Milesians claimed as sacred land belonging to Myous but which the Herakleians claimed for themselves.[46] At dispute in this war was also a brickworks and its neighbouring *topos* claimed by the Milesians to lie within the boundaries of Ioniapolis but by Herakleians to be 'their own' (*Milet* I.3 150.81–3). A glance at a map[47] shows at once why Milesian expansion by Myous and Pidasa would alarm Herakleia. Herakleia lay at the eastern end of the Latmian Gulf, backed up against Mount Latmos; its arable territory was limited largely to the plain of Bafa, which occupies the territory from the eastern end of modern Bafa Gölü up to the saddle that separates it from the Euromis and Mylasean territory further east[48] – though at the same time one should not underestimate the importance of the mountain, which was laced with roads, forts and small settlements.[49] Immediately to the north-west, along the shores of the gulf, Miletos pressed against Herakleia by its absorption of Myous, a pressure that surely would have felt all the more intense after the award to Miletos of the disputed

---

[45] Wörrle (1988*b*: 445 n. 92); Gauthier (2001: 123). On Zeuxis see now Ma (1999: 123–30).

[46] *Milet* I.3 150.78–86 (and see now Ager 1996: 290–2, no. 108), which is now dated to 185/4: Errington (1989: 288); Herrmann, *Milet* VI.1 p. 186; and see on the war Ma (2000: 350–1). I follow here the reconstruction of Gauthier (2001: 123–4). It has been suggested that this territory is the same as that awarded by Philip V to Magnesia on the Maiandros in 200 BC after his capture of Myous and returned (as 'sacred territory', ἱερὰ χώρα) in 188 BC to the Milesians in the settlement after Apameia; see Polyb. 16.24.9, where Philip captures Myous and awards τὸ χωρίον to Magnesia in repayment for figs the Magnesians supplied, with 21.46.5: Μιλησίοις δὲ τὴν ἱερὰν χώραν ἀποκατέστησαν, ἧς διὰ τοὺς πολέμους πρότερον ἐξεχώρησαν (see Livy. 38.39.9) with Walbank (1979: 169); Herrmann (1965: 93–6).

[47] A good map at Gauthier (2001: 118). Map 61 in Talbert (2000) is less helpful, since it shows the putative shoreline of the delta of the Maiandros in late antiquity, when the geography had changed radically from the Hellenistic period.

[48] Nicely described, with photographs, by Robert (1978*c*: 510–15).

[49] See now Peschlow (1996) for a good overview.

sacred land. Around the western end of the gulf, on its south shore, was Ioniapolis – also Milesian territory. Pidasa was located at modern Cert Osman Kale on the north-eastern slopes of ancient Mount Grion, about halfway between Ioniapolis and Euromos, almost opposite the high point separating the territories belonging to Miletos and Herakleia from the Euromis valley.⁵⁰ The absorption of Pidasa placed Milesian authority, backed up by Milesian troops, even further toward the south-east, hemming in Herakleia even more. Miletos also enjoyed good relations with several powers great and small in this part of Caria. In 214 BC the Mylaseans had approached the Milesians with a request to establish mutual *isopoliteia*; the Milesians accepted.⁵¹ Recently an inscription published by Jeanne and Louis Robert has been reinterpreted – convincingly, I think – as an *isopoliteia* agreement between Miletos and the two small Carian communities of the Messabeans and the Hymesseans, both of which apparently lay north-west of Mylasa, perhaps on the lower reaches of Mount Latmos.⁵² Moreover, Herakleia had a historical claim to Pidasa itself, in the *sympoliteia* of the late fourth century, by which Pidasa was to have disappeared into Latmos (which became later Herakleia). Finally, we know of interests of Herakleia in the Euromis thanks to an inscription of Mylasa that alludes to conflict, perhaps even war, between Mylasa and Herakleia over Euromos.

Milesian security interests are clear. But Milesian economic interests (in the broad sense) also must have figured in this transaction. Though better endowed with territory than Herakleia, Miletos was nevertheless crammed

---

⁵⁰ The suggestion that Pidasa was at Cert Osman Kale was first made by Cook (1961: 91–6), immediately accepted by Robert (1978c: 493); see now Blümel (1997: 135, with full bibliography at nn. 1–2). For the relations between Miletos and Herakleia see the masterful monograph of Robert (1978c: 502–18), and now also Gauthier (2001: 124–7). On the interest in controlling forts see Ma (2000: 341–3). For Euromis see *Milet* I.3 149.40, where Pidaseans who owned land in the Euromis, ἐνεκτημένοις ἐν τῆι Εὐρωμίδι, were to be allowed to import wine up to 1,000 *metretai* from their own properties at an apparently reduced rate of harbour tax as long as they registered as owners in the Euromis (ll. 40–4). How did Pidaseans come to own land in territory clearly not their own? Baslez (1976: 356), followed by Migeotte (2001: 132), has compared these people to those who owned property on Rheneia near Delos and other groups similarly designated; she sees as comparable the people 'who own land in the chora of Miletos or farm it', τῶν ἐκτημένων ἐν τῆι Μιλησίων χώραι ἢ γεωργούντων (*Milet* I.3 150.73), who are to be permitted to bring cattle from Milesian territory through Herakleia's *chora* or *polis* (a striking image). But the issue is different, because in this case the referent is owners of property within Milesian territory, in the other it is Pidaseans who owned vineyards in the Euromis, controlled neither by Pidasa nor by Miletos. An explanation for this situation may be that Pidasa was recently in *sympoliteia* with Euromos – indeed, perhaps precisely in the late third and early second century – and that this *sympoliteia* may have broken up soon before the Milesians gobbled up Pidasa. I will discuss the evidence and arguments for this view in my Mylasa book. Generally on these groups of 'owners and farmers', see Reger (in press).
⁵¹ *Milet* I.3 146 (Schmitt, *Staatsvertr.* III 539; *I. Mylasa* T 51). For the date see now Wörrle (1988b: 437–9); Herrmann, *Milet* VI.1, p. 178.
⁵² Robert and Robert (1983: 216, no. 27C–D); Pontani (1997), cf. Brixhe, *BE* (1998) 388.

into the peninsula projecting into the sea with Didyma at its southern end. To the south-east, along a convoluted shoreline that hosted several small communities, lay Iasos.[53] Control of Myous brought with it part of the great Maiandros plain; the other direction in which good agricultural territory lay was south-east of Ioniapolis. The nature of the agricultural production that the acquisition of Pidasa entailed can be read in part from the concessions granted to the Pidaseans. Of the crops the Pidaseans grew, olive oil was to be taxed at the same rate as the Milesians paid, but other products were subject only to a nominal tax for five years; animals kept in the Pidasis and beehives enjoyed the same privilege, but for only three years. At the end of this period, taxes would revert to the levels paid by the Milesians (ll. 18–25). Not dissimilar tax concessions on agricultural products and capital investments like plough animals and beehives appear in part of a text uniting a small community with Teos.[54] Yields of property belonging to the gods or to the *demos* were granted the same tax reduction for five years, after which these goods too would pay at the Milesian rate except for grain grown in the sacred hills that had been marked off (τοῦ δὲ ἐν τοῖς ἱεροῖς ὄρεσιν τοῖς περιωρισμένοις γινομένο[υ] σίτου), on which only 1 per cent would be paid, forever (ll. 28–35). Pidaseans were granted a ten-year exemption from liturgies (ll. 35–7) and permanent tax advantages for importing wine up to a generous limit from their own estates in the Euromis (ll. 39–44). The construction of a road suitable for wagons from Pidasa to Ioniapolis facilitated the movement of goods (ll. 44–5). The Milesians were always looking for opportunities to increase their χώρα,[55] and here was an excellent one.

The Milesian–Pidasean *sympoliteia* thus encapsulates many of the advantages that absorption of a neighbour might bring to the predominant partner. To the increased security accorded by the establishment of a new, permanently manned fortified outpost and by the pressure placed on a long-standing local enemy can be added also the acquisition of new potential soldiers. Part of the population of Pidasa – up to 390 persons who had remained at the settlement – were moved to Miletos and provided with housing (ll. 25–8). Myous had lost its independence to Miletos on account of underpopulation, δι' ὀλιγανδρίαν (Strabo 14.1.10 (636)), and among the

---

[53] See now La Rocca *et al.* (1993).
[54] The inscription of Olamış, for which see Robert and Robert (1976: 175–88).
[55] See Louis Robert's (1978c: 515) apt remark (*à propos* the Mylaseans) that the Milesians increased their territory by *sympoliteiai*. This whole discussion, especially about the territories of Miletos and Herakleia, owes much to Robert's penetrating monograph on Herakleia (1987: 502–18). On the fiscal aspects of these clauses see Migeotte (2001).

variety of problems this situation surely created for the viability of Myous as a state, one of them must have been increasing difficulty in defending its territory. Miletos itself accepted a large number of new citizens in the third century, some mercenaries and other foreigners established there, among whom were a number of Pidaseans.[56] While in general it may be true that underpopulation can rarely be proven as a motivation for *sympoliteiai*,[57] concerns about just that problem do seem to hover around this instance.

There can be no doubt that Miletos was the predominant partner in this *sympoliteia*. The very first substantive clause of the inscription is unmistakable: 'The Pidaseans and their children and their wives, such as are Pidaseans by birth or citizens of a Greek *polis*, are to be citizens of the Milesians', εἶναι Πιδασεῖς Μιλησίων πολίτας καὶ τέκνα καὶ γυναῖκας ὅσαι ἂν ὦσιν φύσει Πιδασίδες ἢ πόλεως Ἑλληνίδος πολίτιδες (*Milet* 1.3 149.10–12).[58] But Gauthier points out that the impetus for the *sympoliteia* came, at least insofar as the record reveals, from the Pidaseans, who sent an embassy of ten ambassadors to treat with the officials of Miletos. The accord which they worked out included broad terms favourable to the Pidaseans. In addition to the numerous economic and social concessions granted to the Pidaseans – to which can be added housing in Miletos for Pidaseans who had remained at Pidasa up to the number of 390 persons (ll. 25–8) – the accord includes the clause, rightly emphasized by Gauthier, requiring the Milesians to act as the Pidaseans' advocates concerning land restored to them by the *strategoi* (to whom we shall return) in event of a dispute (ll. 37–9). For Gauthier, it was Pidasean fear of Herakleia that motivated them to seek help from their powerful neighbour, with its own history of hostility to Herakleia. The fundamental impetus toward the *sympoliteia*, in this view, derived from pressing Pidasean interests.

We can now see both the interests of the Milesians in accepting the Pidaseans' proposal and of the Pidaseans in making it, whatever its exact original content.[59] But there is still one more quite important matter. Gauthier has argued that the *sympoliteia* did not cause Pidasa to vanish as an

---

[56] *Milet* 1.3 33–119. For the Pidaseans see the references at Gauthier (2001: 125 n. 45). And see ll. 45–7 of the inscription: μετέχειν δὲ Πιδασέων καὶ τοὺς πεπολιτογραφημένους πρότερον τῶν αὐτῶν πᾶσ[ιν] Πιδασεῦσιν πλὴν <πλὴν> τῆς ἀτελείας τῶν λειτουργιῶν.

[57] As argued by Sartre (1995: 65–8), a good overview.

[58] Gauthier (2001: 119–20), citing as parallels te Riele (1987) (Thür and Taueber 1994: 98–111, no. 9, ll. 3–6) and *SIG*³ 647 with Salviat and Vatin (1977: 77–80). Gauthier also argues (less convincingly, in my view) against the *communis opinio* that the inscription we have is the actual *sympoliteia* agreement, and not a supplement to a fuller agreement in a now lost document. Cf. also Migeotte (2001: 130).

[59] It is possible that the Pidaseans came to the Milesians with a proposal that would have preserved Pidasa's autonomy but still guaranteed Pidasa's security in the face of possible aggression from Herakleia – say, a proposal for a *symmachia*. Negotiations with the Milesians – who, as we have seen,

entity. The Pidaseans seem not to have been distributed into the Milesian tribes, and many Pidaseans clearly continued to live in the former territory of Pidasa, enjoying the protection of the Milesian troops stationed at their former settlement. They seem to have formed a 'communauté à la fois unie à Milet et distincte d'elle' and 'le territoire qui leur a été restitué continuera à leur appartenir'.[60] In other words, the Pidaseans did their best to maintain markers of their own self-identity as a community. They had, of course, an earlier experience of what it would mean to vanish completely into another state; however they achieved freedom from Latmos – whether by Asandros' departure, by failure of the *sympoliteia* to be carried out, or some other means – the example surely remained fresh in their collective political memory. But they were hardly the only community in Caria to seek continued self-identity and limited autonomy within the context of unification with a predominant partner. Myous itself enjoyed similar status with respect to Miletos, as Peter Herrmann has argued.[61] But this view must not be pushed too far. It is certainly true that the Pidaseans enjoyed at least five markers of continued self-identity: residence in their territory (though not in the old urban centre of Pidasa), the right to pay reduced taxes forever on the grain grown on certain properties belonging to the Pidasean gods and *demos*, an indefinite claim on Milesian advocacy for the property returned to them, the permanent right to import wine from their properties in the Euromis at an advantageous tax rate, and, if Gauthier's arguments are accepted, incorporation into the Milesian civic body as a group rather than being distributed one by one among its tribes. At the same time, however, other such markers – the rest of their tax exemptions and the freedom from service in liturgies – disappeared after set terms; in these respects, the Pidaseans would eventually merge with the rest of the Milesian civic body. And once the *sympoliteia* had been formalized by oath, Milesians would be free to buy property in the old Pidasis and to marry into Pidasean families – processes that, over time, would surely reduce, and surely in some cases wholly submerge, Pidasean identity for individuals. What would finally be left, interestingly enough, would be the right of importing wine from estates in the Euromis (which by marriage and sale might eventually fall into 'Milesian' hands) and the rights to pay reduced taxes on grain grown on the public and sacred properties of the former Pidasa.

had their own interests in this matter – could have resulted in an agreement to absorb Pidasa by *sympoliteia* with certain guarantees. Other possibilities can also be imagined.
[60] Gauthier (2001: 126).
[61] Herrmann (1965: 91–6). See further below. Gauthier (2001: 127) cites Myous too.

IV

For many of the little *poleis* of Asia Minor, self-identity as an independent entity stretched well back into the fifth century or beyond (as a glance at the entries in the Athenian Tribute Lists, with their masses of names, in some cases of polities otherwise entirely unknown, will show). Their sense of self-identity was tied up with their history, their land and most especially their cults, and they were often reluctant to see that identity disappear into the ethnic of some greater Miletos or Mylasa. In a recent article on the absorption of Lebedos by Teos ordered by Antigonos Monophthalmos, Sheila Ager has stressed the resistance of the Lebendians and their efforts to protect their own identity in the face of threatened extinction; they ultimately prevailed, preserving their *polis* as an independent entity for the next several centuries.[62] This same striving to retain self-identity, even to the point of keeping the organs of *polis*-life, like assemblies, magistracies, and even more extreme forms of self-assertion (as we will see in the case of Olymos), can be found throughout the Hellenistic world, as has been repeatedly remarked in recent years.[63]

How smaller partners achieved the preservation of self-identity can sometimes be seen in the very terms of the agreements by which the predominant partner incorporated them. In the late third or early second century the two Lokrian towns of Myania and Hypnia joined in a political union. Some of the terms survive in an inscription.[64] The agreement goes to great lengths to define the continued rights of Hypnia, clearly the junior partner; its citizens had a claim on public offices, foreign courts might be invited to settle differences between the two towns, each town guarded its own land (though watchtowers and border forts were manned in common), and at one point regulations even indicated what should be done if an archon failed to manage properly the business of the *poleis* (εἰ δὲ μὴ διοικέοι τὰ τῶν πολίων, col. II, ll. 12–13). The sense of persistent separate self-identity here is very strong indeed. Within Asia Minor (indeed, within Caria) the *sympoliteia* between Plarasa and Aphrodisias shows similar traces of a continuing sense of self-identity of the two partners. The *sympoliteia* probably was created some time in the second century BC;[65] our first evidence for it is probably the coins bearing the 'double ethnic', which conventionally are

---

[62] Ager (1998).
[63] For the cities of Crete involved in *sympoliteia*, see Chaniotis (1996b: 107), with multiple examples; Hansen and Nielsen (2000: 145–6) on Drystos; generally, Hansen (1997: 37).
[64] Bousquet (1965: 665–81, date at 670–1). Cf. Schmitt (1994). On the different impact on habitation patterns of various *sympoliteiai* in Phokis and Lokris see the remarks of Rousset (1999: 57 n. 115).
[65] See Robert (1962: 64).

put after 166 BC.⁶⁶ Our first epigraphical evidence comes in (probably) the late 120s BC as an oath consecrated 'on behalf of the alliance and eternal harmony and brotherhood that exists toward each other', ὑπὲρ τῆς πρὸς ἀλλήλους ο[ὔσης] συμμαχίας καὶ ὁμονοίας [αἰ]ωνίου καὶ ἀδελφότητος (ll. 7–9), between Plarasa/Aphrodisias and the *poleis* of Kibyra and Tabai. The text speaks of 'the *demoi* of the Plaraseans and the Aphrodiseans and the (*demos*) of the Kibyratians and the (*demos*) of the Tabenoi', οἱ δῆμοι οἵ τε [? ν.] Πλαρασέων καὶ Ἀφροδισ[ι]έων καὶ ὁ Κιβυράτων καὶ ὁ Ταβηνῶν (ll. 2–5).⁶⁷ The use of the plural of *demoi* in reference to Plarasa and Aphrodisias, followed by the careful iteration of the singular article ὁ before the ethnics of Kibyra and Tabai, expresses exquisitely the sense that, despite the arrangements that had created a combination of these two communities, they continued to regard themselves in at least some respects as separate: the *demoi* of the Plaraseans and the Aphrodiseans. The same feeling emerges from a later inscription which, in speaking of the 'magistrates, *boule*, *demos* of the Plaraseis and the Aphrodisieis', Πλαρασέων καὶ Ἀφροδεισιέων ἄρχουσιν, βουλῇ, δήμῳ,⁶⁸ at once illustrates concretely one element of the institutional combination of the towns – political structures – and the persistent separate self-identity. The persistence of the double ethnic at Aphrodisias until roughly the reign of Augustus bespeaks the length of time required for the populations of the two constituent states finally to submerge their identity into a single 'Aphrodisias' – but with habitation continuing at Bingeç, generally agreed to be the site of Plarasa.⁶⁹

Another example of a *sympoliteia* in which the identity of the partners remains preserved in the name of the new, combined entity appears in

---

⁶⁶ Head (1896: 25–8); MacDonald (1992: 59–73). The existence of Plarasa as an independent community before the *sympoliteia* is attested by a single type with ΠΛΑΡΑΣΕΩΝ alone in the legend; MacDonald (1992: 59).
⁶⁷ Reynolds (1982: 6–11, no. 1, ll. 2–5). For a date for this inscription in the 120s see Bresson, Brun and Varinlioğlu in *HTC* p. 187, with further references. For the restoration ο[ὔσης] in place of φ[ύσει] I am indebted to Riet Van Bremen, who drew my attention to the clear trace of *omicron* (not *phi*) on the published photograph.
⁶⁸ Reynolds (1982: 16–20, no. 3, ll. a3–5), of soon after 85 BC.
⁶⁹ The double ethnic appears in Reynolds (1982): no. 1, ll. 2–4, quoted in the text; 16–20, no. 3, l. 5 (quoted in text above), soon after 85 BC; 20–6, no. 4, ll. 1–2 (restored, but certain), late second/early first century BC (p. 26); 41–8, no. 6a, ll. 8–9, under Octavian; 48–54, no. 7, ll. 3–4, Triumviral period; 54–91, no. 8, ll. 21, etc. (the famous *senatus consultum*); 92, no. 8a, line 5 (restored); 92–6, no. 9, l. 6, etc.; 99–101, no. 11, l. 1. Aphrodisias only in 26–32, no. 5, l. 12; Reynolds comments: 'It cannot . . . be taken as quite certain that the reference to the *demos* of Aphrodisias is not a slip (or shorthand) for the *demos* of Plarasa/Aphrodisias; the formula would then be the earliest evidence for a tendency, which reached its conclusion in the Augustan period, when Plarasa dropped from the city's name altogether' (31). This list is not meant to be exhaustive. I am in agreement with Chaniotis (forthcoming: n. 13) in preferring the views of Reynolds (1982) to Reynolds (1985) about the character of the *sympoliteia* between Plarasa and Aphrodisias.

the combination of two small towns in southern Caria, Pisye and Pladasa. Inscriptions of the late fourth century attest to the independent existence of Pladasa as a *polis*. The town was located near the Gulf of Akbük on the Gulf of Keramos, and controlled a port. By some time in the middle of the third century, however (between 275 and 225 BC), a part of the population of Pladasa had joined with Pisye in a combination called τὸ πλῆθος or τὸ κοινὸν τὸ Πισυητῶν καὶ Πλαδασέων τῶν μετὰ Πισυητῶν. This designation persisted as late as the first century AD. We do not know the exact circumstances that brought about this union of Pisye with part of Pladasa, though it may have had something to do with the financial troubles that Pladasa was having in the late fourth century. It is clear, however, that Pisye – which was located about 15 km north-east of Pladasa, in the interior – gained a port in the bargain; the interest of Pisye in obtaining access to the sea may help explain the bargaining power of the Pladaseans in the arrangement which preserved their identity in the new designation of the unified community. The same was not true of other entities, like the Koloneis and the Londeis which Pisye had likewise absorbed, possibly before taking part of Pladasa (as their territories lay between Pisye and Pladasa).[70]

We can obtain another view of this sense of persisting self-identity by investigating in rather more detail the character of the *sympoliteia* between Mylasa in Caria and its near neighbour and junior partner Olymos.[71] In this *sympoliteia* we can trace something of what the arrangement meant to

---

[70] For independent Pladasa see Bresson, Brun and Varinlioğlu in *HTC* no. 47 (pp. 157–9: *polis* at ll. 6–7) of 319/18 BC, and no. 48 (*ibid.* 159–71). The earliest inscription with the combined community, in which the unified entity is called a *plethos*, is no. 1 (*ibid.* 95–105) of 275–225 BC; the latest, in which it is a *koinon*, dated to between 50 BC and AD 50, is no. 37 (*ibid.* 144–5); other instances: no. 3 (106–7) of 150–100 BC; no. 5 (110–11) of the first century BC; no. 4 (108–10) of the second half of the first century BC. An exception appears in no. 42 (153–4), in which the *koinon* is designated as of the Piseteis without the Pladaseis; there is no obvious explanation (see the commentary at p. 153). The absorption of the Londeis and the Koloneis (whose localization at Yeniköy-Küçükbelen is likely but not absolutely certain: see *ibid.* p. 154) by Pisye is attested by 275–225 BC in the inscription just mentioned (no. 1); on the location of these sites see the map and the discussion by Brun in *HTC* (26–9 Pisye, 43–4 Londeis, 45–6 Koloneis? and 52–64 Pladasa). See also Gabrielsen (2000a: 131–4). It remains possible (though in my view less likely) that Pisye and Pladasa were not coterminous if territory belonging to Panamara interceded between them through the third century; see now for a discussion of this problem Debord (2001a) and van Bremen in this volume. Bresson, Brun and Varinlioğlu in *HTC* (pp. 165–6) suggest that the balance of the Pladaseis was absorbed by Keramos.

[71] *I. Mylasa* 861, first published as Le Bas and Waddington (1870: no. 339). An unpublished inscription mentioning the *sympoliteia* was reported by Robert (1935: 159); Robert (1945: 27), (1962: 55 n. 3), and *I. Mylasa* II, pp. 51–2 and nos. 892–3 all refer to this inscription. Not all the texts relevant to this matter have yet been published. I plan a full treatment of this *sympoliteia* in the context of Mylasean expansionism of the later third and early second centuries BC in my book on Mylasa. Debord (2001b: 29 n. 62) notes the impact of the absorption of Labraunda by Mylasa; for a recent treatment of the whole episode see now Dignas (2002: 59–69). The views expressed here were developed in part in

the Olymeans on the basis of a series of documents, even though we do not have the inscription (if one ever existed) on which the terms of the arrangement were spelled out. Discussion must now start with *I. Mylasa* 866, first published by W. Blümel in 1988. The stone was damaged recently and rendered almost unreadable in the middle, but Blümel and E. Varinlioğlu were able to produce a good text. The inscription dates clearly to the third century BC on the basis of its lettering, language and orthography. It bears the decree of the Olymean *demos*, passed in a *kyria ekklesia*, for one Polites of the unidentified city of Terssogassa. He is granted typical honours, including citizenship, and is to be enrolled in the tribe of his choice, [εἶ]ναι [δὲ α]ὐτὸν φυλῆς ἧς ἂν [αὐτὸ]ς θέληι (ll. 7–8).[72] Since we know that the *phylai* of Olymos were demoted to *syngeneiai* of Mylasa when the Mylaseans absorbed their neighbour, this decree is undoubtedly a document dating to before the *sympoliteia*, when Olymos was still an independent city.[73] The simplicity of the opening formula of this inscription is worth noting. There is no dating by *stephanephoros* or other eponymous official and no indication of who proposed the motion, only the bare, 'It has pleased the Olymeans, the *ekklesia* having been *kyria*', [Ἔδο]ξεν Ὀλυμεῦσιν, ἐγκλησίας κυρί[ας γενομένης] (l. 1). Later Olymean decrees passed after the *sympoliteia* inevitably include the name of the eponymous *stephanephoros* and usually the name of the man who proposed the decree.[74]

This change in the habits of the Olymeans after their absorption by Mylasa provides the key to understanding the considerable importance of three other Olymean inscriptions, hitherto partly unpublished. A stone bearing the right side of one text (*I. Mylasa* 872) and the left of a second (*I. Mylasa* 868) was found and published by E. Hula and E. Szanto.[75] On 9 October 1934, Louis Robert refound this stone and another which bore the right side of one text (868) and the left half of a new third decree.[76] The formulae of all three decrees were identical; in his papers on Mylasa

---

a presentation to John Ma's graduate seminar at Princeton University in 1999. I am grateful to him and his students for useful comments.
[72] The Τερσσωγασσεῖς may appear also in a fourth-century list of ambassadors, *I. Mylasa* 8.7; see also Blümel (1998: 181).
[73] *I. Mylasa* 867, awarding citizenship and the right to own land to an *euergetes* (there is room to restore an ethnic at l. 2, ΙΣ – – –) and inscribed on the same block as 866, has a different formula – the *kyria ekklesia* is absent – but on the other hand, unlike later decrees issued after the *sympoliteia*, lacks a date by eponymous *stephanephoros*. The text is too incomplete to say whether the honorand was enrolled in a tribe or a *syngeneia*. The lettering on the two inscriptions is very similar.
[74] For example, *I. Mylasa* 861, 801, 802, etc., and now also Blümel (1995: 40–1, no. 3); the *stephanephoros* can be restored in the first line.
[75] Hula and Szanto (1895) II 7, no. 5, as left column (872) and 7–8, no. 5, as right column (868).
[76] Robert (1935: 158–9). The precise date derives from Robert's contemporary field notes.

Robert was able to restore all three almost *in toto*. Wolfgang Blümel has now refound the second stone (till now unpublished) and provided texts for all three decrees.[77] These inscriptions point to a new political environment for Olymos, betrayed in the first place by the dating formulae. The presence of the name of the *stephanephoros*, a date by month and day, and the expression Ὀλυμέων τῶι δήμωι, along with the absence of a *kyria ekklesia*, suggest that these three decrees were all passed after the *sympoliteia* with Mylasa.[78] Decisive confirmation comes from the enrolment of the honorands into the *syngeneia*, not tribe, of their choice: for the Olymean tribes were demoted to Mylasean *syngeneiai* as part of the *sympoliteia*. Since the letter forms of these three new decrees belong unequivocally to the third century, though certainly somewhat later than those of *I. Mylasa* 866, the *sympoliteia* can be dated with absolute confidence to that century, and certainly to the second half, since the freedom of Mylasa in 246 BC provides the *terminus post quem*.

These three decrees, passed after Olymos had been absorbed into the Mylasean state, grant citizenship: πολιτεία. The fact that they are decrees of the Olymean *demos* and not of Mylasa guarantees that this citizenship is Olymean only, not Mylasean. It is also remarkable that when the honorands are named with their full names at the beginning, no ethnic is given. This absence would be inexplicable if the honorands were actually foreigners, citizens of another state;[79] it must mean that the honorands were already in some sense 'citizens' of Olymos when 'citizenship' was awarded, and this can only be the case if Olymos had already joined Mylasa in its *sympoliteia* and the honorands were themselves citizens of Mylasa. An inscription of Myous that dates to the late third century BC provides a useful parallel. The Myesians honour Apollodoros Metrophanes, *stephanephoros* at Miletos in 212/11 BC, without an ethnic because, as a Milesian, he is at once

---

[77] Blümel (2000*b*); see also Blümel (1998*c*: 392–3) (preliminary text of the new inscription).

[78] The opinion of J. and L. Robert, *BE* (1939) 370, that 'le décret d'Olymos Hula-Szanto, n. 5 remonte à une époque bien antérieure au synécisme avec Mylasa, au IIIe siècle', was based on their view that the *sympoliteia* occurred in the later second century. They of course did not have the decrees of independent Olymos now available and discussed above. Errington (1995: especially 36) has recently shown that the expression *kyria ekklesia* fell out of use by the early second century at the latest, but the historical inferences drawn from that demonstration have been rejected by Philippe Gauthier, *BE* (1996) 121. Domingo Gygax (2001: 127–9) argues that this institution should be attributed to Hekatomnid times. For another view – that the presence of a *kyria ekklesia* marks a polity with some real autonomy, especially over financial matters – see Behrwald (2000: 51–62).

[79] When Mylasa grants foreigners citizenship, it always gives the ethnic; see, e.g., *I. Mylasa* 118.13, 14, 16 (Koan), 126.3 (Rhodian), 133.2 (Alabandan), etc. And see the important remarks of Robert (1983: 503), on an inscription from Apollonia by the Maiandros: 'un élément capital qui n'a pas été remarqué, observation négative inéluctable. Si Mardonios était de Chios et que la copie eût été envoyée dans sa ville, on lirait nécessairement son ethnique, etc.' See also Reger (1998: 15 with n. 19).

a fellow-citizen and a foreigner.⁸⁰ Precisely the same circumstances recur in *I. Mylasa* 876. A commission of Olymeans was 'elected by the *demos* of the Olymeans according to decree (for the purpose of) distributing those who have become Olymeans into *syngeneia* and *patra*', ἐπικλη[ρῶσαι] τοὺς γεγενημένους [Ὀλ]υμεῖς ἐπί τε συγγένειαν καὶ πάτραν (ll. 8–9). The absence of a *phyle* guarantees that we are in the period after the *sympoliteia*, but the reference to people 'who have become Olymeans' indicates the granting of Olymean citizenship. This procedure, whatever its exact 'constitutional' value, was clearly no rarity at Olymos.

Why would the Olymeans want or need to grant their fellow-citizens citizenship? The explanation lies in the nature of the relationship between Olymos and Mylasa that the *sympoliteia* created. Olymos, as an entity, did not simply cease to exist after the *sympoliteia*, even though its tribes were reduced to *syngeneiai* of Mylasa, any 'foreign policy' it may have pursued ended, and its citizens enjoyed full participation in the civic life of Mylasa. Many institutions of independent Olymos continued to function much as they had before. Most notably, the chief civic cult of Apollo and Artemis enjoyed a striking revival; in the course of the following decades, much new property was assigned to these gods.⁸¹ The Olymeans were very concerned that the cult not be desecrated by participation by inappropriate persons (*I. Mylasa* 861), and the priesthoods of these deities seem to have been reserved for Olymean families. The Olymeans continued to think of themselves as a *demos*; the Olymean *ekklesia* met regularly to pass decrees honouring their citizens (*I. Mylasa* 869–71) and to deal with the purchase by Apollo and Artemis of agricultural estates. There is good evidence to suggest that the Olymean aristocracy worked to maintain a separate identity even after the *sympoliteia*.⁸² A parallel can be found in an inscription from Lindos on Rhodes. A decree of the Lindians from the late fourth century BC honoured two boards of Lindian officials who had seen to it 'that the elections occur in Lindos of priests and *hierothytai* and *hieropoioi* and the others who are put in charge of common matters from the Lindians themselves according to the provisions written in the laws, and that no one participate in the rites in Lindos who did not also participate before', ὅπως ταὶ αἱρέσιες γίνωνται ἐν Λίνδωι τῶν ἱερέων κ[αὶ] ἱεροθυτᾶν κα[ὶ]

---

⁸⁰ Herrmann (1965: 91–6), with Herrmann's excellent commentary (more on the relations of Myous and Miletos below). I thank John Ma for reminding me of the relevance of this text.
⁸¹ See Chandezon (1998) and Dignas (2000), (2002: 95–106) for recent studies of these transfers, with earlier bibliography. A number of these texts are yet to be published (see n. 1).
⁸² My views on this topic were developed very provisionally in 'Agriculture and the rural landscape of Hellenistic Mylasa', read at the Annual Meeting of the American Philological Association, 27–30, December 1996.

ἱεροποιῶν καὶ τῶν ἄλλων τῶν ἐπὶ τὰ κοινὰ τασσομέν[ω]ν ἐξ αὐτῶν Λινδίων καθ' ἃ καὶ ἐν τοῖς νόμοις γέγραπται κα[ὶ μὴ] μετέχωντι τῶν ἐν Λίνδωι ἱερῶν οἳ μὴ καὶ πρότερον μετεῖχον.[83] The Lindians had fought a court case against the other constituent *poleis* of the *polis* of Rhodes to confirm these rights to local exclusivity in religious office and participation; in precisely the same way the Olymeans exerted their claims to exclusive control of their sanctuary of Apollo and Artemis over against the Mylaseans who were technically, but not fully, their fellow-citizens. These examples show clearly the persistent sense of local identity of the less powerful entities in a *sympoliteia*, especially where religious matters were concerned.

The *sympoliteia* between Mylasa and Olymos was permanent. After the great spate of Olymean inscriptions, including the land-transfer texts, which tell us so much about Olymos and its interests, silence prevails; we do not even hear anything more about the sanctuary whose rights the first generations of Olymeans become Mylaseans worked so hard to preserve. Perhaps, as the memory of independence faded, as young people grew up who thought of themselves as Mylaseans only, the sense of Olymean identity disappeared. The older generations' struggles may have ultimately been a failure.

But not all *sympoliteiai* lasted forever.[84] An inscription mentioned several times before of probably the early second century attests to a one-time union between Mylasa and Euromos. This union no doubt followed on that with Olymos, since it was probably only with the absorption of Olymos that Mylasean territory came to border on that of Euromos. We are ignorant of the circumstances of the union (except that it seems to fit in a general period of territorial expansion by Mylasa), but it is clear from our one text that the *sympoliteia* excited the hostility of Herakleia. A citizen of Mylasa, Moschion, was honoured for his long career of public service; among his duties was an embassy: 'When the Euromeans were in *sympoliteia* with the *demos* (sc. of Mylasa), and sacred equipment and private property of individuals were still being held in Herakleia, he was dispatched to the

---

[83] *IG* XII.1 761.38–43. On the date see Pugliese Carratelli (1949: 158) and Fraser (1952: 194). Generally now Gabrielsen (1997: 132). Note also the successful efforts of the Carian Telmisseans, in the second century, to preserve the privileges of their sanctuary of Apollo against attempts by the *polis* to which they belonged (surely Theangela) to encroach; Hicks (1894) with Şahin and Engelmann (1979: 220), Debord (2003: 143–4).

[84] As perhaps the suppositious *sympoliteia* of the Lorenoi with Gordos (see Peter Herrmann, *TAM* v, p. 255, with further references), a discussion of which prompted the Roberts to observe that 'une sympolitie pouvait avoir des formes assez différentes tout en étant une vraie sympolitie. C'est une histoire avec changements rapides que celle des ces toutes petites villes avec des synécismes, des sympolities, des autonomies recouvrées...' (*BE* (1977) 450).

Herakleians and managed well the interests of the *polis*', Εὐρωμέων τε συμπολιτευομένων τῶι δήμωι, τῶν τε ἱερῶν κατασκευασμάτων ἔτ[ι] δὲ καὶ τῶν ἰδίων ἑκάστου ὑπαρχόντων κατεχομένων ἐν Ἡρακλεία[ι], ἐξαποσταλεὶς πρὸς Ἡρακλεώτας κατῳκονομήσατο τὰ συμφέροντα τῆι πόλει (*I. Mylasa* 102.14–18). The Herakleians also took the property of a particular Mylasean who had either taken up residence or, perhaps more likely, owned property in Euromos. Moschion got it back (ll. 18–23). The Mylasean–Euromean *sympoliteia* would have created a common boundary between Mylasa and Herakleia, and apparently led to hostilities, perhaps even a minor war.[85] It is no surprise that Mylasa should have welcomed good relations with Miletos, another erstwhile enemy of Herakleia.[86]

Another example is provided by the temporary *sympoliteia* of Keramos and an unnamed partner. Our knowledge of this arrangement comes from an inscription of Keramos in honour of a Keramean citizen which obviously recounts many events in a long and illustrious career, rather like the famous Athenian decree for Kephisodoros (*ISE* I 33 with *ISE* III, pp. XIV–XV). The relevant text reads:

in the time of the *sympoliteia* he continued to say and do everything on behalf of what was advantageous, making the most powerful displays of his own good disposition to the whole people, and he behaved lovingly to the citizens who met him individually about matters about which they cared; and after these things, when the state fell into a difficult situation, he, undeterred by the quite-certain threatening of some, tried to increase his good disposition toward the people by saying and doing everything nobly and truthfully.

ἔν τε τῷ τῆς συνπολιτείας χρόνῳ διετέλει πάντα κα[ὶ λέγ]ων καὶ πράσσων ὑπὲρ τῶν συμφερόντων, παντὶ τῷ πλήθει τῆς ἰδίας εὐνοίας τὰς κρατί[στα]ς ἀποδείξεις ποιούμενος ἰδίᾳ τε τοῖς ἐντυγχάνουσιν τῶν πολιτῶν ὑπὲρ ὧν προηροῦν[το] προσεφέρετο φιλοστόργως· μετά τε ταῦτα ἐν δυσχερεῖ καταστάσει γενομένου τοῦ πο[λ]ιτεύματος οὐ καταπλαγεὶς τὴν τινῶν ἀνάτασιν πολὺ βεβαιοτέραν ἐπειρᾶτο τὴν πρὸς τὸ πλῆθος αὔξειν εὔνοιαν γνησίως καὶ ἀληθινῶς ἅπαντα καὶ λέγων καὶ πράσσων. (*I. Keramos* 6.4–9)

The precise historical circumstances alluded to here escape us now;[87] but for our purposes there are important implications for understanding what

---

[85] W. Blümel in his comm. on this passage (*I. Mylasa* I, p. 27) infers 'Raub und Plünderung'. The best treatment still in a few pages by Robert (1978c: 515–18). Recently Brixhe (*BE* (1995) 527) has suggested that a Euromean decree for one Amyntes (Errington 1993: 28–9, no. 7) was issued during the period of *sympoliteia* with Mylasa; cf., however, the doubts of Gabrielsen (2000a: 169 n. 133), whose own reconstruction of Euromean history in this period is in turn fragile; I will return to these questions in detail in the book on Mylasa mentioned at n. 1 above.

[86] *Milet* 1.3 146 (*Staatsvertr.* III 539; *I. Mylasa* T 51). For the date see Wörrle (1988b: 437–9).

[87] Spanu (1997: 17–18), who places the *sympoliteia* some time after 167 on the basis of his interpretation and dating of Keramean coinage (32–4); in Reger (1999: 84–5) I had suggested very tentatively

breaking a *sympoliteia* might mean. The honorand had worked hard during the *sympoliteia* on behalf of both the polity as a whole and individuals. The phrase τοῖς ἐντυγχάνουσιν τῶν πολιτῶν is intriguing, for it appears often in decrees honouring foreigners in other *poleis* who helped citizens of the honouring *polis*, and so carries here a distinct flavour of the honorand not being at home when he helped fellow-citizens who came to him; but the phrase – and the situation – is ambiguous, so it is impossible to say with confidence whether the honorand of this inscription was living away from Keramos when he undertook these services.[88] After the *sympoliteia* was terminated, he worked even more actively to restore the Keramean polity, which was apparently thrown into confusion by the change. It is not hard to imagine what sort of confusion might be created by the dissolution of a political arrangement that had allowed people now suddenly foreigners to (say) buy land in Keramos, participate in cult, intermarry, and otherwise impinge on the status of Kerameans.

Reasons for the failure of some *sympoliteiai* to hold over the long term were no doubt complex. In cases in which the *sympoliteia* resulted from royal decisions, it may well be that once royal authority disappeared, the glue that held the partners together simply came unstuck. This was clearly the case with Teos and Lebedos, which snapped back to their original

---

another set of historical circumstances in the 240s, if the attribution of Stratonikeia to Rhodes belongs in this period. There has been strenuous debate recently about these matters (see the works cited in *ibid.* 95 n. 25, to which now add Bringmann and von Steuben (1995: 238–9), the *non liquet* of Gabrielsen (2000a: 172), and n. 14 above, *ad fin.*). At the risk of sounding wishy-washy, I must stress that my suggestion was offered only as another possibility. Rereading the inscription today, I am now struck by how much the stress on the honorand's role in establishing an alliance with the Rhodians, which Keramos judged 'crucial for itself', [καὶ τοῦ] δήμου κρίναντος ἀναγκαιοτάτην εἶναι ἑαυτῷ τὴν πρὸς Ῥοδίους συμμαχία[ν] (ll. 13–14), seems to echo the circumstances of 188, when we know that other Carian states petitioned the Rhodians for special consideration (see Reger 1999: 97 n. 48). Moreover, it is important to remember that the view that the *sympoliteia* of the Kerameans was with Stratonikeia is merely a theory, behind which stands the authority of Louis Robert (1962: 60–1). See now Debord (2001a: 165) for a restatement of Robert's views.

[88] In *IG* XII.6 120, an honorary decree for the *strategos epi Karias*, the Samians recall his benefits [καὶ] ἰδίαι τοῖς ἐντυγχάνουσι Σαμίων (l. 4) and elect an embassy to take a copy of the decree to him (ll. 29–30): so he was evidently not at Samos when he helped Samians who came to him. Herodes, citizen of Priene, seems to have assisted fellow-citizens while he was at Pergamon, but the context is highly problematic (*I. Priene* 109.100); see also the Athenian Kallias who, while stationed at Halikarnassos, continued to help privately Athenians who came individually to him: ἰδί[αι ἑ]κ[άστου τῶν] πολιτῶν τῶν τε παραγιγνομένων πρὸς αὐτὸν [τὴν πᾶσαν ἐπ]ιμέλειαν ποιούμενος (Shear 1978: 4, ll. 70–6, ll. 74–6 quoted here). On the other hand, Diokles son of Ameinias, also a citizen of Priene, behaved honourably καὶ [κοινῆι παντὶ τῶι δήμωι] ἰδίαι τε τοῖς ἐντυγχάνου[σιν αὐτῶι τῶν πολιτῶν] (ll. 12–13) apparently while at home in Priene; it is later that the inscription apparently mentions an embassy, see now the composite text of *I. Priene* 82 in Ma (1999: 348–9, no. 33). More commonly τοῖς ἐντυγχάνουσιν *vel sim.* is used in decrees of persons from the honouring *polis* meeting honorands from another *polis*: *IG* XI.4 716.6–7, Delians honouring Nabis king of Sparta; *IG* XII.6 30.6–7 (*SIG*³ 333), Samians honouring a Lycian who had helped them in exile; *I. Priene* 65.7–8.

configuration after the death of Antigonos Monophthalmos, and was surely also the case with Kolophon and Lebedos (but not Phygela), which resumed independent lives once the interests of Lysimachos were removed.[89] When *sympoliteiai* did break up, much would seem to depend on the success of the smaller partners in maintaining their identity in the face of the larger polity. The Olymeans struggled mightily to do so but ultimately, it would seem, failed; the Lebedeans succeeded.

In this context it is perhaps worth saying a few words about the later Hellenistic and Roman imperial *sympoliteiai* of Lycia. These have been well studied by Martin Zimmermann, to whose discussion I have little to add.[90] But there is one feature of these *sympoliteiai* that distinguishes them strikingly from those we have been studying, and that is that the very citizenship formula which they deploy preserves explicitly the identity of the smaller member *poleis*. For example, an inscription from Idebessos records honours voted for a Roman by 'the *demos* of the Idebesseans which is in *sympoliteia* with the Akalisseans and the Kormeis', Ἰδεβησσέων ὁ δῆμος συμπολιτευόμενος Ἀκαλισσεῦσι καὶ Κορμεῦσι (*TAM* II 830 = *IGR* III 646). Through its league Lycia had of course a long tradition of federal government that did not subsume the identities of its individual *poleis*, which continued to act as at least semi-independent entities; they even awarded each other *isopoliteia*, as a recently published text reminds us.[91] Perhaps it was this tradition, along with a sensitivity to the jealousy of the smaller partners, that helped make the Lycian *sympoliteiai* of the imperial period work.

One striking feature of many of the *sympoliteiai* so far discussed, and which Louis and Jeanne Robert stressed many times, is the persistence of local identity of the component *poleis*, and particularly of the lesser partners in the arrangement, which had the most to lose in the submergence of their identity into that of the larger and more powerful partner. This tendency created a tension that, as we have seen, could destroy the new polity the *sympoliteia* aimed to fashion, especially when an outside force – like a king – was responsible in the first place. How did successful *sympoliteiai* negotiate this tension? In some cases it was by the eventual submersion of the junior partner. But another approach was to recognize, explicitly, the longings of the smaller partner to retain a separate identity, and not just by temporary arrangements, but in a more permanent, structural way.

---

[89] Ager (1998: 14–15) (Lebedos); Robert and Robert (1989: 83–4) (Kolophon).
[90] Zimmermann (1992: 123–44). See now also Behrwald (2000: *passim*) and Domingo Gygax (2001: 116) on Arneai as the centre of a *sympoliteia*. See also Hatzopoulos (1993: 168–9) on a similar institution at Gazoros in Macedonia.
[91] Bousquet and Gauthier (1994: 319–47). See now also Wörrle (1999: 359–61).

We saw some of that in the continuing concessions to Hypnia when it was absorbed. Another mechanism may have been borrowed from an institutional arrangement prominent in a very successful local *sympoliteia* in south-western Asia Minor: the *sympas demos* of Rhodes.

V

The phrase σύμπας δῆμος recurs in decrees and statue bases from a number of towns in western and southern Asia Minor and on islands off the Asia Minor coast. Its basic thrust was illuminated long ago in a lapidary remark of Maurice Holleaux, who wrote of an inscription from Stratonikeia in Caria in which it appeared that 'Manifestement, elle désigne l'ensemble du peuple de Stratonicée par opposition aux différents dèmes.'[92] Holleaux did not observe, however, that the expression seems to be closely tied to states which had been created out of formerly independent *poleis*, or had formerly independent *poleis* which still enjoyed a certain degree of self-government as constituent parts. An inscription of Plarasa/Aphrodisias in Caria of soon after 88 BC affirms that 'our whole *demos* with our wives and children and all our wealth' is ready to support Quintus Oppius, proconsul of Cilicia in 88 BC and an important figure in the early stages of the Mithridatic War.[93] The expression is not identical here (πᾶς, not σύμπας), and so may not be technical; but since Plarasa and Aphrodisias were united in the *sympoliteia* whose administrative features appear in this text, it is possible that this is an instance of the use of the phrase to refer to the whole sympolitized state in contradistinction to its constituent parts.

An inscription of the late third century BC bears a decree of Kalymna honouring a citizen who participated valiantly in the defence of the island in the first Cretan War of 205 BC. The Kalymnians describe the war as 'against the whole *demos*' (τῶι σύμπαντι δήμωι) even as they refer to themselves as 'the *polis* and the *chora* and the islands of the Kalymnians' (ἐπὶ τὰν πόλιν καὶ τὰν χώραν καὶ τὰς νάσος τὰς Κα[λυμνίων]).[94] At this time the Koans and the Kalymnians were linked in the *homopoliteia* discussed above. The

---

[92] Holleaux (1904: 363). Louis Robert chose not to republish this page of Holleaux's article in the collected *Etudes* (vol. IV (1952); cf. 204 n. 1). The inscription is *IS* 7, discussed further below. The phrase has been restored in an inscription from Mytilene dated by its most recent editor to 332 BC (Labarre 1996: 252–5, no. 2, l. 39; the inscription, readily available as *OGIS* 2, has been republished many times). The analysis offered below gives reason to suspect this restoration, though I have no alternative to offer.

[93] Reynolds (1982: 11–16, no. 2, col. 2 ll. 11–12): πᾶς ὁ δῆμος ἡμῶν σὺν γύναιξι καὶ τέκνοις καὶ τῶι πάντι βίῳ. See also the interesting expression at *TAM* II 905 VIII 102–3.

[94] *Tit. Cam.* 64 ll. 9–10 (*SIG*[3] 567); see Sherk (1990: 263–4). On the war and the circumstances see Baker (1991). In the *ed. pr.*, Herzog (1902: 318) took the phrase σύμπας δῆμος and the words *polis* and *demos* to refer all to the Koans.

subdivisions of Kos on the island also used the expression to distinguish their own actions from those of the state as a whole. A decree of Halasarna, for example, passed around 200 BC to regulate access to the rites of the sanctuaries of Apollo and Herakles at Halasarna, included only foreigners 'to whom citizenship had been given by a common law or decree of the whole *damos*', οἷς <δὲ> δέδοται ἁ πολιτεία, κατὰ τίνα νόμον ἢ δόγμα κοινὸν τοῦ παντὸς δάμου.[95] This 'whole *damos*' is of course the Koan state, as can be seen in a newly published honorary decree of the second century BC praising a *dikastagogos* sent to Smyrna who 'guarded . . . the trust voted him by the *sympas demos*', διαφυλάξας . . . τὰν ἐνχειρισθεῖσαν αὐτῶι πίστιν ὑπὸ τοῦ σύμπαντος δάμου.[96] Susan Sherwin-White has linked this usage, rightly in my view, with the *synoikismos* of Kos that brought together previously separate entities into one polity. Its appearance at Halasarna may add some slight weight to the notion that, like Astypalaia, Halasarna too may have been an independent state on Kos before 366 BC.[97]

The phrase appears in the Mylasean inscription discussed above in connection with Euromos. Early on the decree remarks that the honorand Moschion was predisposed from youth 'to be useful privately to each of the citizens and in the commonweal to put together things advantageous to the whole *demos*', ἰδίαι μὲν ἑκάστωι τῶν πολιτῶν εὔχρηστος γ[ί]νεσθαι, κατὰ κοινὴν δὲ τῶι σύμπαντι δήμωι τὰ συμφέροντα συνκατασκευάζειν (*I. Mylasa* 102.11–13, cf. also l. 14). The expression *sympas demos* recurs in *I. Mylasa* 109, a decree of the tribe of the Otorkondeis for a Mylasean who served as ambassador to Marcus Iunius Silanos, governor of Asia in 76/5 BC.

The appearance of *sympas demos* in these two texts has been used to support the view that the *sympoliteia* between Mylasa and Euromos should be dated to roughly this time, i.e. the first decades of the first century BC.[98] But the situation in Mylasa was more complicated than simply absorbing Euromos. Two other decrees of the Mylasean tribe Otorkondeis note that the honorand had served in office 'worthily not only of the tribe but also of the whole *demos*', ἀξίως οὐ μόνον τῆς [φυλῆς ἀλλὰ καὶ] τοῦ

---

[95] Pugliese Carratelli (1963–4: 183–201, no. XXVI A37–41); *SIG*³ 1023; Paton and Hicks (1891: 367).
[96] Crowther, Habicht and Hallof and Hallof (1998: 88–95, no. 1 ll. 23–5).
[97] Sherwin-White (1978: 181–2); on Halasarna as perhaps independent (1978: 58 with 61–3), and now Reger (2001: 174 with n. 88). It is worth noting the relations between Halasarna and the whole Koan state as expressed in the honorary decree for Herodotos son of Herakleitos (now fully published as Hallof and Hallof and Habicht 1998: 121–4, no. 13), especially at ll. 20–6. The appearance of the expression τῶι σύμπαντι δήμωι in a fragmentary inscription of Iasos (*I. Iasos* 4 1 15) leads to the suspicion that Iasos too may once have absorbed one or more neighbours by *sympoliteia*. On Samos, σύμπαντος δήμου ὁμονοίας (*IG* XII.6 13a22), in an obscure context.
[98] Cf. Blümel's commentary *ad loc*.

σύμπαντος δήμου.⁹⁹ Another tribal decree carries exactly the same expression (*I. Mylasa* 110, ll. 6–7). The famous Mylasean decrees of the mid-fourth century BC condemning individuals who had conspired to assassinate Maussolos during a celebration at the sanctuary of Zeus Labraundos required that the verdict be confirmed by the three Mylasean tribes (*I. Mylasa* 1, ll. 2–3; *SIG*³ 167). While the precise situation remains unclear, these inscriptions show that the Mylasean tribes enjoyed real political authority in the 350s, at least in some contexts, whatever the ultimate source of that authority may have been, and whatever changes it may have undergone over the centuries – though certainly there are no further examples of Mylasean decrees 'ratified' by the tribes.¹⁰⁰ In any case the important point for our purposes is that even as late as the Hellenistic period the tribes that made up Mylasa, or at least the Otorkondeis, the most prominent one, continued to feel the articulations between their identity and that of the state as a whole. The later addition to Mylasa by *sympoliteia* of Olymos, other small communities absorbed by the Mylaseans, and (temporarily) Euromos can only have heightened the feeling that the Mylasean state was composed of a series of previously independent (or perhaps in the case of the tribes, quasi-independent) entities which continued to insist on exercising some of the privileges of independent states. It comes as no surprise then to find *sympas demos* recurring especially in tribal decrees throughout the Hellenistic period.

In a decree from the sanctuary of Panamara in the territory of Carian Stratonikeia the *koinon* of the Panamareis praised Leon son of Chrysaor for having persuaded 'the whole *demos*', τὸν σύμπαντα δῆμον, to accept certain sacrifices in honour of Zeus Panamaros. Moreover, the *koinon* elected a representative to go before the *boule* and the *demos* to relate the honours voted 'in order that the whole *demos* recognize the honours given by the *koinon*', ὅπως δὲ καὶ ὁ σύμπας δῆμος ἐπιγνῶι τὰ δεδογμένα τῶ[ι] κοινῶι τῶι Παναμαρέων (*IS* 7.6 and 27–8).¹⁰¹ Although the precise

---

⁹⁹ *I. Mylasa* 106.6; the recurrence of the phrase at the Otorkondeis' second decree guarantees the restoration, 107.5.

¹⁰⁰ Behrwald (2000: 54 n. 157) attributes the notion of a growth in autonomy of the tribes across the Hellenistic period to Hornblower (1982: 69 with n. 120), but Hornblower simply notes that we have no more instances of decisions ratified by all three tribes, rather the 'later inscriptions record decisions only of the individual tribes'. But these are not decrees of independent entities; they are tribal decrees, passed within the political framework of the *polis* of Mylasa. For a recent attempt to provide an integrated account of the role of the tribes in Mylasean political life see Caldesi Valeri (1998). One may now compare the recently published decree of Mylasa: Gauthier (1999: 17–36).

¹⁰¹ See now van Bremen (this volume); also Reger (1998: 11–17), with further bibliography and discussion. Other examples of the phrase: *IS* 344.1–2 (partly restored, but probably rightly); 512.24–5, of Lagina. Gabrielsen (2000a: 166) takes *sympas demos* to refer to 'a federal assembly', presumably that

manner in which the territory of Stratonikeia was constructed by the Seleucids in the later 270s or 260s remains unclear, there can be no doubt that Stratonikeia was created by the assembly, whether through *sympoliteiai* or *synoikismoi*, of the pre-existing settlements now well attested epigraphically and in several cases located archaeologically.[102]

P.M. Fraser and G.E. Bean suggested many years ago that the use of the phrase *sympas demos* at Panamara in Stratonikeia might indicate Rhodian influence.[103] There is indeed no doubt that it is at Rhodes where the expression occurs most frequently. On Rhodes σύμπας δᾶμος refers to the Rhodian state as a whole in contradistinction to the δᾶμοι of its three constituent *poleis* after the *synoikismos* of 408/7 BC.[104] However, it is not clear at what point the phrase came to be the standard designation for the whole Rhodian state. An early decree of Lindos, passed some time around the Rhodian *synoikismos* – but possibly before 411 – refers to a person as *proxenos* 'of all the Rhodians', Ῥο[δ]ίων πάντων (*Lindos* 16.6).[105] An inscription honouring Nikagoras who was general in the Peraia during the war against Philip V indicates that he served 'from all', ἐκ πάντων (*Lindos* 151), which has been taken as equivalent to *sympas damos*.[106] This may be doubted, for other examples occur of the phrase 'having served as general from all', στραταγήσας ἐκ πάντων, in inscriptions from Kamiros of the later third and first centuries BC,[107] when the phrase *ho sympas damos* is

---

of the *koinon* of the Chrysaoreans (so perhaps Debord (2001*b*: 33)). But such an interpretation does not sit well with the other evidence we have for the use of this term in Caria at this date. Many years ago Larsen (1945: 77–9) saw the Chrysaorean League as a *sympoliteia* of the *Bundesstaat*-type, with typical 'double citizenship' marked by ethnics like Χρυσαορεὺς [ἀπ]ὸ Μυ[λασῶν] (*IG* II² 2315.24); some scholars have followed this view (Mastrocinque 1979: 220), others have been more cautious (Spanu 1997: 22, 'ciò è possibile, ma non certo'). But, as we have seen, this type of organization – if accepted as the basis of the Chrysaorean League – is different from the *sympoliteiai* that are our concern here. On the League see now Gabrielsen (2000*b*: 157–61).

[102] For a good brief introduction with bibliography see Cohen (1995: 268–73), and now van Bremen (2000) on the organization of the territory of Stratonikeia, with full bibliography.

[103] Fraser and Bean (1954: 128–9 n. 4).

[104] See, e.g., van Gelder (1900: 234), citing Ross (1846: 191), as the first to make this identification; Papachristodoulou (1989: 51); Gabrielsen (1997: 26) and now Gabrielsen (2000*b*: 190–1). Sometimes ὁ σύμπας δῆμος comes to be used in a way that verges on, or even becomes identical with, *ekklesia*: e.g. when a deme elects a man to ask 'in the *sympas demos*', ἐν τῶι σύμπαντι δάμωι, about the gift of a crown and the erection of a stele (*IG* XII.1 1032.32–3; *Lindos* p. 1009); see Gabrielsen (1994: 117–35). But this usage clearly derived from and is explained by the more basic function of the expression as a way of designating the whole Rhodian state as opposed to its constituent parts.

[105] This inscripton must now be considered in light of the cautionary remarks of Gabrielsen (2000*b*: 179–80).

[106] Cf. Blinkenberg, *Lindos* p. 400, citing F. Hiller von Gaertringen, *SIG*³ 586 n. 5 (*IG* XII.1 1036) and 673 n. 2 (*IG* XII.3 103 of Nisyros). See now, however, Dmitriev (1999: 243–53) and on the Nikagoras dossier Gabrielsen (2000*a*: 153–6).

[107] E.g. *Tit. Cam.* 76 (*IG* XII.1 700), which Segre put after the mid-third century (*LGPN* I, s.v. Ἀλεξίμαχος [49] gives second century BC without explanation), and 78 (much improved text over

used in contemporary texts in a different context. Here the emphasis lies on the fact that the honorand was elected from the whole civic body of the Rhodians, not just from the members of the *polis* of Kamiros. *Sympas damos* carries a different flavour.

The earliest well-dated use of the phrase at Lindos does not come until slightly before 154 BC, in a decree in which the *demos* of the Nettidai honours Astymedes son of Theaidetos who has been well disposed εἴς τε τὸν σύμπαντα δᾶμον καὶ εἰς τὸν Νεττιδᾶν (*Lindos* 216).[108] Other occurrences are notably later, as in *IG* XII.1 762.6 (Sokolowski, *LSCG* 235–6, no. 137), a decree of the Lindians which confirms a decree of ὁ σύμπας δῆμος (l. A6),[109] or in the famous statue base for Athanodoros son of Hagesandros but by adoption of Dionysios,[110] who was priest of Athena Lindia in 22 BC (*Lindos* I J 1.38–9), honoured because of the piety, excellence, good will and love of good reputation that he showed 'toward the people of Lindos and the whole *damos*', εἰς τὸ πλέθος τὸ Λινδίων καὶ εἰς τὸν σύμπαντα δᾶμον (*IG* XII.1 847.14–15).[111] At Kamiros Segre restored the phrase in *Tit. Cam.* 71.4, a fragmentary inscription honouring the commander of undecked ships (*aphraktoi*); from the lettering it looks to belong to the earlier second century, or perhaps even the third, but too little is preserved to be sure. The earliest certain instance from Kamiros is *Tit. Cam.* 86.12–13: εἰ[ς] τὸ πλῆθος τὸ Καμιρέων καὶ τὸν σύνπαντα δᾶμον, a text not dated by the editor but coming from a statue base honouring one Sulla son of Sulla, Kasareus, who is not likely to have lived earlier than the first century BC.[112] There are other

---

IG XII.1 701 based on Hiller's revisions for the never published second edition of *IG* XII.1), which Hiller von Gaertringen associated with the Roman civil wars of the mid-first century; see Jacobsthal (1933: 24–5, no. 1), quoting Hiller followed by Segre. Other examples: *Tit. Cam.* 74, of ca 100 BC (see Kontorini 1983: 67–71, no. 8, with the date at 68–9) and 75. On the other hand, the context assures that εἰς τὸ σύμπαν in *Lindos* 389a of about AD 7 (*IG* XII.1 849) is equivalent to *sympas damos*. For Athenian use of the expression for election from the whole Athenian *demos* see Stroud (1998: 4–5, l. 37), with Stroud's brief commentary at p. 68 and further references.

[108] *Lindos* 216 dates to before 154 BC because that year saw the honorand's service as priest of Athena Lindia; cf. *Lindos* p. 121.

[109] The instance of τὸν σύμπαντα δᾶμον restored at *IG* XII.1 829.13 has been eliminated thanks to a join with another fragment; see *Lindos* 384C d.

[110] On these adoptions see most recently Gabrielsen (1997: 112–36).

[111] The same man was honoured, no doubt at the same time, by the Lindians as a whole for his services [εἴς τε τὸ]ν σύμπαντα δᾶμον [καὶ εἰς τὸ π]λῆθος τὸ Λινδίων (*IG* XII.1 856 + 852, as restored at *Lindos* p. 489). Other examples from Lindos: *Lindos* 281a17 and 281b18, ca 100 BC; 297.13, before 74 BC; 305.17, ca 70 BC; 307.13, slightly before 65 BC; 328.7, ca 70–50 BC; 330.15, ca 70–50 BC; 332.8–9, ca 70–50 BC; 333A14–15, ca 50 BC; 338.6, ca 50 BC; 345D, 46 BC; 379b7, ca 25 BC; 384b4, ca 9 BC (important restorations to ll. 15–16, not affecting the argument here, at Fraser and Bean (1954: 2)); 389ab17, ca 7 AD; 392a4 and 392b3, AD 10; 395.7, AD 10; 398.18, ca 10 AD; 404a5–6 and 404b15, ca 20–10 BC; 406.7–8, end of the first century BC; 415.12–13, before AD 20.

[112] *LGPN* I, s.v. Σύλλας, with a date of the first century BC or the first century AD. See also the Sulleia at *IG* XII.1 918, which dates to the first century AD.

examples.¹¹³ Perhaps the earliest instance may come in an inscription from Amos in the Rhodian Peraia. The Amians honoured Xenomenes, elected as general for 'Apeiron and Physkos and the Chersonasos' 'by the whole *damos*', ὑπὸ τοῦ [σ]ύμπαντος δάμου (*I.Rh.Per.* 357.5–6; Bresson 1991: no. 52). In the *editio princeps* Fraser and Bean dated the inscription to 'the earlier part of the second century BC'.¹¹⁴ Alain Bresson is much more cautious, giving a range of 200 years.¹¹⁵ An inscription from Karpathos honouring a Rhodian doctor which mentions the *sympas damos* probably dates to the second century BC; two other Karpathian texts are probably of about the same date and later.¹¹⁶

In 408/7, the three Rhodian *poleis* of Ialysos, Kamiros and Lindos joined to create a new pan-island state with a new capital at Rhodos town. This amalgamation rested on a long history of cooperation recently stressed by Vincent Gabrielsen, nor was it completed all at once.¹¹⁷ The final result, however, was extraordinarily successful. The Rhodians resisted the Athenians in the latter stages of the Peloponnesian War, and while they succumbed for a while to Maussollos, they led the anti-Athenian coalition in the so-called Social War and beat back Demetrios Poliorketes in the famous siege. They supported a burgeoning fleet, had widespread commercial success, enjoyed excellent relations with the Ptolemies, and saw an extraordinary influx of support when the island was devastated by an earthquake in 228/7. Their role in policing the sea earned them the respect of many (though their tactics may not always have been beyond reproach).¹¹⁸ At the same time, as we have seen, the Rhodian *poleis* continued to assert their traditional identities and to protect their traditional privileges, especially in the religious sphere; this independence was institutionalized and partly reflected in the distinction between the *damoi* of Rhodes and the *sympas damos*. It may therefore be reasonable to suppose that the Rhodians, who had been a combined state for almost ninety years by the death of Alexander, may

---

¹¹³ For example, Maiuri (1925: 39–40, no. 25) (*Tit. Cam.* test. 26, incomplete), probably of the first century BC, honours for a woman given by the *sympas demos* (l. 3), and Kontorini (1989: 149–52, no. 63, l. 18), of the first decades of the first century BC.
¹¹⁴ Fraser and Bean (1954: 85), followed slightly imprecisely (as first half of the second century) by Blümel, *ad loc.*
¹¹⁵ Bresson (1991: 83). Likewise *LGPN* I, s.v. Ξενομένης (9).
¹¹⁶ *IG* XII.1 1032, with the mention at l. 32 (see Gabrielsen 1994: 125–6); the doctor appears again with his wife (also a Samian) and son in a Rhodian subscription list, Pugliese Carratelli (1939–40: 167, no. 20 II 21–4); cf. *LGPN* I, s.v. Μηνόκριτος (2) and (3). The other inscriptions are *Lindos* p. 1009, ll. 50–1 (improved text resulting from Segre (1933: 379–82) + *IG* XII.1 1033; see Gabrielsen (1994: 127–8)), which is second century, and *IG* XII.1 1035.10, the latter of which seems to key into *IG* XII.1 46.249 and so to date to *ca* 64 BC.
¹¹⁷ See now Gabrielsen (2000*b*).   ¹¹⁸ See the revisionist article of Gabrielsen (2001).

have provided their neighbours with a model of how to organize a sympolitized state without either crushing the component *poleis* or allowing them so much self-identity that the new polity self-destructed. A possible early copy-cat might be the Koan *metoikesis* of 366/5, which, as in the case of Rhodes, created a single, pan-island state where there had been at least two *poleis* before, and where the expression *sympas demos* recurs.[119] But, of course, the Rhodians owed their political success to much more than the way they articulated the interactions of the three *poleis* of the island. Whether the *poleis* of south-western Asia Minor which may have borrowed their approach also were able to make their *sympoliteiai* successes depended on local political and social situations, not always favourable to the permanence of the arrangement.[120]

VI

Sympoliteiai promoted by kings or their agents seem to aim at obliterating previously existing cities. Antigonos wanted to meld Teos and Lebedos into a single entity. Asandros issued rules governing the submergence of Pidasa into Latmos that sought even to control marriage decisions. An unknown king attached Chalketor and its territory to another city. With Seleucid support Symrna gobbled up Magnesia by Sipylos. These amalgamations were marked by a violence no less real for being merely ideological, directed as it was against civic identity. It is no surprise, then, that these *sympoliteiai* also tended to be less enduring. When the royal power that wanted the unification evaporated, the parties often broke up, sometimes after having resisted the consummation of the union even in the face of royal displeasure. That is to say, *sympoliteiai* promoted by kings served kings' interests. Those interests revolved, as one might expect, around military security and royal income. Local wishes counted for little, but local wishes often had the last word.

Sympoliteiai driven by local concerns show strikingly different features. While the same general worries – local security and economic prosperity – drove cities to unite without apparent outside pressure, the landscape in which these transactions took place had a very different look. For one thing,

---

[119] I am not persuaded by the arguments of Stylianou (1998: 484–5). See Reger (2001: 171–4).
[120] The phrase *sympas demos* appears also in states farther away from Rhodes than the mostly Carian ones canvassed above. For example, *I. Magn. M.* 100.11 (*SIG*³ 695) has τῶι σύνπαντι πλήθει. The expression recurs at Termessos in *TAM* III 3A11–12 of the second century AD; at Gordos (Malay and Petzl (1984) with *BE* (1984) 384) and at Attaleia (Bosch 1947: no. 1 with *BE* (1948) 229). These are all of course late.

the differential in power was not so great; even a Pidasa had some leverage to negotiate the best deal it could with powerful Miletos. And it is clear again and again – in Plarasa and Aphrodisias, in Mylasa and Olymos, in Miletos and Pidasa – that the predominant partner in local *sympoliteiai* (if I may use this shorthand) had some sympathy for the weaker partner's urgency in preserving aspects at least of its identity once the union was established. No surprise that much of this sensibility – as we can see for example in Mylasa and Olymos – focussed on the preservation, as something separate and distinct, of the cults and cultic property of that weaker partner. Cult and *polis* identity were inextricably linked; nothing could have been more difficult for a proud citizen of a little polity undergoing *sympoliteia* than the prospect that the gods would no longer be worshipped in the right way, if at all.

Once again, too, we have another example of the value of the local optic. Under the radar screen of the great struggles among the great powers, local politics thrived. Local concerns, local conflicts, local resentments, local alliances wove the fabric within which the citizens of the Hellenistic cities lived most of their lives. To secure oneself against the predations of one's neighbour – best by gobbling things up first, or at least having some say in who would gobble you up, and how – or to increase one's prosperity by adding to one's *chora* and one's population were obvious aims for any responsible local patriot. As the history that these struggles created emerges more and more from obscurity, we can begin to reclaim some sense of balance *vis-à-vis* the struggles of the great powers, and to obtain a more nuanced understanding of the realities of politics on the local level.

The possibility that Rhodian political culture in the form of the relations between the former Rhodian *poleis* and the amalgamated Rhodian state influenced Carian practices reveals again the crucial role Rhodes played on the mainland. It was not just as proprietor of the Peraia or as the overlord of much of Caria between 188 and 167 that Rhodes exercised its influence: it was, throughout the Hellenistic period, the most important state in southwestern Asia Minor. This importance grew with its alliance with Rome – shattered but not destroyed by missteps in the war with Perseus – but it was not that alliance which created the Rhodian aura in Caria. In part this aura traced back to the Classical period, for Rhodes had always been a great local power, but in part it must also have been owed to the Rhodian role as a counterweight to the great powers, principally the Seleucids and the Ptolemies, who fought repeatedly over Caria. As arbitrator, as ally, as a fellow *polis*, Rhodes was a political player operating with many of the same assumptions as the Carian towns, and on a scale that, though certainly greater than any Carian town could claim, was nevertheless much closer to the *polis* model than the great territorial empires. Rhodes mattered.

The *sympoliteia* between Miletos and Pidasa remarks that the sacred land recently restored to Pidasa was granted to it by the 'generals' (*strategoi*). Louis Robert pointed out a number of times that these 'generals' were not local Milesian officials, but rather Roman magistrates. The newly established date for this inscription (perhaps exactly 187/6) puts events in the immediate aftermath of the war with Antiochos, when Rome was settling Caria, and indeed much of western Asia.[121] Rome did not instigate the *sympoliteia*, but Roman decisions certainly did provide part of the impetus – not only in placing the Pidaseans in a position in which they felt threatened, but in giving Herakleia reason to feel aggrieved. Rome played an increasingly important role in Asia Minor thereafter, and though no direct evidence is known to me, the Romans must have been aware of the readjustments that such combinations created. A systematic treatment of *sympoliteiai* of Asia Minor might well reveal more concretely the character of Roman interests. For example, I have the impression – but it is only an impression – that the rate at which *sympoliteiai* occur falls markedly as Roman presence in Asia becomes more visible. But this needs testing.

Finally, why Caria? Caria exhibits – again, impressionistically – a striking frequency of attested *sympoliteiai*. It is obvious that these cannot be attributed to a single cause, for some of them were promoted by royal authority while others flowed out of purely local considerations. Perhaps Caria's position as a frontier between Seleucid and Ptolemaic dominions may have contributed to the eagerness to unite. Kings on either side of the divide may have found enlarged states easier to control and better able to defend themselves; the patchwork of small *poleis* and other polities that characterized Classical Caria may have seemed to their rulers too vulnerable to attack and conquest by the armies of the other side (such considerations may perhaps lie behind the newly attested *sympoliteia* of Kildara and Thodasa). The Rhodian *synoikismos* of the late fifth century, so successful, may have spurred Carian polities to imitation. But the highly local character of Caria, with its small agricultural plains and plethora of communities nestled in valleys or up in the mountains, full of self-pride and suspicion of greedy neighbours, may have been an important element, too. Answers may come from a study more complete and more systematic than this one.

---

[121] Robert (1962: 62 n. 7), cf. (1978c: 515); Gauthier (2001: 123, with further references at n. 35).

CHAPTER 6

Hellenism on the periphery: the case of Cilicia and an etymology of soloikismos

Giovanni Salmeri

I

Anyone who has the intention of working on topics even remotely connected with solecism and theories of solecism in antiquity has the good fortune to have at their disposal a work by Pierre Flobert[1] which clarifies many of the central points. Above all, this scholar illustrates how in the first phases of their use – the sixth century BC – the meaning of the terms *soloikos* and *soloikizô* was not connected with the linguistic sphere: rather, they channelled in a quite general way notions of the coarse, the clumsy and the incongruous. Flobert demonstrates, moreover, how the logical meaning of solecism (to conduct false reasoning), well attested in Aristotle and Chrysippus, preceded the grammatical one (to commit an error against good syntactic usage); and he has good grounds for arguing that the passage from the logical to the grammatical sphere was effected by Diogenes of Babylon, one of the emblematic figures of Middle Stoicism. As for the two principal ancient etymologies of the term solecism, one of which derives it from *tou soou logou aikismos* and the other which links it to the Cilician city of Soloi, Flobert rightly stresses that these are unfounded, but he has no interest in pursuing their genesis or development.

The paternity of the first etymology, however, owing to its characteristic attempt to reach the sense of a word by breaking it down into elements, can be attributed to the Stoics: to Chrysippus or Diogenes of Babylon. The origin of the second, which connects the term solecism to Soloi of Cilicia, is not easy to trace.[2] I shall attempt this in the present essay by locating the question within a reconstruction of the history of relations and contacts between Cilicia – always a place for the meeting of peoples and the

---

[1] Flobert (1986), cf. also Holtz (1981: 136–62), Özbayoğlu (1999: 209–19) and Irwin (1999).
[2] On the Stoics' methods of etymology see Long (1996: 71–2, 80–3, 91–2, with previous bibliography). Etymologies of the name Soloi by contemporary scholars are not the concern of this work; cf. Burkert (1992: 12).

shunting of goods between East and West – and the Greek world: a history which accelerated rapidly in the centuries following Alexander, when the language and, to a lesser degree, the culture of the Greeks started to become dominant in the region. Similar situations, moreover, determined perhaps more by processes of interaction and acculturation than by the movements of conspicuous groups of Greek-speakers, evolved over a large part of the eastern Mediterranean, with the result that one can say that by the Roman imperial period Greek was the language generally adopted in the area.[3] As for the origin of the etymology of solecism which, connecting the term with the city of Soloi in Cilicia, highlights uncertainty surrounding the Hellenism[4] of the region, this can be referred, in my opinion, to the third century BC when, years after Alexander, the expansion of Greek among the peoples of the eastern Mediterranean was still in full swing.

II

Generally accepted until a few years ago, the idea that significant groups of Greek-speakers were settled in Cilicia at the end of the second millennium BC[5] was founded on a picture of the peopling of the region derived from Greek literary sources.[6]

Firstly, there are two passages in the *Iliad* in which the Cilicians turn out not to be settled in their normal homeland in the eastern Mediterranean, but to live in the Troad governed by Eëtion, the father of Andromache.[7] This location, owing to the uncertainty it creates concerning the identity of the *ethnos*, gave rise to ancient speculation on its origin and formation.[8] From a geographical point of view, however, in the second half of the fifth century BC Cilicia is firmly located in the south-eastern part of Asia Minor, adjacent to Cappadocia, with close ties to the island of Cyprus, its mountainous region facing Egypt.[9] Herodotus also tells us that the inhabitants of Cilicia in ancient times (*to palaion*) were called by the name *Hypachaioi*;[10] later, looking eastwards and putting himself in a long tradition of genealogists, he derives the ethnic name of the Cilicians from the hero Kilix, son

---

[3] See also for later periods Bowersock (1990), Fowden (1993), Millar (1983) and (1993: 270–1, 524–5).
[4] For the notion of Hellenism adopted in this essay see Bowersock (1990) and also Hornblower (1996: 677–9).
[5] See Boardman (1999b: 35–6).
[6] On these sources cf. Desideri and Jasink (1990: 25–48); on the history of Cilicia until the end of the Persian rule, Erzen (1940) is still useful.
[7] *Iliad* 6.397, 415.   [8] See below n. 14.   [9] Hdt. 2.17.1, 34.1; 5.52.2–3, 108.2.
[10] Hdt. 7.91. For different interpretations of the name *Hypachaioi* see Kretschmer (1933) and Levy (1938).

of the Phoenician Agenor.[11] But Herodotus, even though he argues that the Pamphylians reached their homeland as fugitives from Troy under the leadership of Amphilochos and Kalchas, and that Posideion – on the borders between Cilicia and Syria – was founded by the same Amphilochos,[12] does not consider the possibility of a connection between the Homeric Cilicians of the Troad and those of the Levant. He thus confirms his presentation of Cilicia as a region fundamentally disconnected from the Aegean and instead forming part of the Levantine milieu.

Given the silence of Herodotus, links between the Homeric Cilicians of the Troad and those of the Levant are assumed – on the conviction that a simple movement of people lies behind identical geographical terms for places which are far distant[13] – by that branch of ancient ethnography and local historiography interested in reconstructing in detail the ethnic picture of our region. The most important developments in the subject seem to go back to the period following Alexander, and they are synthesized in the *Geography* of Strabo as follows:

Since the Cilicians in the Troad whom Homer mentions are far distant from the Cilicians outside the Taurus, some represent those in Troy as original colonizers of the latter, and point out certain places of the same name there, as, for example, Thebe and Lyrnessos in Pamphylia, whereas others of contrary opinion point out also an Aleïan Plain in the former.[14]

Strabo, moreover – following literary works such as the Hesiodic *Melampodia* and not, as is commonly believed, the seventh-century elegiac poet Callinus – has the Greek heroes Amphilochos and Mopsos leading a march of peoples from the shores of the Aegean to southern Asia Minor and the Levant.[15]

Derived from the need to impose order on the complex map of the peoples of Asia Minor and on a mass of disparate sources,[16] the two reconstructions of the movements of the Cilicians mentioned by Strabo in the passage quoted above are clearly the result of theoretical work inspired by

---

[11] Hdt. 7.91. A different genealogy for Kilix is offered by Pherecydes of Athens (*FGrHist* 3 F86). On the characteristics of Herodotus' 'Eastern' perspective see Thomas (2000: 75–101).

[12] Pamphylians: Hdt. 7.91; Posideion: Hdt. 3.91. On the Argive Amphilochos cf. Krauskopf (1981: 713–17); on the seer Kalchas, Saladino (1990: 931–5).

[13] On this conviction, very popular in ancient ethnography, see Salmeri (2000b: 168–9).

[14] Strabo 14.5.21 (trans. H. L. Jones, Loeb Classical Library).

[15] Strabo 14.1.27 (Hes. fr. 278 MW), 14.4.3, 14.5.16–17 (Hes. fr. 279 MW). In the second passage, instead of Callinus, M.L. West (*Iambi et Elegi Graeci* II² Callin.[8]) rightly suggests reading the name of the historian Callisthenes. On the seer Mopsos cf. Simon (1992: 652–4) and Burkert (1992: 52–3). On the legends dealing with Amphilochos and Mopsos, see Scheer (1993: 153–73, 222–71).

[16] For this exigency in Strabo see Salmeri (2000b: 163–4), Mitchell (2000: 120).

a migrationist model, without doubt the most widespread in the ancient ethnographic tradition. Moreover, notwithstanding the shared characteristics of the Greeks and the Trojans in Homer,[17] the first of the two reconstructions gives no thought to the contradiction implicit in the notion that the Cilicians of Eëtion – allies of the Trojans – were guided to southern Asia Minor by the Greeks Amphilochos and Mopsos. Strabo for his part, in a period in which the process of linguistic Hellenization in Cilicia was reaching its conclusion, seems to have been bent on somehow anchoring the peopling of the region in the Aegean area, through figures such as Mopsos and Amphilochos, as well as attributing the foundation of Soloi and Tarsos respectively to the Rhodians and Achaeans and to the Argives.[18]

Some scholars, mostly classicists, have sought confirmation of the view expressed by Strabo in the Karatepe bilingual,[19] an important epigraphic monument in hieroglyphic Luwian and Phoenician, found in 1947 about 125 km north-east of Adana and datable to between the end of the eighth and the beginning of the seventh centuries BC. 'Muksas' (Phoenician *MPS*), mentioned in the inscription as the founder of an important dynasty, was in fact identified with the Mopsos who, according to Greek sources, led a group of people into Cilicia from the Aegean area of Asia Minor; while the 'Adanawa-URBS' / (people) *DNNYM* in the same inscription were seen as *Danaoi*, i.e. Greeks. However, the attempt to detect in the Karatepe bilingual traces of an ancient migration to Cilicia from the Aegean area did not meet with general approval. In particular it was noted that the 'Adanawa-URBS' / (people) *DNNYM* are terms applied to the inhabitants of Adana and the Cilician plain,[20] in keeping with other ancient sources; and that there is no compelling reason to identify the Mopsos of the bilingual, the founder of a line of neo-Hittite rulers, with the Mopsos of the legendary Greek migration, especially in view of the wide diffusion of the name in Greece and Anatolia from the fifteenth century BC.[21] It is possible instead that the Greeks, once they were in fairly regular contact with the Cilician

---

[17] See Murray (1988–9: 6). Mackie (1996), however, thinks that the different ways the Greeks and the Trojans speak reflect their disparate cultural structures and their relative positions in the Trojan War.
[18] Colonization of Soloi and Tarsos: Strabo 14.5.8, 12; for Amphilochos and Mopsos see above nn. 12 and 15.
[19] For example, Cassola (1957: 110–18) and Boardman (1999*b*: 36). The final publication of the Karatepe bilingual is provided by Çambel (1999); for the hieroglyphic Luwian text see Hawkins (2000: 1, 45–68) (1.1 Karatepe 1). For a new bilingual inscription in hieroglyphic Luwian and Phoenician mentioning 'Muksas' (*MPS*), see below n. 54.
[20] Laroche (1958: 268), Vanschoonwinkel (1990: 195–7), Hawkins (1982: 430) and (2000: 1, 40).
[21] Vanschoonwinkel (1990).

world, incorporated into their own mythological system figures such as the legendary neo-Hittite dynast 'Muksas' (*MPS*).[22] In short, it seems better with E. Laroche[23] to reject the grandiose hypothesis of a Greek migration which places the arrival of the *Danaoi* in Cilicia during the course of the second millennium BC.

Confirmation of the picture of the peopling of Cilicia presented in Strabo's *Geography* has also been sought in finds of Mycenaean-type pottery in the region, datable approximately to the twelfth century BC and thought to have been transported by Mycenaean Greeks.[24] However, even this piece of support has been called into doubt as the result of a detailed study, not only of the material from the excavations at Tarsos conducted by Hetty Goldman,[25] but in particular of the material gathered during a visit to Kazanlı Höyük, some eighty years ago, by Burton Brown[26] and collected in the surveys carried out in Cilicia by Gjerstad and Seton-Williams in 1930 and 1951 respectively.[27]

In the case of Tarsos E. French lays great emphasis on the similarities with the material of the same period from Cyprus and also finds connections with the production of continental Greece, but identifies specific characteristics of the Mycenaean-type pottery from the site.[28] S. Sherratt and J. Crouwel, on the basis of analysis of pottery fragments decorated in LH IIIC style from Kazanlı Höyük, tend to exclude the possibility that these pieces, and other similar material from the region, are to be connected with the arrival of groups of Mycenaeans from the Aegean world.[29] For them it seems preferable to regard the Aegean-type pottery found in Cilicia, attributable to the period immediately following the fall of the Hittite empire, as an index of changing economic and social relationships and of a privileged link with the dynamic urban centres of coastal Cyprus,[30] rather than a sign of the arrival of a significant number of Greek-speakers.[31] Anna Lucia D'Agata, finally, having re-examined the material gathered in the surveys of

---

[22] This may have started with the Hesiodic *Melampodia* (frr. 278–9 MW), dated to *ca* 550 BC in Löffler (1963: 59). See Braun (1982: 30).
[23] Laroche (1958: 275).
[24] Boardman (1999*b*: 35): 'The break-up of Aegean Bronze Age cultures, and the period . . . following the Trojan War, saw the migrations of many people, from West and North, through the countries of the Near East. Some were carriers of Mycenaean pottery, themselves surely Mycenaean Greeks, and to these years may be assigned new Greek settlements in the east . . . The archaeological record shows this most clearly at Tarsus . . .'
[25] Goldman (1956).   [26] Cf. Sherratt and Crouwel (1987: 327).
[27] Gjerstad (1934); Seton Williams (1954).
[28] French (1975); cf. also Mee (1978: 150); Mee (1998: 145).   [29] Sherratt and Crouwel (1987).
[30] Sherratt and Crouwel (1987: 340–6), Sherratt (1994), Sherratt (1998).
[31] Cf. Jean (1999: 31–2).

Gjerstad and Seton-Williams, has concluded that it can no longer be argued that the entire Cilician plain was affected by the circulation of Mycenaean IIIA-B pottery and the subsequent arrival of IIIC pottery, nor can we speak of some Aegeanizing phenomenon for the area. Rather, relations with the Aegean world appear extremely localized throughout all phases of the Late Bronze/Early Iron Age in the Tarsos and Kazanlı area.[32]

III

A second period to which the presence of Greek settlements in Cilicia is commonly attributed is represented by the eighth and seventh centuries BC. In particular, on the basis of information handed down especially by Strabo, there has been a tendency to regard Soloi as a Rhodian – or preferably Lindian – colony, the foundation of which cannot be dated, however, owing to the lack of archaeological research at the site pertaining to the period in question.[33] A further incentive to consider Soloi a colony was provided by the discovery of 'LG pottery, mainly East Greek' in the neighbouring sites of Tarsos and Mersin; it was thought in fact that such material could only come from a colonial centre.[34] It is not possible here to enter into a discussion whether or not there were Greek colonies on the south-east coast of Asia Minor and the Syro-Phoenician coast at the period in which they fell within the confines of the Assyrian empire.[35] But for a useful insight into the role of Soloi, it is worth recalling that for a single centre in the Levant the existence of a Greek settlement in the middle decades of the eighth century BC has been hypothesized, and not unanimously. The place in question is Al Mina at the mouth of the Orontes,[36] which for the final

---

[32] See Salmeri and D'Agata (2003); also Salmeri, D'Agata, Falesi and Buxton (2002).

[33] See Ruge (1927: 936) and Jeffery (1976: 197). At any rate, in Strabo 14.5.8 Soloi is presented as 'a *ktisma* of the Achaeans and of the Rhodians of Lindos'; in Polyb. 21.24.10 and Livy 37.56.7, on the other hand, she is said by the Rhodians to be descended from Argos just as they were. See also Mela 1.71. Regular excavations on the site of Soloi (Viranşehir) were started in 2000 by R. Yağci.

[34] Boardman (1965: 15) and Coldstream (1977: 95, 359). But see below at n. 38.

[35] Against the existence of a Greek colonial movement towards the Levant in the eighth and seventh centuries BC, comparable to the westward one, see Liverani (1988: 876–8). In favour of the presence of Greek colonies on the southern coast of Asia Minor (Phaselis, Nagidos, Kelenderis) we find, for example, Graham (1982: 93) and Baurain (1997: 301) (here also Soloi is considered a Greek colony), but both scholars rule out this possibility for Al Mina. Specifically on Cilicia see now Arslan (2001).

[36] Popham (1994) and Boardman (1999*b*: 38–46) assert the presence of a settlement of Greeks at Al Mina, in the eighth century BC, consisting chiefly of Euboeans, while Perreault (1993: 63–8) and Snodgrass (1994: 4–5) tend rather to rule it out on the basis of a different interpretation of the pottery finds. Kearsley (1999: 127–30) seeks to demonstrate that around the mid-eighth century BC 'a mercenary group mainly comprising Euboeans was living briefly at the mouth of the Orontes'. See also Boardman (1999*a*).

part of the eighth century is now described as a port of trade frequented by Greeks, Phoenicians and Cypriots.[37] It should also be remarked that the Late Geometric (and later) pottery from Tarsos and Mersin, which until just a few years ago was an established East Greek import, has now – on the basis of research on similar material found during the excavations at Kinet Höyük (ancient Issos)[38] – come to be regarded as local production, indicative of processes of acculturation rather than Greek settlement. For the moment, then, it is perhaps preferable to avoid attributing to Soloi the status of a late eighth-century Rhodian colony.

This does not mean, however, that every type of Greek intervention or presence in Plain Cilicia is to be excluded. This area, called *Que* by the Assyrians, was marched across during the incursions of Shalmaneser III in the 830s BC and became a province of the empire some time before 710 under Shalmaneser V, or more probably Sargon II.[39] In the first place it is likely that sailors and merchants, not only from Cyprus but from the Greek world too and in particular from the eastern Aegean, stayed in the ports of the region – especially Soloi – given the non-hostile attitude on the part of the provincial Assyrian administration towards foreign trade.[40] Further, in 696 BC, there is evidence for an ill-fated rebellion against the central authority by Kirua, ruler of Illubru, in which Greeks were involved along with the cities of Ingira and Tarzi, and with Rough Cilicia. Assyrian sources tell us that Kirua, defeated by the generals of Sennacherib, was captured and burned alive, while Illubru was taken and turned into an outpost of the empire.[41] The *Chronicle* of Eusebius in Armenian – which goes back to two Greek authors of the late Hellenistic and Roman periods, Alexander Polyhistor and Abydenus, both deriving from the Babylonian Berosus – records the defeat inflicted on the Greeks by the army of Sennacherib.[42] According to Alexander Polyhistor the Greeks, 'having advanced into the land of the Cilicians to make war', were defeated in a land battle that was particularly bloody for both sides.

The formulation 'having advanced into the land of the Cilicians to make war' does not square with the hypothesis that the Greeks in question were permanent residents of the province of *Que*. Rather, they appear to belong

---

[37] Kearsley (1999: 130–1).
[38] Cf. above n. 34; for the Kinet Höyük material see Gates (1999: 308–9).
[39] Hawkins (1982: 395, 415–20) and (2000: I, 41–2).
[40] See Lanfranchi (2000: 10–11, 31–4), although as a whole the work tends to view the Greek presence in the Assyrian world in an excessively triumphalistic light.
[41] Hawkins (1982: 426–7) and (2000: I, 43). Cf. also Dalley (1999).
[42] Euseb. (Arm.) *Chron.* p. 14 Karst (Alexander Polyhistor: *FGrHist* 273 F79), pp. 17–18 Karst (Abydenus: *FGrHist* 685 F5); see Desideri and Jasink (1990: 153–6).

to the same group of Ionians (*ia-ú-na-a*) who had been involved in military activity against Assyrian authority since the 730s BC, when a tablet from Nimrud records them making an incursion into Phoenicia. That is to say, it is most likely that they were mercenaries, given also to piracy, who had perhaps some of their bases on the island of Cyprus.[43] Moreover, the tablets in cuneiform script and neo-Assyrian language found at Tarsos[44] do not in any case point towards the presence of conspicuous groups of Greeks in the province of *Que* in the course of the seventh century BC. There does not seem to be preserved any trace of Greek onomastics in the tablets; the Luwian element is dominant, which may possibly document a remarkable continuity in the composition of the local population with respect to the Hittite period.[45]

Luwian onomastics appears to be dominant at the same period in Rough Cilicia as well,[46] with the result that the picture of the population of the whole of Cilicia turns out to be substantially homogeneous.[47] From the point of view of politics, however, Rough Cilicia presents a quite different picture from the Plain, since it was not a settled possession of the Assyrians. After both areas fell into the hands of Sargon II, the former became the nerve-centre of Kirua's revolt and for a large part of the seventh century BC preserved its independence from the empire.[48] This may also be why the Greeks took their name for the whole region (*Kilikia*) from the Assyrian designation for Rough Cilicia (*Hilakku*), but it is impossible to be certain.[49] On the basis of the excavations at Kelenderis, however, and the material they produced, it can be stated with relative security that there were no western-type colonies in Rough Cilicia in the eighth and seventh centuries.[50] In the region as a whole, then, in the two centuries in question the Greeks were nothing if not a marginal element; if in centres like Kinet Höyük, Tarsos or Kelenderis the inhabitants followed the fashions in table-ware from Miletos, Chios or Rhodes, this is to be regarded as the product of

---

[43] A new edition of the text (Nimrud Letter 69), with appropriate commentary, in Parker (2000). On Greek mercenaries in the East see Kearsley (1999: 118–19).

[44] Goetze (1939).

[45] Goetze (1962: 54). The Luwian element in Cilicia reasserted itself in the Assyrian period after the influx of the Hurrians, particularly powerful in the latter half of the second millennium BC, began to wane; by the first millennium BC the Hurrian language was no longer spoken, although some of its personal names were still used: see Giorgieri (2000: 283).

[46] Consider the absolute predominance of Luwian names in the Phoenician inscription from Cebel Ire Dağı: see Mosca and Russell (1987) and below n. 56.

[47] On the interaction between Rough and Plain Cilicia in the ancient world see Jean (2001a: 5–7). In general on the entire region, with a *longue durée* perspective, see Mutafian (1988).

[48] Hawkins (1982: 431–3) and Hawkins (2000: I, 42–3).   [49] Cf. Desideri and Jasink (1990: 12).

[50] For Kelenderis see Zoroğlu (1994: 14–21) (in Mela 1.77 she is said to be a foundation of Samos). In general see Arslan (2001).

processes of acculturation in which Cyprus and her Greek cities certainly performed an important mediating role.[51]

The use of the Phoenician language and alphabetic script in inscriptions found in Cilicia and dating back to the eighth and seventh centuries BC is to be handled similarly; that is to say, by locating it at the centre of a dynamic process of interaction and acculturation.[52] The most famous of these inscriptions is without doubt the Karatepe bilingual, in hieroglyphic Luwian and Phoenician, datable to somewhere between the end of the eighth and the beginning of the seventh centuries BC, and erected by Azatiwatas, a local dynast. Having been promoted by Awarikus, king of Adana, he boasts of having secured the succession to the throne of the family of his *seigneur*, the house of 'Muksas' (*MPS*), and of having restored the fortunes of the kingdom.[53] Awarikus speaks for himself in another hieroglyphic Luwian–Phoenician bilingual found in 1998 at Çineköy, in the area of Karataş to the south-west of Adana.[54] In the inscription, which is earlier than the one at Karatepe, the king speaks of himself as descendant of 'Muksas' (*MPS*), describes his own achievements with great pomp and gives a glimpse into an alliance established between himself and the Assyrians.

Two inscriptions in Phoenician alone are to be added to the bilinguals. The first is fragmentary, found at Hassan-Beyli on the western slopes of Mount Amanos;[55] the second, datable to around the end of the seventh century BC, comes from Cebel Ires Dağı, in Rough Cilicia not far from Alanya, and records a text set down by the scribe *PHL'S* dealing with land allocations.[56] There is also a series of seals which give names, for the most part Luwian, in Phoenician script,[57] while two other inscriptions in Phoenician come from an area just outside the eastern limits of Cilicia: from Zincirli we have a text of Kilamuwa, king of Sam'al, datable to around 825 BC,[58] and from Incirli a badly worn basalt stele from the final period of the eighth century BC which gives a text in Phoenician – perhaps again by Awarikus – accompanied by faint traces of cuneiform and hieroglyphic Luwian.[59] At Ivriz, finally, just beyond the Tauros to the north-west of Tarsos, there was discovered a further bilingual in hieroglyphic Luwian and Phoenician, from around the end of the eighth century BC, in which there is mention of the king Warpalawas of Tuwana.[60]

---

[51] Gates (1999: 308–9). Unfounded is the hypothesis advanced by Bing (1971) presenting Tarsos as 'a forgotten colony of Lindos'.
[52] See Gras, Rouillard and Teixidor (1989: 32–5), Lemaire (1991) and (2001: 188–9).
[53] Above, nn. 19–21.   [54] Tekoğlu and Lemaire (2000).   [55] Lemaire (1983).
[56] Mosca and Russell (1987).   [57] Lemaire (2001: 188–9).   [58] Tropper (1993: 27–46).
[59] Carter (1998).   [60] Hawkins (2000: II, 526) (x.46 Ivriz 2).

The Phoenician used in many of these texts is characterized by such a distinctive form, especially as regards the script, that in view also of the absence of Phoenician names and the overwhelming prevalence of Luwian ones, the Phoenician inscriptions of Cilicia tend to be considered as the product of local scribes whose first language was non-Semitic.[61] In the initial diffusion of Phoenician in the region during the course of the ninth century, if not already in the tenth century BC, a role may have been played by the enlargement of the commercial sphere of Tyre towards the north and the west, into the area of the neo-Hittite kingdoms of northern Syria and Cilicia.[62] It seems, however, that it was the indisputable prestige of the language that was the prevailing factor, rather than the presence of large Phoenician settlements which has not so far been proven. In the north of Syria, moreover, in a multilingual environment – of which Yariris, the ruler of Carchemish, 'claiming a degree of literacy in various scripts as well as proficiency in many foreign languages', is the most eminent representative[63] – Phoenician fitted in well, also because its alphabet adapted itself in a satisfactory way to the dominant language, Aramaic. In Cilicia the Phoenician language, favoured owing to the practicality of its alphabetic script, soon caught up with hieroglyphic Luwian as a language of internal communication.[64] Indeed, in the period of Assyrian domination in the region during the seventh century BC, when the hieroglyphic tradition had dried up, Phoenician seems to have kept its position as a written language next to the cuneiform Assyrian and alphabetic Aramaic attested at Tarsos.[65]

In such a multilingual context on the fringes of the Assyrian empire the language of the Greeks, in keeping with the marginal presence of its speakers, is not attested; this did not, however, prevent L.H. Jeffery from supposing that in the first half of the eighth century the Greeks took their alphabet from the area which includes northern Syria and Cilicia, where the Phoenician language and script were rooted as a medium of communication.[66] It is not possible to deal with such a complex question here, but in support of Jeffery's hypothesis it may at least be emphasized that in order for processes such as the transmission of an alphabet to take place, even

---

[61] See Lemaire (1991: 139–46).
[62] See Gras, Rouillard and Teixidor (1989: 34–5), Lemaire (1991: 137–8).
[63] See Hawkins (1982: 406).   [64] Lemaire (1991: 140).
[65] Lemaire (2001: 189). In relation to a 'Tontafel' found in the course of excavations at Sirkeli Höyük and dated between 750 and 600 BC, Haider (1999: 179) writes: 'Somit dürfte mit der Sirkeli-Tafel . . . ein erstes Zeugnis für ein bodenständiges kilikisches Schriftsystem . . . vorliegen. Ihr Verfasser scheint sich vielleicht einzelner Silbenzeichen aus dem zeitgleichen zyprischen Syllabar bedient zu haben.'
[66] Jeffery (1982: 819–33, especially 832–3), Jeffery (1990: 10–11). Johnston in Jeffery (1990: 425–6) argues the role of Cyprus as a catalyst between Greeks and Phoenicians.

a marginal presence of the receiving party suffices; the Levant, moreover, with its long history of linguistic and alphabetic interaction, seems a more likely candidate than Crete[67] to play the role of place of origin of the Greek alphabet. Cilicia in particular, as we have tried to show, over and above its substantially Luwian population, was a privileged seat of exchange and contact between 'East' and 'West' from the ninth to the seventh centuries BC on account of its intermediate position between the world of imperial Mesopotamia and that of Anatolia, and its regular contacts with both Greek and Phoenician Cyprus. Its candidacy as the place of introduction of the Greek alphabet is surely strengthened by the fact that the Phrygians, independently of the Greeks but not without some interference, seem also to have taken their alphabet from there.[68]

IV

After the end of Assyrian rule Cilicia makes her appearance on the political scene of the eastern Mediterranean with the participation of the king Syennesis as guarantor, along with the Babylonian 'Labynetos', at peace negotiations between the Lydians and the Medes in 585 BC.[69] This Syennesis – the first in a line of Cilician dynasts bearing this name down to the end of the fifth century BC – was in all likelihood the master of *Hilakku*, the mountainous western part of the region which, just as in the Assyrian period, maintained a substantial independence under the Babylonians also, taking the name *Pirindu* and perhaps extending its territory. Plain Cilicia, the *Que* of the Assyrians, was known in turn as *Hume*, and may have been for some periods under Babylonian rule.[70]

In the second half of the sixth century BC it is not easy to identify the moment at which our region, insofar as there seems not to have been a true campaign of conquest, entered into the orbit of the Persian empire of Cyrus the Great: there is, however, a proposal to date the process to a period between the pacification 'campaign' in Caria, a little later than the capture of Sardis in 546, and the conquest of Babylon in 539 BC.[71] As for the role of Cilicia in the empire from a political and administrative point of view, we should not allow ourselves to be misled by the existence of the

---

[67] For Crete see Guarducci (1978).
[68] On this point see Brixhe (1995). It must, however, be stressed that the candidacy of Cilicia as place of origin of the Greek alphabet does not in fact conflict with that of northern Syria.
[69] Hdt. 1.74.3.
[70] Syennesis: Asheri (1991: 45–6), Casabonne (1995) and Briant (1996: 515). For Cilicia in the Babylonian period see Hawkins (1982: 433–4) and (2000: I, 43–4).
[71] Casabonne (2000: 21).

dynasty of Syennesis into considering the integration of our region into the Achaemenid area as purely theoretical. In fact Cilicia, even though retaining its traditional function as a link between Mesopotamia and Anatolia, paid to Darius a tribute of 360 white horses and 500 talents of silver; and she furnished to the army of Xerxes troops and 100 ships, more than the Lycians and the Carians and as many as the Ionians. Under Persian rule Cilicia was more or less a vassal kingdom, with a few special prerogatives, but *not* thereby granted autonomy or governed – from the perspective of the imperial centre – on principles different from those of a satrapy.[72]

With regard to the presence of a Greek element in Cilicia in the Persian period, by far the most important testimony is provided by silver coins which began to be struck a little after the middle of the fifth century BC in the principal centres of the region: from Nagidos, Kelenderis and Holmoi in Rough Cilicia, to Issos, Mallos, Soloi and Tarsos in the Plain. On the coins, as has been well written, 'un filo rosso di grecità linguistica e figurativa corre . . . evidente anche se in realtà discontinuo, e non sempre della stessa forza e spessore'.[73] The local coins of Cilicia turn out in fact to be marked with a toponymic legend for the most part in the Greek language and alphabet, except that in the case of Tarsos the prevalent language is Aramaic, which may have been intended to support some dynastic agenda. The iconography of the coins in cases such as Nagidos and Kelenderis is decidedly Greek, as also in the case of pieces from Soloi with the helmeted head of Athena on the obverse; while Tarsos again stands out in presenting subjects of Persian derivation.[74] Beyond these differences, all the Cilician coins in question were nevertheless struck on the Persian standard, with the result that they have been interpreted as Persian double *sigloi* and seen as a manifestation of Achaemenid power in the region.[75] This hypothesis seems fragile, but it is undeniable that the decision to adopt the same monetary unit – first of all in Cyprus, then in Cilicia and Pamphylia, and also at Arados and Phaselis – based on a stater of original weight between 11 and 11.3 g, can be seen as indicative of a tendency towards integration under Persian authority on the south-eastern coast of Asia Minor.[76] But how did the urban centres of Cilicia, which cannot be described as Greek in the seventh and sixth centuries BC from the perspective of political and social organization, arrive at the use of Greek legends and iconography on their coins?

---

[72] Tribute paid to Darius: Hdt. 3.90.3; troops and ships furnished to Xerxes: Hdt. 7.91. See Asheri (1991) and Briant (1996: 514–15), and more in general Casabonne (1999).
[73] Capecchi (1991: 67).   [74] See Kraay (1976: 278–86), Capecchi (1991) and Casabonne (2000).
[75] Davesne (1989: 161).   [76] Casabonne (2000: 54).

It is prudent to exclude the possibility that the coin production in question was determined by large migrations of Greek-speakers into Cilicia between the sixth and the fifth centuries BC, a movement for which there is no real evidence;[77] on the contrary, the coin production could have been a result of the network of connections that had been established between Cilicia and the Greek world, especially after contingents from the region had taken part in the expedition of Xerxes against Greece. To this of course can be added the enormous influence that Greek coinage – in particular that of Athens – had in Cilicia and in the rest of the Mediterranean on account of its conspicuous artistic quality and wide circulation.[78]

One of the earliest opportunities for contact between the Cilicians and the Greek world, after the Persian Wars, was created by the expeditions of Kimon to the eastern Mediterranean. The son of Miltiades, he defeated the Persians in or about 466 BC in a land and sea battle around the mouth of the Eurymedon in Pamphylia; in 450 he launched a campaign against Cyprus during the course of which – after his own death – the Athenians defeated the Cypriots and the Cilicians around Salamis once again in a land and sea battle.[79] In the case of the first expedition in particular, the cities confronted by the Athenians were faced with a serious problem as to which side they should take, and it is significant that Phaselis, a foundation of Lindos on the eastern fringe of Lycia, remained loyal to the Persians and suffered harsh treatment as a result. Nevertheless, having paid ten talents the city soon reached an accord with Kimon by the mediation of the Chians, and in the first assessment (454/3 BC) of the Delian League emerged with a tribute of six talents.[80] To the east of Phaselis another urban centre, on the southern coast of Asia Minor, appears to have belonged to the Delian League: Kelenderis, in Rough Cilicia, which is included in the extravagant assessment of 425 BC, and was probably assessed also in 454/3 BC.[81] A little more than a decade later, between 440 and 430 BC, Kelenderis would have been one of the first centres in our region to produce silver staters,[82] but it is not possible on the basis of the documentation at our disposal to establish any connection between this fact and the admission of the city to the League. The material belonging to the Classical period found in the

---

[77] On Greeks in the Persian empire see Miller (1997: 97–108).
[78] For the presence of Attic coins in Cilician hoards see Casabonne (2000: 27–31); for the imitations of Attic coins also in Cilicia, Figueira (1998: 528–35).
[79] Battle of the Eurymedon: Thuc. 1.100, Plut. *Cim.* 12.5–8 and Badian (1993: 2–10, 100); campaign against Cyprus: Thuc. 1.112, and Badian (1993: 19–20, 103) with discussion of other sources.
[80] Plut. *Cim.* 12.3–4 and Blackman (1981). Phaselis, according to Hdt. 2.178, took part in the construction of the *Hellenion* at Naukratis.
[81] Meiggs (1972: 102, 329). On Kelenderis cf. above n. 50.   [82] Casabonne (2000: 39).

excavations of the city's necropolis deserves instead some attention: apart from Attic red-figured lekythoi it includes a large amount of non-Attic vases, among which stand out Cypriot imports, bowls of local manufacture, and Phoenician transport amphoras.[83] The society that we glimpse lying behind this mixed collection is not one dominated by Greeks. The red-figured Attic lekythoi are in fact prestige items adopted by the local elite in their burial practice, just as, on a more general level, the 'reference' on local coinage to Greek numismatic production – perhaps through the influence of Cyprus and Phaselis – represents one of the ways in which Kelenderis could affirm herself in the regional context of Cilicia.

The networks which tie Soloi, another Cilician centre remarkable for its coinage,[84] to the Greek world extend along routes which – somewhat differently from Kelenderis – are directed on one side towards Cyprus and on the other towards Rhodes. With Cyprus, which was separated from the city by a short stretch of water, there was a constant stream of trade and contacts. Here we cite the information given by Isocrates, according to which Evagoras, the future king of the Greek Salamis, shortly before 411 BC – while the city was in the hands of the tyrant Abdemon of Tyre – went into exile at Soloi. Having conquered and consolidated control of Salamis, King Evagoras was able – in response to the actions of the Great King, and certainly exploiting contacts formed during his exile – to annex areas of Cilicia, creating serious problems for the Persian empire in the decade between 391 and 381 BC, and further confirming the strategic potential of the axis between Cyprus and the area of Asia Minor that faces it.[85]

The link between Soloi and Rhodes appears to be of an essentially cultural and religious type. Important evidence for this is found in the Lindian *Temple Chronicle*, where for a year that cannot be pinned down with certainty – perhaps around the beginning of the fifth century BC – we read that the people of Soloi offered to Athena Lindia a golden *phiala* as a tithe of the booty which, together with Amphilochos, they had taken from some neighbouring peoples whose names are difficult to restore.[86] A short text, but one which provokes a whole series of questions related to the tradition concerning the foundation of the city, a tradition condensed as follows by Strabo: 'Soloi is a *ktisma* of the Achaeans and the Rhodians of Lindos.'[87]

---

[83] Zoroğlu (1994: 61–63) and (2000).

[84] On the coinage of Soloi see most recently Casabonne (2000: 40, 47).

[85] Exile: Isocr. *Euag.* 27–8; annexation of Cilicia: *ibid.* 62. On Evagoras' political perspective see Costa (1974), Collombier (1990) and Briant (1996: 628–9, 666–8, 671).

[86] The entry in the Lindian *Temple Chronicle* dealing with Soloi (33) is referred with some doubt to the Archaic period in Blinkenberg (1915: 29) and *Lindos* II.1 col. 177. The Amphilochos of this text does not seem to have anything to do with the Argive hero (above n. 12).

[87] Strabo 14.5.8, but cf. also above n. 33.

As for the Rhodians, this tradition seems to have its roots in the same decades of the early fifth century to which, in my view, the offering of the *phiala* to Athena Lindia by the people of Soloi also dates. At that time, as we know from Herodotus, the town of Posideion, south of the Orontes, claimed to have been founded by the Argive hero Amphilochos;[88] and King Xerxes and the Persians, under whose control both Posideion and Soloi fell, considered themselves to be descendants of the Argives through Perseus.[89] In this context it is easy to understand the decision of the people of Soloi to send an offering to Lindos, traditionally considered a colony of Argos, and to establish a connection with Argos by parading a homonym of the mythical Amphilochos, who according to the Hesiodic *Melampodia* was killed by Apollo just near Soloi.[90]

During the course of the fifth century BC, the cities of Cilicia – represented here by Kelenderis and Soloi – show every sign of being bound to the Greek world by a network of relationships that were, on the whole, well established. As far as regards the population of these cities, on the basis of the data at our disposal, no distinct Greek presence can be reconstructed. Apart from the coin inscriptions already mentioned, no other significant traces of Greek writing from fifth-century Cilicia can be quoted.

Quite different is the case of Aramaic, which is attested in the interior of the region in a dozen inscriptions from the fifth and fourth centuries BC. The oldest was identified in Rough Cilicia and comprises a commemorative text of a local chief or dynast; there follows a series of boundary stones, funerary inscriptions and even a *dâta*, or law, from the fortress of Meydancıkkale located in the Taurus.[91] This use of Aramaic as a written language in Cilicia has precedents which go back a few centuries earlier, to the periods of Assyrian and Babylonian domination; and the language, generally adopted for administrative purposes throughout the Persian empire, in Cilicia in particular came more or less to take the place of Phoenician, which we saw accompanying hieroglyphic Luwian in the Karatepe and Çineköy bilinguals.[92] For these reasons there is no call for surprise at the diffusion of Aramaic in our region in the final century of Persian control, or at the fact that bearers of Iranian, Semitic and Luwian names made use

---

[88] Hdt. 3.91. For the identification of Posideion with Ras el Bassit see Courbin (1986: 187–8).
[89] Hdt. 7.150.
[90] See Strabo 14.5.17 (Hes. fr. 279 MW). Soloi is said to be a colony of Argos by Polybius and Livy, cf. above n. 33.
[91] The inscriptions are listed and discussed in Lemaire and Lozachmeur (1996: 102–6). For the inscription from Meydancıkkale see especially Lemaire and Lozachmeur (1998: 308–14). On the meaning of the term *dâta* see Briant (1996: 526–8).
[92] On the use of Aramaic in the Persian empire see Briant (1996: 523–4, 981) (with bibliography). For the use of Phoenician in Cilicia cf. above nn. 52–65.

of it.⁹³ It is clear, nevertheless, that the normal language of use in Cilicia must have remained Luwian for a long time, even after the abandonment of the hieroglyphic script at the beginning of the seventh century BC.

Still on the subject of the diffusion of Aramaic in Cilicia, but in a field somewhat removed from monumental texts, it is worth mentioning the inscriptions in this language which appear on a particular class of local coins: these so-called caranic coins were struck at several of the city mints by Persian military commanders such as Tiribazos and Pharnabazos, charged in the 380s and 370s with expeditions against Evagoras and the Egyptian rebellion respectively. These coins, destined to pay the mercenary troops employed in expeditions and also perhaps for the building of supplementary ships for the fleet, have been well studied and classified.⁹⁴ For our purposes, however, two groups are of special interest. The first, attributed to Tiribazos and struck in four mints in Plain Cilicia (Soloi, Tarsos, Mallos, Issos), shows the same types on both obverse (Baal standing with a bird – perhaps an eagle – on his right arm), and reverse (bust of Ahuramazda emerging from a winged sun), while the legend in most cases consists of the name of Tiribazos in Aramaic (*TRBZW*) on the obverse, sometimes accompanied by the abbreviation in Greek letters of the city where the mint was located.⁹⁵ Thus the intention must have been on the one hand to give a semblance of unity to the coin production of at least a part of Cilicia, and on the other – by means of the iconographic choice – to underline the strong commitment of the Great King to support the action of his general. The other group which attracts attention is attributed to Pharnabazos and presents markedly Hellenizing types on both obverse and reverse: a three-quarter head of Arethusa and a bearded head with helmet respectively. As for the legend, this consists of the name of Pharnabazos in Aramaic (*PRNBZW*) followed by that of Cilicia in the same language (*HLK*).⁹⁶ With the coinage of Pharnabazos, then, just as with that of Tiribazos, the aim was to present a unitary image of Cilicia, in this case giving the name in the legend as well; but from an iconographic perspective the coinage of Pharnabazos shows a greater degree of Greek influence, especially in the choice of types.

Cilicia, in short, by reason of its strategic position and its use as a point of departure and support for Persian military expeditions, saw its unitary character as a region underlined on its caranic coinage in the first half of the fourth century BC, and, at the same time, through the use of specific

---

⁹³ See Lemaire (1994: 94–5); Lemaire and Lozachmeur (1996: 105).
⁹⁴ See Davesne (1989), Casabonne (2000: 31–6, 60), De Callataÿ (2000). The adjective caranic, used for example in Casabonne (2000), is formed from the Greek word *karanos*.
⁹⁵ Casabonne (2000: 31–4).   ⁹⁶ Casabonne (2000: 34–7).

iconography and of Aramaic for the legend, found that its ties to the imperial centre were made clear. The translation of all this into administrative terms is represented by the transfer of Cilicia to the condition *tout court* of satrapy in the final phase of Persian control.[97] But such geopolitical and administrative tendencies should not obscure the Hellenizing stylistic elements and the decidedly Greek types, adopted by Pharnabazos, which characterize caranic coinage. These features may find an explanation in the fact that the coin production of Tiribazos and Pharnabazos was undertaken mainly to pay the mercenary troops in their service – troops largely made up of Greeks, who, in any case, do not seem to have developed lasting relations with the local population.[98]

Two Attic funerary stelae, with appropriate inscriptions, found in the area of Soloi are a sign of a Greek presence in the region which begins to look more stable. Both pieces date to the second quarter of the fourth century BC, and their inscriptions are characterized by the use of the Attic dialect, except for one name in Doric (*Athanodotos*).[99] But these traces are too exiguous to support hypotheses on the manner and mechanisms by which the Greeks consolidated their presence at Soloi, which along with Kelenderis was always the community in Persian Cilicia most integrated into the diverse world of Greek culture and tradition. On a more general and political level, however, one is obliged to agree with Pierre Briant, who interprets as propaganda the passage in Isocrates' *Panegyricus* – referring to 380 BC – in which the orator alleges that most of the cities of Cilicia were on the side of the Greeks and their allies, and that the remainder were easily detachable from the Persians. Rather than reflecting the real situation, Isocrates wishes to incite his compatriots to war.[100]

The picture of Cilicia under the Achaemenids, which presents the Greek component in a subordinate and marginal position, finds an exact parallel in certain Greek texts which are ascribable (they or their sources) to the fourth century BC or the first decade of the third. In the first place Ephorus, in his division of the peoples (*genê*) of Asia Minor into Greeks and barbarians, with a special category for those of mixed race (*khôris tôn migadôn*), has no hesitation in placing the Cilicians in the second group.[101] In the *Periplous* of Ps.-Scylax, on the other hand, the only community of Rough and Plain Cilicia, apart from Holmoi, which earns the definition *hellênis* is Soloi.[102]

---

[97] Briant (1996: 730).
[98] Xenophon's *Anabasis* offers a good picture of the type of relations obtaining between Greek troops in the service of the Persians and local populations of Asia Minor.
[99] von Gladiss (1973–4: 177) (*Athanodotos*), Hermary (1987: 227–9): see Jones and Russell (1993: 297).
[100] Isocr. *Paneg*. 161, Briant (1996: 669).   [101] Eph. in Strabo 14.5.23, on which see Desideri (1992).
[102] Ps.-Scylax 102. In Xenophon's *Anabasis* (1.2.24) Soloi is simply presented as a maritime city.

Finally, in the section of Arrian's *Anabasis* dedicated to the march of Alexander along the southern coast of Asia Minor, and derived from Ptolemy I and Aristoboulus, the author presents a picture of ethnic and cultural diversity in which it is difficult to identify clearly the space occupied by the Greeks.[103] In the chapters on Cilicia, for example, the peoples occupying the Tauros, against whom Alexander prepares a week-long expedition starting from Soloi, are introduced as crude mountain folk, while for Anchialos and Tarsos the tradition that they owed their foundation to the Assyrian king 'Sardanapalus' is accepted without dispute,[104] though all possibility of annexing the cities to the Greek camp is thereby excluded. As for Soloi, far from alluding to the city as a *polis hellênis* as the author of the *Periplous* had done, the *Anabasis* maintains that Alexander punished her with a fine of 200 silver talents for its philo-Persian sentiments, and provided for the establishment of a constitutional (non-tyrannical) government.[105] Only in the case of Mallos, owing to its vaunted Argive foundation, was there talk of Hellenism – and, more importantly, of her relationship with Alexander, who also claimed descent from the Argos of the Herakleidai.[106] Thus began in the Hellenistic age a second chapter in the fortunes of Argos in Cilicia, which reveals the aspiration to Hellenization on the part of certain cities in the region.

v

Before the time of Alexander's expedition, then, the Hellenism of Cilicia does not present the same pronounced character as in the western area of Asia Minor; on the contrary, it turns out to be in a position of clear inferiority compared to the other ethnic and linguistic elements in the region. It principally concerns port cities such as Soloi, from where contact with the Greek centres of Cyprus was easy; and by and large its manifestations appear to derive from processes of interaction and acculturation rather than from the actions of a significant core of Greek residents.

After the expedition of Alexander it is clear that the Greek presence in the region did not materialize suddenly. A fundamental role in this regard was played by the 'colonizing' activity of the Seleucids and Ptolemies in the

---

[103] Arr. *Anab.* 1.26–2.5, on which see Bosworth (1980: I, 164–98).
[104] 'Cilicians living on the mountains': Arr. *Anab.* 2.5.6; Tarsos and Anchialos: 2.5.4. In Curt. 3.7.3 the inhabitants of Soloi, and those of the area in general, are presented as *barbari*.
[105] Fine: Arr. *Anab.* 2.5.5; establishment of a constitutional (in the sense of non-tyrannical) government (*dêmokrateisthai edôken*): 2.5.8. For the interpretation of *dêmokrateisthai* in the sense proposed here, and not of democracy *tout court*, see Corsaro (1997: 36).
[106] Arr. *Anab.* 2.5.8.

course of the third century BC, which was continued even through the conflicts that characterized their relations in Cilicia as elsewhere.[107] Without taking into account cases such as Tarsos, which was renamed Antioch on the Kydnos, the most significant Seleucid intervention was the foundation of Seleukeia on the Kalykadnos in Rough Cilicia by Seleukos I.[108] In this city, according to Strabo, were settled the inhabitants of the neighbouring Holmoi, most likely along with those of other Greek communities of Asia Minor.[109] On this basis Seleukeia was described as 'well-peopled' (*eu synoikoumenê*) and 'standing far aloof from the Cilician and Pamphylian usages'.[110] As for the Ptolemies, most significant is the foundation by the *stratêgos* Aetos of a city called Arsinoe, not far from Nagidos in Rough Cilicia, between 279 and 253 BC.[111] During the course of the reign of Ptolemy III Euergetes (246–221 BC), in a decree from Nagidos, the event was recalled with words[112] which are in general indicative of the promotional function of the Greek element stressed by the colonizing activities of the Hellenistic kings, to the detriment of indigenous elements.

The route followed by Soloi to consolidate and reinforce her own Hellenism was different. The city had been given a constitutional (non-tyrannical) government by Alexander and – counting on an ancient relationship with Rhodes and, perhaps through Rhodes, with Argos[113] – already by the end of the fourth century BC had, just like Aspendos, established kinship-ties (*syngeneia*) with the city of the Herakleidai,[114] from whom Alexander claimed descent. We can add that through the intervention of Rhodes in 189 BC, on the eve of Apameia, Soloi sought to free herself from the Seleucids by winning *eleutheria* from the Romans, but without success.[115] Thus a general strategy of Hellenization 'by diplomacy'[116] on the part of Soloi is clear; it is not, however, possible to delineate in detail the progress of Hellenization, linguistic or otherwise, in the city after Alexander, owing to the lack of excavation and the limitations of the epigraphic

---

[107] See Cohen (1995: 55–7); for the conflicts between Seleucids and Ptolemies in Cilicia, see Will (1979: I, 140, 239, 255, 259), Jones and Habicht (1989: 335–7). Plutarch (*De Alex. Magni fort. aut virt.* 328 E) underlines the civilizing function of the cities established by Alexander in the East. See also Jos. *Ant.* 1.121.
[108] Cohen (1995: 358–60, Antioch on the Kydnos; 369–71, Seleukeia on the Kalykadnos).
[109] See Strabo 14.5.4. Holmoi, as we have already remarked (above at n. 102), is defined *hellênis* in the *Periplous* of Ps.-Scylax.
[110] Strabo 14.5.4.   [111] Jones and Habicht (1989), Cohen (1995: 363–4).
[112] Jones and Habicht (1989: 320, ll. 22–4).   [113] See above nn. 33, 86, 105.
[114] Cf. the inscription found at Nemea and published in Stroud (1984: 197, l. 7). See Curty (1995: 7–9).
[115] Polyb. 21.24.10, Livy 37.56.7 and above, n. 33. In Polybius the relationship between Soloi and Rhodos is defined as *adelphikê syngeneia*, Argos being the common ancestor.
[116] A 'kinship diplomacy', to use C. Jones's (1999*b*) formula.

material at our disposal. We are well informed, by contrast, on the contribution of Soloi to Hellenistic culture, a contribution which for the most part flowed into Athens. This was in fact the destination of two men of letters and one philosopher from Soloi: the comic poet Philemon, who received citizenship towards the end of the fourth century; Aratus, author of the *Phainomena*, who, before his move to Macedonia and to the court of Antigonos Gonatas, hobnobbed in Athens with Callimachus and Zeno; and finally Chrysippus, who was head of the Stoa.[117]

This connection with Athens through her poets and philosophers proved to be a certificate of Hellenism of the first importance for Soloi. It is likely, moreover, that the remodelling of the tradition regarding the city's origins by Euphorion in his poem *Alexander* (second half of the third century BC) can be traced to this relationship: according to Stephanus of Byzantium, it was claimed in the poem that Soloi took her name from Solon.[118] On the wider content of the *Alexander* very little can be said, and it is not even clear whether the object of the work was Alexander of Chalkis, son of Krateros, to whose widow the poet was greatly indebted, or Alexander the Great. If the latter, a reference to Soloi as the foundation of Solon – a tribute above all to Aratus, a poet greatly admired by Euphorion – would have been well placed in the verses dealing with Alexander's expedition against the Persians.[119]

Without dwelling further on the presence of Soloi in Euphorion's *Alexander*, it may be observed that the Athenian origin of the city supposed in the poem and her on-going diplomatic offensive aimed at Argos and Rhodes need not, given the difference in context, appear contradictory. Indeed, the former fits in with the normal practice of refined and erudite Hellenistic poetry, which was always in search of novelty. At any rate, the phonetic similarity between the names of Soloi and Solon is undeniable, and at the time Euphorion composed his *Alexander*, the tradition that Solon played a

---

[117] For the origin from Soloi of Philemon, Aratus and Chrysippus see Strabo 14.5.8. At any rate, in *Suda* φ 327 Philemon is said to be from Syracuse. Another philosopher from Soloi based at Athens at the beginning of the third century BC was the Academic Krantor. On the contribution of Soloi to Hellenistic culture see Ingholt (1967–8).

[118] Steph. Byz. s.v. Soloi. Euphorion's fragment is discussed in van Groningen (1977: 20–1). In the Aristotelian *Soleôn Politeia* (Arist. fr. 582 Rose) a Solon of Lindos is considered the founder of Soloi. We cannot trace back the origins of this tradition with any exactitude.

[119] On Euphorion's *Alexander* see van Groningen (1977: 20–1) and Treves (1955: 34–5). In Curt. 3.7.3 reference is made to games held in honour of Aesculapius and Minerva and celebrated by Alexander at Soloi (see Arr. *Anab.* 2.5.8 where only Asklepios is named): this could have been the context in which Euphorion asserted his claim that Soloi was founded by the great Solon. On the games celebrated by Alexander at Soloi, especially for the role of Minerva at Soloi, see Atkinson (1980: 173–5, 466–9) and Bing (1991: 163–4).

role in the foundation of the Cypriot Soloi must have already been widely known.[120] It cannot, then, have been a particularly daring move on the part of the poet to connect Cilician Soloi with the Athenian legislator, by means of a simple application of poetic *variatio*.

With firm connections to the Greek world established by various means, Soloi saw the etymology of the term solecism attached to herself through one of these connections: Athens. The etymology is attested for the first time in Strabo,[121] and is explicated as follows in the first book of Diogenes Laertius: Solon, having left Croesus, 'lived in Cilicia and founded a city which he called Soloi after his name. In it he settled some few Athenians, who in process of time corrupted the purity of Attic and were said to solecize.'[122]

To establish the date of the birth of this etymology an important clue is provided by Strabo, who does not speak of it as a novelty in his day, and presents it as though in competition with others; among these must have been the one that wished to derive the term from the string *tou soou logou aikismos* and which, as we have seen, most likely goes back to the Stoics Chrysippus or Diogenes of Babylon;[123] hence, with a reasonable margin of error, to the final part of the third century BC. The etymology which connects the term solecism to Cilician Soloi may also, in my view, be assigned to the final decades of the third century BC, a little after the appearance of Euphorion's *Alexander*. We shall now try to demonstrate this by means of a reading of the passage of Diogenes Laertius cited above.

In this passage the etymology is explained by taking as a starting point the conviction, widespread in antiquity, that an inexorable process of corruption is triggered in a language when its speakers come into contact with foreign peoples, particularly if they find themselves in a situation of isolation.[124] A first manifestation of this sentiment – perhaps not a coincidence – is to be found in some verses of Solon, in which he claims to have brought back to Athens a certain number of Athenian citizens who had been sold more or less legally or constrained by necessity to abandon their homeland; these people, on account of their wanderings, no longer spoke the Attic dialect.[125] But in the ancient world the man who considered these and similar realities of interaction in the greatest detail was Herodotus, the Greek historian most given to the investigation of language in all its aspects.[126] Of the Sauromatae, descendants of the Amazons, for example, he writes

---

[120] See Gallo (1975: 185–201), Gallo (1976: 31–5) and also Irwin (1999: 187–9).
[121] Strabo 14.2.28.   [122] Diog. Laert. 1.51 (trans. R.D. Hicks, Loeb Classical Library).
[123] Cf. above n. 2.   [124] See Asheri (1983: 25–6).   [125] Fr. 36.8–12 W.
[126] See Werner (1992: 10–11), Salmeri (1994: 91–2), Salmeri (2000b: 179).

'they use the Scythian language, but incorrectly by the standards of the primitive form, since the Amazons never succeeded in learning it properly'; of the inhabitants of Gelonus in Scythia he notes that, since they were of Greek origin and then merged with the Budini, they spoke half Greek and half Scythian.[127] After Herodotus the expedition of Alexander stimulated a reawakening of interest in changes in the Greek language caused by contact with foreign peoples; on his march he encountered groups of Greeks who had been deported by the Persian King,[128] and who after centuries of living in an alien environment had lost, or had gone a good way to losing their distinctive characteristics, starting with language. The examples of the Eretrians and the Branchidai reported by Curtius are sufficient.[129] A paradigmatic case, finally, is that of the Sidetans as related in Arrian: the first of them arrived in Pamphylia from Kyme in Aeolis with the intention of founding a city, and had scarcely installed themselves when they forgot Greek and started to speak a language that was completely their own, different also from that of the local peoples.[130]

This, then, is the tradition of thinking about language in which the explanation reported in Diogenes Laertius on the origin of the meaning of the term solecism is to be located: an explanation centred on the fate of the Athenians who – abandoned by Solon in Soloi in conditions of isolation – corrupted their language. Although such an interpretative proposal would hardly be acceptable today, it might nevertheless be interesting to attempt to identify what exactly provided the impetus for its formulation. A plausible hypothesis is the presence in Athens of Chrysippus of Soloi, the man responsible for the advancement of the study of solecism in the sphere of logic,[131] but who at the same time was also the object of criticism in the city – an echo of which reached even Galen in the second century AD – for not having invested the necessary care into mastering Greek in his native land and for the numerous 'mistakes' he made in speaking.[132] On the basis of this, one of the professional enemies of Chrysippus, or the inevitable grammarian-defender of Attic purity, eliding the positive air that the legend of Soloi's foundation by Solon seems to have in Euphorion, could have cooked up the etymology which linked the term solecism with Soloi and the poor quality of the Greek that the Athenians, abandoned by Solon, had

---

[127] Sauromatai: Hdt. 4.117; Geloni: Hdt. 4.108. On the Budini see Thomas (2000: 286–8).
[128] On deportations in the Persian empire see Asheri (1983: 30–4) and Briant (1996: 521–3).
[129] Eretrians: Hdt. 6.107.2, 115, 119, Curt. 4.12.11, Philostr. *VA* 1.23–5, see Grosso (1958). Branchidai: Strabo 11.11.4, 14.1.5, Curt. 7.5.28–35.
[130] Arr. *Anab.* 1.26.5, on which see Bosworth (1980: I, 167) and Nollé (1993: 43–7). Beyond Arrian's words, on the language of Side, see Neumann (1980: 173).
[131] Above § I.   [132] Gal. *De diff. puls.* 2.10 (8.631–2 K).

with time started to speak.¹³³ Now, this is merely a hypothesis which, even if it does not correspond exactly to the truth, has perhaps the merit of throwing light on the uncertainties in Chrysippus' command of Greek about a century after the end of Persian control in Cilicia. At any rate, taking a longer view, it cannot be denied that the etymology of solecism proposed in Diogenes Laertius, at whatever level of consciousness it was formulated, amply reflects the fortunes of Hellenism in Cilicia between the seventh and the third centuries BC: a Hellenism that was feeble and uncertain, felt itself under siege and was in constant search of legitimization.

VI

Nevertheless, at the beginning of the second century BC the process of linguistic Hellenization appears already firmly in motion in our region, and could be said to be complete, at least in the urban areas and along the coastal belt, some time before the territory of Rough Cilicia was added to the province of Cilicia by Pompey in the 60s BC.¹³⁴ This process of linguistic Hellenization is to be located within a wider process in Asia Minor, by which, in the time of Strabo, the tendency to abandon local languages in favour of Greek had culminated in the victory of the latter in southern and western regions such as Lydia, Caria and Lycia: in the central-eastern area, on the contrary, the local languages of Galatia and Cappadocia seem to have remained almost unaffected.¹³⁵ A general reading in historical terms of the linguistic dynamics in Asia Minor between the third and first centuries BC, with a view to identifying the political, social and even economic reasons behind it, is still lacking. The analysis, however, of situations such as those obtaining in Lydia, Caria and Lycia – of vicarious interest for Cilicia – could start from a passage of seminal importance in Strabo.¹³⁶ Here, speaking with specific reference to central-western Asia Minor, the author assigns the general disappearance of the local languages and onomastics to the period of the Roman presence which began with the formation of the province of Asia (129 BC). This remark is not generally taken into account by Anatolian language specialists, perhaps because it is considered somewhat impressionistic; but what Strabo says seems to offer the definitive picture

---

¹³³ Cf. Irwin (1999: 192–3), although she follows a somewhat different line.
¹³⁴ After defeating the pirates in 67 BC. For the 'province' of Cilicia from its origins as a military command until after Sulla's reorganization of Asia Minor see Syme (1939) and (1995: 118–20), Sherwin-White (1983: 97–101, 152–3), Freeman (1986), Campanile (2001). The province, at any rate until the campaigns of Pompey in the 60s, did not include any part of Cilicia proper.
¹³⁵ Salmeri (2000b: 171–8).   ¹³⁶ Strabo 12.4.6.

of the dissolution of local languages in the areas in question, a process decisively set in motion in the decades following Alexander's expedition. Furthermore, demonstrating an interest in linguistic phenomena that is far from superficial, Strabo adduces factors of a political and administrative order to explain the disappearance of local Anatolian languages. His reasoning is substantially as follows: the arrival of the Romans, introducing new territorial divisions into Asia Minor (the *conventus*), dealt a mortal blow to the coherence of the world of the *ethnê*, and in such a way favoured the *poleis* and thus the ultimate success of Greek.[137] Similarly in the case of Cilicia the victory of Greek in the urban areas and along the coastal belt can be attributed to the fact that during the Hellenistic period they were integrated into imperial states, such as those of the Ptolemies and, to a larger extent, of the Seleucids. As well as reorganizing the territory and putting it under the control of their own governors, the Seleucids, at least until the reign of Antiochos IV Epiphanes, continued their work of establishing colonies and refounding cities, a policy always inclined to favour the Greek element.[138] When in 83 BC the Armenian king Tigranes invaded the Cilician plain he found himself confronted by cities which are defined in literary sources simply as Greek; their inhabitants were chosen by the king to be the principal vehicles of the Hellenization of his new capital, Tigranocerta.[139]

The adoption of Greek as the spoken language of the cities of Cilicia does not imply, however, that the region can be described as Hellenized *tout court* during the imperial period. For a start, there are a few reservations in the writings of the grammarians concerning the purity of the Greek spoken in Cilicia which, in line with the etymology of *soloikismos* analysed in the previous pages, tends to be viewed as an object of the corrupting influences of neighbouring languages.[140] In Tarsos there is evidence not only for a Jewish community, most likely settled during the Seleucid period, but also for a substantial group of linen-workers, whom Dio of Prusa presents as situated on the margins of civic life, and who are considered by Rostovtzeff 'as descendants of serfs who originally had been attached to the temple-factories'.[141] Furthermore, the fact that a building as symbolic of Hellenization as the theatre, after an initial spread during the Hellenistic

---

[137] See also Strabo 13.4.12. On Strabo's linguistic interests see Salmeri (2000*b*: 171–8).
[138] Cf. above nn. 107–12.
[139] Strabo 11.14.15, Plut. *Luc.* 26.1, Dio Cass. 36.2.3, 37.6 and Plut. *Pomp.* 28, see Ruge (1927: 936), Will (1982: II, 457–9, 500).
[140] Cf. Latte (1915: 387 n. 1).
[141] On the Jewish community at Tarsus see Schürer (1986: III.1, 33–4). Tarsus was also the place of birth of the apostle Paul: Hengel (1992: 29–33); and Paul's trade, if understood as that of 'tentmaker'

Hellenism on the periphery: Cilicia

period, achieved a moderate success in the cities of Cilicia only from the middle of the second century AD, could be considered an index of the region's late and uncanonical acquisition of Greek customs.[142] On a more general level there is evidence throughout Cilicia, but particularly in Rough Cilicia and in areas which were mountainous and lacking in urban centres, for the survival in some measure of Luwian onomastics and of local cults.[143] And on top of all this there is the perception that the Greek world had of Cilicia and her inhabitants – a perception which, for the period in question, is attested in a series of proverbs and epigrams and in writers such as Dio of Prusa or Lucian.[144] On the basis also of recent historical precedents[145] the inhabitants of the region were generally presented as bandits, pirates, liars, dishonest and debauched – and as such located on the margins of Hellenism.[146] Dio, for example, in an oration delivered before the inhabitants of Tarsos, questions whether his audience – widely considered colonists of Argos in the imperial period – should be regarded as colonists of Arados and the Phoenicians rather than Greeks, owing to their excessive passion for lascivious Phoenician music and their wild politics.[147] It is clear that the orator in posing his question is not arguing, against the general opinion of the time, that Tarsos was a foundation of Arados instead of Argos; rather, he wants to rouse the pride of his listeners by means of this provocation, and stimulate them to adopt better morals and wiser politics.[148] But the assimilation to Arados in neighbouring Phoenicia is in itself indicative of Dio's assessment of Tarsos as a city where Hellenism was in danger; where disorder and vice reigned and the inhabitants inclined to debauchery.

In a Cilicia that in the second century AD was Hellenized linguistically, but not completely in other respects, it is easy to identify in analysis of

---

(*skênopoios*: *Act.* 18.3), is interestingly appropriate to his Cilician origin: Hemer (1990: 119). On the linen-workers of Dio (*Or.* 34.21–3) see Rostovtzeff (1957: 179), Jones (1978: 81), Salmeri (2000*a*: 75–6 n. 112).

[142] See Spanu (2001). On the festivals held in the region see Ziegler (1985).
[143] See Hopwood (1990), and Houwink Ten Cate (1965) especially for the Hellenistic period.
[144] See North (1996). The Lncianic *Pseudosophistês ê Soloikistês* is not relevant.
[145] Rough Cilicia, for example, was the home of the pirates defeated by Pompey in 67 BC.
[146] Cf. above n. 144.
[147] Dio, *Or.* 33.41–2. For the claim of the inhabitants of Tarsos to be colonists of Argos, see the same passage and also the first paragraph of the speech. Of course, the claim has no historical basis but represents rather the result of the longing for Hellenization that had already taken root in some centres of Cilicia before Alexander; see Robert (1977: 108, 111) and above § IV. For the problems raised by the two speeches (*Or.* 33–4) delivered by Dio in Tarsos towards the end of his life, in the first decade of the second century AD, see Jones (1978: 72–82, 136), Swain (1996: 214–19), Salmeri (2000*a*: 78–9 n. 126, 83–4).
[148] Robert (1977: 132).

the epigraphic and numismatic material a movement on the part of the local ruling groups to consolidate the claims of their respective cities to Hellenism. This phenomenon turns out to be perfectly integrated into the cultural climate of rediscovery on the part of the Greeks of the Empire of 'self and unity' which constituted the fertile soil in which the *Panhellenion* flourished.[149] None of the cities of Cilicia or the Near East, however, on the basis of the material at our disposal, seems to have joined the Athenian assembly, most probably since the Hellenism of the area could not be considered above suspicion.[150] In Tarsos and Aigai, as though to counter this defect, and following a regional tradition that can be traced back to the Persian period, as has been superbly shown by Louis Robert, there was insistence on a connection with Argos.[151] At Soloi – which became Pompeiopolis in 66 or 65 BC on the wishes of Pompey, who repopulated her with a nucleus of the pirates he had defeated and granted her *eleutheria*[152] – they chose a different route. After the visit of Hadrian in AD 130 there arose a desire to embellish the appearance of the city and make her comparable to any of the illustrious centres of Hellenism. They started the construction of a monumental harbour, which was completed under Antoninus Pius,[153] and made plans for a colonnaded street, which would have been among the most imposing in the eastern Mediterranean.[154] The city, like many others in the Greek world, also erected a statue of Hadrian in the precinct of the Olympieion at Athens,[155] and repeatedly featured her illustrious sons Aratus and Chrysippus on her coinage in the second half of the second and the first decades of the third centuries AD,[156] the portraits being intended to point out her rightful place in the Greek cultural orbit. But none of this was sufficient for Soloi – despite having changed her name to Pompeiopolis[157] – to succeed, in the following centuries, in shaking off the etymology which connected her with the term solecism[158] and underlined her doubtful claim to Hellenism. The history of Cilicia, in which languages had always met and interacted, weighed heavily upon her.

---

[149] Jones (1996: 47). [150] See Spawforth (1999: 347–50).
[151] Robert (1977: 88–132) and above nn. 89–90 and 113–16. Dio Chrysostom (*Or.* 44.6) defines Athens, Sparta and Argos as the most famous (*endoxótatai*) among the Greek cities of his time.
[152] Above n. 139, *IGR* III 869 and Jones (2001: 234). [153] Boyce (1958).
[154] Peschlow-Bindokat (1975), Bejor (1999: 72–3). [155] *IG* II/III² 3302, see Paus. 1.18.6.
[156] See Ingholt (1967–8) and also Bacchielli (1979).
[157] Cf. above n. 152. However, some of the authors of the imperial period, such as Plutarch, continue to use the old name, see Jones (2001: 234).
[158] See Irwin (1999).

CHAPTER 7

Leon son of Chrysaor and the religious identity of Stratonikeia in Caria*

Riet Van Bremen

The publication, in 1995, of two Hellenistic decrees found at the sanctuary of Zeus at Panamara in Caria, honouring the Stratonikeian citizen Leon son of Chrysaor for his role as priest of Zeus Karios, has already generated a fair amount of interest among scholars. Understandably, immediate attention has focussed on the problem of the identity of the honouring community in one of the texts: the thus far unknown *koinon* of the Laodikeis.[1] There is, however, a great deal more in these decrees to deserve further investigation. The two new texts complement a third, which was found at Panamara almost a century ago.[2] Together they now make up a small dossier which is of some importance for our understanding of the process of city formation in this part of Asia Minor, in that it throws light on the relationship between

---

* Much of the research for this article was done in the excellent library of the Kommision für Alte Geschichte und Epigraphik des Deutsches Archäologisches Institut in Munich. I am grateful to its director, M. Wörrle, for his kindness and hospitality. I wish to thank B. Dignas, H. Müller and G. Reger for comments and discussion, and particularly A. Bresson for allowing me to consult the epigraphic section of *Les hautes terres de Carie* (referred to here as *HTC*) before publication and for making me look differently at many aspects of Stratonikeia's role in this part of Caria. The Leverhulme Foundation generously funded a year's research leave in 1999–2000.
   This article was largely completed in 2001. Since then, articles, books and new inscriptions have appeared that are of relevance to its content. I have tried where possible to include references to these in the text or footnotes. Among these I single out the new Chrysaoric decree found at Lagina and published by M. Ç. Şahin. It is too late to incorporate a discussion of this problematic text here. Most importantly, I have had access to G. Cousin's notebooks in the Ecole française in Athens, which has forced me to rethink the dating of one or two inscriptions. I have resisted the temptation of a major rewrite of some sections and have tried to incorporate these changes as inobtrusively as possible within my argument.

[1] Publication of the decrees by Şahin (1995: nos. 1 and 2 with pl. 18) (*SEG* XLV 1556 and 1557). Republication of both decrees in *HTC* as nos. 84 (Kallipolis) and 89 (Laodikeis) with translation and commentary. Articles on the identity of the Laodikeis by Corsten (1995), Ma (1997) and Reger (1998). Gabrielsen (2000a) discusses the texts more generally in the context of the political development of communities in the Rhodian Peraia: 140–1 (Kallipolis), 144–6 (Laodikeis) and 165–6 (Leon).

[2] Published by Cousin (1904: 350–1, no. 6) (*IS* 7) together with a number of other Hellenistic decrees from this sanctuary (Cousin's nos. 1, 2 joined with 3, 4, 5 and 7 are now in *IS* as 3, 4, 5, 6 and 8 respectively). Discussions of Leon by Holleaux (1904: 361–2), Oppermann (1924: 24–30), who dated the decree (*IS* 7) to 197 BC; Laumonier (1958: 237–8) and (1937: 238, no. 1, dated 'un peu avant... 189'); Chaniotis (1988: 302–3); Debord (1994: 114–15).

a Seleucid foundation, Stratonikeia, which went on to become one of the major cities in this area, and the Carian communities and sanctuaries that formed its building blocks. More specifically it raises questions about the impact that integration into the larger organizational structures of a *polis* had on the local identity and role of an existing sanctuary and, indirectly, about the way in which a newly founded city's religious identity took shape.[3]

I. THE LEON DECREES

All three texts (in the Appendix, with translations) were found at Panamara. They bring to nine the total number of honorific decrees from the sanctuary that are datable to somewhere between the last year of the third and the middle of the second century BC.[4] Of these, six were issued by the *koinon* of the Panamareis, two by other Carian *koina*,[5] and one by the Carian city of Kallipolis.[6] Of the earliest two decrees, both issued by the *koinon* of the Panamareis, one is in honour of the Macedonian king, Philip V, issued at the time of his campaigns in the area,[7] and the other in honour of the king's *epistates* over the sanctuary, Asklepiades (*IS* 3 and 4, dated to 201 and 198 BC respectively). Three further decrees, also issued by the *koinon* of the Panamareis, are in honour of Rhodians (*IS* 5, 6 and 9); one decree

---

[3] I do not intend to discuss here the overall development of local cults within the wider context of Stratonikeia, which requires more space, nor do I discuss in any detail the city's role within the larger organization of the Chrysaoric League (in my opinion predominantly a religious organization – *pace* Gabrielsen 2000*a*: 157–61) or the implications of the interesting early presence of a Sarapieion and a sanctuary of the Samothrakian gods in the civic centre (Sarapieion: Varinlioğlu 1994, dated to the early second century BC; the Samothrakion is referred to in *IS* 1004, of the same date). On these see now Debord (2001*a*: 158–62).

[4] This is in striking contrast to the dearth of Hellenistic inscriptions from the civic centre of Stratonikeia, an imbalance already remarked upon by J. and L. Robert (1955: 553), and one which the excavations of the last twenty-odd years have not changed.

[5] The term *koinon* in this part of Caria in the Hellenistic period appears to denote a community, or a group of communities, which is/are politically organized into a *demos*, with an *ekklesia* (but without a *boule*), a number of officials and a decision-making process closely resembling that of a *polis*, and which was sometimes organized around a central sanctuary. See in general Francotte (1906: 1–11, 20); Oppermann (1924: 4–6, 13–17); Gabrielsen (2000*a*: 132–4); *HTC passim*, but especially the discussion on pp. 82–3 and at no. 1, the *neoria* inscription. Some see a lack of political independence as one of its main determining features, and the transition from *polis* to *koinon* status as part of the process of loss of political autonomy. Within the Rhodian 'subject' Peraia this model appears to fit. It cannot, however, be shown that elsewhere, too, the change in status, from *polis* to *koinon*, was always generated by the community's subordination to a higher authority, or its integration into a larger *polis* (e.g. Stratonikeia or Mylasa). Thus, for instance, the citizens of Olymos, while still independent, before their absorption by Mylasa in the late third century BC, already referred to themselves as a *koinon* (*I. Mylasa* 866. 4; on the date of the Mylasa–Olymos *sympoliteia* see Reger in this volume), although the use of the word in this decree is not entirely unambiguous.

[6] On the south-eastern shore of the Gulf of Keramos. On the site see most recently Descat (1994: 205–14), who shows that its territory stretched from Gelibolu along the coast to Ferek and inland to Duran Çiftlik and discusses the remains of fortifications at Ferek and Çetibeli.

[7] On the campaigns of Philip V in Caria see most recently Reger (1999: 86–8), with further refs.

(*IS* 8) was issued by the *koinon* of the Londeis, located some 10 km to the south of Panamara. The decrees honouring Leon were issued by the *koinon* of the Panamareis (*IS* 7), the *polis* of the Kallipolitai (*EA* no. 1), and the *koinon* of the Laodikeis (*EA* no. 2). The latter two are inscribed on the same stele. All three must have been issued soon after the end of Leon's priesthood.[8]

Of the three, only the decree issued by the Laodikeis has a dating formula. Since it is dated ἐπὶ ἱερέως Εὐδάμου καὶ ἀρχόντων ἐν <Λα>οδικείαι κτλ., i.e. by the Rhodian priest of Helios as well as the local Laodikeian magistrates, one's first instinct would be to place it within those decades of the second century BC (between 188 and 167) when Stratonikeia and Panamara, together with most of Caria south of the Maiandros, were under the direct control of the island of Rhodes.[9] It would, on the other hand, make considerably more historical sense to see renewed Stratonikeian activity in the region only after the city's liberation from Rhodian control. There are, in fact, supporting arguments for a later date. The letter forms of the decrees, though compatible with a date in the first half of the second century BC, tend towards the latter part of that period.[10] It has further been shown, by G. Reger, that the priest Eudamos is a man well known from Rhodian amphora stamps whose date is thought to lie somewhere between 175 and 150 BC. Guided by the lower chronology for Virginia Grace's Period I–IV Rhodian amphoras recently proposed by G. Finkielsztejn, Reger now points out the possibility of dating the Leon inscriptions even more

---

[8] *IS* 7 l. 20, Kallipolis ll. 7–8, Laodikeis ll. 5–6. There is a – not very clear – photograph of the two new texts in *EA* 25, pl. 18. No photograph or squeeze exists of *IS* 7 though the majuscule drawing in *BCH* 28 (1904) 350–1 aims to approximate characteristics of the inscription's lettering. This drawing differs at several points from what can be made out of the letter forms on the photograph of the other two Leon decrees. Almost all its *alpha*s have straight cross-bars (two broken), while the photograph shows broken cross-bars throughout; the *omicron*s on the photograph are smaller than those of the drawing; the right *hasta* of its *pi*s does not touch down to base whereas most of those in the drawing do (though some do not, which again suggests that some care was taken in reproducing the letter forms). *Theta*s in both have a central cross-bar. It would be unsafe to conclude from this comparison alone that *IS* 7 is of a much earlier date than the other two texts, but it is possible that it was inscribed somewhat earlier.

[9] Reger (1999: 89–93, with further refs) on the rewarding of Rhodes with Caria south of the Maiandros in the treaty of Apameia, and on the subsequent relations between Rhodes and Caria.

[10] See above, n. 8. For comparison see the photographs of two inscriptions almost certainly datable to the first decades of the second century: *IS* 504 from Lagina, in Schober (1933: 13, pl. 2) (probably 190s BC but possibly earlier: *alpha*s with straight cross-bars, *theta*s with central dot) in which a priest of Hekate is reappointed by Stratonikeia's *boule* to the priesthood of Helios and Rhodes; cf. also *IS* 9, the decree for a Rhodian *epistates* (dated to between 197 and 167 BC) in *MDAI* 25 (1975) pl. 60, no. 3 (straight-barred *alpha*s). There is further *IS* 1003, in Robert (1937: pl. 17, no. 1): 'fin du IIIe siècle, au plus tard au début du IIe' on Robert's estimate, based on letter forms only, though very likely somewhat later: *alpha*s with broken cross-bars throughout; the recently published fragment in Varinlioğlu (1994: 189–91, photo on p. 191, fig. 1) has identical lettering: both are from Stratonikeia's city walls, but need not be contemporary with their construction.

specifically, to 150–148 BC, i.e. almost two decades *after* the period of Rhodian domination.¹¹ But even without Finkielsztejn's redating one could safely opt for a date within the context of the city's recently regained autonomy. That the Laodikeis continued to be subordinated to Rhodes in the period after 167 BC simply confirms that the Rhodians did not lose all their possessions on the Carian mainland at this date but only those they had acquired at the peace of Apameia in 188 BC; it also suggests that Laodikeia, though doubtless originally a Seleucid foundation, had already come under Rhodian control at some point before 188. All this, of course, narrows down the possible location and identification of this community.¹² I discuss the Rhodian connection and this *koinon's* relationship to Stratonikeia more fully below.

In all probability, then, Leon's priesthood fell more or less a century after the city's foundation (in the 260s or 250s BC).¹³ That Leon son of Chrysaor son of Zoilos son of Polyperchon was a citizen of Stratonikeia is no longer a matter of dispute: the text of the Kallipolis decree specifically refers to him in those terms (ll. 23 and 28).¹⁴ That he was also very likely a descendant of one of the city's Macedonian settler families is suggested not only by the fact that his descent is – unusually for this time – traced back three generations, but also by his great-grandfather's Macedonian name.¹⁵ That it was the Stratonikeis rather than the *koinon* of the Panamareis who

---

¹¹ Reger (1998) and personal communication. Along the same lines also A. Bresson in *HTC* at no. 89, pp. 213–14, who supports a date after 167 BC on grounds of historical plausibility, linking Leon's activities with a revival of Stratonikeia's autonomy. On the redating see Finkielsztejn (1995) and (1993), and see now Finkielsztejn (2001).

¹² See now in particular the discussion in *HTC* at no. 89 and, on the wider issue of Rhodian control in this region, see especially the introductory remarks on pp. 82–3, the discussion of the *neoria* inscription from Pisye (no. 1) and further under individual entries. I return to the question of the location and possible date of the foundation at the end of this chapter. Debord (2001a: 167–70) argues that the Laodikeia in question was Laodikeia on the Lykos, demoted to *koinon* status after the peace of Apameia. This would be unparalleled for a Hellenistic city foundation (the alleged parallel of Hyllarima adduced by Debord concerns a very different kind of development). The board of three *archontes* (and one *grammateus*) mentioned in the decree of our Laodikeis is unknown from the city on the Lykos, but is a familiar feature in Lycia and in parts of south-west Caria (with variations in their number), cf. the *koinon* of the Tarmianoi (*I.Rh.Per.* 781; *HTC* 62), which had three *archontes* plus one *grammateus*; an unspecified number of *archontes* in *IS* 8 (the *koinon* of the Londeis) and Koranza (two, then one: *IS* 503, 549); on Lycian boards of *archontes* see Wörrle (1988a: 119–23) and Bresson (1999: 115 with n. 150).

¹³ On the date of the foundation see the next section.

¹⁴ This decree has put paid to the suggestion, first made by H. Oppermann, and most recently championed by Chaniotis (1988: 202–3), that Leon was identical with the historian Leon of Alabanda: it refers to him specifically as Stratonikeian and congratulates the Stratonikeis on having appointed him priest (Kallipolis ll. 23 and 28). Debord (1994: 115), without knowledge of the new texts, assumed rightly that Leon was a Stratonikeus, as did already Holleaux (1904: 361–2).

¹⁵ Debord (1994: 115) makes a plausible case for Leon's settler descent. If right, this further supports a date around the middle of the second century.

had appointed him to this, 'the most prominent sanctuary', also emerges from the Kallipolis decree (ll. 29–31: καὶ ἐπαινέσει αὐτοὺς ἐπ[ὶ τ]ῶι καλὸν [κ]αγαθὸν ἄνδρα καθεστακέναι ἐν τῶι ἐπιφανεστάτωι ἱερῶι. We do not know what was the nature of the priesthood before the Stratonikeis took control of the appointing process, nor do we know whether Leon was the first priest thus appointed.[16]

In the decree issued by the *koinon* of the Panamareis Leon is praised for having made great efforts to raise the prestige of Panamaran Zeus – in these texts always referred to as Zeus Karios – by trying to persuade, first, the entire people (*sympas demos*) to increase the splendour of the sacrifices (ll. 6–7: ἔπεισεν τὸν σύνπαντα δῆμον εἰς τ[ὸ] τὰς θυσίας ἐπιφανεστέρας καὶ μείζονας συντελεῖν), and then a number of individual *demoi*, whose identity is left vague (l. 8: ἐπελθών τε ἐπί τινας δήμους ἔπεισε καὶ ἐκείνους συνθύειν), to join in the sacrificing.[17] His attempt to convince the *sympas demos* of the importance of this local Zeus was made with the aid of extracts from historians and old documents, from which he reconstructed the honours and the grants of *asylia* that had formerly adhered to the sanctuary; the decree he is said to have handed over must have contained a resolution of the Panamareis to persuade the *sympas demos* to act on Leon's advice (ll. 3–6: ψή]φισμα ἀποδοὺς καὶ παραθεὶς ἔκ τε [τ]ῶ[ν ἐπιστολῶ]ν καὶ ἀρχαίων γραμμάτων καὶ συστησά[μενος τὰς ἄν]ωθεν τιμὰς καὶ ἀσυλίας ὑπαρχούσας τῶι Διὶ καὶ Παναμαρεῦσιν). In all this, he allegedly spared neither danger nor cost nor suffering.[18] The grateful *koinon* honoured its benefactor with a bronze statue, a gold crown, *politeia*, and a share in everything the Panamareis had a share in, for himself and his descendants (ll. 13–23). A man was delegated from the *koinon* to the *sympas demos* to inform it of the *koinon*'s decision 'so that the whole *demos* may know what has been decided by the Panamareis' (ll. 27–8).

The decrees issued by the Laodikeis and the Kallipolitai appear to refer to the same general events and are phrased in very similar language. That of the Kallipolitai, first on the stone and badly damaged down to l. 15,

---

[16] A priest (to whom the *koinon* gives instructions) is very likely referred to in the decree for Philip V (*IS* 3, l. 7), on which see my discussion below. There is nothing to suggest the presence of a dynasty of priests at Panamara as it is known, e.g., from the sanctuary of Zeus at Labraunda (*Labraunda* III. 2, ch. 12) or from that of Sinuri near Mylasa (Robert 1945: 19, no. 5).

[17] On *synthyein* and the status of *synthytes* see most recently Jones (1998), who concentrates mainly on the Roman period but who usefully sets out the general structures of the institution.

[18] A formula that may be banal in one sense, in that many parallels can be given for it, but which nevertheless reflects the precariousness of the diplomatic activities undertaken by men like Leon. An example from the same region and close in date is *I. Keramos* 6, l. 3, referring to similar hazardous circumstances. It seems to me not at all certain that the *sympoliteia* referred to in this decree was with Stratonikeia, as was first suggested by L. Robert (1962: 60–1).

can be partly reconstructed using the decree of the Laodikeis, second on the stone, which is perfectly preserved but only half as long. Both decrees refer to Leon's care and good treatment of their own citizens when they visited the sanctuary (Laodikeis, ll. 5–7: ἱερατεύσας ἐμ Παναμάροις εὐσεβῶς καὶ φιλαγάθως πᾶσι τοῖς παραγεγενημένοις τῶμ πολιτῶν εἰς τὸ ἱερὸν φιλόδοξον αὑτὸμ παρείχετο; only the first part of this sentence is preserved in the Kallipolis decree). The decree of the Kallipolitai in addition has the words τῶν ἱκετευόντων, the suppliants, in the – otherwise illegible – line following immediately after this one (10). Both also mention Leon's continuous efforts at 'reconciling those who disagreed about the oaths' (Kallipolitai 12–13; Laodikeis 7–8) and emphasize the danger, cost and hardship braved by Leon (the words used closely reflect those in ll. 10–11 of the Panamareis' own decree, where they immediately follow upon his attempt at persuading the *sympas demos* to increase the splendour of the sacrifices and his appeal to certain *demoi* to participate in the sacrificing). The use of the definite article in both texts, 'those who disagreed about *the* oaths', presupposes a common enterprise during which, or for whose ratification, oaths needed to be sworn by the various parties. The oaths could have been bilateral: linked to an agreement (following a dispute?) between the Kallipolitai and the Laodikeis, or multilateral: focussed on the sanctuary itself and involving other communities as well (I return to this issue).

What basic information can we extract from these texts about the relationship between the sanctuary and *koinon* of the Panamareis and the city of Stratonikeia, approximately one hundred years after the latter's foundation? First of all, from the two new decrees, it is now clear (as it was not before) that the Stratonikeis were in charge of appointing the priest at Panamara. Second, at the same time, there existed a *koinon* around the sanctuary which called itself the Panamareis and which functioned in the manner of a political community: meeting in assembly, taking decisions, issuing decrees, granting *politeia* and other privileges. Third, a clear constitutional relationship existed between the *demos* that constituted the *koinon* of the Panamareis and the *sympas demos* assembled in Stratonikeia: decisions taken by the former were imparted to the latter as a matter of organizational efficiency: 'so that the *sympas demos* may know what was decided' (*IS* 7, l. 27).[19] Fourth, a Stratonikeian citizen of Macedonian descent, having become priest of Zeus Karios at Panamara, did his utmost for

---

[19] To be compared with the formal diplomatic rituals observed by the Kallipolitai (Kallipolis ll. 27–31). I do not agree with Gabrielsen (2000a: 166), who sees in the *sympas demos* that of the Chrysaoric League. For one thing, no *boule* is attested for this organization. And why, if the Kallipolitai conveyed

the sake of his deity and the community that was associated with the cult. There is no overt attempt to claim this particular Zeus as 'Stratonikeian', rather, the city's *sympas demos* is persuaded to increase the splendour of its sacrifices to the local god, and other *demoi* (on whose identity further below) are persuaded to join in. It appears that the cult at Panamara still had at this time a distinct and separate identity. Lastly, the sanctuary appears to have served as a focus for an area beyond Stratonikeia's territory, namely the region to the south and south-east of Panamara, down to the Gulf of Keramos.

The skeletal facts presented here are not in themselves controversial. Their interpretation and further implications do, however, fit uneasily with what has been written, or assumed, about the territorial and political relationship between the *koinon* and sanctuary at Panamara, on the one hand, and the newly created Seleucid city on the other, about the nature of the new city itself, and about the impact of a 'Greek city' on 'indigenous' cult. Before tackling these issues, however, it is necessary briefly to set out the circumstances of Stratonikeia's foundation and to attempt a reconstruction of the sanctuary's early, pre-Stratonikeian, history.

2. THE CITY OF STRATONIKEIA

The city of Stratonikeia, named after Stratonike, the wife of Antiochos I (and mother of Antiochos II), was a Seleucid foundation, most likely dated to the 260s or 250s BC. Strabo refers to it as a '*katoikia* (a settlement) of Macedonians'.[20] As so often with this kind of foundation, we know nothing about the size and nature of the original Macedonian settlement, or about its precise location, but it is thought that it was relatively small, and that

---

their honours to the Stratonikeis, would the Panamareis have conveyed theirs to the Chrysaoreis? On the Chrysaoreis see Gabrielsen (2000a: 157–61); J. and L. Robert (1983: 217–26); Boffo (1985: 128–34); a new Chrysaoric decree has just been published by Şahin (2003).

[20] On the date of the foundation see most recently van Bremen (2000: 389), with references to earlier publications. John Ma's recent suggestion (Ma 1999: 41 n. 53 and Appendix 5) that Antiochos II, rather than Antiochos I, was the founder is not unpersuasive. His further assertion that until the former's reconquest in the early 250s the region was continuously under Ptolemaic control cannot be maintained. Even though it is now clearer than it was before, that the communities on the site of the future city, as well as Panamara, were under Ptolemaic control in the 270s (attested by *IS* 1002, an inscription from Eskihisar, dated by Ptolemaic regnal year to 276 BC, and by a fragment of a decree copied at Panamara dated probably to the same year), to assume that this control continued throughout the 260s flies in the face of the evidence. It requires Ma to argue that an honorific inscription found in a house at Yatağan, near Stratonikeia, which honours a man from Koliorga, and which is dated by Seleucid era and kings to 268 BC (*IS* 1030) was a 'pierre errante from eastern Karia' (Ma 1999: 277). All that can be said with reasonable certainty is that the city was founded some time after 276 and before 254. On Ptolemaic control in the 270s see now van Bremen (2003).

the new city was predominantly formed through a merger of existing local communities, either imposed on the region by the Seleucid founder, or granted by him at the request of the communities themselves.[21] It is impossible to say whether the merger involved the physical movement of people, but it is more likely that only a new administrative and political centre was created and that the formerly independent communities remained as centres of habitation.[22]

In inscriptions from the late second century BC onwards – there are no earlier examples to date – a Stratonikeian citizen was referred to by his name, his patronymic and his demotic.[23] This usage continued well into the third century AD. Five demotics dominate in the inscriptions even though these five did not at all times constitute between them the total territory of Stratonikeia. P. Debord has suggested that they were the five communities of the original *synoikismos*, which he dates to the time of the city's foundation.[24] Three of the five names (Koranza, Koliorga and Hierakome) belong to communities that are attested as *poleis* in the fourth century BC; nothing is known about the former status of the other two (Koraia and Lobolda).[25] The location of only one of these (Koranza, to the north-west of the urban centre) has been established with reasonable certainty; that of Hierakome and Koliorga is still uncertain.[26] The locations of Koraia and Lobolda are

---

[21] Debord (1994: 111, 118–19) and (2001a: 161) reiterates an earlier suggestion by Şahin (1976) that the principal settlement was located on the site of Hierakome and that it was on its territory that the city's urban centre developed. Şahin (1976: 1–15) argued that the deme of Hierakome received its name upon the city's foundation, on the grounds that it was here that the sanctuary of Zeus Chrysaoreus was located. This cannot be right, at least in a chronological sense: Hierakome is among the *poleis* in the recent Sekköy inscriptions of the mid-fourth century BC (Blümel 1990: 32–42, nos. 1 and 2 – allocated nos. 11 and 12 in *I. Mylasa*; cf. *SEG* XL 991 and 992; *HTC* nos. 90 and 91). The association between Zeus Chrysaoreus and Hierakome is unclear, since we do not know the location of the former's sanctuary or even how far back the cult can be dated.

[22] See van Bremen (2000) for a more detailed discussion.

[23] The earliest attested use of demotics dates to the late second century BC. But note Debord's announcement (1994: 117 n. 62) of a still unpublished inscription dated to the period of Rhodian control in which all five main demotics are mentioned.

[24] See the map in Debord (1994: 121), showing the hypothetical location of the five main demes, and a table showing the list of demes, with corrections to earlier versions. For a general discussion cf. 112–16, with all further references. See further van Bremen (2000), and, on *sympoliteia* and *synoikismos*, G. Reger in this volume.

[25] Koranzeis, Hierokomitai and Koliorgeis are listed as *poleis*, among many others, great and small, in the fourth-century inscriptions from Sekköy (above, n. 21). Koranza is also attested specifically as a *polis* in *IS* 503, l. 9, dated to 318 BC.

[26] Debord proposed to locate Koliorga at Kürbet Köy, where there are the remains of a temple and where *IS* 801, a decree of a *koinon*, was found (1994: 111). Şahin's 'Beschluss des koinon der [------] eis' at 801 is misleading: that word-ending is not on the stone, and e.g. [*Hierokomitai*] cannot be excluded. On the possible location of Koliorga and Koraia see also below, n. 110.

also unknown, though physical remains of settlements at Gibye, Bozarmut, Süleyman Bey Çiftlik, Elekçi, Kafaca, Kürbet Köy and Elmacık all come into consideration.²⁷ Since no systematic survey of this area has taken place, little more can be said. It is, however, a fair guess that all five main demes will have been in close proximity to the civic centre and that the map drawn up by P. Debord is correct at least in its indication of the areas where they were most likely located.

It is generally agreed that Panamara cannot have been a party to the original Stratonikeian *sympoliteia*. The striking absence of the letters ΠΑ as a demotic abbreviation in the epigraphic record of the city has been taken by many as an indication of the Panamareis' inclusion only at a relatively late date.²⁸ But the virtual absence of 'Panamareis' from Stratonikeia's records *at all times* – despite the great, and steadily increasing, importance of the sanctuary itself, as well as the fact that, among the almost three hundred priests (male and female) of Zeus Karios/Panamaros on record between the mid-second century BC (when priestly dedications at the sanctuary begin) and the mid-third century AD (when they gradually peter out), there is not a single *Panamareus* – requires a different explanation. What became of the Panamareis when the sanctuary was incorporated is a question that has not been adequately addressed.²⁹

3. PANAMARA BEFORE THE FOUNDATION OF STRATONIKEIA

The sanctuary of Zeus Karios (increasingly referred to as 'Panamaros' from the late first century BC onwards)³⁰ at Panamara was located some 12 km to

---

[27] The approximate location of these modern communities can be identified on the map in *IS* II.1 and in the map in Debord (1994: 121), and see this vol. Map 1.

[28] The abbreviation ΠΑ occurs in *IS* 227, l. 12 (from Panamara, late second century AD), as the demotic of the priest's wife. In *IS* 615, in a priest list from Lagina (first century BC?), the priest is Διοκλῆς Καλλίου Κολιοργεὺς καθ' ὑοθεσίαν δὲ Φανίου Παναμαρεύς; in *IS* 846, from Kafaca/Akçehisar (where there are ruins of a Hellenistic temple), the priest is Δαμόνικος Ἡρῴδου ΠΑ(ναμαρεύς); the priestess has the demotic ΚΟ(λιοργίς). This text was dated to the later imperial period by Laumonier (1958: 212).

[29] Oppermann (1924: 30) merely noted this fact, as did Roussel (1927: 130 n. 3). The majority of priests, with only a handful of exceptions, came from one of the five main Stratonikeian demes (about 160 male priests are known and 120 female).

[30] Within the Stratonikeia/Panamara context the epithet Panamaros appears first in the so-called Miracle text (*IS* 10) of 39 BC or soon after, as well as in a priest's (?) dedication of about the same time (*IS* 55); the title Zeus Karios, found in earlier decrees and dedications from the sanctuary, continued in use during the first century AD. The epithet Panamaros already occurs, however, in a dedication from Hyllarima dated by L. Robert to the second century BC (1937: 513–15), and may have been a way of referring to the deity outside the immediate context of the sanctuary itself. Laumonier

the south-east of Stratonikeia's urban centre, in wooded country on a level platform at the top of a ridge, along one side of which runs a deep ravine. The sanctuary's enclosure is a rectangular space of *ca* 100 by 85 m, within which, on a second, elevated, rocky platform of about 50 by 50 m, the main temple was located. Laumonier also describes a large open space: 'une esplanade assez longue', suited for processional display and the pitching of tents during festivals. The enclosure is surrounded by massive walls, large stretches of which survive.[31] Its appearance has been likened to a 'terraced fortress'[32] and ancient texts refer to the sanctuary as a *chorion*, a fortified place.[33] The temple within the enclosure was, as I shall argue below, already in existence at the beginning of the third century BC and thus very likely predates the city of Stratonikeia itself, not only as a 'lieu de culte', but also as a monumental structure. No archaeological investigation of this site has ever been carried out, and no date has been proposed for the walls and the sanctuary complex on the basis of an analysis of the remaining structures.[34]

Panamara's location is a key to understanding its history. It was not self-evidently a part of the nexus of communities that were to synoikize into the new *polis* of Stratonikeia immediately to its north, but belonged inherently to the mountainous region of small communities extending south from the Mylasa–Stratonikeia road down to the Gulf of Keramos: the part of Caria commonly referred to as the Rhodian 'subject Peraia'. Its neighbours to the south and south-east were *koina*: some small, like the

---

(1958: 241) saw in the use of 'Panamaros' a continuation of the deity's original, indigenous name, in use only 'dans les milieux purement indigènes', while the use of 'Karios' was due to the Hellenizing assumptions of those in the new 'Macedonian' city. By the end of the first century, 'Greek' and 'Carian' had sufficiently fused to warrant a return to the original name. Oppermann (1924: 85) similarly attempted to link the use of the epithet Karios to the foundation of the new colony: 'Als Stratonikeia gegründet wurde, kam durch die griechisch-makedonischen kolonisten Ζεὺς Κάριος in Übung. Sie stellten auf diese Weise den Gott in Gegensatz zum griechischen Zeus.' Debord (2001*a*: 167) links the name to a wider organization.

[31] Descriptions: Laumonier (1936: 324–7 with pl. 41); and *idem* (1958: 221–7); Roussel (1931: 93–4). Certain passages in the Miracle text give a good impression of the sanctuary's unscalable walls, of the ravine, and of the mountainous landscape around the site. It is remarkable that the only site drawing available appears still to be the rather primitive sketch made by Laumonier to illustrate his description of the site (Laumonier 1936: pl. 41), on which the 'champ de blé en pente légère' indicates the large open space suitable for processions, etc.

[32] Laumonier (1958: 223): 'une forteresse à étages'.

[33] *IS* 9, l. 9; *IS* 10 (Miracle text), ll. 11, 19, 24.

[34] The encroaching menace of the surface mining for brown coal, which has been devastating much of this area in the past decade, has now reached the immediate surroundings of Panamara, so that little can be made any longer of the ancient (or modern) settlements around the sanctuary or its connections within the larger region. For an account of the damage see Özgan (1999: 17–20), cf. also Varinlioğlu (1997: 297 and 303 with n. 47).

Leukoideis (at Çırpı, immediately to the sanctuary's south) and the Londeis (at Çiftlik) and Koloneis (probably at Yeniköy) beyond. Others were or became part of larger *koinon*-structures, such as that of the Tarmianoi, based around Muğla and extending in a north-westerly direction, or the 'Pisyetai and Pladaseis united with the Pisyetai' (the former's centre at Yeşilyurt was clearly an important focus; the latter's was near the coast at Sarnıç with its harbour at Akbük) whose north-westernmost settlement, at Selvili Çeşme, lay at a distance of only about 10 km south-east of Panamara. In the course of the third century BC many of these communities came under Rhodian control or stood in some kind of dependent relationship to the island-state.[35] Throughout the Hellenistic period Rhodians predominate to a remarkable extent in the honorific decrees, the dedications and the funerary inscriptions of this region, and it was doubtless the continuing dependence on Rhodes which 'froze' an existing situation and prevented any of its larger *koina*-structures from developing into *poleis*. Unlike the neighbouring *koina*, the Panamareis do not appear to have come under Rhodian control other than for a brief period, but they could easily have shared the fate of their neighbours and become part of the 'subject' Peraia more permanently, thus continuing as a *koinon* well into the first century BC. Indeed, in the case of Panamara, one may rightly wonder what it was that tipped the balance in favour of Stratonikeia, not Rhodes.

The position of Stratonikeia itself, though successfully transformed from a grouping of similar small communities into a *polis* through an act of royal foundation, was equally constrained by the immediate proximity of Rhodian-dominated territory more or less from the time of its foundation, and Stratonikeia was, for a while, itself incorporated into that territory. For a period of almost two centuries, between the date of the city's foundation and the *senatus consultum* of 81 BC – in which the Stratonikeis were granted, in reward for having sided with Rome against Mithridates, among other things the city and territory of Keramos, on the coast, with its *choria*, villages and harbours[36] – the new city found itself on the edge of a region which was almost entirely dominated and/or controlled by Rhodes, without

---

[35] On all this, in much greater detail than it is possible to go into here, see now the descriptions and discussions in *HTC* 11–18 for an introduction to the geography of the region, parts III and V for the individual sites and their inscriptions. On the meaning and definition of 'subject Peraia' see Fraser and Bean (1954: 53, 70–8, 98–117); Reger (1999: 78–81); and Gabrielsen (2000a) *passim* (critical of the concept). On Rhodes and Caria see now also Bresson (2003).

[36] Doubtless various communities in between: Themessos is mentioned but has not been located, and there is space in the text for another community's name. *IS* 505, Sherk, *RGE* no. 63, with translation.

apparently being able to make any inroads into it.³⁷ The entire subject-Peraia formed a buffer between Stratonikeia and the sea, with Rhodian-dominated *koina* on either side of the main route along the valley of the Marsyas down to the sea at Idyma; the same applied for the alternative route via Pisye along the valley of the Kartal Deresi (Kocaçay) down to Sarnıç and to the sea at Akbük, which was moreover lined with a series of fortresses.³⁸

The sanctuary at Panamara, because of its location, must from an early date have functioned as a cult centre for this region.³⁹ The name of Zeus Karios suggests this wider appeal, even if it was not necessarily pan-Carian.⁴⁰ How far back can we trace the existence of a sanctuary at Panamara? Most scholars leave this question open, taking the decrees for Philip V and Asklepiades (*IS* 3 and 4, dated to 201 BC and 198 BC respectively) as the starting point of their discussion of the cult and the sanctuary.⁴¹ There are clear pointers, however, both in the decree of the Panamareis for Leon and in those for Philip V and his *epistates*, to the existence of a cult and a sanctuary well before the late third century. The *epistates* Asklepiades,

---

³⁷ The Tarmianoi, for instance, were still honouring Rhodians – one for his δικαιοσύνη towards themselves, another for whom naval and military positions are listed – in the early to mid-first century BC (*I.Rh.Per.* nos. 781 and 782; *HTC* nos. 62, 63, as redated by A. Bresson); cf. similarly the entries for the Leukoideis and many of the inscriptions found in the territory of Pisye (*I.Rh.Per.* and *HTC* s.v.). On the possible earlier *sympoliteia* between Stratonikeia and Keramos see above, n. 18.

³⁸ See the description in Varinlioğlu (1997: 297 and 301–2), retracing the route taken by the Rhodian commander Nikagoras in order to recapture territory gained by Philip V. For a description of the fortresses see Fraser and Bean (1954: 75–7), Paton and Myres (1896: 189–90, with pl. 10). On a possible route connecting Stratonikeia and Keramos see Paton and Myres (1896: 189): the road will have gone first to Panamara. From there it is said to have gone via Gevenez/Kavenas to the head of the Kay Dere and thence 'across the Marishal Dagh to Pirnari and Keramos' (it must, however, have skirted the western flank of that mountain rather than crossed it).

³⁹ There appear to have been few other sanctuaries of any size. For a possible sanctuary at Çandüsüren, originally part of the *polis* of the Pladaseis (whose deity has not been identified), see *HTC*, commentary at no. 48.

⁴⁰ One of the decrees set up at Panamara (*IS* 8: first half of the second century BC, on letter forms) was a decree of the neighbouring *koinon* of the Londeis in honour of a man whose identity is lost but who cannot himself have been a Londeus. He may have been a Lomeus (one of the constituent communities of the nearby *koinon* of the Tarmianoi, on which see above, n. 12). The general context of this decree, which appears to be dated by a local eponym, is uncertain. It was long thought to have been a decree of the Londargeis (and therefore of Stratonikeia – though the identity and location of this 'deme' is far from clear), but see now *HTC*, comments at no. 39. For the restoration [δήμ]αρχος in ll. 10–11 of this decree see below, n. 85. *HTC* no. 39 itself is a dedication (found at Çiftlik and dated to 150–100 BC) of a fountain and a Nymphaion, by two *hierotamiai* to 'Zeus Karios and the Londeis'.

⁴¹ Debord (1994: 114–15) begins his discussion with Panamara being a '*koinon* autonome' at the time of Philip V. Oppermann's discussion is guided by the existing Panamaran inscriptions (1924: 4–5, 18–31); Laumonier (1958: 234–5) presupposes the existence of the cult at the time of Stratonikeia's foundation but takes it to have been insignificant and local (see below, n. 45).

in 198 BC, restored the walls that 'had been destroyed in the earthquake' (ll. 16–17)[42], while in ll. 11–12 of the decree for Philip we read: 'to inscribe [this decree] on the *parastas* [of the temple of Zeus]'.[43] The attention of Philip V, furthermore, who offered φιάλας καὶ κάδον (libation bowls and a vessel) to the god,[44] implies that at that time the sanctuary had attained a certain local reputation, even if its strategic importance may not have been far from the king's mind.[45] It is doubtless this reputation that was reflected in the *asylia* and other privileges mentioned in the Panamareis' decree for Leon.

What is significant is that these previous *asyliai* explicitly pertained to 'Zeus *and* the Panamareis' without any reference to Stratonikeia: καὶ συστησά[μενος τὰς ἄν]ωθεν τιμὰς καὶ ἀσυλίας ὑπαρχούσας τῶι Διὶ καὶ Παναμαρεῦσιν.[46] When were they first granted? Is it likely that *asylia* for the sanctuary at Panamara would have been sought, and recognized, precisely at the time of the new city's foundation but without letting that city in any way share in its prestige? If so, the very fact of the granting must have served to underline the sanctuary's, and especially the *koinon*'s, detachment from Stratonikeia. And who, other than the city's Seleucid founder, would have been in a position to concede this special status? It may be thought more likely that the *asylia*, together with other privileges (*ateleia, hikesia*?), was granted before the foundation of the city, in which case either a Ptolemaic or a Seleucid ruler could be considered as a possible royal grantor. Claims of an even earlier grant should not, however, be excluded.[47] Unfortunately, Leon's use of 'old (*archaia*) documents'

---

[42] Most likely the earthquake of 199/8, so Holleaux (1904: 358–9).
[43] εἰς τὴν παραστά[δα τοῦ ναοῦ τοῦ Διὸς?] (as restored by Holleaux, 1904: 354–6). The age as well as the longevity of the temple was pointed out already by Laumonier (1958: 223 n. 6).
[44] *IS* 3, l. 5.
[45] According to Laumonier (1958: 235), the visit of the Macedonian king showed that Panamara had been incorporated by Stratonikeia from the time of the city's foundation and as a result had developed from an insignificant, rural sanctuary to one worthy of a royal visit: the king 'ne se serait pas dérangé pour un petit sanctuaire rustique'. On Laumonier's view of the integration of sanctuary and city see further below.
[46] *IS* 7, ll. 5–6. Leon presents a decree (presumably of the Panamareis) and the findings of his historical researches (in the sanctuary's archives) to the *sympas demos*.
[47] Cf. the claims invoked by several cities before the Roman Senate in AD 22 of Persian precedents for the *asylia* of their temples (Tac. *Ann.* 3. 60ff.). Cf. also a mid-fourth-century BC decree of the Tralleis, reinscribed in the early first century AD (*I. Tralleis* 3), documenting the ἱκετηρία of Dionysos Bakchios. See Hornblower (1982: 365), M4, and, on the date 41–3, Debord (1999: 68, 136). The fact that the decree is dated to the seventh year of Idrieus does not warrant Debord's 'l'acte de reconnaissance de l'asile de Dionysos Bacchios par Idrieus au nom d'Artaxerxès'; Rigsby (1996: 416–17) rejects the decree's authenticity. For Ptolemaic control at Panamara in the 270s see now van Bremen (2003).

(*IS* 7, ll. 3–6) cannot be pressed into telling precisely how 'old' these documents were perceived to be. It is relevant to note the even more emphatic use of ἀρχαιότατος in connection with *asylia* and *ateleia* in another, much damaged, document from the sanctuary (*IS* 20). Its date is, however, probably in the first century BC, ('petites lettres' wrote Cousin, but the copy in his notebook shows letters typical of the first century).[48] A third decree (*IS* 19), of the second century BC (? Cousin: 'petites lettres de bonne époque') and equally damaged, has the word τὸ ἄσυ[λον?] in l. 7, [ἐν] Παναμάροις in l. 6 and ὁ δῆμος ὁ Σ[τρατονικέων] in l. 5.[49] Both are surely recognitions of the sanctuary's previous *asylia* status and therefore concerned with its present renewal. *IS* 19 may well be a Stratonikeian acknowledgement of the neighbouring sanctuary's status, in response to an initiative of the Panamareis, while *IS* 20 most likely belongs in a Roman context and may be concerned with Rome's acknowledgement of the sanctuary's status – the reference to ἀρχαιότατος fits the general context of the two (?) *senatusconsulta* of 39 BC, *IS* nos. 11 and 12.[50]

Support both for the existence of a sanctuary at Panamara in the early third century and for a pre-Stratonikeian context for the privileges granted to the sanctuary may be found in an inscription from Labraunda. In this inscription (*I. Labraunda* III.2, no. 44), probably dated to the early 260s BC and mentioning a king Ptolemy, the name Panamara occurs in connection with the word *hieron* (l. 2):

[------c.20---ἱ]ερὸν [--c.5--] Παναμαρα [--c.5--]

This text, which, like almost all Labraunda inscriptions, is extremely worn and difficult to interpret, appears to be concerned with the granting of privileges, including immunity (the word *ateleia* may just be legible in l. 10) by Ptolemy Philadelphos (mentioned in l. 6 as *basileus Ptolemaios*) to the sanctuary at Labraunda, the name of whose presiding deity, Zeus Labraundos, can perhaps be read in l. 7.[51] There is no easy way of connecting

---

[48] 'Un document de date incertain' wrote L. Robert (1937) 520 n. 3. Cousin's notebooks are kept at the Ecole française in Athens. The reference for *IS* 20 is AS 10, no. 315.
[49] On the oddity of the sentence in which the word ἄσυ[λον and of the word itself, see Rigsby (1996) 424. Cousin's notebook AS 10, no. 279.
[50] *IS* 20 ll. 3–4 mention the god's ἐν]αργεῖς ἐπι[φανείας ?]; l. 7 contains the word ἀρχαιότατου, l. 8 has]ου καὶ ἀσύλου καὶ ἀτε[--- ; the decree foresees the setting up of two *stelai*, one in the sanctuary of Zeus Karios (l. 15), the other appears to involve the *prytaneis* (or the *prytaneion*) and therefore presumably a location within the city walls (l. 16).
[51] The editor, J. Crampa, suggested that the text was probably a decree of the Chrysaoric League, like the text preceding it on the stone, no. 43. Crampa dated the text to 267 BC, noting the similarity of this text's letter forms to those of no. 43, which he dated to that year (discussion on p. 56).

the inscription's uncertain first two lines (nothing is left of lines 3, 4 and 5) with lines 6–10, which are concerned with Labraunda. If the context is that of the Chrysaoric League, as was suggested by its editor, J. Crampa, then Panamara as well as Labraunda may at this time have been among that League's sanctuaries.[52] The Chrysaoric context of the text is, however, so uncertain that nothing specific can really be derived from it. Yet it is tempting to think that Panamara had been held up by the priesthood at Labraunda as a precedent of a nearby sanctuary to which similar privileges (*ateleia, hikesia, asylia*?) had previously been granted by Ptolemy himself – whether in a Chrysaoric context or not.[53]

The letter from a *basileus Seleukos* to an anonymous community on or near the site of the future Stratonikeia, whose ambassadors had appeared before the king (*IS* 1001), is also of relevance, for if the king in question is Seleukos I (as the letter forms suggest)[54] rather than Seleukos II (preferred by some on grounds of historical plausibility)[55] it provides evidence of contact between the communities in this area and the Seleucid dynasty already in 281, and an early context for the granting of privileges to local communities and/or sanctuaries.[56] In a study of *asylia* K. Rigsby has recently argued that no grants of *asylia* are known to have occurred before the 240s, only of *ateleia* and other similar privileges. In doing so he dismissed the case made previously by L. Robert that it was Seleukos I, with his son Antiochos, who first granted, in a letter dated to 281 BC, *hikesia, asylia* and *ateleia* to the Athymbrianoi for their sanctuary of Plouton and Kore, shortly before they became part of the newly founded city of Nysa.[57] An early grant to

---

[52] J. and L. Robert (1983: 223–6) on the League's community of cult. On the Chrysaoric League see now Gabrielsen (2000a: see above, n. 3).

[53] F. Piejko's restoration of l. 2 implying that the decree had also been set up in the sanctuary at Panamara is unconvincing: if the decree itself is meant, it would be highly unusual to have such an arrangement at its beginning; its implication, that Panamara was in Ptolemaic hands at the time, has now found confirmation: see van Bremen (2003).

[54] A photograph of this text in *ZPE* 39 (1980) pl. v.1. Comparison with the photograph of *IS* 1030 (*ibidem*, pl. v.2), securely dated to 268 BC, strongly suggests that *IS* 1001 is earlier. Its letter forms are very close to those of *IS* 1002 of 277/6 BC (photo: J. and L. Robert 1983: 121, fig. 6).

[55] Ma (1999: 39 n. 48): 'I. Stratonikeia 1001 should be dated to Seleukos II rather than Seleukos I.' Cf also Cohen (1995: 271). A letter of Seleukos II at Labraunda (*Labraunda* III.1, no. 1 with photo) may be compared. The argument is always that Seleukos I, between the battle of Kouroupedion early in 281 and his death six months later, would not have had enough time to organize his newly acquired possessions in Caria and Lycia. But one can take this kind of argument too far, and it is moreover entirely likely that ambassadors from this region would have gone to Seleukos after his victory at Kouroupedion in order to confirm existing privileges or seek new ones.

[56] For *IS* 1001 is clearly from a sanctuary even if probably not from Panamara. I aim to discuss this text elsewhere.

[57] Whose founder may have been Antiochos I. See Cohen (1995: 256–9). L. Robert took these privileges to be the *hikesia, asylia* and *ateleia* referred to and renewed several times in later documents inscribed

Panamara (by Seleukos, or Antiochos I) would, however, provide support for Robert's interpretation and cast doubt on the rigidity of the chronology suggested by Rigsby.

About the date and context of any later renewal(s?) we remain completely in the dark, but the fact that Leon's investigations concerning earlier *asyliai* clearly involve no reference to Stratonikeia at all suggests that they, too, pertained to the sanctuary and to the *koinon* and were made entirely without reference to the city.

4. CITY AND CULT

Even if no chronological precision is possible, it looks as if the sanctuary at Panamara had a local reputation of its own already before the foundation of Stratonikeia and had been the subject of royal, and possibly satrapal, privileges in its own right. It must now be asked what happened to the Panamareis and their sanctuary after the city was founded; whether, at any time between the 260s or 250s BC and 167 BC, the date of Stratonikeia's liberation from Rhodian control, attempts at incorporation of sanctuary and *koinon* into the new city were made, or whether Leon's activities indeed marked a crucial moment in the history of both.

For some, the case is unproblematic. The integration of the sanctuary at Panamara into the new Seleucid city was a straightforward case of Hellenizing the rural and the indigenous: a 'take-over' that occurred immediately after Stratonikeia had come into being. At the root of this view is the more general – though seldom articulated – assumption that in the process of city foundation in Asia Minor new cities functioned as Hellenizing centres to a predominantly indigenous countryside. The process of cities gradually annexing so-called indigenous sanctuaries is part of a familiar historical discourse for this period: cities emerging and proliferating through colonization, new foundations, *synoikismos*, *sympoliteia*, and through a system

---

on the same temple wall as the text of the letter. K. Rigsby doubts whether *asylia* would have been granted this early, 'with Nysa anticipating cities like Smyrna and Cos', and prefers *ateleia* only (400). Cf. J. and L. Robert (1983: 144); Rigsby (1996: 399–406). Rigsby also rejects all other cases of early grants or acknowledgments: he is sceptical about the Sardians' claim, before the Senate in AD 22, that *asylia* was granted to them by Alexander the Great in 334 BC (434, and see above n. 47 for even earlier claims). His conclusion (423–7), reached after a lengthy and careful discussion of all the evidence, that *asylia* was not granted to Panamaran Zeus until 39 BC and that therefore the relevant Stratonikeian inscriptions all belong in the imperial period, fits awkwardly with the main drift of his discussion. Nor do I agree with his assessment of the relative importance of Lagina and Panamara in the first century BC: Strabo's failure to mention Panamara (14.2.25) has been much over-interpreted for this purpose.

of political 'upgrading' generated a dissolution of earlier, indigenous, political and religious organizational forms; the result was a gradual conforming to the familiar city/territory model.[58]

Along these lines, A. Laumonier, in his *Cultes indigènes en Carie* of 1958, assumed that the incorporation of the cult at Panamara took place when the city was founded: 'la simple présence de documents épigraphiques sur marbre à Panamara au IIIe siècle suffit à prouver que le sanctuaire fut rattaché à la ville dès sa fondation'.[59] He saw the new city as having generated a 'renouvellement complet du culte, qui, de local et rustique, devient municipal et national'.[60] Laumonier's near-contemporary, P. Roussel, too, spoke of 'l'emprise de la cité macédonienne sur l'antique sanctuaire carien'.[61] In both these descriptions a separate cultural identity of city and sanctuary is assumed, and equally a superiority of one over the other: of the central and secular over the peripheral, the indigenous, the religious, with the latter supposedly changing under the impact of the former.

That the city should be the Hellenizing centre to a predominantly indigenous countryside is, however, an interpretation that is as inappropriate in a Carian context as it is for many other regions of Asia Minor. Stratonikeia's constituent *demoi* were, as we have seen, pre-existing Carian communities who themselves had, already in the fourth century BC, borrowed Greek constitutional ideas, increasingly used the Greek language in a public context and given Greek names to themselves and to their local deities.[62] Whatever the size of the new Macedonian settlement at Stratonikeia, or whatever its level of 'Hellenization', there is nothing to justify this artificial opposition between centre and periphery, or to indicate that the new city at the centre made attempts symbolically to appropriate the 'indigenous' cults in what was now 'her' territory, to bring its deities within 'her' walls or subject them to a new, Greek set of cultic prescriptions and rituals. Even to speak of a symbiosis between 'new city' and 'old sanctuary' is to misunderstand, fundamentally, the nature of the new city itself.

It is worth reviewing the evidence on which Laumonier based his reconstruction of the process of integration:

---

[58] Debord (1982: summary on pp. 291–3).   [59] Laumonier (1958: 235).

[60] For a more specific discussion of Laumonier's reconstruction see below. Similar assumptions governed his discussion of the incorporation of Lagina. I hope to deal elsewhere with Hekate's sanctuary at Lagina (whose relationship to the new city was very different from that of Panamara).

[61] Roussel (1927: 124). Cf. also J. Hatzfeld in *BCH* 51 (1927) 68: 'la mainmise de la jeune cité macédonienne sur les vieux sanctuaires de la confédération Chrysaôrique'. There are reverberations of this in L. Robert's description of the region before the city's foundation, when 'les bourgades cariennes n'avaient pas été soumises à la nouvelle ville grecque' (1937: 570).

[62] On the Hellenizing influence of the Hekatomnid satraps on this part of Caria see in particular Hornblower (1982: ch. 12 and *passim*). But Rhodes and Kos, too, were important influences.

Au cours du IIIe siècle avant J.-C. est fondée la colonie macédonienne de Stratonicée, à laquelle furent jointes sans doute en même temps, par sympolitie ou synoecisme, les bourgades cariennes voisines. Les cultes de Lagina et de Panamara durent être dès ce moment rattachés à la ville par des fêtes annuelles, comportant avant tout une procession qui perpétuait le souvenir de la première entrée des dieux dans la nouvelle ville et leur retour dans les sanctuaires de la campagne et de la montagne. Ainsi ont dû apparaître, parallèlement à la klidagogie d'Hékate, les Panamareia de Zeus. Un calendrier rituel est établi, attestant l'importance du sacrifice du boeuf et de la musique dans les rites mensuels. Une fête triétérique est déjà consacrée à Héra dès cette époque. Un fragment de *lex sacra*, interdisant, entre autres choses, l'apport des armes de guerre dans le sanctuaire, paraît remonter à la même époque, celle du renouvellement complet du culte qui, de local et rustique, devient municipal et national. (Laumonier 1958: 234–5)

Some of this reconstruction is based on conflation of evidence, projecting back later developments to a much earlier period: the annual festivals and the processions between the sanctuaries and the civic centre are well documented for the imperial period, with evidence for the *kleidophoria*, the procession of Hekate's key, first attested around the middle of the first century BC; for the Panamareia and for Zeus' procession on horseback into the city the first attestation is in the first century AD.[63] First attestations should not, of course, be understood as providing a secure *terminus post quem* of what actually went on, but to project the later evidence back almost three hundred years to the early third century BC is methodologically unsound.

The only apparently contemporary evidence on which Laumonier's interpretation of an early takeover by the 'Macedonian' city of the cults in 'her' territory is based consists of two inscriptions found at Panamara: one a sacrificial calendar ('sacrifice du boeuf et de la musique dans les rites mensuels'), the other a fragment listing objects not to be brought into the sanctuary: Laumonier's *lex sacra* (*IS* 1 and 2 respectively). *IS* 2, on which only the prohibition on the carrying in of weapons can be made out,[64] was dated by Laumonier to the third century BC. Even if the dating were

---

[63] The earliest attested *kleidophoros*: *IS* 1048, with the additional fragment in *IS* II.2 34, no. 22 (for the date see below, n. 67). The granting of *asylia* to the temple at Lagina in 81 BC (*IS* 504), possibly the building of the new temple, or the institution of penteteric *Hekatesia* all provide a likely context for Hekate's procession, although in some form or other, it may well go back earlier. The restoration κλ[ειδοφόρου] in a new inscription from Lagina dated to the first century BC (Şahin 1999: 35–6) should be changed to: κα[θ' υἱοθεσίαν]. Zeus's entrance into the city: Oppermann (1924: 58–62); Laumonier (1958: 292, 298, 305, cf. 234); Boffo (1985: 300).

[64] σίδ]ηρο[ν] μὴ εἰσφέρε[ιν] πολεμίστριον (further restorations are uncertain); Cousin's copy, notebook AS 6, no 231, shows letters of the second or first century BC. See also Sokolowski, *LSAM* no. 68 and *BE* (1939) 376.

right, the inscription cannot show the impact of central authority: it is more probable that it was set up on the authority of the *koinon* of the Panamareis.

The text of the sacrificial calendar (*IS* 1, in which the above-mentioned μολπὴν καὶ βουθυσίαν feature repeatedly) is central to Laumonier's proposition that there was a close connection between city and cult already in the mid-third century BC. Since it also attests the existence of a joint cult of Zeus and Hera at Panamara, it is further used to show that a local, 'Carian' Zeus had a 'Greek' or Hellenized adjunct at a relatively early time, with her own trieteric festival, the *Heraia* (ll. 7–8: ὅταν δὲ Ἡραῖα συν[τελῆται κατὰ] τριετηρίδα κτλ.).[65] The date of this very fragmentary text is, however, nowhere near as secure as has been assumed. The early dating, which was accepted by Laumonier and Sokolowski, and retained by M.Ç. Şahin at *IS* no. 1, is, in fact, based solely on what its first editor, Hatzfeld, wrote about its letter forms.[66] From the photograph of part of this text (*IS* 1(a)) which Th. Drew-Bear and Th. Schwertfeger have since published (in 1979), there is little doubt, however, that its letters belong to the first century BC, most likely the second half.[67]

The two parts of this so-called calendar do not, in any case, belong together. 1(a) is inscribed on a block 40 cm deep, while the thickness of 1(b) is only 11 cm; but Hatzfeld's assumption that they were part of the same calendar has never been questioned. Since Cousin's notebook copy of 1(b) (AS 6, no. 216) shows letters of the second/first century BC for this text, it, too, is definitely later than has been assumed. So we lose the only seemingly unambiguous piece of evidence for the city's early attempt at integrating the sanctuary and especially at reorganizing the cult. Even if Sokolowski's (very speculative) restoration of [τῆι δὲ ἀναβά]σι τοῦ θεοῦ in ll. 8–9 of this text were correct, the god's *anabasis* – on horseback, returning from the city to Panamara[68] – would belong in the second or first century BC,

---

[65] In the Roman period, the *Heraia* were celebrated in the *Heraion* within the sanctuary's enclosure. See the examples and discussion in Oppermann (1924: 75–7); Laumonier (1958: 307–11). The first reference to a *Heraion* is in the Miracle text (*IS* 10, l. 26) which is thought to refer to the attack on the sanctuary by Labienus and his troops in 41 BC.

[66] *BCH* 51 (1927) 68 n. 1: 'on notera que dans le calendrier sacré . . . qui, d'après l'écriture, doit être placé à une date assez ancienne et peut-être au milieu du IIIe siècle av. J.C.'. Already *SEG* IV 266; Laumonier (1958: 223, 234–5); Sokolowski, *LSAM* no. 67. Rigsby (1996: 423): 'late third century'.

[67] Drew-Bear and Schwertfeger (1979: pl. 10b), not commented on by the editors nor by M.Ç. Şahin despite a reference to the photograph. The letters are close to, e.g., those of *IS* 1038 (pl. 14) dated by Şahin as 'hellenistisch, wohl 1. Jhr. v. Chr.' and to those of some recently published inscriptions which were dated, again by Şahin, to the middle of the first century BC. Important to compare are the very similar letter forms of *EA* 12 (1988) 82, pl. 1, no. 2, with its companion fragment *IS* 1048, pl. 15, for a *kleidophoros kata pentaeterida*: a title which is unlikely to be earlier than 38 BC, when it was first appended to the priest's name (cf. Laumonier 1938a: 252, and see *IS* 609).

[68] *LSAM* no. 67.

not in the third. Since it is no longer possible to date the *Heraia* or even the presence of Hera herself at Panamara to the third century, we can no longer see her introduction (or the renaming of an existing, indigenous deity)[69] as integral to the 'renouvellement complet du culte' postulated by Laumonier. There are, in fact, no good grounds for assuming that Hera was from the beginning companion to Zeus. There are no Carian attestations of the Zeus/Hera couple before the late second century BC: most Carian Zeuses appear to have operated without a 'parèdre': nearby Zeus Labraundos held out on his own throughout the Hellenistic period, as did Mylasan Zeus Osogo (or Osogollis).[70] And while it is not unthinkable that a region which had joint cults of Apollo and Artemis already in the fourth century BC would have associated a Hera with one of its local Zeuses from an early date, this simply appears not to have been the case. What certainly cannot be shown is that it was the impact of the city's foundation that generated the change.

When precisely the cult of Hera was added to that of Zeus at Panamara therefore cannot be established with certainty. Among the sanctuary's early surviving 'end of office' dedications by priests, the earliest, that of Androsthenes son of Zoilos (first half of the second century BC?)[71] is a simple dedication to Zeus Karios, while another, somewhat later, of Menippos son of Leon is dedicated to Zeus and Hera, and that of Hekaton son of Leon is dedicated to 'Zeus, Hera and the [*demos*]'.[72] Even though it is not possible to date Hekaton very closely, the transition, not only from Zeus alone to Zeus and Hera but also the inclusion of the *demos* (of Stratonikeia) in the dedication, may point to changes in the cult related to wider organizational changes at this time. The evidence is, however, too thin to be certain that these are developments rather than coincidences.[73]

---

[69] Laumonier's (1958: 59) suggestion that Hera at Panamara, as well as the Hera attested as companion of Zeus Stratios at neighbouring Mylasa, was originally an indigenous Anatolian goddess ('une parèdre primitive'), assimilated and Hellenized through her association with Zeus, seems unfounded. (*I. Mylasa* 204, l. 16: a priest of Zeus Stratios and of Hera, late second century BC.)

[70] See especially Crampa's discussion of Zeus Labraundos in *Labraunda* III. 2 194 (against Laumonier 1958: 59–62) and *ibid.* on the problematic association of Zeus Stratios with Zeus Labraundos. On the name of Zeus Osogo(llis) see now Blümel (1990: 30–2).

[71] *IS* 101, *ed. pr.* Cousin-Deschamps (1888: 251, no. 25): 'petite stèle, jolie gravure, lettres de bonne époque'. Laumonier (1937: 238, no. 3) cautiously dates it to 'avant l'empire', but more can be derived from Cousin's description than this. Notebook AS 6, no. 114.

[72] Menippos Leontos *Korazeus*, *IS* 104: 'gravure soignée, caractères de bonne époque' (Cousin-Deschamps 1888: 250, no. 23); Hekaton Leontos, to Zeus and Hera and the [*demos*], *IS* 102: 'petites lettres' (Cousin-Deschamps 1888: no. 27). Notebook AS 10, nos. 171 and 69 respectively.

[73] Androsthenes has no demotic, while Menippos and Hekaton both have one (unabbreviated) in addition to their name and patronymic: a transition which, again, may point at wider organizational changes of Stratonikeia's territory. The fact that Menippos and Hekaton, of two different demes,

A further anachronistic element in the cult at Panamara was introduced by M. Holleaux, who assumed that there was a priestess at the sanctuary at the time of the visit of Philip V. Holleaux restored ll. 8–10 of *IS* 3, the decree issued by the *koinon* of the Panamareis for Philip V in 201 BC, as follows: ἐπεύξασθ[αι δὲ τὸν ἱερέα μετὰ τῆς ἱερεί]ας ὑπὲρ τῆς σωτηρία[ς τοῦ τε βασιλέως καὶ τῆς βασιλίσ]σης καὶ τῶν τέκνων α[ὐτῶν καὶ ἐπὶ ταῖς εὐχαῖς παρα]στῆσαι τὴν θυσίαν τ[ὴν πάτριον. κτλ.]: 'la restitution [μετὰ τῆς ἱερεί]ας ne me paraît point douteuse; il est constamment parlé de "la prêtresse" dans les inscriptions de Panamara'.[74] In fact, the inscriptions of the pre-Augustan period never talk of a priestess, and, more generally, the occurrence of priestly couples – and the later priest and priestess at Panamara were always that – is not a feature of the Hellenistic period. In other words, her presence would need a special explanation, which is not easily found, and the restoration has to be rejected.[75]

We should, then, think of the cult at Panamara at the time of Stratonikeia's foundation and afterwards, most likely until the time of Leon's revivalist efforts, as a cult of Zeus Karios/Panamaros, served by a single priest who would have been chosen from among the members of the *koinon* of the Panamareis and administered by that *koinon*. The introduction of Hera as 'parèdre' of Zeus, whenever it occurred, may have been part of a conscious reform but need not have been connected with the foundation of the nearby Seleucid city.

5. CITY AND *KOINON*

Whether the above reconstruction is in conflict with the idea of some form of political dependence on, if not integration into, Stratonikeia at all times

---

are both sons of a Leon shows sufficiently that any speculations about family links involving the all too common name Leon are pointless. It is tempting, however, to see a connection between Androsthenes son of Zoilos and Leon son of Chrysaor son of Zoilos, since the latter name is far less common.

[74] Holleaux (1904: 354 n. 1). In neighbouring Labraunda, at approximately the same time, a sacrifice was brought on behalf of King Philip to various Zeuses (*Labraunda* III. 1 6, ll. 7–8): καὶ θυσίαν προσαγαγε[ῖν ὑπ]ὲρ τε τοῦ βα[σι]λέως Φιλίππου καὶ ὑπὲρ ἡμ[ῶν Δ]ιὶ Ὀσογωι καὶ Διὶ [Λα]βραύνδωι καὶ Διὶ Ἐλευθερί[ωι κτλ., and one would expect a reference to sacrifice in our case, too, but to restore, e.g., καὶ συντελεῖν θυσί]ας ὑπὲρ κτλ. is problematic because of the plural ending; for ἐπεύξασθ[αι δὲ τὸν ἱερέα μετὰ θυσί]ας no immediate parallels are available. A specification of the frequency and timing of the priest's prayers might also be possible.

[75] van Bremen (1996: 115–25). Not even postulating an early presence of Hera could explain a priestess: later, in the imperial period when the presence of a priestess alongside the priest was the norm, she never specifically served Hera: it was always the priest of Zeus who officiated during the *Heraia*. The role of the priestess appears to have been that of feasting the female worshippers, but again not specifically during the *Heraia*.

before 167 BC now needs to be discussed. There is certainly much disagreement about the nature and the timing of the integration of *koinon* and cult into the larger *polis* organization. This is partly a result of confusion about the interpretation of the constitutional language of the early decrees from the sanctuary (*IS* 3, 4, 5, 6, 7 and 9) and partly of disagreement about the nature and timing of Rhodian control over both city and sanctuary. I shall first deal with the former, then briefly discuss the Rhodian context.

Indicators within the texts have been variously used to show Panamara's independence from, or dependence on, the new city. H. Oppermann's assessment may be taken as an example. Along with most other scholars, he took as his starting point the surviving decrees, from which he deduced that, at the time of Philip V's campaigns, Panamara was 'somehow' dependent on Stratonikeia 'but was formally autonomous'. In 197, the Rhodians, having received the city from Antiochos III after themselves besieging the city in vain in order to 'liberate' it from Philip V, then 'assumed Stratonikeia's position' so that, at that time, Panamara was 'somehow dependent on Rhodes', but still 'formally autonomous'.[76] At some point between 167, when Rhodian control over Caria ended, and 81 BC, the date of the *senatus consultum* which rewarded the city for having supported Sulla in the Mithridatic wars, Panamara 'came to Stratonikeia', the *koinon* disappeared, and Zeus Panamaros became one of Stratonikeia's two principal deities, together with Hekate of Lagina.

The indicators on which this assessment is based are, first, in the decree for Philip's *epistates* (*IS* 4, 198 BC) the dating by a stephanephorate (held by the god Apollo: ll. 3–4 'for the third? time')[77] which Oppermann plausibly assumed to have been that of Stratonikeia.[78] Then, in one of the three Rhodian decrees (*IS* 9; the dating formula in the other two, 5 and 6, is lost), the dating by the Rhodian priest of Helios and the title of the honorand – *epistates* in charge of guarding the *chorion*, a man who had also adjudicated in disputes between citizens of the *koinon* (ll. 7–13) – led to the 'somehow dependent on Rhodes'. Panamara's 'autonomy', on the other hand, seemed evident from the very existence of the decrees, their language, the honours conferred (which include *politeia* and *proxenia*), the reference to the *koinon* meeting (*IS* 3, 5 and 7; in *ekklesia kyria* in *IS* 4, ll. 5–6, *IS* 9, ll. 2–3) for the purpose of taking collective decisions and the sending

[76] Oppermann (1924: 30–1, with discussion of the individual decrees at 18–30). On Rhodes' receiving the city in 197 see below.
[77] ἐπὶ σ[τεφα]νηφόρου Ἀπόλλωνος [τὸ τρί]τον as suggested by Şahin. In *IS* 15, l. 1, dated to the Hadrianic period, Apollo is *stephanephoros* for the fourth time.
[78] The *stephanephoros* was the Stratonikeian eponym.

of ambassadors (*IS* 5, 6).⁷⁹ The *demarchos* in *IS* 6 (l. 13) was explained by Oppermann as the highest official of an autonomous *koinon* rather than as an indicator of Panamara's integration (as a deme) into the larger structure of the Stratonikeian *polis*.⁸⁰

Like Oppermann, most scholars have preferred a relatively late date for Panamara's incorporation precisely because of the kind of political activity that emerges from the decrees issued by the *koinon* in the late third and early second century BC. They have found it particularly hard to accept that a community capable of bestowing *politeia* could at the same time be a subunit of a larger *polis* structure. Thus P. Debord argued in a recent article that the Panamareis were an autonomous *koinon* at the time of the expedition of Philip V, which led him to deny that the *stephanephoros* by which the decree for Asklepiades was dated was that of Stratonikeia.⁸¹ Gabrielsen, writing on the Rhodian Peraia, argued that Panamara was an autonomous *polis*, independent of Stratonikeia until well after 167, precisely on the basis of its ability to grant *politeia* to Leon. The three decrees for Rhodians, including that for an *epistates* sent to guard the *chorion* which is dated by the Rhodian priest of Helios, further show, according to Gabrielsen, that Panamara was 'closely tied' to Rhodes or within its 'sphere of influence' but not necessarily that it was under the island's control.⁸² Others prefer

---

⁷⁹ Errington (1995: 30), whose conclusions on the use of the term *ekklesia kyria* are interesting (it was associated with the introduction of democratic structures and was largely limited to Caria and adjoining areas, more often than not under the aegis of a king, satrap or local dynast – though on the latter see the reservations of P. Gauthier, *BE* (1996) 121), but whose interpretation of *ekklesia kyria* as the equivalent of a quorum-requirement is not persuasive finds it hard to fit the two Panamaran examples into his overall scheme. His 'Koroandeis' (on pp. 28 and 30) is a variant spelling of the admittedly chameleon-like Koarendeis/Ko(a)ra(n)zeis. The name has, however, not (yet) been attested in any ancient text.

⁸⁰ Oppermann (1924) with further examples which are, however, not convincing, as was pointed out by M. Wörrle (1988a: 145–6). Our present knowledge of the *koina* in this part of Caria does not support Oppermann's assumption. A board of *Komarchoi* is now attested for the *koinon* of the Leukoideis, south of Panamara, cf. *HTC* no. 36, dated to 107–80 BC, but among the many *koina* now known, none appears to have been headed by a *demarchos*. On the strength of the *demarchos* in *IS* 6, M. Holleaux argued that Panamara had become a deme of Stratonikeia (1904: 361).

⁸¹ Debord (1994: 114).

⁸² Gabrielsen (2000a: 163–7). His 'friendly' view of the Rhodians' role in this part of Caria leads him to deny the necessity of dating two of the decrees, *IS* 5 and 6, to between 197 and 167 BC. Certainly the first two Panamaran decrees are not clearly in honour of *epistatai*, nor are they visibly dated by the Rhodian priest of Helios, but this is of course partly the result of the loss of their first lines. I agree with Gabrielsen's caution about dating these two decrees, but suggest that they may well be earlier – not later – than *IS* 9. The latter, on which the name of the Rhodian *epistates* is erased, is the only inscription of which a photograph exists, in Roos (1975: pl. 60, 3). Its letters point distinctly to a date in the early decades of the second century. The date given for the priest (Archidamos) confirms this: between 210 and 175 BC (*LGPN* I, s.v.). The *epistates* was not, as G. writes, in charge of guarding 'a' *chorion*: the sanctuary itself is thus designated, and, given its nature and position, was clearly a site of some strategic importance for the Rhodians. On unfriendly feelings towards Rhodes after 167 see below, n. 96.

not to render the situation too exactly: so for instance Th. Drew-Bear and Th. Schwertfeger, who write: 'Das Heiligtum ... war, wie Lagina zeitweise ein zu Stratonikeia gehörendes Heiligtum, zu anderen Zeiten selbständiger Mittelpunkt eines bedeutsamen karischen Kultes.'[83]

As this last quotation sufficiently shows, any assessment of territorial and political incorporation and any definition of 'autonomy' or 'Selbständigkeit' have obvious implications for how we perceive the identity of sanctuary and cult, and the extent to which the Stratonikeis were able to integrate this Zeus as one of their city's major deities, exercising central control over cultic regulations and festivals, appointing their own citizens as priests, and, doubtless, profiting from the income generated by festivals. In the new decrees for Leon, significantly, it is a religious aspect which plays havoc with assumptions about political 'autonomy'. It is precisely the Stratonikeis' apparent right to appoint the priest at Panamara which affects our assessment of the local community's 'autonomy'. For while displaying all those characteristics of 'autonomous' behaviour (embodied here in the granting of *politeia* to Leon), the Panamareis apparently no longer had any control over one of the most central aspects of their communal existence: that of appointing a priest for their deity.

The nearest comparison for the constitutional relationship between *koinon* and city as we find it in the decree of the Panamareis for Leon comes from a neighbouring Carian city, Mylasa; it is discussed more fully in G. Reger's chapter on *sympoliteia* elsewhere in this volume. In the *sympoliteia* between Mylasa and the smaller neighbouring city of Olymos, the latter's *demos*, after its incorporation into the greater Mylasan state in the late third century BC, while dating its decrees by that city's *stephanephoros*, still met in *ekklesia* and still granted *politeia* to those it honoured, including citizens of Mylasa itself. And it is in complex, 'aggregate' *poleis* like Mylasa (or Rhodes) that the term *sympas demos* is used frequently to refer to the central decision-making body of the whole *polis* in the separate decrees of those who formed its constituent parts.[84]

If the elements of meeting in assembly, taking decisions, granting decrees, granting *politeia* and other privileges which signalled 'autonomy' to many scholars, must now be balanced against the control exercised by Stratonikeia over the appointing of Zeus's priest, then we can no longer be so sure that the appearance of all those elements in earlier decrees is in

---

[83] Drew-Bear and Schwertfeger (1979: 195).
[84] See again, more fully, G. Reger, elsewhere in this volume. It is precisely this well-attested usage which speaks against any idea of seeing in the *sympas demos* that of an over-arching organization like the Chrysaoreis.

itself sufficient ground for the argument that Panamara was 'formally' autonomous, even if first somehow dependent on Stratonikeia (though indirectly, of course, on the Macedonian king while he held both the city and the *chorion* at Panamara) then on Rhodes. The fact that, while under the control of Philip's *epistates*, the Panamareis dated their decrees by the *stephanephoros* of Stratonikeia, which was, of course, itself in the hands of the Macedonian king, *might* mean that there had been a previous dependence which was retained, but it is equally possible that it was the Macedonian occupation of Stratonikeia and of the sanctuary-fortress to its south-east which created the situation and imposed the convention. The reference, in this very inscription, to the Panamareis meeting in *ekklesia kyria* clearly cannot in itself be an indication of the community's independence from Stratonikeia, if the same decree is dated by that city's *stephanephoros*.

It follows that the dating of Panamaran decrees, after 197, by the Rhodian eponym, not that of Stratonikeia, cannot in itself suggest that the sanctuary had been 'detached' from the new city by the Rhodians: Stratonikeia's own decrees of this period – which, if they existed, have not survived – would have been dated by the same priest of Helios, not by the city's own *stephanephoros*. A double dependency, of sanctuary on city and city on island state, seems possible in theory. There is, in other words, nothing in the constitutional language of these decrees alone to provide conclusive proof either of incorporation or of – relative – autonomy. In a constitutional sense, only the *demarchos* in *IS* 6, one of the decrees for a Rhodian, continues to confound. In support of seeing this official as an indicator of the incorporation of the Panamareis as a *demos* into the wider *polis* structure, one could point to the occurrence of another *demarchos*, at roughly the same time, as official of a *koinon* located on the site of Kürbet Köy, where one of Stratonikeia's main constituent demes is likely to have been located.[85] For the time being, the position is simply too unclear and the *demarchos* too fragile an indicator to let the decision of Panamara's incorporation into Stratonikeia depend on it alone.

We must now deal briefly with the issue of Rhodian control before 197 BC, an unresolved problem on which debate continues. At its core is Polybius'

---

[85] Were the *demarchoi* perhaps a feature of the Rhodian organization of Stratonikeia between 197 and 167 (or earlier still: see the next section on the Rhodian take-over of the city) which was later abandoned? On the site, and the identity of Koliorga, see above n. 26. The restoration of αἱρεθεὶς δὲ δήμ]αρχος πρῶτο[ς in the problematic decree *IS* 8, set up in the sanctuary at Panamara by the *koinon* of the Londeis, to Panamara's south, for an honorand of another *koinon*, is too uncertain, and the status and dating of the decree too unclear, to use it either in support of, or against, the *demarchos* argument, but it is interesting that it, too, appears to date from the first decades of the second century.

passage (30.31.6) in which the Rhodian envoy before the Roman Senate, in 166 BC, bemoaning the Rhodians' loss of Kaunos and Stratonikeia, claims that they had received Stratonikeia ἐν μεγάλῃ χάριτι παρ' Ἀντιόχου καὶ Σελεύκου. The statement allows for a number of interpretations as to the identity of the kings and thus the date of the gift, almost all of which are problematic. It needs to be considered together with Livy's description of how, in the spring of 197 BC, the Rhodians tried to regain (*vindicare*) their ancestral possessions in the Peraia which Philip had detached during his campaigns, how they failed to take Stratonikeia when that would have been easy (*si confestim victores Stratoniceam petissent, recipi eam urbem sine certamine potuisse*) and then, having lost their opportunity, unsuccessfully besieged the city, only managing to (re-?)gain (*recipi*) it 'somewhat later' (*aliquanto post*) 'through the help of Antiochos' (*per Antiochum*).[86]

Of the 'real-life' pairs proposed as donors (Antiochos I and his son Seleukos, Seleukos II and Antiochos Hierax, Antiochos III and his son Seleukos IV), only Seleukos II and Antiochos Hierax, before the latter's rebellion against his brother *ca* 240, are in any way plausible,[87] although the interval between the city's foundation and its giving away seems exceedingly short, especially if a foundation by Antiochos II is favoured.[88] The virtual consensus in recent discussions has been to opt for a non-contemporary pair of kings, interpreting the construction in the Polybius passage in a *proteron-hysteron* sense, putting the most recent event first. On this interpretation, the Rhodians originally received Stratonikeia from Seleukos II (possibly as a reward for assistance against Hierax), and then again, having briefly lost it to Philip V between 201 and 197, from Antiochos III. The arguments are, however, not convincing, for not only does it seem problematic in itself to see the term ἐν μεγάλῃ χάριτι as applying to two separate gifts, but there are further considerations which, to my mind, make it unlikely that the expression could have been used with reference to Antiochos III (see below).[89]

---

[86] Livy 33.18.1–3 and 22.
[87] See the extensive discussions of all the possibilities in J. and L. Robert (1955: 564–5, *OMS* v = 461–2), Cohen (1995: 271–2), Walbank (1979: ad loc.) and Reger (1999: 83–4), all with full refs. See also Gabrielsen (2000*a*: 171–4). Arguing for the pair Seleukos II and Antiochos Hierax, van Gelder (1900: 197–8) suggested the gift was a reward for Rhodes' assistance to Seleukos in the Laodikeian war of 246–241 BC. Holleaux (1904: 353 n. 2) and (1931: 8 with n. 6) favoured a single gift, by Antiochos III and his son Seleukos IV, dated alternatively to 197 or 193 BC, with different justifications for the son's association with his father. Debord (2001*a*: 163), prefers a single gift by Antiochos III.
[88] The usual explanation given for the inversion of the names is that it was done to avoid hiatus.
[89] The most recent advocates of a 'double' gift are Ma (1999: Appendix 5) and Reger (1999: 82–5), both with references to earlier discussions, but following in particular J. and L. Robert (1955: 564–5 = *OMS* v, 461–2), who themselves revived an earlier proposal by A. Aymard.

The main arguments adduced for a single, early gift are of course broadly the same as those for a 'double' one. Both are based largely on seeing Livy's '*vindicare*' and '*recipi*' as renderings of the Greek (and Polybian) ἀνακτάομαι ('reconquer, retake'), and therefore as proof that the Rhodians, in 197, were *re*-taking what had previously been theirs. Even those who admit that '*recipere*' can also just mean 'to gain, to capture', still argue that the general context of the '*vindicare*' passage and the prominent place given in it to the taking of forts in Stratonikeian territory and the besieging of the city must mean that Stratonikeia was part of the possessions which the Rhodian commander set out to reconquer.[90] An additional point made is that in 201 Philip mostly kept away from Seleucid possessions, and would not have taken the city had it belonged to Antiochos.[91] It is, however, possible to add yet a further argument to those usually given. At the negotiations between Philip and Rome at Nikaia, in autumn 198, a number of conditions were imposed upon Philip at the demand of Rome's allies, among whom were the Rhodians (Polyb. 18.2.3). Among other things, he was to evacuate the Peraia and withdraw his troops from Iasos, Bargylia and Euromos.[92] During the negotiations following his defeat at Kynoskephalai in spring 197, Philip again accepted these same conditions (Polyb. 18.38.2). What is striking is that Stratonikeia is never specifically mentioned, even though we know that in 198 the city was still in Philip's possession. The omission to list by name a city so energetically fought over can only mean that it was considered part of the Rhodian Peraia when Philip took it and was therefore included in the demands for a general withdrawal from that whole region rather than listed among the individual cities.[93]

If this is accepted, it is possible to go further and argue that, in the general context of the negotiations between Rome, her allies and Philip, and the Roman demands to evacuate the Peraia, it would have been most peculiar for the Rhodians to have stated in a speech *addressed to the Roman Senate* that they had received the city ἐν μεγάλῃ χάριτι from Antiochos III. Livy's neutral *nec recipi nisi aliquanto post per Antiochum potuit* must instead reflect the fact that the king had been somehow instrumental in the transmission of the city back to the Rhodians in compliance with the

---

[90] So Reger (1999: 83 with n. 23). I do not think that the so-called 'Nikagoras-dossier' can by itself be used to prove or disprove previous Rhodian possession of Stratonikeia (a discussion of the dossier in Gabrielsen 2000*a*: 153–6).
[91] Ma (1999: 278); Reger (1999: 84).   [92] At Polyb. 18.6.3, Philip agrees to clear the Peraia.
[93] In the *senatus consultum* of 196, mentioned at Polyb. 18.44.4, withdrawal from Iasos, Bargylia and Euromos (as well as Pidasa) is still stipulated but the Peraia is no longer mentioned: by that date it had been fully recovered by the Rhodians, including Stratonikeia, 'through Antiochos'.

general conditions imposed on the Antigonid king (it is not necessary to assume that he had recovered it through force). Ideologically, a straight and first-time 'gift' to Rhodes of an important city, which carried moreover a dynastic Seleucid name, is hard to reconcile with Antiochos' widely proclaimed and vigorously pursued aims of recovering his ancestral possessions, but his handing over of the city becomes more acceptable if it is seen as a restoration of what those ancestors had themselves earlier granted to Rhodes, ἐν μεγάλῃ χάριτι.

In the end, no absolute certainty is possible on the present state of the evidence, but the cumulative force of the arguments in favour of an early gift, and especially against a gift only in 197, is considerable. It is obvious that any designs which the Stratonikeis may have had on the sanctuary at Panamara will have been affected by such an early dependence on Rhodes. Rhodian control over the city so soon after its foundation must have precluded any attempt at expansion.

On balance, some form of integration of *koinon* and cult into Stratonikeia must have taken place before the middle of the second century. 'Constitutional' evidence cannot prove Panamara's autonomy, while all that the *asylia* argument can suggest is that Stratonikeia had not at any time between the date of its foundation and the time of Leon been able actively to incorporate the sanctuary at Panamara, though it had possibly acknowledged an earlier *asylia*-request by the Panamareis themselves (*IS* 19). What seems distinctly possible is that the occupation of both sanctuary and city by the Macedonian king in 201 BC led the latter to implement an enforced royal 'rationalization' not uncommon in western Asia Minor: enlarging the territory of the city by adding to it the strategically important site at Panamara.[94] This would explain the dating of *IS* 4 by the Stratonikeian *stephanephoros*. The Rhodian takeover of both city and sanctuary after Philip's defeat in 197 would not necessarily have changed this situation, and, as I have argued, neither the dating of *IS* 9 by the Rhodian eponym nor the apparent indicators of Panamaran 'autonomy' contradict such a relationship, which furthermore need not be incompatible with the stationing of a special *epistates* at the sanctuary. Since the Rhodians had no reason to think they would lose the city, a deliberate detaching of the sanctuary might not have made much sense.[95] On this scenario, after the removal of Rhodian control,

---

[94] On synoikisms imposed from above see now Reger in this volume.
[95] Separate arrangements were apparently made for the defence of the civic centre of Stratonikeia: some form of Rhodian control within the civic centre of Stratonikeia is implied by Debord (2001*a*:

the Stratonikeis would have been able to exploit what had, after more than thirty years, become the 'normal' situation.⁹⁶

6. THE REVIVAL OF THE CULT AND THE DISSOLUTION OF THE *KOINON*

The decree of the Panamareis in honour of Leon, not surprisingly, emphasizes the man's efforts on behalf of their sanctuary. His attempts at reviving its earlier importance and at widening, once again, the circle of those who took part in its festivals and who, as newly joined *synthytai*, offered their communities' sacrifice, are presented as great benefactions to the Panamareis. But if we read only a little below the surface of the Panamaran rhetoric it becomes clear that the greatest beneficiaries of the cult's renewed flourishing would be the Stratonikeis who now controlled the sanctuary and appointed its priests. If the Kallipolitai and the Laodikeis were among the 'certain *demoi*' that Leon visited in order to persuade them to join in the sacrificing (as I suggest they were),⁹⁷ then the Kallipolitai's reference to the Stratonikeis being their 'friends and kinsmen' is telling for its focus on the city rather than the *koinon* and for its implication that a network of *synthytai* was being set up at whose centre were the Stratonikeis as well as the Panamareis.

Much has been made of the fact that the decrees of the two communities – one, Kallipolis, an autonomous city on the coast, the other, Laodikeia, a Rhodian dependency somewhere in the subject Peraia – were inscribed on the same stone.⁹⁸ The fact that both texts are in parts virtually identical,

---

162, 164), with reference to unpublished inscriptions. There was a garrison within the city walls at least by 167 (Polyb. 30.21.3–50) but there is no good reason to assume from this, with Gabrielsen (2000*a*: 171–4), that it was only in that year that the city was garrisoned. Stratonikeia is not known to have had a *hegemon* as did Kaunos. The fact that Panamara is never specifically mentioned could mean that Rhodes both received, and lost, the sanctuary-site as part of the Stratonikeian 'package'. As for the *epistates,* so little appears to be known with certainty about this official's position outside Rhodes that one cannot derive much from it about Panamara's status. Cf. Fraser and Bean (1954: 86–94) and Gabrielsen (2000*a*: 136–7), playing down the military role of the *epistates*.

⁹⁶ The erasing of the name of the Rhodian *epistates* in *IS* 9 speaks of hostile feelings. For a different opinion: Gabrielsen (2000*a*: 165). Alternatively, after their liberation from Rhodian control, the Panamareis, aware of the precariousness of their new autonomy on the edge of Rhodian-controlled territory, themselves sought protection by joining up with the Stratonikeis.

⁹⁷ The contrast with the *sympas demos* in *IS* 7, ll. 6–9 is too deliberate to see in the τινας δήμους constituent communities of Stratonikeia: the phrase must refer to other communities, *koina* or *poleis* in the sanctuary's vicinity. Moreover, Leon's 'danger, cost and suffering' might be thought somewhat excessive if referring only to the context of Stratonikeia's constituent *demoi*.

⁹⁸ Debord (2001*a*: 168): 'Le fait que les deux décrets soient gravés sur la même stèle indique bien qu'ils ne peuvent être dissociés', but his subsequent argument, that the Laodikeia in question was

and that both refer to Leon's achieving of a settlement 'between those who disagreed about the oaths', suggests at first sight that the disagreements may have been between these two communities. But their juxtaposition on the stone may not be all that deliberate: there may have been more *demoi* responding to Leon's invitation in much the same way, using similar language, and therefore other stelaí on which more than one decree was inscribed. Instead of focussing on these two communities, it seems vital not to lose sight of the connection between the *three* surviving decrees: between what Leon was trying to achieve and what the Kallipolitai and Laodikeis were responding to. If other responses had survived, then the whole series might be able to shed more light on the details of Leon's mission; but that its aim was the setting up of a cult community focussed on the sanctuary, whose members shared in the festivals and cultic activities at Panamara, seems uncontroversial even now. The reference to τῶν ἱκετευόντων in the Kallipolis decree (l. 10) further implies that Leon's attempts at renewing the sanctuary's *asylia* status had been successful. The swearing of oaths in the process of setting up this kind of common network is to be expected; the specific use of the definite article 'the' in both decrees implies they were shared, and we should not let the fact that they survive only in these two decrees unduly narrow our interpretation of what was being aimed at more generally.[99] It would, in any case, be hard to imagine a situation in which a dispute either within the *koinon* of the Laodikeis, or between that *koinon* and another community, would not have been settled by a Rhodian judge at a time when the Laodikeis were subject to Rhodes. To think that a citizen of Stratonikeia could have been invited to act as judge in such a context defies all logic.

Why the Kallipolitai, why the Laodikeis: two communities whose position could not have been more different, one autonomous, the other dating its decrees by the Rhodian priest, and demoted from a Seleucid *polis* to a subject *koinon*? Why, further, the difference in diplomatic language and protocol when addressing the Stratonikeis?[100] The answer to these

---

Laodikeia on the Lykos (on which see above, n. 12) to all intents and purposes does precisely that: it never explains what it was that made the inscribing of its decree and that of the Kallipolitai on the same stone so imperative, or what was the association between the two cities. A. Bresson, *HTC* 214–15, thinks in terms of geographical proximity.

[99] The interpretation of P. Fraser (quoted in Şahin 1995) that Leon, in his capacity as priest, functioned as judge between these two communities disengages what is written in the two decrees from the wider context referred to in *IS* 8.

[100] Reger (1998: 14–15), for instance, suggested that the omission of Leon's ethnic in the Laodikeis' decree pointed to the community's incorporation (as a 'satellite') into the wider Stratonikeian organization ('the ethnic is inevitable when one *polis* honours a citizen of another *polis*'), as did the

questions lies in Stratonikeia's position in this part of Caria: in the city's dual identity as a Seleucid foundation and a cluster of synoikized Carian communities, but also in its precarious location on the edge of the Rhodian subject Peraia. However forceful the appeal of cultic and ethnic ties may have been, political and territorial considerations cannot have been far from the mind of those who set out to make Zeus Karios and Panamara great once more. When attempting any kind of territorial expansion, or gaining access to the sea, the Stratonikeis were bound to trespass on Rhodian territory and offend Rhodian sensibilities. The city's incorporation (or retaining) of Panamara must have seemed to the Rhodians a first step in this direction, and contacts with Kallipolis on the coast as an attempt at establishing a corridor down to the sea. Any appeals to neighbouring *demoi* in the name of the common, ancestral Zeus Karios would have been seen as potentially hostile acts and would have risked conflict.[101] Part of the precariousness of Leon's mission must have lain precisely in this approaching of communities that were now under Rhodian control. In that context both the οὔτε κίνδυνον οὔτε δαπάνην οὔτε [κακοπ]αθίαν οὐδεμίαν ὑφορώμενος and the almost apotropaic imprecision of the ἐπελθών τε ἐπί τινας δήμους may find an explanation: specifying on stone, in a sanctuary on the edge of the Rhodian subject Peraia, in a region where Rhodians abounded, that which was bound to displease those very Rhodians, may have seemed like asking for trouble.[102] A similar reticence very likely explains the difference in style between the two decrees of the Kallipolitai and the Laodikeis: the omission of Leon's ethnic *Stratonikeus*, and of any further passages such as 'praising the Stratonikeis on having appointed a good and noble man' which is found in the adjoining decree, seems like a careful, diplomatic way of avoiding the name of the city towards which the Rhodians were said to have felt hatred: ἀπέχθεια.[103]

---

fact that no ambassador was sent or permission asked for erecting the stele. Instead, it was to be set up 'wherever Leon preferred'. Both of these are pertinent observations, but they can be otherwise explained. Gabrielsen (2000a: 145–6) thought that the omissions could be explained by the fact that the decrees were abbreviated versions of the originals, so that the ethnic *Stratonikeus* did not need to be repeated in the second decree.

[101] Much the same would have applied to Stratonikeia and Mylasa. A conflict between the two cities over territory, possibly settled by Rome, is dated to the mid-second century: *I. Mylasa* 134; Ager (1996: no. 101).

[102] That the conflict between the Stratonikeis and Rhodes was very real at this time is shown in the arbitration of Bargylia in an unspecified conflict between the two cities, and the Bargylian negotiator's success in keeping the parties from appealing to Rome (*ca* 130 BC): the term ἀπέχθεια is used to describe the Rhodians' sentiments towards Stratonikeia: *I. Iasos* 612; Ager (1996: no. 161).

[103] Previous note. The vagueness of the directions for setting up of the stele – 'wherever he prefers' – may have a similar origin, and is different from that of the Kallipolitai. It is, however, to be noted

The appeal Leon made to neighbouring communities was partly based on their shared Carian – and possibly Chrysaorian – identity,[104] to which could be added, in the case of Laodikeia, the further appeal of a shared Seleucid identity. The same double identity that Strabo so interestingly, though rather wrong-headedly, described in the case of Stratonikeia must have pertained to Laodikeia too: Στρατονίκεια δ'ἐστὶ κατοικία Μακεδόνων... καὶ Στρατονικεῖς δὲ τοῦ συστήματος μετέχουσιν, οὐκ ὄντες τοῦ Καρικοῦ γένους, ἀλλ' ὅτι κώμας ἔχουσι τοῦ Χρυσαορικοῦ συστήματος.[105] Although absorbed early on into the Rhodian political system and no longer itself a *polis*, the awareness of this double *syngeneia* must have been a strong reason for responding to Leon's requests, even if, at the same time, it seemed inadvisable to spell it out publicly on stone. In fact, the most extraordinary aspect of the Laodikeis' decree is precisely the omission of such obvious points of common reference.[106]

What, finally, happened to the Panamareis? The absence of the demotic from Stratonikeia's records despite the great, and steadily increasing, importance of the sanctuary itself, and the fact that among the almost three hundred priests (male and female) of Zeus Karios/Panamaros on record between the mid-second century BC and the mid-third century AD there is not a single *Panamareus*, have already been mentioned. M.Ç. Şahin was right to emphasize, on the analogy of the structure of neighbouring *koina* like the Tarmianoi or Pisyetai, that the *koinon* of the Panamareis, too, must have consisted of several communities in the vicinity of the sanctuary, and not only of the site of the sanctuary itself (the *chorion*).[107] The most probable development seems to me a physical incorporation of these communities

---

that neither community apparently needed permission to erect a stele in the sanctuary at Panamara. Perhaps this can be explained by their status as participants in the cultic community based at the sanctuary.

[104] Known members of the Chrysaoreis are Amyzon, Alabanda, Alinda, Mylasa, Thera, Stratonikeia and Keramos. See most recently Gabrielsen (2000a: 158–9) with references.

[105] Strabo 14.2 (660).

[106] Whatever the location of Laodikeia, like Stratonikeia it must have been founded, for its strategic position and accessibility to Seleucid troops, along an important route – probably that along the Marsyas valley, leading south from the Maiandros plain. A location somewhere to the north-west of Muğla and Pisye seems most likely, rather than, as has been suggested, further south (and thus deeper into Rhodian territory). It is tempting to think in terms of a 'twin' foundation by Antiochos II, in honour of both his mother and his wife. This clearly has implications for the date of the foundation, i.e. both must have been founded before Antiochos' divorce from Laodike in 254, a timing which does not altogether fit the reconstruction of Antiochos' activities proposed by Ma (1999: 41–2), who dates the king's inroads into this part of Caria to after 254. For a different opinion about the location of Laodikeia (further south, near Idyma and Kallipolis) see A. Bresson, *HTC* at no. 89.

[107] Şahin (1976: 24 n. 78).

into the territories of the nearest of Stratonikeia's *demoi* (in other words, the breaking up of the *koinon*), or at least a constitutional distribution of their inhabitants over the city's existing demes (*phylai*?). Only the site of the sanctuary itself – which was small – may have retained the name of Panamara, thus explaining the mere handful of attestations of the 'demotic' *Panamareus* in the later record.

Despite large gaps in our evidence, especially for the crucial second century BC,[108] the pattern that emerges from what can be established of the origins of the priests of Zeus Karios/Panamaros supports this interpretation. It shows that during the first centuries BC and AD a large majority of priests came from only two out of five of Stratonikeia's main demes: Koraia and Koliorga.[109] The location of either deme has not so far been established with certainty, but this evidence suggests that these two were very likely the demes nearest the sanctuary. If they did indeed incorporate the members of the *koinon* of the Panamareis, one would expect the preponderance of priests originating from them to have been even greater in the second century BC. What is interesting is that long after the absorption of the sanctuary within the larger structure of the *polis*, there was still a strong association between localities and cult. Instead of a takeover of the periphery by the centre, we see a very slow transition, within the wider *polis* context, from a domination of the priesthoods by those who lived in the sanctuary's vicinity, to a more evenly distributed participation across the whole territory later in the Roman period.

This case study has tried to show that Stratonikeia's religious identity during the first hundred years of its existence was much less clear-cut, less unified, and much more diffuse and localized than might appear from

---

[108] The earliest known priests, apart from Leon himself and his possible relative Androsthenes son of Zoilos, whose demotics are unknown but who were not Panamareis, are a man from Koranza and one from Koraia, both probably second century BC, see above, n. 73.

[109] On my provisional count, based on Laumonier's prosopographical lists (Laumonier 1937 and 1938*b*), and which may well change slightly as dates are refined and all the evidence has been entered into a database of priests, the figures for these centuries are as follows (M = male, F = female, T = total): Koraia: 16M + 7F = 23T; Koliorga: 12M + 12F = 24T; Koranza: 7M + 3F = 10T; Hierakome: 11M + 2F = 13T; Lobolda: 3M + 4F = 7T. A total of forty-seven priests out of seventy-seven or *c.* 61 per cent came from two of the demes. If one allows for the fact that Koranza and Hierakome were among the more important of the demes, the effect becomes more striking. Again, a comparison with the total figures given in Debord (1994: 113), following calculations by Şahin (which may be in need of some recounting) of the number of demotics explicitly attested in the whole of the epigraphic corpus, is instructive: Hierakome, Koliorga and Koranza lead, with little difference between them (85, 95 and 81 attestations respectively) but Koraia lags well behind with 55. My work has not progressed sufficiently to make precise comparisons with developments in the priesthoods at Lagina.

reconstructions based on evidence pertaining to the first three centuries AD, in which the focus is exclusively on the two patron deities, Panamaran Zeus and Hekate at Lagina, and on the interaction between 'centre' and 'periphery'. By concentrating on Panamara, only one aspect of the city's development could be discussed here. But once similar reassessments have been attempted for the entire network of local sanctuaries in the Stratonikeia region, for the emergence of Hekate at Koranza, the early cults in the civic centre, and the elusive Zeus Chrysaoreus, the religious, political and cultural history of this city may be more clearly understood.

APPENDIX

Decree of the koinon *of the Panamareis in honour of Leon (*IS 7*)*

[— — — — — — — — — — — — — — — — πα]ρασκευὰς . . . α . .
[— — — — — — — — — — — — —]ε συμμέτρων αἴ[ς] συντε
[— — — — — — — — — — — ψή]φισμα ἀποδοὺς καὶ παραθεὶς ἔκ τε [τ]ῶ[ν]
4 [ἐπιστολῶ]ν καὶ τῶν ἀρχαίων γραμμάτων καὶ συστησά[με]-
[νος τὰς ἄν]ωθεν τιμὰς καὶ ἀσυλίας ὑπαρχούσας τῶι Διὶ
καὶ Παναμαρεῦσιν ἔπεισεν τὸν σύνπαντα δῆμον εἰς τ[ὸ]
τὰς θυσίας ἐπιφανέστερας καὶ μείζονας συντελεῖν, ἐ-
8 πελθών τε ἐπί τινας δήμους ἔπεισε καὶ ἐκείνους συνθύειν, καθόλου τε ἔσπευδεν ὑπέρ τε τοῦ θεοῦ καὶ τοῦ κοινοῦ
τοῦ Παναμαρέων οὔτε κίνδυνον οὔτε δαπάνην οὔτε [κα]-
[κοπ]αθίαν οὐδεμίαν ὑφορώμενος· ὅπως οὖν καὶ Παναμα-
12 ρεῖς φαίνωνται τοῖς καλοῖς καὶ ἀγαθοῖς ἀνδράσιν τὰς
καταξίας χάριτας ἀποδιδόντες· δεδόχθαι τῶι κοινῶι·
ἐπῃνῆσθαι Λέοντα Χρυσάορος τοῦ Ζωίλου τοῦ Πολυπέρχοντος καὶ στεφανῶσαι αὐτὸν χρυσῶι στεφάνωι ἀρετῆς
16 ἕνεκεν καὶ εὐσεβείας εἶναι δὲ αὐτῶι καὶ ἐκγόνοις πολιτεί-
αν καὶ μετουσίαν πάντων ὧν καὶ Παναμαρεῖς μετέχουσιν
στῆσαι δὲ αὐτοῦ καὶ εἰκόνα χαλκήν ἐν ὧι ἂν αὐτὸς βούλη-
ται τόπωι καὶ ἐπιγράψαι ἐπιγραφὴν τήνδε· τὸ κοινὸν
20 τὸ Παναμαρέων ἐτίμησεν ἱερατεύσαντα Λέοντα
Χρυσάορος τοῦ Ζωίλου τοῦ Πολυπέρχοντος ἐπαίνωι χ[ρυ]-
σῶι στεφάνωι εἰκόνι χαλκῇ ἀρετῆς ἕνεκεν καὶ εὐσε-
βείας· ἀναγράψαι δὲ {δὲ} τόδε τὸ ψήφισμα εἰς
24 στήλην λιθίνην καὶ ἀναθεῖναι ἐν τῶι ἱερῶι τοῦ Διὸς τοῦ Καρίου ἐν τῶι ἐπιφανεστάτωι τόπωι τὸ δὲ τέ-
λεσμα τὸ εἰς τὰ προγεγραμένα ὑπαρχέτω ἐξ ἐπαγγελίας·
ὅπως δὲ καὶ ὁ σύνπας δῆμος ἐπιγνῶι τὰ δεδογμένα τῶ[ι]
28 κοινῶι τῶι Παναμαρέων ἑλέσθαι ἄνδρα· ὁ δὲ αἱρεθεὶς ἀ-
ποδότω τόδε τὸ ψήφισμα καὶ ἐπελθών ἐπί τε τὴν βουλὴν

καὶ τὸν δῆμον διαλεγήτω ὑπὲρ τῶν δεδογμένων
τῶι κοινῶι. ἡρέθη Καλλιμήδης Πολυάρχου

... providing for ...
... of. ... (things?) in due proportion/commensurate, with which
... restoring. ..., handing over the decree and providing alongside it (evidence)

4   from the [letter]s? and from the old documents, and having reconstructed
    that the above-mentioned honours and (grants of) *asylia* adhered to Zeus
    and to the Panamareis, he persuaded the entire people to
    make the sacrifices more splendid and better
8   and going to certain *demoi* he persuaded them, too, to participate in the sacrificing;
    (in all this) he zealously promoted the cause of the god and of the *koinon*
    of the Panamareis not sparing danger or cost or
    suffering. So that then also the Panamareis
12 may be seen to render appropriate honours to excellent men,
    the *koinon* decided:
    to praise Leon, son of Chrysaor son of Zoilos son of Polyperchon
    and to crown him with a gold crown for his virtue
16 and his piety; to grant to him and his descendants citizenship
    and a share in everything the Panamareis have a share in,
    to erect a bronze statue of him, in whichever place
    he wishes, and to inscribe it as follows: 'the *koinon*
20 of the Panamareis honours Leon, son of
    Chrysaor son of Zoilos son of Polyperchon, after his priesthood,
    with praise, a gold crown, and a bronze statue, for his virtue and piety'.
    To inscribe this decree on
24 a stone stele and to set it up in the sanctuary of
    Zeus Karios in the most prominent place, the money for
    the aforementioned is to come from a promised contribution.
    So that the entire *demos* may know what has been decided by
28 the *koinon* of the Panamareis, a man will be elected. The elected person is to
    deliver this decree and upon arrival at the *boule*
    and *demos* he is to set out the things decided by the *koinon*.
    Elected was Kallimedes son of Polyarches.

Decree of the Kallipolitai (EA 1995 no. 1; HTC no. 84; SEG XLV, no. 1556)

[– –]
[– –]
[– – – – – – κ]λ[ἐ]ου[ς – – – – – – – – – – –]

4   [--------]ΣΥ[-]Χρυσαορικ[--]Ο[- ἔδοξε]
    [Καλλιπολιτῶν τῆι β]ουλῆι καὶ τῶι δήμω[ι· ἐπειδὴ Λέων]
    [Χρυσάορο]ς τοῦ Ζωίλου τοῦ Πολυ[πέρχοντος Στρατο]-
    νικεὺς ἱερ]ατεύσας [ἐ]μ Παναμάρο[ις εὐσεβῶς καὶ φι]-
8   λοτίμως] καὶ μεγαλο[πρεπ]ῶς [τοὺς παραγεγενημένους τῶν]
    [πολ]ιτῶν εἰς τὸ ἱερὸν [-----------------]
    [--]τῶν ἱκετευόντων [----------------]
    [--] πρόνοιαν ἐποιεῖτο [----------------]
12 [----]ΑΣ[--]ΤΩΝΤΑΙ αὐτοὺς [---- καὶ τοὺς διαφερο]-
    [μένο]υς ὑπὲρ τῶν ὅρκων συλλύων [διετέλει --------]
    [----]δεν Υ[--]ΤΩ[--]ΜΕΤΕ[--]Ν ΩΣ[-------]
    [οὔτε κ]ίνδυ[νο]ν οὔ[τ]ε δαπάνην οὔτε κ[ακοπαθίαν οὐδε]-
16 [μίαν ὑφο]ρώμενος· ὅπως οὖγ καὶ ὁ δῆ[μος φαίνηται ἀπο]-
    [διδοὺς τὰς καταξίας χάρ]ιτας· δεδόχθαι· ἐπ[ηινῆσθαι αὐτὸν εὐ]-
    [ν]ο[ίας ἕ]νεκεν καὶ εὐσεβείας καὶ στε[φανῶσαι]
    [θ]αλλοῦ σ[τε]φάνωι, ἀναγορεῦσαι δὲ τ[ὸν στέφανον τοὺς]
20 [ε]ἰσιόντας [πρυτ]άνε[ι]ς ἐν ταῖς ἀρχα[ιρεσί]αις ποιουμέ-
    νους τὴν ἀναγ[όρευσιν τήνδε]· ὁ δῆμος ὁ Καλ<λ>ιπολιτῶν
    [ἐ]παινεῖ καὶ στεφανοῖ Λέ[οντα Χ]ρυσάορος τοῦ Ζωίλου
    τοῦ Πολυπέρχοντος Στρατ[ονικέα] ἀρετῆς ἕνεκεν καὶ εὐνο-
24 ίας, ἣν ἔχων διατελεῖ εἰς τὸν δ[ῆμ]ον τὸγ Καλλιπολιτῶ[ν]·
    ἀναγ{ι}ράψαι δὲ τόδε τὸ ψήφισμα εἰς [στήλη]ν λιθίνην καὶ ἀ-
    ν]αθεῖναι ἐν τῶι ἱερῶι τοῦ Διὸς τοῦ [Καρίο]υ τοῦ ἐμ Πανα-
    [μ]άροις· ἑλέσθαι δὲ καὶ πρεσβευτήν, ὃς [ἀ]φικόμενος πρὸς
28 Στρατ{ρ}ονικεῖς φίλους καὶ συγγενεῖς ὄν[τ]ας τό τε ψήφισ-
    μα ἀποδώσει καὶ ἐπαινέσει αὐτοὺς ἐπ[ὶ τ]ῶι καλὸν
    [κ]ἀγαθὸν ἄνδρα καθεστακέναι ἐν τῶι ἐπιφανεστά-
    τωι ἱερῶι· ᾑρέθη Ἀριστόνικος Ζηνοδότου.

    4. ed. pr. [--------] σὺ[ν] Χρυσάορι κ[αὶ -] Ο [-]
    5. ed. pr. [ἔδοξε τῆι β]ουλῆι

    [-------------------------------]
    [------------- opinion-------------]
    [-------------k]l[e]ou[s-----------]
4   [-------------]sr[-]Chrysaorik[--]O
    [was decided by the c]ouncil and the *demos* of the Kallipolitai. [Since Leon]
    [son of Chrysaor] son of Zoilos son of Poly[perchon, Stratonikeus]
    [having held the pr]iesthood in Panamara [piously and]
8   [generously] and lavishly [those of the citizens? who had gone]
    to the sanctuary [------------------------]
    [----] of the suppliants
    he made? care/forethought
12 [----] [--] *tontai* them between [those who disagreed on]
    the oaths he achieved a settlement
    [------------------------------]
    avoiding neither danger nor cost nor [suffering]

16 so that therefore the *demos* may be seen to [render]
    [the appropriate gra]titude it was decided to [praise him]
    for his benevolence and piety and to crown him
    with a crown of leaves, that the *prytaneis* entering office
20 during the main assembly make
    the following announcement: 'the *demos* of the Kallipolitai
    praises and crowns Leon son of Chrysaor son of Zoilos
    son of Polyperchon Strat[onikeus] for his virtue and bene-
24 volence which he continuously held for the *demos* of the Kallipolitai.
    To inscribe this decree on a stone stele and
    to place it in the sanctuary of Zeus Karios in Pana-
    mara. To elect also an ambassador, who, having arrived
28 at the Stratonikeis, who are friends and kinsmen, will hand over
    the decree and praise them for having appointed
    an excellent man as priest in the most prominent
    sanctuary. Aristonikos son of Zenodotos was elected.

Decree of the Laodikeis (EA 1995 no. 2, HTC no. 89; SEG XLV, no. 1557)

Ἐπ' ἱερέως Εὐδάμου καὶ ἀρχόντων ἐν <Λα>οδικείαι Μενεκράτ[ου]
[τ]οῦ Θαργηλίου, Μυωνίδου τοῦ Πανταλέοντος, Νίκωνος τοῦ Νικομά-
[χ]ου, γραμματεύοντος Φανία τοῦ Καλλίου, Ζμινθίου δευτέραι·
4   [ἔ]δοξε Λαοδικέων τῶι κοινῶι· ἀρχόντων γνώμη· ἐπειδὴ Λέων
    Χρυσάορος τοῦ Ζωίλου τοῦ Πολυπέρχοντος ἱερατεύσας ἐμ Πα-
    ναμάροις εὐσεβῶς καὶ φιλαγάθως πᾶσι τοῖς παραγεγενημένοις
    τῶμ πολιτῶν εἰς τὸ ἱερὸν φιλόδοξον αὐτὸμ παρείχετο καὶ τοὺς διαφερο-
8   [μ]ένους ὑπὲρ τῶν ὅρκων συλλύων διετέλει, καθόλου τε ἐμ πᾶσιν ἐγί-
    [ν]ετο ἐκτενὴς καὶ φιλότιμος, οὐδεμίαν κακοπάθιαν οὐδὲ δαπάνην
    [ὑφ]ορώμενος, ὅπως οὖν καὶ ὁ δῆμος φαίνηται ἀποδιδοὺς τοῖς καλοῖς
    [κ]ἀγαθοῖς καὶ φιλοδόξοις ἀνδράσιν τὰς καταξίας χάριτας δεδόχθα[ι].
12 [ἐ]πηνῆσθαι Λέοντα Χρυσάορος τοῦ Ζωίλου <τοῦ> Πολυπέρχοντος καὶ στε-
    φανῶσαι αὐτὸν θαλλοῦ στεφάνωι, ἀναθεῖναι δὲ καὶ στήλην λιθί-
    [ν]ην, εἰς ἣν ἀναγραφήσεται τόδε τὸ ψήφισμα, τὴν δὲ στήλην
    ἀναθέτω{ι} οὗ ἂν αὐτὸς βούληται, τὸ δὲ εἰς αὐτὴν τέλεσμα
16   ὑπαρχέτω{ι} ἐξ ἐπαγγελίας

During the priesthood of Eudamos, and while Menekrates son of Thargelios,
Myonides son of Pantaleon, and Nikon son of
Nikomachos were *archontes* in Laodikeia, and Phanias son of Kallion
grammateus
4   the *koinon* of the Laodikeis decided, on the advice of the *archontes*: since
    Leon, son of Chrysaor son of Zoilos son of Polyperchon, while holding the priesthood in
    Panamara piously and well, disported himself generously to all of our
    citizens who came to the sanctuary and achieved a settlement between

8 those who disagreed about the oaths, and was altogether
   hard-working and zealous and did not avoid hardship or expenses,
   so that the *demos* will be seen to be giving the appropriate gratitude
   to excellent and glory-loving men, it was decided:
12 to praise Leon son of Chrysaor son of Zoilos son of Polyperchon and to
   crown him with a crown of leaves and to set up a stone stele
   on which this decree will be inscribed, and the stele
   will be erected wherever he wishes, and the money for it
16 will come out of a promised contribution.

Bibliography

Ager, S.L. (1996), *Interstate Arbitration in the Greek World, 337–90 B.C.* (Berkeley, Los Angeles and London).
  (1998), 'Civic identity in the Hellenistic world: the case of Lebedos', *GRBS* 39, 5–21.
Alföldy, G. (1984), *Römische Sozialgeschichte³* (Wiesbaden).
  (1985), *The Social History of Rome*, trans. D. Braund and F. Pollock (London).
Alford, R.D. (1988), *Naming and Identity: A Cross-cultural Study of Personal Naming Practices* (New Haven, Conn.).
Alzinger, W. (1970), 'Ephesos', *RE* Suppl. XII, cols. 1588–1704.
Anagnostou-Canas, B. (1998), '"Justice" oraculaire dans l'Égypte hellénistique et romaine', *RHD* 76, 1–16.
Anderson, J.G.C. (1913), 'Festivals of Mên Askaênos in the Roman colonia at Antioch of Pisidia', *JRS* 3, 267–300.
André, J. (1995), *Etre médecin à Rome²* (Paris).
Arangio-Ruiz, V. and Olivieri, A. (1925), *Inscriptiones Graecae Siciliae et Infimae Italiae ad ius pertinentes* (Milan).
Arslan, N. (2001), 'Kilikia bölgesindeki grek kolonizasyonu', *Olba* 4, 1–17.
Asheri, D. (1983), *Fra Ellenismo e Iranismo* (Bologna).
  (1991), 'Divagazioni erodotee sulla Cilicia persiana', *Quaderni Storici* 76, 35–65.
Assmann, J. (1997), 'Eine liturgische Inszenierung des Totengerichts aus dem Mittleren Reich. Altägyptische Vorstellungen von Schuld, Person und künftigem Leben', in J. Assmann and T. Sundermeier (eds), *Schuld, Gewissen und Person. Studien zur Geschichte des inneren Menschen* (Gütersloh), 27–63.
Atkinson, J.E. (1980), *A Commentary on Q. Curtius Rufus' Historiae Alexandri Magni* (Amsterdam).
Bacchielli, L. (1979), 'Arato o Crisippo? Nuove ipotesi per un vecchio problema', *Quad. di Arch. della Libia* 10, 26–48.
Badian, E. (1993), *From Plataea to Potidaea* (Baltimore and London).
Bagnall, R. (1976), *The Administration of Ptolemaic Possessions outside Egypt* (Leiden).
Baker, P. (1991), *Cos et Calymnos* (Quebec).
Barton, S.C. and Horsley, G.H.R. (1981), 'A Hellenistic cult group and the New Testament church', *JbAC* 24, 7–41.

Baslez, M.-F. (1976), 'Déliens et étrangers domiciliés à Délos', *REG* 89, 343–60.
Baurain, C. (1997), *Les Grecs et la Mediterranée orientale* (Paris).
Bean, G. (1948), 'Notes and inscriptions from Lycia', *JHS* 70, 40–58.
Bechtel, F. (1917a), *Die historischen Personennamen des Griechischen bis zur Kaiserzeit* (Halle).
 (1917b), *Namenstudien* (Halle): repr. in his *Kleine Onomastische Studien* (Königstein 1981).
Beck, H. (1997), *Polis und Koinon. Untersuchungen zur Geschichte und Struktur der griechischen Bundesstaaten im 4. Jahrhundert v. Chr.* (*Historia* Einzelschrift 114, Stuttgart).
Bejor, G. (1999), *Vie colonnate. Paesaggi urbani del mondo antico* (Suppl. *RdA* 22, Rome).
Bellinger, A.R. (1949), *The Excavations at Dura-Europos, Final Report* VI: *The Coins* (New Haven, Conn.).
Below, K.-H. (1953), *Der Arzt im römischen Recht* (Munich).
Berhwald, R. (2000), *Das lykische Bund. Untersuchungen zu Geschichte und Verfassung* (Bonn).
Berranger, D. (1992), *Recherches sur l'histoire et la prosopographie de Paros à l'époque archaïque* (Clermont-Ferrand).
Berranger-Auserve, D. (2000). *Paros* II: *Prosopographie générale et étude historique du début de la période classique jusqu'à la fin de l'époque romaine* (Clermont-Ferrand).
Billows, R.A. (1990), *Antigonos the One-Eyed and the Creation of the Hellenistic State* (Berkeley).
Bing, J.D. (1971), 'Tarsus: a forgotten colony of Lindos', *JNES* 30, 99–103.
 (1991), 'Alexander's sacrifice *dis praesidibus loci* before the battle of Issus', *JHS* 111, 161–5.
Björck, G. (1938), *Der Fluch des Christen Sabinus* (Uppsala).
Blackman, D. (1981), 'Brief history of the city, based on the ancient sources', in *Phaselis* (*Ist. Mitt.*, Beiheft 24, Tübingen), 31–7.
Blinkenberg, C. (1915), *Die lindische Tempelchronik* (Bonn).
Blümel, W. (1990), 'Zwei neue Inschriften aus Mylasa aus der Zeit des Maussollos', *EA* 16, 29–42.
 (1992), *Die Inschriften von Knidos* I (*IGSK* XLI, Bonn).
 (1995), 'Inschriften aus Karien I', *EA* 25, 35–64.
 (1997), 'Ein Vertrag zwischen Latmos und Pidasa', *EA* 29, 135–42.
 (1998a), 'Einheimische Ortsnamen in Karien', *EA* 30, 163–82.
 (1998b), 'Addendum zu dem Vertrag zwischen Latmos und Pidasa: fratôrion', *EA* 30, 185.
 (1998c), 'Epigraphische Forschungen im westen Kariens 1996', *XV. Araştırma Sonuçları Toplantısı* I (Ankara), 387–95.
 (2000a), 'Rhodisches Dekret in Bargylia', *EA* 32, 94–6.
 (2000b), 'Ehrendekrete aus Olymos', *EA* 32, 97–100.
Boardman, J. (1965), 'Tarsus, Al Mina and Greek chronology', *JHS* 85, 5–15.
 (1999a), 'The excavated history of Al Mina', in Tsetskhladze (1999), 135–61.
 (1999b), *The Greeks Overseas*[4] (London).

Boffo, L. (1985), *I re ellenistici e i centri religiosi dell' Asia Minore* (Pavia).
Bosch, E. (1947), 'Antalya kitabeleri', *Belleten* 11, 88–125.
(1967), *Quellen zur Geschichte der Stadt Ankara im Altertum* (Ankara).
Bosworth, A.B. (1980), *A Historical Commentary on Arrian's History of Alexander* I (Oxford).
Bousquet, J. (1965), 'Convention entre Myania et Hypnia', *BCH* 89, 665–81.
(1988), 'La stèle des Kyténiens au Létôon de Xanthos', *REG* 101, 12–53.
and Gauthier, P. (1994), 'Inscriptions du Létôon de Xanthos', *REG* 107, 319–61.
Bowersock, G.W. (1990), *Hellenism in Late Antiquity* (Cambridge).
Boyce, A.A. (1958), 'The harbor of Pompeiopolis', *AJA* 62, 67–78.
Braun, T.F.R.G. (1982), 'The Greeks in the Near East', *CAH* III.3^2, 1–31.
Breasted, J.H. (1924), *Oriental Forerunners of Byzantine Painting* (Chicago).
Bresson, A. (1991), *Recueil des inscriptions de la Pérée rhodienne* (Besançon and Paris).
(1999), 'Rhodes and Lycia in Hellenistic Times', in Gabrielsen (1999) (ed.), 98–131.
(2003), 'Les intérêts rhodiens en Carie à l'époque hellénistique, jusqu'en 167 av. J.-C.', in F. Prost (ed.), *L'Orient méditerranéen, de la mort d'Alexandre aux campagnes de Pompée. Cités et royaumes à l'époque hellénistique* (Rennes), 169–91.
and Descat, P. (eds) (2001), *Les cités d'Asie Mineure occidentale au IIe siècle a.C.* (Bordeaux).
Briant, P. (1996), *Histoire de l'empire perse de Cyrus à Alexandre* (Paris).
Bringmann, K. and Von Steuben, H. (1995), *Schenkungen hellenistischer Herrscher an griechische Städte und Heiligtümer* (Berlin).
Briscoe, J. (1973), *Commentary on Livy Books* XXXI–XXXIII (Oxford).
Brixhe, C. (1987), *Essai sur le grec anatolien au début de notre ère*^{2} (Nancy).
(1995), 'Les Grecs, les Phrygiens et l'alphabet', in *Studia in honorem Georgii Mihailov* (Sofia), 101–14.
(1997), 'Deux épitaphes de Phrygie et de Lycaonie', in C. Brixhe (ed.), *Poikila Epigraphika* (Nancy), 59–65.
(1999), 'Du lycien au grec: lexique de la famille et de la société', in A. Blanc and A. Christol (eds), *Langues en contact dans l'Antiquité: aspects lexicaux* (Nancy), 81–105.
and Drew-Bear, T. (1997), 'Huit inscriptions néo-phrygiennes', in R. Gusmani, M. Salvini and P. Vannicelli (eds), *Frigi e Frigio. Atti del 1° Simposio Internazionale, Roma, 16–17 ottobre 1995* (Rome), 71–113.
Bryce, T.R. (1986), *The Lycians* (Copenhagen).
Buckler, W.H. (1914–16), 'Some Lydian propitiatory inscriptions', *ABSA* 21, 169–83.
Buraselis, K. (1995), 'Zu Caracallas Strafmaßnahmen in Alexandrien (215/6)', *ZPE* 108, 166–88.
Burkert, W. (1992), *The Orientalizing Revolution. Near Eastern Influence on Greek Culture in the Early Archaic Age* (Cambridge, Mass.).
(1996), *Creation of the Sacred. Tracks of Biology in Early Religions* (Cambridge, Mass.).

Butcher, K. (1996), 'Coinage and currency in Syria and Palestine to the reign of Gallienus', in C.E. King and D.G. Wigg (eds), *Coin Finds and Coin Use in the Roman World* (Berlin), 101–12.

Calder, W.M. (1912), 'Colonia Caesarea Antiocheia', *JRS* 2, 70–109.

Caldesi Valeri, V. (1998), 'Le assemblee di Mylasa', *Patavium* 12, 93–109.

Çambel, H. (1999), *Karatepe-Aslantaş. The Inscriptions* (*Corpus of Hieroglyphic Luwian Inscriptions* II, Berlin and New York).

Campanile, M.D. (2001), '*Provincialis molestia*. Note su Cicerone proconsole', *Studi ellenistici* 13, 243–74.

Capecchi, G. (1991), 'Grecità linguistica e grecità figurativa nella più antica monetazione di Cilicia', *Quaderni Storici* 76, 67–103.

Carter, E. (1998), *A Preliminary Report on the Incirli Stela* (http://www.humnet.ucla.edu/humnet/nelc/stelasite/report.html).

Carradice, I. (1983), *Coinage and Finances in the Reign of Domitian:* AD *81–96* (Oxford).

and Cowell, M. (1987), 'The minting of Roman Imperial coins for circulation in the East: Vespasian to Trajan', *Numismatic Chronicle* 147, 26–50.

Casabonne, O. (1995), 'Le *syennésis* cilicien et Cyrus: l'apport des sources numismatiques', *Pallas* 43, 147–72.

(1999), 'Local powers and Persian model in Achaemenid Cilicia: a reassessment', *Olba* 2, 57–62.

(2000), 'Conquête perse et phénomène monétaire: l'example cilicien', in Casabonne (ed.) (2000), 21–91.

(ed.) (2000), *Mécanismes et innovations monétaires dans l'Anatolie achéménide. Numismatique et histoire* (Varia Anatolica 12, Paris).

Casanova, G. (1997), 'Συνίστωρ – συνιστορέω. Osservazioni su "complice" ed "essere complice"', *Aegyptus* 77, 27–42.

Cassola, F. (1957), *La Ionia nel mondo miceneo* (Naples).

Chandezon, C. (1998), 'Paysage et économie rurale en Asie Mineure à l'époque hellénistique. A partir de quelques baux de Mylasa (2e–1er siècle avant J.-C.)', *Histoire et sociétés rurales* 9, 33–56.

Chaniotis, A. (1990), 'Drei kleinasiatische Inschriften zur griechischen Religion', *EA* 15, 127–33.

(1988), *Historie und Historiker in den griechischen Inschriften* (Stuttgart).

(1995), 'Illness and cures in the Greek propitiatory inscriptions and dedications of Lydia and Phrygia', in H.F.J. Horstmanshoff, P.J. van der Eijk, and P.H. Schrijvers (eds), *Ancient Medicine in its Socio-cultural Context. Papers read at the Congress held at Leiden University, 13–15 April 1992* (Amsterdam and Atlanta), II, 323–44.

(1996a), 'Conflicting authorities: Greek asylia between secular and sacred law', *Kernos* 9, 65–86.

(1996b), *Die Verträge zwischen kretischen Poleis in der hellenistischen Zeit* (Stuttgart).

(1997a), 'Tempeljustiz im kaiserzeitlichen Kleinasien: Rechtliche Aspekte der Beichtinschriften', in G. Thür and J. Vélissaropoulos-Karakostas (eds),

Symposion 1995. Vorträge zur griechischen und hellenistischen Rechtsgeschichte (Korfu, 1.–5. September 1995) (Cologne, Weimar and Vienna), 353–84.

(1997*b*), 'Reinheit des Körpers – Reinheit der Seele in den griechischen Kultgesetzen', in J. Assmann and T. Sundermeier (eds), *Schuld, Gewissen und Person* (Gütersloh), 142–79.

(forthcoming), 'Inscriptions from Aphrodisias (1995–2001)', *AJA*.

Chastagnol, A. (1992), *Le sénat romain à l'époque impériale* (Paris).

Christensen, A. and Johansen, C. (1971), *Hama: fouilles et recherches 1931–1938* III.2: *Les poteries hellénistiques et les terres sigillées orientales* (Copenhagen).

Christol, M. (1975), '*CIL*, XIII, 6754 (Mayence). Caracalla en Germanie Supérieure: empereur-soleil ou empereur victorieux?', *Bonner Jahrbücher* 175, 129–39.

(1993), 'Le préfet d'Egypte Titus Pactumeius Magnus et la diffusion de la cité romaine', *RHD* 71, 405–10.

and Drew-Bear, T. (1987), *Un castellum romain près d'Apamée de Phrygie* (*TAM* Ergänzungsband 12, Vienna).

and Drew-Bear, T. (1991), 'D. Fonteius Fronto, proconsul de Lycie-Pamphylie', *GRBS* 32, 397–413.

and Drew-Bear, T. (1995), 'Inscriptions militaires d'*Aulutrene* et d'Apamée de Phrygie', in Y. Le Bohec (ed.), *La hiérarchie (Rangordnung) de l'armée romaine sous le Haut-Empire (Actes du Congrès de Lyon, 15–18 septembre 1994)* (Paris), 57–92.

and Drew-Bear, T. (2000), 'Une inscription d'Ancyre relative au *sacer comitatus*', in Y. Le Bohec (ed.), *Les légions de Rome sous le Haut-Empire (Actes du Colloque de Lyon, 1998)* (Paris), 529–39.

Clogg, R. (1992), *A Concise History of Greece* (Cambridge).

Cohen, G.M. (1995), *The Hellenistic Settlements in Europe, the Islands and Asia Minor* (Berkeley).

Coldstream, J.N. (1977), *Geometric Greece* (London).

Colledge, M.A. (1977), *Parthian Art* (London).

Collombier, A.M. (1990), 'Organisation du territoire et pouvoirs locaux dans l'île de Chypre à l'époque perse', *Transeuphratène* 4, 21–43.

Cook, J.M. (1961), 'Some sites of the Milesian territory', *BSA* 56, 90–101.

(1973), *The Troad. An Archaeological and Topographical Study* (Oxford).

Corell, J. (1994), 'Drei defixionum tabellae aus Sagunt (Valencia)', *ZPE* 101, 280–6.

Corsaro, M. (1997), 'I Greci d'Asia', in S. Settis (ed.), *I Greci* (Turin), II.2, 27–59.

Corsten, T. (1995), 'Das Koinon der Laodikener in Panamara', *EA* 25, 87–8.

(1999), *Vom Stamm zum Bund. Gründung und territoriale Organisation griechischer Bundesstaaten* (Munich).

Costa, E.A. Jr (1974), 'Evagoras I and the Persians, ca. 411 to 391 BC', *Historia* 23, 40–56.

Courbin, P. (1986), 'Bassit', *Syria* 63, 175–220.

Cousin, G. (1904), 'Inscriptions du sanctuaire de Zeus Panamaros. II, Décrets', *BCH* 28, 345–52.

and Deschamps, G. (1888), 'Inscriptions du temple de Zeus Panamaros. Ex-voto et dédicaces', *BCH* 12, 249–73.

Cox, D.H. (1949), *The Excavations at Dura-Europos, Final Report* IV.1, fasc. 2: *The Greek and Roman Pottery* (New Haven, Conn.).
Crampa, J. (1968), 'Some remarks on Welles, *Royal Correspondence*, 29', *Opuscula Atheniensia* 8, 171–6.
Crook, J. (1955), *Consilium principis. Imperial Councils and Counsellors from Augustus to Diocletian* (Cambridge).
Crowther, C., Habicht, C. and Hallof, K. and L. (1998), 'Aus der Arbeit der *Inscriptiones Graecae* I. Drei Dekrete aus Kos für δικασταγωγοί', *Chiron* 28, 87–100.
Curty, O. (1995), *Les parentés légendaires entre cités grecques* (Geneva).
Dain, A. (1933), *Inscriptions grecques du Musée du Louvre: les textes inédites* (Paris).
Dalley, S. (1999), 'Sennacherib and Tarsus', *AS* 49, 73–8.
Davesne, A. (1989), 'La circulation monétaire en Cilicie à l'époque achéménide', *REA* 91, 157–68.
Debord, P. (1982), *Aspects sociaux et économiques de la vie religieuse dans l'Anatolie gréco-romaine* (Leiden).
  (1994), 'Essai sur la géographie historique de la région de Stratonicée', in M.-M. Mactoux and E. Geny (eds), *Mélanges Pierre Lévêque* (Paris), VIII, 107–21.
  (1997), 'Hiérapolis: du sanctuaire-état à la cité', *REA* 99, 415–26.
  (2001*a*), 'Questions stratonicéennes', in Bresson and Descat (eds) (2000), 157–73.
  (2001*b*), 'Sur quelques Zeus Cariens: religion et politique,' *Studi ellenistici* 13, 19–37.
  (2003), 'Cité grecque – village carién. Des usages du mot *koinon*', *Studi ellenistici* 15, 115–80.
De Callataÿ, F. (2000), 'Les monnayages ciliciens du premier quart du IVe s. av. J.-C.', in Casabonne (ed.) (2000), 93–127.
Decourt, J.C. (1990), 'Décret de Pharsale pour une politographie', *ZPE* 81, 163–84.
Degrassi, A. (1921), 'Aurellius', *Athenaeum* 5, 292–9 (= *Scritti vari di Antichità* I, Rome 1962, 467–72).
De Hoz, M.P. (1999), *Die lydischen Kulte im Lichte der griechischen Inschriften* (*Asia Minor Studien* 36, Bonn).
Demand, N. (1990), *Urban Relocation in Archaic and Classical Greece. Flight and Consolidation* (Norman, Okla.).
Demougin, S. (1992), *Prosopographie des chevaliers romains julio-claudiens* (Rome).
Descat, R. (1994), 'Les forteresses de Théra et de Kallipolis de Carie', *REA* 96, 205–14.
  (1997), 'A propos d'un citoyen de Philippes à Théangela', *REA* 99, 411–13.
  (1998), 'La carrière d'Eupolemos, stratège macédonien en Asie Mineure', *REA* 100, 167–90.
Desideri, P. (1992), 'Eforo e Strabone sui popoli misti', in M. Sordi (ed.), *Autocoscienza e rappresentazione dei popoli nell'antichità* (*CISA* 18, Milan), 19–31.
  and Jasink, A.M. (1990), *La Cilicia. Dall'età di Kizzuwatna alla conquista macedone* (Florence).
Devijver, H. (1996), 'Social elite, equestrians and senators: a social history of Roman Sagalassos', *Anc. Soc.* 27, 105–102.

Dignas, B. (2000), 'The leases of sacred property at Mylasa: an alimentary scheme for the gods', *Kernos* 13, 117–26.
  (2002), *Economy of the Sacred in Hellenistic and Roman Asia Minor* (Oxford).
Dirven, L. (1999), *The Palmyrenes of Dura-Europos* (Leiden).
Dmitriev, S. (1997), 'Οἱ ἐπώνυμοι and αἱ ἐπώνυμοι ἀρχαί in the cities of Hellenistic and Roman Asia Minor', *REA* 99: 525–34.
  (1999), 'The στραταγὸς ἐκ πάντων in Rhodian inscriptions', *Historia* 48, 243–53.
Domingo Gygax, M. (2001), *Untersuchungen zu den lykischen Gemeinwesen in klassischer und hellenistischer Zeit* (Bonn).
Dow, S. (1937), 'The Egyptian cults in Athens', *HThR* 30, 183–232.
Downey, S.B. (1988), *Mesopotamian Religious Architecture* (Princeton).
Dressler, W. (1966), 'Zu den sigmatischen Nominativbildungen und der Dentalflexion von Frauennamen auf -α, -η', *Wiener Studien* 79 (*Festschrift Lesky*), 263–72.
Drew-Bear, T. (1979), 'The city of Temenouthyrai in Phrygia', *Chiron* 9, 275–302.
  and Schwertfeger, T. (1979), 'Zur Topographie und Epigraphik von Panamara in Karien', *ZPE* 36, 195–205.
Dreyer, B. (2001), 'Der "Raubvertrag" des Jahres 203/2 v. Chr.: Das Inschriftenfragment von Bargylia und der Brief von Amyzon', *EA* 34, 119–38.
Dušanič, S. (1978), 'Notes épigraphiques sur l'histoire arcadienne du IVe s.', *BCH* 102, 333–58.
Dyson, S.L. (1968), *The Excavations at Dura-Europos, Final Report* IV.1, fasc. 3: *The Commonware Pottery; the Brittle Ware* (Locust Valley, New York).
Eger, O. (1939), 'Eid und Fluch in den maionischen und phrygischen Sühneinschriften', in *Festschrift Paul Koschaker* (Weimar), III, 281–93.
Ehrhardt, N. (forthcoming), 'Die politischen Beziehungen zwischen den griechischen Schwartzmeergründungen und ihre Mutterstädten', in A. Fol (ed.), *Acta Centri Historiae. Terra antiqua Balcanica* (Sofia), II, 78–117.
Eichner, H. (2000), 'Kyberniskos, der lykische Anführer in der Flotte des Xerxes bei Salamis (Herodot VII 98)', in F. Beutler and W. Hameter (eds), *Und das nächste Jahrtausend beginnt: FS Ekkehard Weber* (Vienna), 25–7.
Empereur, J.-Y. and Garlan, Y. (1997), *Bulletin Archéologique*, nos. 101, 102, *REG* 110, 183–4.
Erkelenz, D. (2001), '*Patria, civis, condecurio* – Zur Identifizierung der Herkunft von Rittern und Senatoren in der römischen Kaiserzeit', *ZPE* 137, 271–9.
Errington, R.M. (1986), 'Antiochos III., Zeuxis, und Euromos', *EA* 8, 1–7.
  (1989), 'The peace treaty between Miletus and Magnesia (I. Milet 148)', *Chiron* 19, 279–88.
  (1993), 'Inschriften von Euromos', *EA* 21, 15–32.
  (1995), 'Ἐκκλησίας κυρίας γενομένης', *Chiron* 25, 19–42.
Erzen, A. (1940), *Kilikien bis zum Ende der Perserherrschaft* (Leipzig).
Etienne, R. and Migeotte, L. (1998), 'Colophon et les abus des fermiers des taxes', *BCH* 122, 143–57.
Figueira, T. (1998), *The Power of Money. Coinage and Politics in the Athenian Empire* (Philadelphia).

Finkielsztejn, G. (1993), *Amphores et timbres d'amphores importées en Palestine à l'époque hellénistique: études de chronologie et d'histoire* (Diss. Univ. de Paris I).

—— (1995), 'Chronologie basse des timbres amphoriques rhodiens et évaluation des exportations d'amphores', in T. Fischer-Hansen (ed.) (1995), 279–302.

—— (2001), *Chronologie détaillée et révisée des éponymes amphoriques rhodiens, de 270 à 108 av. J.-C. environ* (BAR International Series 990, Oxford).

Fischer-Hansen, T. (ed.) (1995), *Ancient Sicily* (*Acta Hyperborea*, Danish Studies in Classical Archaeology 6, Copenhagen).

Flobert, P. (1986), 'La théorie du solécisme dans l'antiquité: de la logique à la syntaxe', *RPh* 60, 173–81.

Fowden, G. (1993), *The Egyptian Hermes*² (Princeton).

Francotte, H. (1906), *L'organisation des cités à Rhodes et en Carie* (Louvain and Paris).

Fraser, P.M. (1952), 'Alexander and the Rhodian constitution', *PP* 7, 192–206.

—— and Bean, G.E. (1954), *The Rhodian Peraea and Islands* (Oxford).

Freeman, P. (1986), 'The province of Cilicia and its origins', in P. Freeman and D. Kennedy (eds), *The Defence of the Roman and Byzantine East* 1 (*BAR* International series 279, Oxford), 253–75.

French, D.H. (1981), *Roman Roads and Milestones of Asia Minor* 1: *The Pilgrim's Road* (*BAR* International series 105, Oxford).

French, E. (1975), 'A reassessment of the Mycenaean pottery at Tarsus', *AS* 25, 53–75.

Frézouls, E. and Morant, M.-J. (1985), 'Inscriptions de Sidyma et de Kadyanda I', *Ktema* 10, 233–43.

Frisch, P. (1983), 'Über die lydisch-phrygischen Steininschriften und die "confessiones" des Augustinus', *EA* 2, 41–5.

Fugier, H. (1963), *Recherches sur l'expression du sacré dans la langue latine* (Paris).

Gabrielsen, V. (1994), 'Subdivisions of the state and their decrees in Hellenistic Rhodes', *C&M* 45, 117–35.

—— (1997), *The Naval Aristocracy of Hellenistic Rhodes* (Aarhus).

—— (1999) (ed.), *Hellenistic Rhodes. Politics, Culture and Society* (Studies in Hellenistic Civilization 9, Aarhus).

—— (2000a), 'The Rhodian Peraia in the third and second centuries B.C.', *C&M* 51, 129–83.

—— (2000b), 'The synoikized polis of Rhodos', in P. Flensted-Jensen, T. Heine Nielsen and L. Rubinstein (eds), *Polis and Politics. Studies in Ancient Greek History Presented to Mogens Herman Hansen on his Sixtieth Birthday* (Copenhagen), 177–205.

—— (2001), 'Economic activity, maritime trade and piracy in the Hellenistic Aegean', *REA* 103, 219–40.

Gagarin, M. (1997), 'Oaths and oath-challenges in Greek law', in G. Thür and J. Vélissaropoulos-Karakostas (eds), *Symposion 1995. Vorträge zur griechischen und hellenistischen Rechtsgeschichte (Korfu, 1.–5. September 1995)* (Cologne, Weimar and Vienna), 125–34.

Gallo, I. (1975), *Frammenti biografici da papiri* I (Rome).
  (1976), 'Solone a Soli', *QUCC* 21, 29–36.
Gates, M.H. (1999), 'Kinet Höyük in eastern Cilicia: a case study for acculturation in ancient harbors', *Olba* 2, 303–12.
Gauthier, P. (1989), *Nouvelles inscriptions de Sardes* II (Geneva).
  (1999), 'Nouvelles inscriptions de Claros: décrets d'Aigai et de Mylasa pour juges colophoniens', *REG* 112, 1–36.
  (2001), 'Les Pidaséens entrent en sympolitie avec les Milésiens: la procédure et les modalités institutionnelles', in A. Bresson and R. Descat (eds) (2001), 117–27.
Gélin, M. (2000), 'De l'Euphrate à l'Oxus: exemples de l'utilisation de la brique cuite à Doura-Europos et à Termez', in *La brique antique et médiévale: production et commercialisation d'un matériau* (Collection de l'Ecole Française de Rome 272), 53–75.
Ghiron-Bistagne, P. (1988), 'Le nom et le surnom dans l'onomastique grecque: étude de littérature et d'épigraphie', in S. Gély (ed.), *Sens et pouvoirs de la nomination dans les cultures hellénique et romaine* (Montpellier), 5–19.
Giorgieri, M. (2000), 'L'onomastica hurrita', *PdP* 55, 278–95.
Giovannini, A. (1971), *Untersuchungen über die Natur und die Anfänge der bundesstaatlichen Sympolitie in Griechenland* (Göttingen).
Gjerstad, E. (1934), 'Cilician studies', *RA* 3, 156–203.
Gnoli, T. and Thornton, J. (1997), 'Σῶζε τὴν κατοικίαν. Società e religione nella Frigia romana. Note introductive', in R. Gusmani, M. Salvini and P. Vannicelli (eds), *Frigi e Frigio. Atti del I° Simposio Internazionale, Roma, 16–17 ottobre 1995* (Rome), 153–200.
Goetze, A. (1939), 'Cuneiform inscriptions from Tarsus', *JAOS* 59, 1–16.
  (1954), 'The linguistic continuity of Anatolia as shown by its proper names', *JCS* 8, 74–81.
  (1962), 'Cilicians', *JCS* 16, 48–58.
Goldman, H. (1956), *Excavations at Gözlü Kule, Tarsus* II: *From the Neolithic through the Bronze Age* (Princeton).
Graf, F. (1993), 'Dionysian and Orphic eschatology: new texts and old questions', in T.H. Carpenter and C. Faraone (eds), *Masks of Dionysus* (Ithaca and London), 240–58.
  (1996), *Gottesnähe und Schadenzauber. Die Magie in der griechisch-römischen Antike* (Munich).
Graham, A.J. (1982), 'The colonial expansion of Greece', *CAH* III.3^2, 83–162.
Grainger, J.D. (1990), *The Cities of Seleukid Syria* (Oxford).
  (1997), *A Seleukid Prosopography and Gazetteer* (Leiden).
  (1999), *The League of the Aitolians* (Leiden).
Gras, M., Rouillard, P. and Teixidor, J. (1989), *L'Univers phénicien* (Paris).
Grosso, F. (1958), 'Gli Eretriesi deportati in Persia', *RFIC* 86, 350–73.
Grottanelli, C. (1991), 'Do ut des?', in G. Bartoloni, G. Colonna and C. Grottanelli (eds), *Atti del convegno internazionale "Anathema". Regime delle offerte e vita dei santuari nel mediterraneo antico, Roma 15–18 giugno 1989* (*Scienze dell'antichità* 3–4, 1989/90, Rome), 45–55.

Gschnitzer, F. (1989), 'Bemerkungen zum Zusammenwirken von Magistraten und Priestern in der griechischen Welt', *Ktema* 14, 31–8.
Guarducci, M. (1978), 'La culla dell'alfabeto greco', *RAL* 33 (s. 8), 381–8.
Guthrie, W.K.C. (1971), *The Sophists* (Cambridge).
Habicht, C. (1996), 'Neue Inschriften aus Kos', *ZPE* 112, 83–94.
 (1998), 'Zum Vertrag zwischen Latmos und Pidasa', *EA* 30, 9–10.
Haider, P.W. (1999), 'Mitteilung', *Kadmos* 38, 179.
Halfmann, H. (1986), *Itinera principum. Geschichte und Typologie der Kaiserreisen im Römischen Reich* (Stuttgart).
 (1982), 'Die Senatoren aus den Kleinasiatischen Provinzen des römischen Reiches vom 1. bis 3. Jahrhundert', *Tituli* v: *Atti del colloquio internazionale AIEGL su epigrafia e ordine senatorio* (Rome) II, 603–50.
Hallof, L. and K., and Habicht, C. (1998), 'Aus der Arbeit der *Inscriptiones Graecae* II. Ehrendekrete aus dem Asklepieion von Kos', *Chiron* 28, 101–42.
Hansen, M.H. (1997), 'The *polis* as an urban centre. The literary and epigraphical evidence', in *idem* (ed.), *The Polis as an Urban Centre and as a Political Community* (Copenhagen), 9–86.
 and Nielsen, T.H. (2000), 'The use of the word *polis* in the fragments of some historians', in P. Flensted-Jensen (ed.), *Further Studies in the Ancient Greek Polis* (Stuttgart), 141–50.
Harper, R.P. (1970), 'Podandus and the Via Tauri', *AS* 20, 149–53.
Harrison, T. (2000), *Divinity and History: The Religion of Herodotus* (Oxford).
Hassall, M.W.C. and Tomlin, R.S.O. (1994), 'Roman Britain in 1993. II. Inscriptions', *Britannia* 25, 293–314.
 (1995), 'Roman Britain in 1994. II. Inscriptions', *Britannia* 26, 371–90.
 (1996), 'Roman Britain in 1995. II. Inscriptions', *Britannia* 27, 439–57.
Hatzopoulos, M. (1993), 'Epigraphie et villages en Grèce du Nord: *ethnos, polis* et *kome*, Macédoine', in A. Calbi, A. Donati and G. Poma (eds), *L'epigrafia del villaggio* (Faenza), 151–71.
Hawkins, J.D. (1982), 'The Neo-Hittite states in Syria and Anatolia', in *CAH* III.1^2, 372–441.
 (2000), *Inscriptions of the Iron Age* I–III (*Corpus of Hieroglyphic Luwian Inscriptions* I, Berlin and New York).
Hayes, J.W. (1985), 'Sigillata orientale A', in *Enciclopedia dell'arte antica: atlante delle forme ceramiche* (Rome), 9–48.
Head, B.V. (1896), *A Catalogue of the Greek Coins in the British Museum. Catalogue of the Greek Coins of Caria, Cos, Rhodes, etc.* (London, repr. Bologna 1964).
Hemer, C.J. (1990), *The Book of Acts in the Setting of Hellenistic History* (Winona Lake, Ind.).
Hengel, M. (1992), 'Pre-Christian Paul', in J. Lieu, J. North and T. Rajak (eds), *The Jews among Pagans and Christians in the Roman Empire* (London and New York), 29–52.
Hermary, A. (1987), 'Une nouvelle stèle funéraire attique trouvée à Soloi', in G. Dagron and D. Feissel (eds), *Inscriptions de Cilicie* (Paris), 227–9.
Herrmann, P. (1962), *Ergebnisse einer Reise in Nordostlydien* (Vienna).

(1965), 'Neue Urkunden zur Geschichte von Milet im 2. Jahrhundert v. Chr.', *Ist. Mitt.* 15, 71–117.

(1978), 'Men, Herr von Axiotta', in S. Şahin, E. Schwertheim and J. Wagner (eds), *Studien zur Religion und Kultur Kleinasiens. Festschrift für Friedrich Karl Dörner zum 65. Geburtstag am 28. Februar 1976* (Leiden), 1. 415–23.

(1985), 'Sühn- und Grabinschriften aus der Katakekaumene im archäologischen Museum von Izmir', *AAWW* 122, 248–61.

and Varinlioğlu, E. (1984), 'Theoi Pereudenoi. Eine Gruppe von Weihungen und Sühneinschriften aus der Katakekaumene', *EA* 3, 1–17.

Herzog, R. (1902), 'κρητικὸς πόλεμος', *Klio* 2, 316–33.

(1942), 'Symbolae Calymniae et Coae', *RFIC* 20, 1–20.

Hicks, E.L. (1894), 'Inscription on a limestone block', *JHS* 14, 377–80.

Hirschfeld, O. (1905), *Die kaiserliche Verwaltungsbeamten bis auf Diokletian*[2] (Berlin).

Hirzel, R. (1902), *Der Eid. Ein Beitrag zu seiner Geschichte* (Leipzig).

Hoffman, O. (1906), *Die Makedonen* (Göttingen).

Höghammar, K. (1993), *Sculpture and Society* (Uppsala).

Holleaux, M. (1904), 'Remarques sur des décrets trouvés dans le sanctuaire de Zeus Panamaros', *BCH* 28, 353–63 (pp. 353–9 repr. in Holleaux, *Etudes*, IV, 204–10).

(1931), 'Les additions annalistiques au traité de 196 (Tite Live 33, 60, 6–11)', *Rev. Phil.* 57, 5–19 (repr. in Holleaux, *Etudes* V, 104–20).

(1938–68), *Etudes d'épigraphie et d'histoire grecques* (6 vols, ed. L. Robert, Paris).

Holz, L. (1981), *Donat et la tradition de l'enseignement grammatical* (Paris).

Hopwood, K.R. (1990), 'The indigenous population of Roman Rough Cilicia', in *X Türk Tarih Kongresi* (Ankara), 337–45.

Hornblower, S. (1982), *Mausolus* (Oxford).

(1996), 'Hellenism, Hellenization', *OCD*[3], 677–9.

Hornum, M.B. (1993), *Nemesis, the Roman state, and the Games* (Leiden, New York and Cologne).

Horsley, G.H.R. (1997), 'A Pisidian poet', *EA* 29, 45–57.

Houwink Ten Cate, H.J. (1965), *The Luwian Population Groups of Lycia and Cilicia Aspera during the Hellenistic Period* (Leiden).

Howgego, C.J. (1982), 'Coinage and military finance: the Imperial bronze coinage of the Augustan East', *Numismatic Chronicle* 142, 1–22.

(1985), *Greek Imperial Countermarks: Studies in the Provincial Coinage of the Roman Empire* (London).

Hula, E. and Szanto, E. (1895), 'Bericht über eine Reise in Karien', II Abhandlung (*SB Akad. Wien* 132, Vienna).

Ingholt, H. (1967–68), 'Aratos and Chrysippos on a lead medallion from a Beirut collection', *Berytus* 17, 143–77.

İplikçioğlu, B. (1991), *Epigraphische Forschungen in Termessos und seinem Territorium* 1 (*SB Akad. Wien* 575, Vienna).

Irwin, E. (1999), 'Solecising in Solon's colony', *BICS* 43, 187–93.

Jacobsthal, B. (1933), *Diskoi* (Berlin).

Jacoby, F. (1959), *Diagoras ὁ Ἄθεος* (Berlin).
Jean, E. (1999), 'The "Greeks" in Cilicia at the end of the 2nd millennium BC: classical sources and archaeological evidence', *Olba* 2, 27–39.
— (ed.) (2001), *La Cilicie: espaces et pouvoirs locaux* (Varia Anatolica 13, Paris).
— (2001*a*), 'La Cilicie: pluralité et unité', in Jean (ed.) (2001), 5–12.
Jeffery, L.H. (1976), *Archaic Greece. The City-States c. 700–500 BC* (London).
— (1982), 'Greek alphabetic writing', in *CAH* III.1^2, 819–33.
— (1990), *The Local Scripts of Archaic Greece*, revised edition with a supplement by A.W. Johnston (Oxford).
Johnston, S.I. (1999), *Restless Dead. Encounters between the Living and the Dead in Ancient Greece* (Berkeley).
Jones, A.H.M. (1939), *The Greek City from Alexander to Justinian* (Oxford).
Jones, C.P. (1977–8), 'Some new inscriptions from Bubon', *Ist. Mitt.* 27–8, 267–96.
— (1978), *The Roman World of Dio Chrysostom* (Cambridge, Mass.).
— (1982), 'A family of Pisidian Antioch', *Phoenix* 36, 264–71.
— (1992), 'Hellenistic history in Chariton of Aphrodisias', *Chiron* 22, 91–102.
— (1996), 'The Panhellenion', *Chiron* 26, 29–47.
— (1998), '"Joint sacrifice" at Iasus and Side', *JHS* 118, 183–6.
— (1999*a*), 'The union of Latmos and Pidasa', *EA* 31, 1–7.
— (1999*b*), *Kinship Diplomacy in the Ancient World* (Cambridge, Mass.).
— (2001), 'Appia in Phrygia and Appius Claudius Pulcher, *cos.* 54 BCE', *Studi ellenistici* 13, 233–41.
— and Habicht, C. (1989), 'A Hellenistic inscription from Arsinoe in Cilicia', *Phoenix* 43, 317–46.
— and Russell, J. (1993), 'Two new inscriptions from Nagidos in Cilicia', *Phoenix* 47, 293–304.
Jones, J.W. (1956), *The Law and Legal Theory of the Greeks* (Oxford).
Judeich, W. (1927), 'Politische Namengabung in Athen', in *Epitymbion H. Swoboda dargebracht* (Reichenberg), 99–106.
Junghölter, U. (1989), *Zur Komposition der Lagina-Friese und zur Deutung des Nordfrieses* (Europäische Hochschulschriften, series 38, Archäologie 29, Frankfurt am Main).
Kantzia, C. (1997), 'Εὐχὴ κατακλιτικὴ κατὰ τοῦ Ἑρμία Πυθιάδος. Ἕνας εἰκονογραφημένος κατάδεσμος ἀπὸ τὴν Κῶ', in A.P. Christidis and D.R. Jordan (eds), Γλῶσσα καὶ μαγεία. Κείμενα ἀπὸ τὴν ἀρχαιότητα (Athens), 170–92.
Karwiese, S. (1989), 'Erster vorläufiger Grabungsbericht über die Wiederaufnahme der archäologischen Untersuchungen der Marienkirche in Ephesos', *Denkschr. Wien* 200.
— (1995), 'The church of Mary and the temple of Hadrian Olympius', in H. Koester (ed.), *Ephesos, Metropolis of Asia. An Interdisciplinary Approach to its Archaeology, Religion, and Culture* (Valley Forge, Penn.), 311–19.
Kaser, M. (1971), *Das römische Privatrecht. Erster Abschnitt. Das altrömische, das vorklassische und klassische Recht*^{2} (Munich).
— (1975), *Das römische Privatrecht. Zweiter Abschnitt. Die nachklassischen Entwicklungen*^{2} (Munich).

Kearsley, R.A. (1999), 'Greeks overseas in the 8th century BC: Euboeans, Al Mina and Assyrian imperialism', in Tsetskhladze (ed.) (1999), 110–34.
Keen, A.G. (1993), 'Gateway from the Mediterranean to the Aegean: the strategic value of Lycia down to the fourth century BC', in J. Borchardt and G. Dobesch (eds), *Akten des II. Int. Lykien-Symposions* (Vienna), 1, 70–7.
—— (1998), *Dynastic Lycia: A Political History of the Lycians and their Relations with Foreign Powers, c. 545–362 B.C.* (Leiden).
Keil, J. (1905), 'Ärzteinschriften aus Ephesos', *JÖAI* 8, 123–38.
—— (1912), 'Vorläufiger Bericht über die Arbeiten in Ephesos 1912', *JÖAI* 15, Beibl., 183–211.
—— and Premerstein, A. von (1911), *Bericht über eine zweite Reise in Lydien* (Vienna).
Kenrick, P. (1981), 'Finewares of the Hellenistic and Roman periods', in J. Matthers (ed.), *The River Qoueiq, Northern Syria, and its Catchment* (Oxford), part 2, 439–58.
Kienast, D. (1996), *Römische Kaisertabelle. Grundzüge einer römischen Kaisergeschichte²* (Darmstadt).
Klauck, H.-J. (1996), 'Die kleinasiatischen Beichtinschriften und das Neue Testament', in H. Cancik, H. Lichtenberger and P. Schäfer (eds), *Geschichte – Tradition – Reflexion. Festschrift für Martin Hengel zum 70. Geburtstag* (Tübingen), III, 63–87.
Knibbe, D. (1998), ΕΦΕΣΟΣ. *Geschichte einer bedeutenden antiken Stadt und Porträt einer modernen Großgrabung* (Frankfurt am Main).
Knoll, F. (1932), 'Baubeschreibung', in E. Reisch (ed.), *Die Marienkirche in Ephesos: Forschungen in Ephesos* (Vienna), IV.1, 13–78.
Kobes, J. (1995), 'Mylasa und Kildara in ptolemäischer Hand? Überlegungen zu zwei hellenistischen Inschriften aus Karien', *EA* 24, 1–6.
Kolendo, J. and Bozilova, V. (eds) (1997), *Inscriptions grecques et latines de Novae (Mésie Inférieure); Inscriptions latines* by J. Kolendo and V. Bozilova; *Inscriptions grecques* by A. Bresson and T. Drew-Bear (Bordeaux).
Kontorini, V. (1983), *Inscriptions inédites relatives à l'histoire et aux cultes de Rhodes au IIe et au Ier s. av. J.-C.* (Louvain-la-Neuve and Providence).
—— (1989), *Anékdotes epigrafés Ródou* II (Athens).
Korpela, J. (1987), *Das Medizinalpersonal im antiken Rom. Eine sozialgeschichtliche Untersuchung* (Helsinki).
Kraay, C.M. (1976), *Archaic and Classical Greek Coins* (London).
Krause, J.-U. (1995), *Witwen und Waisen im römischen Reich* III. *Rechtliche und soziale Stellung von Waisen* (Stuttgart).
Krauskopf, I. (1981), 'Amphilochos', *LIMC* I, 713–17.
Kretschmer, P. (1933), 'Die Hypachäer', *Glotta* 21, 213–57.
Krob, E. (1997), 'Serments et institutions civiques à Cos à l'époque hellénistique', *REG* 110, 434–53.
Krzyzanowska, A. (1970), *Monnaies coloniales d'Antioche de Pisidie* (Warsaw).
Kudlien, F. (1986), *Die Stellung des Arztes in der römischen Gesellschaft* (Stuttgart).
Labarre, G. (1996), *Les cités de Lesbos aux époques hellénistique et impériale* I (Paris).

Landucci Gattinoni, F. (1992), *Lisimaco di Tracia. Un sovrano nella prospettiva del primo ellenismo* (Milan).
Lanfranchi, G.B. (2000), 'The ideological and political impact of the Assyrian imperial expansion on the Greek world in the 8th and 7th centuries BC', in S. Aro and R.M. Whiting (eds), *The Heirs of Assyria* (Melammu Symposia 1, Helsinki), 7–34.
La Rocca, E. *et al.* (1993), 'Sinus Iasicus I. Il territorio di Iaso: ricognizioni archeologice 1988–1989', *ASNP* 23, 847–998.
Laroche, E. (1951), *Recueil d'onomastique hittite* (Paris).
  (1958), 'Etudes sur les hiéroglyphes hittites', *Syria* 35, 252–83.
  (1979), 'L'inscription lycienne', *Fouilles de Xanthos* 6 (Paris), 49–127.
  (1980), 'Les dieux de la Lycie classique d'après les textes lyciens', in H. Metzger (ed.), *Actes du colloque sur la Lycie antique* (Paris), 1–6.
Larsen, C.P. (1945), 'Representative democracy in Hellenistic federations', *CPh* 40, 65–97.
Lassère, J.-M. (1988), 'Onomastique et acculturation dans le monde romain', in S. Gély (ed.), *Sens et pouvoirs de la nomination dans les cultures hellénique et romaine* (Montpellier), 87–102.
Latte, K. (1915), 'Zur Bestimmung des Antiatticista', *Hermes* 50, 373–94.
  (1920), *Heiliges Recht. Untersuchungen zur Geschichte der sakralen Rechtsformen in Griechenland* (Tübingen).
  (1931), 'Meineid', *RE* XV.1, 346–57 (= *Kleine Schriften zu Religion, Recht, Literatur und Sprache der Griechen und Römer* (Munich 1968), 367–79).
Laumonier, A. (1934), 'Inscriptions de Carie', *BCH* 58, 291–380.
  (1936), 'Archéologie carienne', *BCH* 60, 286–335.
  (1937), 'Recherches sur la chronologie des prêtres de Panamara', *BCH* 62, 236–98.
  (1938*a*), 'Recherches sur la chronologie des prêtres de Lagina', *BCH* 62, 251–84.
  (1938*b*), 'Complément aux recherches sur la chronologie des prêtres de Panamara', *BCH* 62, 167–79.
  (1958), *Les cultes indigènes en Carie* (Bibliothèque des Ecoles françaises d'Athènes et de Rome 88, Paris).
Le Bas, P. and Waddington, W.H. (1870), *Voyage archéologique en Grèce et Asie Mineure* III.5 (Paris).
Lemaire, A. (1983), 'L'inscription phénicienne de Hassan-Beyli reconsidérée', *RStudFen* 11, 9–19.
  (1991), 'L'écriture phénicienne en Cilicie et la diffusion des écritures alphabétiques', in C. Baurain, C. Bonnet and V. Krings (eds), *Phoinikeia grammata. Lire et écrire en Mediterranée* (Namur), 133–46.
  (1994), 'Deux nouvelles stèles funéraires araméens de Cilicie orientale', *EA* 23, 91–8.
  (2001), 'Les langues du Royaume de Sam'al au IXe–VIII^{e}s. av. J.-C. et leurs relations avec le Royaume de Qué', in Jean (ed.) (2001), 185–92.
  and Lozachmeur, H. (1996), 'Remarques sur le plurilinguisme en Asie Mineure à l'époque perse', in F. Briquel-Chatonnet (ed.), *Mosaïque de langues, mosaïque culturelle. Le bilinguisme dans le Proche-Orient ancien* (Antiquités Sémitiques 1, Paris), 91–123.

(1998), 'Les inscriptions araméens', in *Gülnar* (Paris), 1, 308–49.
Lemerle, P. (1935), 'Inscriptions latines et grecques de Philippes', *BCH* 59, 126–64.
Levick, B. (1958*a*), 'Two Pisidian colonial families', *JRS* 48, 74–8.
— (1958*b*), 'An honorific inscription from Pisidian Antioch', *AS* 8, 219–22.
— (1967*a*), 'Unpublished inscriptions from Pisidian Antioch', *AS* 17, 101–21.
— (1967*b*), *Roman Colonies in Southern Asia Minor* (Oxford).
— (1968), 'Antiocheia (Pisid.)', *RE* Suppl. XI, cols. 49–61.
— and Jameson, S. (1964), 'C. Crepereius Gallus and his Gens', *JRS* 54, 97–106.
Levy, I. (1938), '*Hypachaioi*', in *Mélanges Emile Boisacq* II (Brussels), 119–27.
Lewis, N. (1981), 'Literati in the service of Roman emperors: politics before culture', in L. Casson and M. Price (eds), *Coins, Culture and History in the Ancient World. Studies in Honor of Bluma Trell* (Detroit), 149–58.
— (1989), *The Documents from the Bar Kokhba Period in the Cave of Letters. Greek Papyri* (Jerusalem).
LiDonnici, L.R. (1995), *The Epidaurian Miracle Inscriptions. Text, Translation, and Commentary* (Atlanta).
Liverani, M. (1988), *Antico Oriente. Storia, società, economia* (Rome and Bari).
Lloyd-Jones, H. (1983), *The Justice of Zeus* (Berkeley).
Löffler, I. (1963), *Die Melampodie. Versuch einer Rekonstruktion des Inhalts* (Meisenheim am Glan).
Long, A.A. (1996), *Stoic Studies* (Cambridge).
Luce, J.-M. (1998), 'Thésée, le synoecisme et l'Agora d'Athènes', *RA* 1, 3–31.
Lund, H.S. (1992), *Lysimachus. A Study in Early Hellenistic Kingship* (London).
Lund, J. (1995*a*), 'A fresh look at the Roman and Late Roman fine wares from the Danish excavations at Hama, Syria', in H. Meyza and J. Mlynarczyk (eds), *Hellenistic and Roman Pottery in the Eastern Mediterranean – Advances in Scientific Studies* (Acts of the II Nieborów Pottery Workshop, Warsaw), 135–61.
— (1995*b*), 'Response to G. Finkielsztejn', in T. Fischer Hansen (ed.) (1995), 297–302.
Ma, J. (1997), 'The Koinon of the Laodikeis in the Rhodian Peraia', *EA* 28, 9–10.
— (1999), *Antiochos III and the Cities of Western Asia Minor* (Oxford).
— (2000), 'The fighting poleis of the Hellenistic world', in H. van Wees (ed.), *War and Violence in Ancient Greece* (London), 337–76.
— (2002), *Antiochos III and the Cities of Western Asia Minor²* (Oxford).
MacDonald, D. (1992), *The Coinage of Aphrodisias* (Royal Numismatic Society Special Publication 23, London).
Mackie, H. (1996), *Talking Trojan. Speech and Community in the* Iliad (Lanham, Md).
Magioncalda, A. (1991), *Il sviluppo della titolatura imperiale da Augusto a Giustiniano attraverso le testimonianze epigrafiche* (Turin).
Maiuri, A. (1925), *Nuova silloge epigrafica de Rodi e Cos* (Florence).
Malay, H. (1988), 'New confession-inscriptions in the Manisa and Bergama Museums', *EA* 12, 147–52.
— (1992), 'Θυμολυτεῖν and θυμολυσία and the cult of Apollon Axyros in Lydia', *EA* 20, 75–6.

(1994), *Greek and Latin Inscriptions in the Manisa Museum* (*TAM* Ergänzungsband 19, Vienna).

(1999), *Researches in Lydia, Mysia and Aiolis* (*TAM* Ergänzungsband 23, Vienna).

and Petzl, G. (1984), 'Ehrenbeschlüsse für den Sohn des Anaximbrotos aus Gordos', *EA* 3, 157–65.

(1985), 'Neue Inschriften aus den Museen Manisa, Izmir und Bergama', *EA* 6, 55–68.

Manganaro, G. (1997), 'Nuove tavolette di piombo inscritte siceliote', *PdP* 52, 306–47.

Marasco, G. (1998*a*), 'I medici di corte nella società imperiale', *Chiron* 28, 267–85.

(1998*b*), 'I medici di corte nell'impero romano: prosopografia e ruolo culturale', *Prometheus* 24, 243–63.

Marek, C. (1982), 'Ein ptolemäischer Strategos in Karien', *Chiron* 12, 119–23.

(2000), 'Der höchste, beste, größte, allmächtige Gott. Inschriften aus Nordkleinasien', *EA* 32, 129–46.

Maschke, R. (1926), *Die Willenslehre im griechischen Recht* (Berlin).

Mason, D.J.P. (1990), 'The use of earthenware tubes in Roman vault construction: an example from Chester', *Britannia* 21, 215–22.

Masson, O. (1980), 'Quelques anthroponymes rares chez Thucydide', in *Mélanges E. Manni* IV.1479–88 (= *Onomastica Graeca Selecta* (Paris) I, 321–30).

(1996), 'Nouvelles notes d'anthroponymie grecque', *ZPE* 112, 143–50 (= *Onomastica Graeca Selecta* (Paris), III, 256–63).

Mastino, A. (1981), *Le titolature di Caracalla e Geta attraverso le iscrizioni* (Bologna).

McNicoll, A.W. (1997), *Hellenistic Fortifications from the Aegean to the Euphrates* (Oxford).

Mee, C. (1978), 'Aegean trade and settlement in Anatolia in the second millennium BC', *AS* 28, 121–56.

(1998), 'Anatolia and the Aegean in the Late Bronze Age', in E.H. Cline and D. Harris-Cline (eds), *The Aegean and the Orient in the Second Millennium* (*Aegaeum* 18, Liège), 137–45.

Meiggs, R. (1972), *The Athenian Empire* (Oxford).

Merkelbach, R. (1995), *Isis regina – Zeus Sarapis. Die griechisch-ägyptische Religion nach den Quellen dargestellt* (Stuttgart and Leipzig).

and Stauber, J. (1998), *Steinepigramme aus dem griechischen Osten* I: *Die Westküste Kleinasiens von Knidos bis Ilion* (Leipzig).

Migeotte, L. (1992), *Les souscriptions publiques dans les cités grecques* (Geneva and Paris).

(2001), 'Le traité entre Milet et Pidasa (Delphinion 149). Les clauses financières', in A. Bresson and R. Descat (eds) (2001), 129–35.

Mikalson, J.D. (1983), *Athenian Popular Religion* (Chapel Hill).

(1991), *Honor thy Gods. Popular Religion in Greek Tragedy* (Chapel Hill).

Millar, F. (1977), *The Emperor in the Roman World* (London).

(1983), 'The Phoenician cities: a case-study of Hellenisation', *PCPS* 29, 55–71.

(1993), *The Roman Near East* (Cambridge, Mass.).

Miller, M. (1997), *Athens and Persia in the Fifth Century* BC. *A Study in Cultural Receptivity* (Cambridge).
Miltner, F. (1958), *Ephesos, Stadt der Artemis und des Johannes* (Vienna).
Mitchell S. (1993a), *Anatolia. Land, Men and Gods in Asia Minor* I: *The Celts in Anatolia and the Impact of Roman Rule* (Oxford).
— (1993b), *Anatolia. Land, Men and Gods in Asia Minor* II: *The Rise of the Church* (Oxford).
— (2000), 'Ethnicity, acculturation and empire in the Roman and Late Roman Asia Minor', in S. Mitchell and G. Greatrex (eds), *Ethnicity and Culture in Late Antiquity* (London and Swansea), 117–50.
— and Waelkens, M. (1998), *Pisidian Antioch. The Site and its Monuments* (London).
Mommsen, T. (1884), *Ephemeris epigraphica* 5.
Mosca, P.G. and Russell, J. (1987), 'A Phoenician inscription from Cebel Ires Daği in Rough Cilicia', *EA* 9, 1–27.
Murray, O. (1988–9), 'Omero e l'etnografia', *Kokalos* 34–5, 1–13.
Mutafian, C. (1988), *La Cilicie au carrefour des empires* I–II (Paris).
Muttelsee, M. (1925), *Zur Verfassungsgeschichte Kretas im Zeitalter des Hellenismus* (Hamburg).
Neumann, G. (1978), 'Spätluwische Namen', *Zeitschrift für vergleichende Sprachforschung* 92, 26–131.
— (1979), 'Namen und Epiklesen lykischer Götter', in *Florilegium Anatolicum: Mélanges offerts à E. Laroche* (Paris), 259–71.
— (1980), 'Kleinasien', in G. Neumann and J. Untermann (eds), *Die Sprachen im Römischen Reich der Kaiserzeit* (Bonner Jahrbücher Beih. 40), 167–85.
— (1985), 'Beitrage zum Lykischen vii', *Sprache* 31, 243–8.
— (1996), 'Griechische Personennamen in lykischen Texten', in *Fremde Zeiten: Festschrift J. Borchhardt* (Vienna), I, 145–51.
Nielsen, I. (1993), *Thermae et Balnea. The Architecture and Cultural History of Roman Public Baths*[2] (Aarhus).
Nielsen, T.H. (1999), 'The concept of Arkadia – the people, their land, and their organisation', in T.H. Nielsen and J. Roy (eds), *Defining Ancient Arkadia* (Copenhagen), 16–79.
Nollé, J. (1993), *Side im Altertum* (*IGSK* XLIII, Bonn).
Nörr, D. (1986), *Causa mortis. Auf den Spuren einer Redewendung* (Munich).
North, J.L. (1996), 'Paul's protest that he does not lie in the light of his Cilician origin', *JThS* 47, 439–63.
Nutton, V. (1969), 'The doctor and the oracle', *RBPh* 47, 37–48.
— (1971a), 'Two notes on immunities: *Digest* 27, 1, 6, 10 and 11', *JRS* 61, 52–63.
— (1971b), 'L. Gellius Maximus, physician and procurator', *CQ* 21, 262–72.
— (1977), 'Archiatri and the medical profession in antiquity', *PBSR* 45, 191–226.
Oppermann, H. (1924), *Zeus Panamaros* (Giessen).
O'Sullivan, L. (1997), 'Asander, Athens and IG II^2 450: a new interpretation', *ZPE* 119, 107–16.
Özbayoğlu, E. (1999), 'Soli (Cilicia) ve "Soloecismus"', *Olba* 2, 209–19.

Özgan, R. (1999), *Die Skulpturen von Stratonikeia* (*Asia Minor Studien* 32, Bonn).
Papachristodoulou, I.C. (1989), Οἱ ἀρχαῖοι ῥοδιακοὶ δῆμοι. Ἱστωρικὴ ἐπισκώπηση – Ἡ Ἰαλυσία (Athens).
Parker, B.J. (2000), 'The earliest known reference to the Ionians in the Cuneiform sources', *AHB* 14.3, 69–77.
Parker, R. (1983), *Miasma. Pollution and Purification in Early Greek Religion* (Oxford).
Paton, W.R. and Hicks, E.L. (1891), *The Inscriptions of Cos* (Oxford).
 and Myres, J.L. (1896), 'Karian sites and inscriptions', *JHS* 16, 188–271.
Pembroke, S. (1964), 'The last of the matriarchs: a study in the inscriptions of Lycia', *JESHO* 8, 217–47.
Perkins, A.L. (1973), *The Art of Dura-Europos* (Oxford).
Perreault, J.Y. (1993), 'Les *emporia* grecs du Levant: mythe ou realité?', in A. Bresson and A. Rouillard (eds), *L'emporion* (Paris), 59–83.
Peschlow-Bindokat, A. (1975), 'Zur Säulenstrasse von Pompeiopolis in Kilikien', *Ist. Mitt.* 25, 373–91.
 (1977–8), 'Ioniapolis. Zur Topographie einer milesischen Hafenstadt am latmischen Golf', *Ist. Mitt.* 27–8, 131–6.
 (1996), *Der Latmos. Eine unbekannte Gebirgslandschaft an der türkischen Westküste* (Mainz am Rhein).
Petrakos, B.C. (1997), Οἱ ἐπιγραφὲς τοῦ Ὠρωποῦ (Athens).
Pettazzoni, R. (1936), *La confessione dei pecati* III: *Siria, Hittiti, Asia Minore, Grecia* (Bologna).
 (1954), 'Confession of sins and the Classics', in *Essays on the History of Religion* (Leiden), 55–67.
Petzl, G. (1988), 'Sünde, Strafe, Wiedergutmachung', *EA* 12, 155–66.
 (1991), 'Lukians Podagra und die Beichtinschriften Kleinasiens', *Métis* 6, 131–45.
 (1992), 'Ein frühes Zeugnis für den Hosios-Dikaios-Kult', *EA* 20, 143–6.
 (1994), *Die Beichtinschriften Westkleinasiens* (*EA* 22, Bonn).
 (1995), 'Ländliche Religiosität in Lydien', in E. Schwertheim (ed.), *Forschungen in Lydien* (*Asia Minor Studien* 17, Bonn), 37–48.
 (1997), 'Neue Inschriften aus Lydien (II). Addenda und Corrigenda zu "Die Beichtinschriften Westkleinasiens"', *EA* 28, 69–79.
 (1998*a*), 'Ein Zeugnis für Sternenglauben in Lydien', *Chiron* 28, 65–75.
 (1998*b*), *Die Beichtinschriften im römischen Kleinasien und der Fromme und Gerechte Gott* (Opladen).
 and Malay, H. (1987), 'A new confession inscription from the Katakekaumene', *GRBS* 28, 459–72.
Pfister, R. and Bellinger, L. (1945), *The Excavations at Dura-Europos, Final Report* IV.2: *The Textiles* (New Haven, Conn.).
Pflaum, H.-G. (1950), *Les procurateurs équestres sous le Haut-Empire romain* (Paris).
 (1960), *Les carrières procuratoriennes équestres sous le Haut-Empire romain* (Paris).
Plassart, A. (1915), 'Orchomène d'Arcadie. Fouilles de 1913. Inscriptions (2e article)', *BCH* 39, 53–124.

Plescia, J. (1970), *The Oath and Perjury in Ancient Greece* (Tallahassee).
Poland, F. (1909), *Das griechische Vereinswesen* (Leipzig).
Pollard, N. (2000), *Soldiers, Cities and Civilians in Roman Syria* (Ann Arbor).
Pontani, F. (1997), 'I. Amyzon 27 C–D: Teil eines milesischen Isopolitievertrags', *EA* 28, 5–8.
Popham, M. (1994), 'Precolonization: early Greek contact with the East', in Tsetskhladze and De Angelis (eds) (1994), 11–34.
Potter, D.S. (1991), 'The inscriptions of the bronze Herakles from Messene', *ZPE* 88, 277–90.
Pouilloux, J. (1989), 'Akératos de Thasos: poésie et histoire', in R. Etienne, M.-T. Le Dinahet and M. Yon (eds), *Architecture et poésie dans le monde grec: hommage à Georges Roux* (Lyon), 193–204.
Pugliese-Carratelli, G. 1939–40. 'Per la storia delle associazioni in Rodi antica', *Annuario* n.s. 1–2, 147–200.
  (1949), 'Alessandro e la constituzione rodia', *PdP* 4, 154–71.
  (1963–4), 'Il damos coo di Isthmos', *Annuario* n.s. 25–6, 147–200.
Quaegebeur, J. (1993), 'La justice à la porte des temples et le toponyme Premit', in C. Cannuyer and J.-M. Kruchten (eds), *Individu, société et spiritualité dans l'Égypte pharaonique et copte. Mélanges égyptologiques offerts au Professeur Aristide Théodoridès* (Athens, Brussels and Mons), 201–20.
Ramsay, W.M. (1895), *The Cities and Bishoprics of Phrygia* (Oxford).
  (1916), 'Colonia Caesarea (Pisidian Antioch) in the Augustan age', *JRS* 6, 83–134.
  (1919), 'A noble Anatolian family of the fourth century', *CR* 33, 1–9.
  (1924), 'Studies in the Roman province Galatia, VI. Some inscriptions of Colonia Caearea Antiochea', *JRS* 14, 172–205.
  (1933), Review of *SEG* 6 (1932), *JHS* 53, 313–18.
Reger, G. (1998), 'The koinon of the Laodikeis in Karia', *EA* 30, 11–17.
  (1999), 'The relations between Rhodes and Caria from 246 to 167 BC', in Gabrielsen (ed.) (1999), 76–98.
  (2001), 'The Mykonian synoikismos', *REA* 103, 157–81.
  (forthcoming), 'Aspects of the economic role of merchants in the Hellenistic world', in A. Giardina and C. Zaccagnini (eds), *Mercanti e politica nel mondo antico* (Rome).
Reisch, E. (1932), 'Zur Geschichte der Bauten auf dem Ruinenfeld der Marienkirche', in E. Reisch (ed.), *Die Marienkirche in Ephesos: Forschungen in Ephesos* (Vienna), IV.1, 1–12.
Reynolds, J. (1982), *Aphrodisias and Rome* (London).
  (1985), 'The politeia of Plarasa and Aphrodisias', *REA* 87, 213–18.
  (1998), 'An ordinary Aphrodisian family: the message of a stone', in G. Schmeling (ed.), *Qui miscuit utile dulci. Festschrift Essays for Paul Lachlan MacKendrick* (Wauconda), 287–97.
Ricl, M. (1991a), 'Hosios kai Dikaios. Première partie: Catalogue des inscriptions', *EA* 18, 1–70.
  (1991b), 'Meonsi πιττάκιον u Zenevi?', in P.H. Ilievski and V. Mitevski (eds), *Greek–Roman Antiquity in Yugoslavia and in the Balkans. Proceedings of the 5th*

Yugoslav Congress on Classical Studies held in Skopje on 26–29 Sept. 1989 (*Ziva Antika* Monographs 9, Skopje), 201–6.
(1992*a*), 'Hosios kai Dikaios. Seconde partie: analyse', *EA* 19, 71–102.
(1992*b*), 'Hosios kai Dikaios. Nouvaux monuments', *EA* 20, 95–100.
(1994), 'Inscriptions votives inédites au Musée d'Eskişehir', *Ziva Antika* 44, 157–74.
(1995), 'The appeal to divine justice in the Lydian confession-inscriptions', in E. Schwertheim (ed.), *Forschungen in Lydien* (*Asia Minor Studien* 17, Bonn), 67–76.
(1997), 'CIG 4142 – A forgotten confession inscription from north-west Phrygia', *EA* 29, 35–43.

Riele, G.-J.M.G. Te (1987), 'Hélisson entre en sympolitie avec Mantinée. Une nouvelle inscription d'Arcadie', *BCH* 111, 167–90.

Rigsby, K.J. (1996), *Asylia. Territorial Inviolability in the Hellenistic World* (Berkeley).

Ritterling, E. (1924), 'Legio (III Aug.)', *RE* xii, cols 1494–1505.

Robert, L. (1934), 'Hellenistica', *REA* 36, 521–6.
(1935), 'Rapport sommaire sur un second voyage en Carie', *RA*, 152–63.
(1936), *Collection Froehner* i: *Inscriptions grecques* (Paris).
(1937), *Etudes anatoliennes* (Paris).
(1938), *Etudes épigraphiques et philologiques* (Paris): ch. 3, 'Noms grecs et anatoliens' (pp. 151–217).
(1945), *Le sanctuaire de Sinuri près de Mylasa, première partie: les inscriptions grecques* (Paris).
(1949), 'Divinités d'Anatolie', *Hellenica. Recueil d'épigraphie, de numismatique et d'antiquités grecques* vii (Paris), 50–8.
(1951), *Etudes de numismatique grecque* (Paris).
(1960), 'Inscription agonistique d'Ancyre. Concours d'Ancyre', *Hellenica. Recueil d'épigraphie, de numismatique et d'antiquités grecques* xi–xii (Paris), 350–68.
(1962), *Villes d'Asie Mineure*² (Paris).
(1963), *Noms indigènes dans l'Asie Mineure gréco-romaine* (Paris).
(1964), *Nouvelles inscriptions de Sardes* (Paris).
(1967), 'Sur des inscriptions de Ephèse', *RPh* 41, 7–84.
(1977), 'Documents d'Asie Mineure', *BCH* 101, 43–132.
(1978*a*), 'Les conquêtes du dynaste lycien Arbinas', *Journal des Savants* 165, 3–48.
(1978*b*), 'Catalogue agonistique des Romaia de Xanthos', *RA*, 277–90.
(1978*c*), 'Documents d'Asie Mineure. v–xvii', *BCH* 102, 395–543.
(1983), 'Documents d'Asie Mineure. xxiii–xxviii', *BCH* 107, 497–599.
(1987), *Documents d'Asie Mineure* (Paris).
(1989), *Opera Minora Selecta* vi (Amsterdam).
and Robert, J. (1954), *La Carie* ii (Paris).
(1955), 'Deux inscriptions de Carie', in *Mélanges I. Lévy* (*Annuaire de l'Institut de philologie et d'histoire orientales et slaves* 13, Brussels), 553–72.
(1976), 'Une inscription grecque de Téos en Ionie. L'union de Téos et de Kyrbissos', *Journal des Savants*, 153–235.

(1983), *Fouilles d'Amyzon en Carie* I: *Exploration, histoire, monnaies et inscriptions* (Paris).
(1989), *Claros* I.1: *Décrets hellénistiques* (Paris).
Robinson, D.M. (1925), 'Notes on inscriptions from Antioch in Pisidia', *JRS* 15, 252–62.
(1926), 'Greek and Latin inscriptions from Asia Minor', *TAPA* 57, 195–237.
Robinson, H.S. (1959), *The Athenian Agora* v: *Pottery of the Roman Period: Chronology* (Princeton).
Rochette, B. (1997), *Le latin dans le monde grec* (Collection Latomus 233, Brussels).
Roos, P. (1975), 'Alte und neue Inschriftenfunde aus Zentralkarien', *MDAI* (I) 25, 335–4.
Ross, L. (1846), 'Inschriften von Lindos auf Rhodos', *RhM* 4, 161–99.
Rostad, A. (2002), 'Confession or reconciliation – the narrative structure of the Lydian and Phrygian "confession inscriptions"', *Symbolae Osloenses* 77, 145–64.
Rostovtzeff, M. (1957), *The Social and Economic History of the Roman Empire*^{2}, ed. P.M. Fraser (Oxford).
Rougé, J. (1969), ' Ὁ θειότατος Αὔγουστος', *RPh* 43, 83–92.
Roussel, P. (1927), 'Les Mystères de Panamara', *BCH* 51, 123–37.
(1931), 'Le miracle de Zeus Panamaros', *BCH* 55, 70–116.
Rousset, D. (1999), 'Centre urbain, frontière et espace rural dans les cités de Grèce centrale', in M. Brunet (ed.), *Territoires des cités grecques. Actes de la table ronde internationale organisée par l'École française d'Athènes* (Athens and Paris), 35–77.
Ruge, W. (1927), 'Soloi 1', *RE* IIIA, cols 935–8.
Rupprecht, H.-A. (1967), *Untersuchungen zu Darlehen im Recht der graecoägyptischen Papyri der Ptolemäerzeit* (Munich).
(1971), *Studien zur Quittung im Recht der graeco-ägyptischen Papyri* (Munich).
Russu, I. (1938), 'Macedonica', *Ephem. Dacoromana* 8, 105–232.
Şahin, M.Ç. (1973), 'Two new inscriptions from Lagina (Koranza)', *Anadolu* 17, 187–95.
(1976), *The Political and Religious Structure in the Territory of Stratonikeia in Caria* (Ankara).
(1995), 'Two new Hellenistic decrees from Panamara', *EA* 25, 83–8.
(1997), 'New inscriptions from Lagina', *EA* 29, 83–105.
(1999), 'The place name of Korazis: a new inscription from Lagina', *EA* 31, 35–6.
and Engelmann, H. (1979), 'Inschriften aus dem Museum von Bodrum', *ZPE* 34, 211–20.
Saladino, V. (1990), 'Kalchas', *LIMC* v, 921–35.
Salmeri, G. (1994), 'I Greci e le lingue indigene d'Asia Minore: il caso del cario', in M. Salvini *et al.* (eds), *La decifrazione del cario* (Rome), 87–99.
(2000*a*), 'Dio, Rome, and the civic life of Asia Minor', in S. Swain (ed.), *Dio Chrysostom. Politics, Letters, and Philosophy* (Oxford), 53–92.
(2000*b*), 'Regioni, popoli e lingue epicorie d'Asia Minore nella *Geografia* di Strabone', in A.M. Biraschi and G. Salmeri (eds), *Strabone e l'Asia Minore* (Naples), 159–88.

and d'Agata, A.L. (2003), 'Cilicia survey 2001', *20. Araştırma Sonuçları Toplantısı* 1, 207–11.

d'Agata, A.L., Falesi, L. and Buxton, B. (2002), 'Cilicia survey 2000', *19. Araştırma Sonuçları Toplantısı* 2, 39–44.

Salviat, F. and Vatin, C. (1971), *Inscriptions de Grèce centrale* (Paris).

Sartre, M. (1995), *L'Asie Mineure et l'Anatolie d'Alexandre à Dioclétien* (Paris).

Scafuro, A.C. (1997), *The Forensic Stage. Settling Disputes in Greco-Roman New Comedy* (Cambridge).

Scarborough, J. (1969), *Roman Medicine* (Ithaca, NY).

Scheer, T.S. (1993), *Mythische Vorväter* (Munich).

Schmitt, H. (1994), 'Überlegungen zur Sympolitie', in G. Thür (ed.), *Symposium 1993. Vorträge zur griechischen und hellenistischen Rechtsgeschichte* (Vienna), 35–44.

Schober, A. (1933), *Der Fries des Hekateions von Lagina* (*Istanbuler Forschungen* 2).

Scholten, J. (2000), *The Politics of Plunder* (Berkeley).

Schuler, C. (1998), *Ländliche Siedlungen und Gemeinden im hellenistischen und römischen Kleinasien* (Munich).

Schürer, E. (1973–87), *The History of the Jewish People in the Age of Jesus Christ* I–III (Edinburgh).

Schürr, D. (1998), 'Kaunos in lykischen Inschriften', *Kadmos* 37, 143–62.

Schweyer, A.-V. (1996), 'Le pays lycien: une étude de géographie historique aux époques classique et hellénistique', *RA*, 3–68.

Segre, M. (1932), 'Due nuovi teste storici', *Riv. Phil.* n.s. 10, 446–61.

— (1933), 'Κρητικὸς πόλεμος', *RFIC* 11, 365–92.

— (1993), *Iscrizioni di Cos*, ed. G. Pugliese Caratelli, 2 vols (Rome).

Seton Williams, M.V. (1954), 'Cilician survey', *AS* 4, 121–74.

Shear, T.L. (1978), *Kallias of Sphettos and the Revolt of Athens in 286 B.C.* (*Hesperia* Suppl. 17, Princeton).

Sherk, R.K. (1990), 'The eponymous officials of Greek cities. Mainland Greece and the adjacent islands', *ZPE* 84, 231–95.

Sherratt, E.S. (1994), 'Patterns of contact between the Aegean and Cyprus in the 13th and in the 12th centuries BC', *Kypr. Arch.* 3, 35–43.

— (1998), '"Sea People" and the economic structure of the late second millennium in the eastern Mediterranean', in S. Gitin, A. Mazar and E. Stern (eds), *Mediterranean Peoples in Transition. Thirteenth to Early Tenth Centuries BCE* (Jerusalem).

— and Crouwel, J.H. (1987), 'Mycenaean pottery from Cilicia in Oxford', *OJA* 6, 325–52.

Sherwin-White, S. (1978), *Ancient Cos. An Historical Study from the Dorian Settlement to the Imperial Period* (Göttingen).

— (1983), *Roman Foreign Policy in the East* (Norman, Okla.).

Sima, A. (1999), 'Kleinasiatische Parallelen zu den altsüdarabischen Buß- und Sühneinschriften', *Altorientalische Forschungen* 26, 140–53.

Simon, E. (1992), 'Mopsos 2', *LIMC* VI, 652–4.

Sittig, E. (1912), *De Graecorum nominibus theophoris* (Halle).

Slane, K.W. (1997), 'The finewares', in S.C. Herbert (ed.), *Tel Anafa* II.1: *The Hellenistic and Roman Pottery* (Ann Arbor), 247–405.
Smith, M.J.F. (1998), 'Excavations at Oinoanda 1997: the new Epicurean texts', *AS* 48, 125–70.
Snodgrass, A.M. (1994), 'The nature and standing of the early western colonies', in Tsetskhladze and De Angelis (eds) (1994), 1–10.
Sotgiu, G. (1961), *Studi sull'epigrafia di Aureliano* (Sassari).
Sourvinou-Inwood, C. (1995), *'Reading' Greek Death to the End of the Classical Period* (Oxford).
Spanu, M. (1997), *Keramos di Karia. Storia e monumenti* (Rome).
— (2001), 'Teatri e edifici da spettacolo in Cilicia', in Jean (ed.) (2001), 445–77.
Spawforth, A.J.S. (1999), 'The Panhellenion again', *Chiron* 29, 339–52.
Stein, A. (1915), *Untersuchungen zur Geschichte und Verwaltung Ägyptens unter römischer Herrschaft* (Stuttgart).
— (1918), 'Gellius 16a', *RE* Suppl. III, col. 542.
— (1927), *Der römische Ritterstand* (Munich).
Steinleitner, F.S. (1913), *Die Beicht im Zusammenhange mit der sakralen Rechtspflege in der Antike* (Munich).
Sterrett, J.R.S. (1888), *An Epigraphical Journey in Asia Minor* (Papers of the American School of Classical Studies Athens 2, Boston).
Stroud, R.S. (1984), 'An Argive decree from Nemea concerning Aspendos', *Hesperia* 53, 191–216.
— (1998), *The Athenian Grain-tax Law of 374/3 B.C.* (Princeton).
Strubbe, J.H.M. (1991), 'Cursed be he that moves my bones', in C.A. Faraone and D. Obbink (eds), *Magika Hiera: Ancient Greek Magic and Religion* (Oxford), 33–59.
— (1997), *Arai epitymbioi: Imprecations against Desecrators of the Grave in the Greek Epitaphs of Asia Minor. A Catalogue* (Bonn).
Stylianou, P.J. (1998), *A Historical Commentary on Diodorus Siculus* (Oxford).
Swain, S. (1996), *Hellenism and Empire* (Oxford).
Syme, R. (1939), 'Observations on the Roman province of Cilicia', in W.M. Calder and J. Keil (eds), *Anatolian Studies presented to W.H. Buckler* (Manchester), 299–332 (repr. in *Roman Papers* I (Oxford 1979), 120–48).
— (1995), *Anatolica. Studies in Strabo* (Oxford).
Talbert, R. (ed.) (2000), *The Barrington Atlas of the Greek and Roman World* (Princeton).
Taşlıalan, M. (1997), *Pisidian Antioch: 'The Journeys of St. Paul to Antioch'* (Ankara).
Tekoğlu, R. and Lemaire, A. (2000), 'La bilingue royale louvito-phénicienne de Çineköy', *CRAI*, 961–1006.
Thomas, R. (2000), *Herodotus in Context. Ethnography, Science and the Art of Persuasion* (Cambridge).
Threatte, L. (1980), *The Grammar of Attic Inscriptions* I (Berlin and New York).
Thür, G. and Taeuber, H. (1994), *Prozeßrechtliche Inschriften der griechischen Poleis: Arkadien* (Vienna).

Toll, N. (1943), *The Excavations at Dura-Europos, Final Report* IV.1, no. 1: The Green-glazed Pottery (New Haven, Conn.).
Tomlin, R.S.O. (1997), 'Roman Britain in 1996, II. Inscriptions', *Britannia* 28, 455–72.
Treves, P. (1955), *Euforione e la storia ellenistica* (Milan and Naples).
Tropper, J. (1993), *Die Inschriften von Zincirli* (Münster).
Tsetskhladze, G.R. (ed.) (1999), *Ancient Greeks West and East* (Leiden).
 and De Angelis, F. (eds) (1994), *The Archaeology of Greek Colonisation. Essays dedicated to Sir John Boardman* (Oxford).
Urban, R. (1978), *Wachstum und Krise des achäischen Bundes. Quellenstudien zur Entwicklung des Bundes von 280 bis 222 v. Chr.* (Wiesbaden).
Van Bremen, R. (1996), *The Limits of Participation. Women and Civic Life in the Greek East in the Hellenistic and Roman Periods* (Amsterdam).
 (2000), 'The demes and phylai of Stratonikeia in Karia', *Chiron* 30, 389–401.
 (2003), 'Ptolemy at Panamara', *EA* 35, 9–14.
Van Gelder, H. (1900), *Geschichte der alten Rhodier* (The Hague).
Van Groningen, B.A. (1977), *Euphorion* (Amsterdam).
Vanschoonwinkel, J. (1990), 'Mopsos: légendes et realité', *Hethitica* 10, 185–211.
Van Straten, F.T. (1976), 'Daikrates' dream: a votive relief from Kos, and some other kat'onar dedications', *BABesch* 51, 1–38.
Varinlioğlu, E. (1983), 'Zeus Orkamaneites and the expiatory inscriptions', *EA* 1, 75–86.
 (1989), 'Eine Gruppe von Sühneinschriften aus dem Museum von Uşak', *EA* 13, 37–50.
 (1991), 'Vier Inschriften aus Lydien', *EA* 18, 91–4.
 (1994), 'La fortification hellénistique de Stratonicée, archéologie et épigraphie', *REA* 96, 189–91.
 (1995), 'An inscription from Panamara', *EA* 25, 91–3.
 (1997), 'Pisye in Caria', *Preatti of the XI International Congress of Greek and Latin Epigraphy* (Rome), 297–307.
Vérilhac, A.-M. and Vial, C. (1998), *Le mariage grec du VIe siècle av. J.-C. à l'époque d'Auguste* (*BCH* Suppl. 32, Paris).
Versnel, H.S. (1991), 'Beyond cursing: the appeal to justice in judicial prayers', in C.A. Faraone and D. Obbink (eds), *Magika Hiera. Ancient Greek Magic and Religion* (Oxford), 60–106.
 (1994), 'Πεπρημένος. The Cnidian curse tablets and ordeal by fire', in R. Hägg (ed.), *Ancient Greek Cult Practice from the Epigraphical Evidence. Proceedings of the Second International Seminar on Ancient Greek Cult, organized by the Swedish Institute at Athens, 22–24 November 1991* (Stockholm), 145–54.
 (1999), 'Κολάσαι τοὺς ἡμᾶς τοιούτους ἡδέως βλέποντες. "Punish those who rejoice in our misery": on curse texts and Schadenfreude', in D.R. Jordan, H. Montgomery and E. Thomassen (eds), *The World of Ancient Magic. Papers from the First International Samson Eitrem Seminar at the Norwegian Institute at Athens, 4–8 May 1997* (Bergen), 125–62.

(2002), 'Writing mortals and reading gods. Appeal to the gods as a dual strategy in social control', in D. Cohen (ed.), *Law, Society, and Social Control* (Munich), 37–76.

Veyne, P. (1962), 'Les honneurs posthumes de Flavia Domitilla et les dédicaces grecques et latines', *Latomus* 21, 49–98.

Vogüé, C.J.M. (1865), *Syrie centrale: architecture civile et religieuse du Ier au VIIIe siècle* (Paris).

Volkmann, H. (1928), 'Studien zum Nemesiskult', *Archiv für Religionswissenschaft* 26, 296–321.

(1934), 'Neue Beiträge zum Nemesiskult', *Archiv für Religionswissenschaft* 31, 57–76.

Von Gladiss, A. (1973–4), 'Ein Denkmal aus Soloi', *Ist. Mitt.* 23–4, 175–81.

Waagé, F.O. (1948), *Antioch-on-the-Orontes* IV.1: *Ceramics* (Princeton).

Wachsmuth, C. (1863), 'Inschriften von Korkyra', *RhM* 18, 537–83.

Walbank, F. (1979), *A Historical Commentary on Polybius* III (Oxford).

Waldmann, H. (1981), 'Neue Inschriften aus Pisidien', *ZPE* 44, 95–102.

Welles, C.B. (1934), *Royal Correspondence in the Hellenistic Period* (London).

Fink, R.O. and Gilliam, J.F. (1959), *The Excavations at Dura-Europos, Final Report* V: *The Parchments and Papyri* (New Haven, Conn.).

Werner, J. (1992), 'Zur Fremdsprachenproblematik in der griechisch-römischen Antike', in *idem et al.* (eds), *Zum Umgang mit fremden Sprachen in der griechisch-römischen Antike* (Stuttgart), 1–20.

Wheeler, M. (1954), *Rome Beyond the Imperial Frontiers* (London).

Whittaker, C.R. (1994), *Frontiers of the Roman Empire: A Social and Economic Study* (Baltimore).

Wiemer, H.-U. (2001), 'Karien am Vorabend des 2. Makedonischen Krieges. Bemerkungen zu einer neuen Inschrift aus Bargylia', *EA* 33, 1–14.

Wilhelm, A. (1931), 'Epigramma ek Lykias', *PAA* 6, 319–34.

Will, E. (1979–82), *Histoire politque du monde hellénistique*^{2} I–II (Nancy).

Wilson, R.J.A. (1992), 'Terracotta vaulting tubes: on their origin and distribution', *JRA* 5, 97–129.

Woeß, F. von (1923), *Das Asylwesen Ägyptens in der Ptolemäerzeit und die spätere Entwicklung* (Munich).

Wörrle, M. (1978), 'Epigraphische Forschungen zur Geschichte Lykiens ii', *Chiron* 8, 201–46.

(1988*a*), *Stadt und Fest im kaiserzeitlichen Kleinasien. Studien zu einer agonistischen Stiftung aus Oinoanda* (Vestigia 39, Munich).

(1988*b*), 'Inschriften von Herakleia am Latmos I: Antiochos III, Zeuxis und Herakleia', *Chiron* 18, 421–76.

(1991), 'Epigraphische Forschungen zur Geschichte Lykiens IV: drei griechische Inschriften aus Limyra', *Chiron* 21, 203–34.

(1996), 'Ein Weihaltar aus Kilepe/Yeşilköy', in F. Blakolmer *et al.* (eds), *Fremde Zeiten. Festschrift Jürgen Borchhardt* (Vienna), 153–60.

(1999), 'Epigraphische Forschungen zur Geschichte Lykiens VII. Asarönü, ein Peripolion von Limyra', *Chiron* 29, 353–70.

Zawadzki, T. (1952–3), 'Quelques remarques sur l'étendue et l'accroissement des domaines des grands temples en Asie Mineure', *Eos* 46, 83–96.

Zgusta, L. (1964), *Kleinasiatische Personennamen* (Prague).

Ziegler, R. (1985), *Städtisches Prestige und kaiserliche Politik. Studien zum Festwesen in Ostkilikien in 2. und 3. Jahrhundert n. Chr.* (Düsseldorf).

Zimmermann, M. (1992), *Untersuchungen zur historischen Landeskunde Zentrallykiens* (Bonn).

Zingerle, J. (1905), 'Fluchinschrift aus Maionien', *JÖAI* 8, 143–4.

—— (1926), 'Heiliges Recht', *JÖAI* 23, Beiblatt: 5–72.

Zoroğlu, L. (1994), *Kelenderis* 1 (Ankara).

—— (2000), 'Kelenderis nekropolu', *Olba* 3, 115–33.

Index

Abydenus 187
Achaean League 146, 148
Achaeans
   in foundation of Soloi 184
Achaios 149
adlectio 111
Aelius Ponticus 102, 103, 116
Aetolian League 146, 148
Agatharchides (*FGrHi*st 86 F16)
Aigai (Cilicia) 206
Akalissos (Lycia) 171
akathartia see purity
Akmonia 4
Al Mina 186
Aleppo/Beroea 124
Alexander the Great 156
   southern Asia Minor, campaign 198
Alexander Polyhistor 187
Alexandreia (Troas) 150
alphabet
   Greek 45; place of adaptation 190–1
   Lycian 45
   Phrygian 191
Amos (Rhodian Peraia) 177
Amphilochos 183–4, 195
Anatolian languages
   disappearance 203–4; *see individual languages*
Anchialos (Cilicia)
   foundation by 'Sardanapalus' 198
Antigonos Monophthalmos 150, 162, 171, 178
Antioch (Pisidia) 85–117
   transferred from Galatia to Lycia-Pamphylia 99
Antioch (Syria) 90
   pottery production 122
Antiochos I 221
Antiochos II 153
Antiochos III 147, 149, 232–4
Apamea 139

Aphrodisias (Caria)
   sympoliteia with Plarasa 162–3, 172, 179
Aphrodite
   Stratonikis 153
Apollo 167, 173, 226
   Lairbenos 4, Lyrboton 36, Tarsios 5, Tiamos 22
   Lycian 58–9
Apollodoros Metrophanes (Miletos) 166
Apollonia (Crete) 148
Apollonis (Lydia) 149
Apollonos Hieron (Lydia) 4
Arados (Phoenicia) 205
Aramaic
   used (written) in Cilicia 190, 192, 195–6
Aratus 200, 206
arbitration 32
archiatros 100, 101, 103, 107
architecture
   Greek influence at Dura 121
   Parthian 132
Argos
   mythological (kinship) ties with Cilicia 198–9; Aigai 206; Soloi 195; Tarsos 184, 206
Aristotle, on solecism 181
Arrian (*Anab.* 1.26–2.5) 197, 202
Arsinoe (Cilicia) 199
Artemis 21, 60–61 (?), 166, 226
   Pergaia 41
Arykanda (Lycia)
   sympoliteia with Tragalassa
Asandros 151–2, 161, 178
Asklepiades 208, 218
Asklepios 105, 108
   patron god of doctors 106
Asklepieion (Pergamum) 106
Assyrian, cuneiform 188, 190
Assyrians
   domination in Cilicia 187–90
asylia 31

Atalanta 63
Athanodoros (priest of Athena Lindia) 176
Athena, Alea 2; Lindia 176
Athens 10
   Athenian (Delian) League 45, 70, 162, 193
Aurelian 85
Aurelius (imperial physician) 114
Aurel(l)ius, orthography 89
Aurelius Gellius Lucius, Iulius 96, 99, 116–17
Axiotta 9

Babrius (*Fab.* 2) 2, 15, 26–32, 36, 41
Banasa (Mauretania) 88–9
barbarians, barbarism
   ancient concept of 44, 197, 198
Bargylia (Caria) 146
baths and bathing technology
   evidence at Dura 119, 132–43, 144
Bellerophon 44, 63
Berosus 187
bilingualism
   Greek and Latin 106
   Greek and Lycian 69
Brecht, Bertolt 1
Britain 9, 142

Callinus 183
Cappadocian languages 203
Caracalla 87–117
   bad health 100, 103
Caria
   influence on Lycia 52
   role of sanctuaries in administration of justice 31–3
   Carian names 49, 63, 67, 69, 223; in Lycia 51, 52, 57, 59
   sympoliteiai 146; *see also sympoliteia*
Carian language
   displaced by Greek 203–4
Chalketor (Caria) 153–5, 178
Chinese silk, at Dura 144
Christians 8, 12, 40
Chrysa (Troas) 150
Chrysaoric League 175, 221
Chrysippus 181, 200, 201, 206
Cicero (*Verr.* 4. 10) 44
Cilicia
   history, Bronze age 182–6; Archaic 186–91; Classical 191–8; Hellenistic 198–203; Roman 203–6
   name derived from Assyrian *Hilakku* 188
   onomastics 67, 188
Claudius (emperor) 45
Claudius Balbillus, Ti. 114, 115
codex Iustinianus (4.1.2) 42; (2.3.9) 41; (8.46.4) 42

coins
   Cilicia 192–3, 194, 196–7, 206
   Parthian coins at Dura 128–30
   Roman coins at Dura 119, 132–43, 144
   countermarks 126, 131
Commodus 88
Corbulo 127
Crete 191
   sympoliteiai 148, 162
curses 8–9, 13–14, 34, 37
   annulment of 34–5, 39
   defixiones (curse tablets) 7, 21; *see also pittakion*
   funerary (epigraphic) 10, 29, 36, 40
   of the guilty by priests 6, 43
Curtius (4.12.11) 202
Cyprus
   connections with Cilicia 185, 188, 189, 191, 194, 198

Daidalos 63
Darius 192
dating formula (epigraphic) 38
Demeter 6–7
Demetrios Poliorketes 177
Diagoras of Melos 1
Dikaiosyne (deity) 10, 11
Dikes Ophthalmos (deity) 10
Dio of Prusa 205
   (*Or.* 34.21–3) 204
Diocletian 114
Diogenes of Babylon 181, 201
Diogenes Laertius (1.51) 8, 201–2
Diogenes of Oinoanda 1
Dioskouroi 64
Dodona 3
Dorylaion 9
ducenarius 114–16
Dura-Europos
   foundation and history 119–21
   evidence of pottery 121–5; of coinage 125–32; of bath technology 132–43

Eëtion 182, 184
Egypt 1, 3, 27, 32, 33, 114
ekklesia kyria 166, 229
Elagabalus 95
Ephesos
   relocation by Lysimachos 150, 155
Ephorus 197
epitaphs 9, 10, 42, 43
   evidence of Hellenization 51
Eudamos 209
Euphorion, *Alexander* 200–1, 202
Euphrates 124

Index

Euromos (Caria) 158
  renamed Philippi 154
  sympoliteia with Mylasa 154–5, 168–9, 173–4
  sympoliteia with Pidasa (?) 158
Eusebius, *Chronicle* (Armenian) 187
Evagoras of Salamis 194

Galatian language 203
Galen 202
Gellius Maximus, Lucius
  physician to Caracalla 91
  honoured by his native city Antioch 95–6; by a grateful citizen of Sagalassos 96–101; as *amicus* of Caracalla 101–3; as priest of Asklepios 103–8; by the city of Sagalassos 109–10
  his son (senator by *adlectio*) 91, 111
Geta 90
Glaukos (mythological hero) 63
gods
  origin of 1
  punishment by 3, 4, 10
  see also sanctuaries
Greek language
  alphabet, place of adaptation 190–1
  corrupted by contact with foreigners 201–3
  cultural prestige 45
  replaces Latin in Asia Minor 111
  spreads in Asia Minor, in Lycia 46, 51–4; in Cilicia 182, 184, 203–4; in Caria 223

Hadrian 206
Halasarna (Kos) 173
Halikarnassos 148
Hama/Epiphania 123, 124
Hampshire 8
Harpagos (Persian general) 45
Hatra 121
Helios 10, 16, 209
  Pantepoptes 10
Hellenization
  Cilicia 184, 197, 198–203, 204–6
  different models 46–7, 222–3
  reflected in Lycian names 51–4, 62
  Roman colonies in the East 107, 111
Hekate 224, 228, 240
Hekatomnids 45
Hera 226
  Zeus, joint cult (Panamara) 225–6
Herakleia under Latmos
  hostile to Mylasa-Euromos 168–9
  relations with Miletos 157–60
  renamed Pleistarcheia 151

Herakles 173
Hermes 61–2
Herodotus (2.17, 2.34; 3.91; 5.52, 5.108, 7.91) 182–3, 195
  languages, interest in (4.117, 4.108) 201
[Hesiod] *Melampodia* 183, 195
Hierakome (Stratonikeia) 214
Hierapytna
  isopoliteia with Itanos 149
Hippolytos 63
Hittite-Luwian language 44, 45, 56
Holmoi (Cilicia) 199
homopoliteia 153
Hosios kai Dikaios 10, 11, 16
Hurrians 188
Hymesseans 158
Hypnia (Lokris) 162, 172
hypocaust 132, 134–5, 142

Ialysos 177
Iason, *strategos* in Caria
Iasos (Caria) 159, 173
Idebessos (Lycia) 171
Iliad 44, 45
  (6.397, 415) 182
imprecations, *see* curses
Indian silk, at Dura 144
Indo-European
  name structure 47, 67
inscriptions
  bilingual, Greek/Lycian 10, 46, 66;
    Luwian/Phoenician 184, 189
  confession or propitiatory 3–6, 7, 11, 16–20, 21, 22, 24–30, 33, 34–8, 39, 43
  see also epitaphs, curses
Ioniapolis 156, 157–9
Isocrates (*Euag.* 27–8, 62) 194; (*Paneg.* 161) 197
isopoliteia 148–9, 158
Itanos
  isopoliteia with Hierapytna 149
Iulia Gordos (Lydia) 43
Iulia Paulla 108
Iuliopolis 89–91
Iulius Vestinus, Lucius 114, 115
Iunius Silanos, M. 173

Jews 4, 204
  synagogues 36

Kabalia 50
Kalchas 183
Kallipolis (Caria) 30, 31, 208
Kalymna
  homopoliteia with Kos 153, 172–3

Kamiros 175–6, 177
Karatepe bilingual 184, 189
Karpathos 177
Katakekaumene (Lydia) 4
Kelenderis (Cilicia) 193
Keramos (Caria) 154
  sympoliteia 169–70
Kibyra
  sympoliteia with Plarasa, Aphrodisias, Tabai 163
Kildara/Killara (Caria) 147, 155, 180
Kilix 182
Kimon 193
Kirua, ruler of Illubru 187–8
kleidophoria 224
Knidos 7
koiné
  in Lycian inscriptions 46
  typical features in Anatolia 46, 56
koinon 208; chapter 7 *passim*
Koliorga (Stratonikeia) 213, 214, 239
Kollyda (Lydia) 15
Koloneis (Caria) 217
  absorbed by Pisye 164
Kolophon
  synoikismos with Ephesos 150, 171
Koraia (Stratonikeia) 214, 239
Koranza (Stratonikeia) 214, 240
Kore 7, 221
Kormeis (Lycia) 171
Kos 10
  homopoliteia with Kalymna 153, 172–3
  metoikesis 178
Kritias 1
Kula (Lydia) 16, 20
Kuprlli (Lycian dynast) 49
Kyaneai 10
Kybele 36
Kydonia (Crete) 148
kyria ekklesia see *ekklesia kyria*
Kyrbissos
  absorbed by Teos 145, 152, 156
Kytinion 44, 63

Labraunda 220–1
Laodikeia/Lykos 27–8, 30, 33, 210
Laodikeis (Caria)
  koinon 209–12
Latin language
  influenced by Greek 90
  use in Roman colonies in the East 95
Latmos
  sympoliteia with Pidasa 151–2, 161, 178
law
  Athenian 2
  criminal 42
  interdependence with religion 3, 5–6, 11, 27–34, 40, 42
  legal terminology 6, 29, 32, 33, 34
Lebedos
  synoikismos with Ephesos 150, 171
  synoikismos with Teos 150, 162, 170, 178
legio III Augusta 143; *X Fretensis* 127; *XV Apollinaris* 127
Leon of Stratonikeia 30–4, 174
  date of priesthood 210
  goals 236–8
  honoured by local communities 211, 212
Lesbos 10
Leto 59–60
Leukodeis (Caria) 217, 218
Lindian *Temple Chronicle* 194–5
Lindos 167, 175–6, 177
  Soloi (alleged role in foundation) 186
Livy (33.18) 232, 233
Lobolda (Stratonikeia) 214
Lokris 162
Londeis (Caria)
  absorbed by Pisye 164
  koinon 209, 217
Lucian 205
  (*Alex*. 44) 41
Lucius Verus 121, 142
Luwian
  cult 205; moon goddess 61
  language, Lycia 45; Cilicia 184, 189, 190, 196
  see also onomastics
Lycia 10, 36
  boundaries 50–1
  considered part of the classical world 44–5
  sympoliteiai 146, 171
Lycian language
  Anatolian language 45
  in the epigraphic record 45
  displaced by Greek 51–4, 69, 203–4
Lycians 44–70
Lydia 3, 4, 5, 6, 9–14, 20, 35, 39; chapter 1, *passim*
  onomastics 67
Lydian language
  displaced by Greek 203–4
Lysimachos 150, 155, 171

Macedonia 10
  Macedonian names 58, 64–5
magic 10, 11, 43
Magnesia/Maiandros 156
Magnesia/Sipylos
  sympoliteia with Smyrna 152–3, 156, 178
Maionia 4, 23–30

Index

Mallus 198
marriage
  between siblings 55
Maussollos 174, 177
Maximian 114
medicine
  cult of the healer god 59
  Greek doctors in the Roman world 106
  guild of doctors 106
  physicians to the Roman elite 102, 106, 111, 114; *see also* L. Gellius Maximus
  secular versus divine healing 40
  see also Asklepios
Megalopolis 149
Memphis 29
Mes 11, 13, 29–35, 62
  Artemidorou 5, 28
  Axiottenos 5, 9, 16, 20, 22, 29–34
  Tiamou 17
Mesopotamia 98, 122, 191
  Parthian 121
Messabeans (Caria) 158
Meter Tarsene 5
miasma *see* purity
Miletos
  sympoliteia with Myous 157–61
  sympoliteia with Pidasa 152, 156–61, 179, 180
Milyas 50
Mithridates (son of Antiochos III)
Mopsos 183–5; *see also* Muksas
Morgantina 141
Moschion (citizen of Mylasa) 173
Mother of the gods 15, 16
mother goddess 60
Muksas 189; *see also* Mopsus
museum (Alexandria)
  membership as a title or honorific 94, 110, 111–16
  Ephesos 112
  Smyrna 112
Myania (Lokris) 162
Mylasa
  sympoliteia with Euromos 154, 168–9, 173–4
  sympoliteia with Olymos 152, 155, 164–8, 179, 230
Myous (Caria)
  sympoliteia with Miletos 157–61, 166
Myrikion (Galatia) 15
Mysia 4, 11
mythology, Greek 44
  as a factor in names 46

names
  copronyms 49–50
  double names 67
  mythological 57, 59, 62
  nicknames 47, 68
  Roman, for new citizens 64, 99
  shortened (Koseformen) 47, 49
  theophoric 57, 58–62, 65
  see also onomastics
Nemesis 10, 11
Neptune 8–9
Nero
  Armenian wars 131
Nerva 88
Nikagoras (Rhodian general) 175
Niskus (deity) 8–9
Nysa 221

oaths, of innocence 31–4, 39
  see also vows
Olymos
  sympoliteia with Mylasa 152, 155, 164–8, 179, 230
Omm-es-Zeitun 138
onomastics
  Asia Minor 203
  Athens 57, 58–64
  Caria 223
  Luwian (Cilicia) 188, 189–90, 205
  Lycia 45–70
  Lydia 67
  Macedonian 58
  Rhodes 57, 61, 63
Oppius, Q. (proconsul in Cilicia) 172
oracles 5, 23–30, 32, 33, 34, 39, 41
Orontes 124
Oropos 8, 9
Otorkondeis (Mylasa) 173–4

Palmyra 121, 131, 139
Pamphylia
  interaction with Lycia 69
Pamphylians
  fugitives from Troy 183
Panamara (Caria) 30–1, 174–5
  Hellenization, models of 222–3
  history and location 215–18
  sanctuary 218–27; joint cult of Zeus and Hera 225–6
Panamareis (*koinon*) 208–12, 222
  Rhodian control 217
Paphlagonia 47
Parthians
  attacked by Caracalla 90
  Parthian coins at Dura 128–30
  Parthian Dura in the Roman economy 119–21
  Parthian Mesopotamia 121
  hairstyle 143
  see also Dura-Europos, pottery

Pednelissos (Pisidia) 35
peprêmenos 7
Persephone 8
Perseus
  ancestor of the Persians 44, 195
Persia
  dominant in Cilicia 191–2, 196–7
Persians 44
  Persian names in Lycia 51, 52, 57, 60
Phaselis (Lycia) 44, 193, 194
Philadelpheia (Lydia) 1, 4
Philemon *comicus* 200
Philip V 155, 175, 208, 219, 233
Phoenician language
  Cilicia 184, 189–90, 195
Phoenicians 205
Phrygia
  alphabet 191
  Greek in Phrygia 46
  onomastics 63, 64, 67
  religious life 4, 5, 6, 11, 20, 39
Phygela/Pygela
  synoikismos with Ephesos 150, 171
Pidasa (Caria)
  sympoliteia with Euromos (?) 158
  sympoliteia with Latmos 151–2, 161, 178
  sympoliteia with Miletos 152, 156–61, 179, 180
Pisidia 35, 85–117
  onomastics 63, 65, 67
Pisye (Caria) 218, 238
  sympoliteia with Pladasa 164, 217
pittakion 9–14, 15, 17
Pladasa (Caria)
  sympoliteia with Pisye 164, 217
Plarasa (Caria)
  sympoliteia with Aphrodisias 162–3, 172, 179
Plato (*Resp.* 364) 2
Pleistarchos 150
  Pleistarcheia (Herakleia under Latmos) 151
pletorin (*praetorium*) 29–35
Pluto (Ploutos, Plouton) 8, 15, 221
Podandos (Cilicia) 90
pollution *see* purity
Polybius (6.56) 1; (4.25) 148; (21.24) 199; (28.14) 147; (30.21.6) 231
Pompey
  establishes province of Syria 119
Posideion (Cilicia/Syria) 183, 195
pottery
  as evidence for trade in Roman empire 119
  Attic, Cypriot and Phoenician at Kelenderis 193
  African red slip at Dura 124, 144
  Eastern Sigillata A (red slip) at Dura 121–4, 144
  Hellenistic black slip at Dura 121
  late Geometric in Cilicia 186
  Mycenaean-type in Cilicia 185
  'Parthian' green-glazed at Dura 121, 122, 125, 144
prayers
  for justice 8, 15, 21, 40
  for revenge 12, 19
priests 36, 38
  appointment 212, 230
  as administrators of justice 5, 21, 23–30, 34, 35, 39, 42
  priesthood restricted 167
  see also sanctuaries
Ptolemy III 199
Ptolemy V 147
purity 4, 11, 23, 24, 28
  akathartia 3
  miasma 3, 9

Rhamnous 10
Rhodes 10
  control of Caria 209–10, 228, 231
  influence on Lycia 45, 69; in Cilicia 194–5
  mythological (kinship) ties with Soloi 199
  Soloi (alleged role in foundation) 184, 186
  synoikismos 146, 175–8, 179–80
rituals, religious 28, 35, 37, 39
Robert, Louis 49, 61, 63, 65, 106, 112, 165, 206, 221
  and Jeanne 62, 145, 158, 171
Roman army (agency in transmitting technology) 142
  see also legiones
Roman empire
  frontier zone 119–20
Rome 10
  influence on *sympoliteiai* 180
  relations with Rhodes 179; and Philip V 233

Sagalassos (Pisidia) 99, 101, 109, 117
Saittai (Lydia) 4, 36
Samos 10
sanctuaries
  asylia (Panamara) 218–22
  important for local identity: in *sympoliteiai* 168, 208, 212, 213, 222, 230;
  access restricted 173
  role in legal disputes 11–38
  social services 32
Sardis 4–26, 149
Sargon II 187, 188
Sarpedon (mythological hero) 44, 45, 63
sceptre (as symbol of imprecation) 13, 21, 29–35, 36

[Scylax] *Periplous* 197
Seleukeia/Kalykadnos 199
Seleukeia/Tigris 121
  coinage 128
Seleukos I 221
Seleukos II 153, 221
Sennacherib 187
Septimius Severus 90
sexual behaviour
  regulated by law/religion 26, 27–9, 42
Shalmaneser III 187
Shalmaneser V 187
Sicily 17
Smyrna 10
  sympoliteia with Magnesia/Sipylos 152–3, 156, 178
Soloi (Cilicia)
  connections with the Greek world 194–5, 199–202, 206
  etymology of *solecism* 181–2, 201–3
  foundation by Rhodians and Achaeans 184, 186
  renamed Pompeiopolis 206
Soloi (Cyprus) 201
Solon (13.25–32W) 2; (36.8–12W) 201
  connection with Soloi 200–1
Spain 15
Stoicism, Middle 181
Stoics
  linguistic theory 181
Strabo (12.4.6) 203–4; (14.1.10) 157; (14.1.27, 14.4.3, 14.5.16, 14.5.21) 183, 185; (14.2.25) 238; (14.2.28) 201; (14.5.8) 186, 194
Stratonike (mother of Seleukos II) 153
Stratonikeia 30, 174
  foundation and *sympoliteia* 155, 213–15, 222
  Rhodian dominance 217
Stratonikis Aphrodite (sanctuary) 153
suffragator 99
Sulla 50
Sura/Euphrates 121
Syennesis 191
sympas demos 172–8, 211–13, 230
sympoliteia
  definition 148–9; *see also homopoliteia, isopoliteia*
  preservation of civic identity within 162–78
  result of royal policy 150–6
  Roman policy 180
synkletos (senate) 29–34
synoikismos
  definition 148–9
  Stratonikeia 214, 222
Syria
  Caracalla's visit 116

Dura 119; *see also* Dura-Europos
Neo-Hittite kingdoms in north 190
Parthian 124
Roman province 119, 122–4

Tabai
  sympoliteia with Kibyra, Plarasa, Aphrodisias 163
Tarraco (Iberia) 97
Tarmianoi (Caria) 217, 218, 238
Tarsos 204
  foundation by Argives 184; by 'Sardanapalus' 198; by Aradus 205
  renamed Antioch on the Kydnos 199
Telmessos 9, 36
Teos 159
  absorbs Kyrbissos 145, 152, 156
  synoikismos with Lebedos 150, 162, 170, 178
Termessos (Pisidia) 41, 60, 65
Terssogassa 165
Theangela (Caria) 147
Themissos 147
Thodasa (Caria) 147, 155, 180
Thrace 10
Tiberiopolis 4
Tigranes 204
Tragalassa (Lycia)
  sympoliteia with Arykanda
Trajan
  eastern conquests 127, 142
Tripolis 4
Troad 182
Trojans 44
Tyre 190

Ulpius Traianus, *legatus pro praetore* 121

vengeance 2
via Sebaste 91
vows 9; *see also* prayers, vows

women
  accused of adultery 42; of poisoning 7, 11, 21, 34
  business transactions/disputes 16, 18, 24
  honorary decrees for 56, 108
  inherit property 9
  in trouble with the law 7, 24, 26, 29, 38
  names and social position in Lycia 54, 55, 56, 67
  set up inscriptions of public record 5, 11, 14, 17, 19, 20, 22, 26, 38, 55

Xenophon (*Anab.* 7.8) 60
Xerxes 192, 195

Yariris 190

Zeus 27–8, 33, 42, 62
    Chrysaoreus 214, 240
    Karios 207, 211, 218, 227, 237
    Labraundos 151, 174, 220, 226
    Olympios 9
    Osogo 226
    Panamaros 174, 215, 228, 240
    Pigindenos 23–30
    Stratios 226
    Hera, joint cult (Panamara) 225–6
Zeuxis (agent of Antiochos III) 157